INTERVENTION

SHAPING THE GLOBAL ORDER

Karen A. Feste

Westport, Connecticut
London

Library of Congress Cataloging-in-Publication Data

Feste, Karen A.
  Intervention : shaping the global order / Karen A. Feste
    p. cm.
  Includes bibliographical references and index.
  ISBN 0–275–95942–2 (alk. paper)
    1. United States—Foreign relations—1989– 2. United States—Foreign relations—2001– 3.
  United States—Military policy. 4. Intervention (International law) 5. Intervention
  (International law)—Case studies. I. Title.
  E840.F475 2003
    327.73′009′049—dc21   2003040375

British Library Cataloguing in Publication Data is available.

Library of Congress Catalog Card Number: 2003040375
ISBN: 0–275–95942–2

First published in 2003

Praeger Publishers, 88 Post Road West, Westport, CT 06881
An imprint of Greenwood Publishing Group, Inc.
www.praeger.com

Printed in the United States of America

∞™

The paper used in this book complies with the
Permanent Paper Standard issued by the National
Information Standards Organization (Z39.48–1984).

10 9 8 7 6 5 4 3 2 1

Copyright Acknowledgments

The author and publisher gratefully acknowledge permission to use the following:

Tables 7.9 and 7.10 are based on material from James Meernik, "Presidential Decision Making and the Political Use of Military Force." *International Studies Quarterly* 38 (1994): 121–138.

Tables 6.2 and 6.3 are based on material from William R. Ayres, "A World Flying Apart? Violent Nationalist Conflict and the End of the Cold Ward." *Journal of Peace Research* 37 (2000): 114 and 115, respectively. Reprinted by permission of Sage Publications Ltd. Copyright © International Peace Research Institute (Oslo), PRIO, 2000.

Tables 7.6 and 7.7 are adapted from copyright © 1999 from "The Structural Shape of Force: Interstate Intervention in the Zones of Peace and Turmoil, 1946–1996." *International Interactions* 25 (1999): 374 and 380, respectively, by Jeffrey Pickering. Reproduced by permission of Taylor & Francis, Inc., http://www.routledge-ny.com

Tables 6.4, 6.5, and 6.6 are based on material from Peter Wallensteen and Margareta Sollenberg, "Armed Conflict, 1989–2000." *Journal of Peace Research* 38 (September 2001): 629–644. Reprinted by permission of Sage Publications Ltd. Copyright © International Peace Research Institute (Oslo), PRIO, 2001.

To

Mother and Dad

also

DS—LK

Contents

Illustrations

Acknowledgments

I am grateful to the University of Denver for a sabbatical leave that gave me the time and energy to produce this work; thankful for two wonderful colleagues who enriched my understanding of the topic, Tom Farer and Tim Sisk; appreciative of all student contributions in my Winter term 2002 Intervention seminar at the Graduate School of International Studies; thank my loyal assistant Millie Van Wyke; and acknowledge the special benefits of thinking space and discussion made possible by life in Reno.

Introduction:
Intervention Centrality—An Argument

Intervention is a key concept for understanding global political dynamics. In broadest form, it refers to deliberate involvement by larger states into the internal affairs of smaller ones using economic leverage, diplomatic techniques, or military means to influence or control target states' policies of governance, their social and economic development programs, and foreign relations. Historically, patterns of intervention by great powers shaped the international system by defining contours of connection between its units, guiding interaction, and creating operational expectations—from imperialism and colonialism to north-south dependency and globalization processes; from Cold War superpower rivalry to post–Cold War unipolarity—each structure illustrates the result of a conscious intervention strategy or the net effects of accumulated intervention activity.

Among symbols of its age, the Berlin Wall best expressed the U.S.-USSR East-West divide carved from superpower intervention practice in the Cold War; another icon, the New York World Trade Center towers, captured the essence of the post–Cold War America-dominated setting of globalization, the corpus of worldwide economic transactions emanating from the superpower's financial center. The fall of the wall in October 1989 and collapse of the towers a dozen years later in September 2001, were carried out for different purposes, through different means, with far reaching, totally opposite consequences in the global system. After the first event, optimistic expectations of a more serene, secure world spread quickly as tension of the Cold War subsided, heralding a major shift in intervention rules. Following the second event, a mood of sobering uncertainty and insecurity unfolded, highlighting significant concern about intervention effects. Both acts of destruction signaled a major change in global relations, dramatizing in part the discontent of groups residing in targeted intervention regions who were seeking fundamental change in local governing leadership by attempting to alter the linkage between a superpower and its clients, and dramatizing more generally a strategy by these groups to change the basic discourse of international politics by breaking intervention power, practice, and expectations.

Berlin, a major metropolitan area located deep within East Germany, had been divided in 1945 after World War II into an east sector, under USSR authority, and a west, U.S.-allied sector. The wall around West Berlin, constructed by the Soviet Union in 1961 at the height of the Cold War, was designed to cut off access to the West for local citizens seeking escape from communist control within the country. It was destroyed by a popular movement arising from local dissatisfaction with regime policies—lack of political and economic freedom and repressive surveillance were major grievances—and was brought down when the Soviet Union decided not to intervene to help the East German government stop the move against it. The air crashes into the twin towers of New York City were masterminded by disaffected individuals opposed to American intervention in the Middle East, ranging from long- standing U.S. economic and military assistance to Israel to military troop stationing in Saudi Arabia, put in place during the Gulf crisis in 1990. The U.S. presence ensured existing regimes in the Islamic and non-Islamic countries, which they felt were following detrimental politics, would remain in power. The airplane hijackers were drawn from Muslim countries of sectors of society where future economic conditions looked grim: those from Saudi Arabia were recruited from its poorest parts where unemployment was common; members of Al Qaida, the supporting terrorist group, were veterans of the long civil war in Afghanistan, who had fought (with U.S. financial backing) against Soviet intervention and now faced few job prospects. In essence, the fall of the wall and fall of the towers, very different events not to be equated with respect to their moral and ethical implications, human suffering, and loss of life that resulted, are similar in this way: all groups of participants believed their personal situation derived from superpower intervention policy, namely the USSR hold over East Germany in the Cold War, U.S.-Soviet competition in Afghanistan's civil war, and American influence in Israel and certain Arab states in the post–Cold War period.

As the Cold War ended, the United States emerged as a confident, sole-standing superpower, spreading its global involvement under a different banner, yet, as before, using military intervention to advance policy. Intervention, a foreign policy tool of strong states seeking to force their will on weaker ones through temporary, limited acts of defined scope was the common currency of competition in international relations between the United States and the Soviet Union from 1945 to 1989. Political, economic, and military intervention tactics of the superpowers—from intimidation to coercion to domination—directed at both aligned and nonaligned countries throughout the last half of the twentieth century depended on national interest configuration, that is, the perceived strategic value of individual states to each party in the context of the American-Soviet balance of power rivalry. This rivalry, now rendered irrelevant, was the cornerstone of superpower intervention strategy which created and maintained the global structure of rules and operating norms including where, when, and why each party could and would intervene. It was a mutually reinforcing situation.

During the evolving post–Cold War era, the international system has transformed from a bipolar structure into a unipolar one, yet the dominant role of
intervention in global affairs continues. American troops were sent abroad frequently in the 1990s to deal with international and civil disturbances in situations perceived to be threatening to world peace and security. For the United
States, lines of justification supporting intervention policy had to be revised;
communist containment, the doctrinal pillar of American foreign policy for
more than four decades, was completely outdated and unsuitable. Issues of instability, now viewed through a lens devoid of ideological overtone and competitive power marking the East-West division, suggested the need for fresh
foreign policy foundations to govern intervention mission objectives.

Prominent in the new thinking was a shift away from exclusive state-based
strategic value calculations—the traditional national interest concept—toward
consideration of people-based interest assessments, a new national identity concept focused around humanitarian issues as a valid reason for the United States
to intervene. Human need was understood as a root cause of instability within
societies due to the scarcity and unequal distribution of resources, a problem that
could be confronted directly now that Cold War politics had passed. Thus, civil
conflicts—violent, destabilizing situations accompanied by rapidly deteriorating
living conditions affecting innocent human life—could be viewed as legitimate
intervention opportunities, in spite of nonintervention norms and the sacred
status of state sovereignty within the international community. Social and economic conditions coupled with repressive political mechanisms perpetuated
poverty and promoted frustration, which led to outbursts of violence and insecurity. Violence produced massive human suffering, which states in crisis could
not handle. Hence, a primary purpose of intervening into an ongoing crisis was
essentially to provide nonpolitical humanitarian assistance: to help suffering
people by donating and delivering emergency medical aid and food and establishing temporary living quarters for displaced persons. A related objective
sometimes accompanying situations of disaster relief was more politically oriented, to facilitate longer-term improvement in human conditions by encouraging development of democratic movements, actively promoting leadership
change, and participating in political institution building. Together, these policies were designed to bring stability to a region and build up overall security at a
global level. From this perspective, international security was conceptualized as
accumulating layers of local peace around the world.

A second main imperative for U.S. intervention was added after the attacks on
American soil in September 2001: following President George W. Bush's directive, countries harboring terrorists or pursuing terrorist-based state policies could
be subject to American interference and punishment; countries seeking to fight
terrorism within their borders could receive military assistance (including
American troops). Thus, the purpose of intervening is national interest, state
based, and essentially coercive: to eliminate an opposition force threatening the
security of the United States. Here, international security has a different meaning, fostering peaceful relations between America and other nation-states, which

conforms to a traditional version of foreign policy goals and intervention rationale.

U.S. INTERVENTION POLICY

The dual basis of post–Cold War U.S. intervention policy in the twenty-first century reflects both continuity and change from previous patterns: as continuity, national interests, that is, state-to-state relations, still provides a foundation for the competitive nature of international politics and a major justification behind intervention acts; as change, humanitarian need is clearly a new element, with its purported unselfish, people-based interest level leading to humanitarian intervention; and as continuity *and* change, active promotion of civil society and nation-building through democratic rule, rather than merely its rhetorical use by policy-makers in the Cold War years, is a strong step toward implementing Wilsonian goals of American foreign policy, initially presented at the close of World War I. This stance represents a hybrid combining traditional national interests with the humanitarian element, blending state-based and people-based perspectives, owing its origins to a normative premise, that individuals are better off in democratic societies, and also an empirical fact, that democracies do not fight one another.

The war in Afghanistan provides a good illustration of an intervention mission serving all objectives. As a national interest rationale: soldiers were originally dispatched to the country *primarily* to capture the enemy—leaders of Al Qaida, the international terrorist group living as guests in Afghanistan where they operated training camps, who were responsible for the hijacked planes crashing into New York City, Washington, D.C., and Pennsylvania that killed several thousand people. As a humanitarian gesture and democratic political change directive: a *secondary* goal of the intervention—punishing governments giving sanctuary to terrorists—led to the downfall of the Taliban, an extremely repressive and unpopular ruling regime in Afghanistan. With subsequent creation of a new, more representative government, U.S. commitment to help rebuild the national society by implementing extensive social and political reform programs and by providing considerable economic aid, the intervention, not unreasonably, could be categorized at some level as a humanitarian gesture, though its origins clearly reside in the basic strategic, vital interest rationale.

As the world moved from a bipolar system into a unipolar-dominant one, the contours and motivational forces of intervention in global politics shifted; however, the centrality of intervention, both as a foreign policy concept and operating theme of international relations, did not change. Why? Because the presumed positive relationship between intervention and security remained untouched. Intervention, help from the outside, is supposed to alleviate suffering on the inside, thereby producing security on the inside and beyond. For the intervener, taking action is supposed to prevent conflict escalation or spillover into neighboring countries, thereby containing insecurity, that is, enhancing security maintenance on the outside by reducing threats from inside. The idea linking intervention to security is based partly on a belief system, partly on cost-benefit and risk analysis, partly on hope: an intervening party assumes its objectives—to separate warring factions, stop violence, prevent its spread, and reduce tensions—will be brought about by implementation of strategic plans and tactical organization to stabilize a conflict situation in the target region. The long-term expectation is that stabilization may lead to dispute resolution, that dispute resolution may open the political landscape to allow introduction of positive nation-building steps, and that nation-building efforts help create an environment of security for the state, for the region, and for the international system.

The operating premise, intervention brings peace and security, is not without challenge. It forms the core of debate on U.S. foreign policy principles and application, reflecting how updated notions of security could or should link to the logic of intervention in the post–Cold War era. During the Cold War, national security was regarded as a scarce resource, which led to the creation of superpower rivalry, a functioning competition of power enhancement efforts whereby America and the Soviet Union sought to solidify their stronghold on countries within their respective geographic spheres of influence and to expand their alliance networks into the frontiers—Southern Europe, the Middle East, Asia, and Africa—to increase their relative sense of security. In the post–Cold War period, national security is gradually being enlarged and remodeled into a social, public good, reflecting both the individual level of human security and a collective international security—a commodity unlimited in supply and available to all. This new concept builds from the assumption that American national security is embedded in, and derives from, both global development and global contentment linked in a structural form. Accordingly, the United States has emphasized two justifications for intervention to encompass these expanded levels: (1) an offensive security goal: alleviate immediate human suffering and help build civil society foundations within countries experiencing violent domestic conflict and/or significant, undemocratic political change; and (2) a defensive security goal: eradicate international terrorism, especially its effect on American national interests.

Policies adopted to pursue these joint goals have not been uncontroversial. With the exception of the early months of intervention into Afghanistan, whenever a U.S. president announces a military intervention decision to the public and outlines its rationale—whether for combat or peacekeeping functions—Congressional and popular reactions often show little support. Specific policies are dissected and critiqued not so much on detail, but for their implications of grandeur in the context of America's role in the world: what its leadership function should be in the new international environment, what national interest parameters should guide future action, and how American intervention behavior broadly conceived might draw down its world reputation, jeopardizing security opportunities. Policies relating exclusively to the defensive security goal provoke less opposition but still raise questions. About six months after the terrorist attacks against America, members of Congress started to complain about the increasingly larger campaign against terrorism, stating that costs were escalating, but there seemed to be no road map behind the U.S. military effort.

SHAPING THE GLOBAL ORDER

A broad debate evolving from recent intervention action has covered a range of important issues, including divisions between those advocating expanded global engagement into more countries requiring emergency social, political, and economic assistance versus those pressing for reduced commitments and fewer obligations (where both sides base their positions on the disappearance of superpower rivalry which enables the United States to decide its foreign policy more freely); the nature and purpose of humanitarian intervention and its relevance to security and national interests; and unilateral vs. multilateral strategic involvement including U.S. policy toward and participation in United Nations (UN) peacekeeping. The centerpiece throughout these discussions is domestic instability around the world: understanding the causes and consequences of contemporary civil wars, their spread, and threats posed by unstable or repressive regimes with respect to their impact on the world community. The lingering issue in this complex maze is whether America has intervened in appropriate places, at appropriate times, in appropriate ways.

Intervention policy choice implies a singular move: a calculated step to interfere in another nation's internal affairs in order to maintain the status quo or to change it. The method of its implementation, though, offers a wide array of models. A smooth and direct linkage between policy and implementation specifics—how operational tactics and mission goals mesh and reach their joint objectives—is key to assessing intervention success or failure. One attempt to specify preconditions for intervention success was identified by George, Hall, and Simons (1971: 216) in their comparative study of coercive diplomacy—U.S. interventions of the 1960s in Laos, Cuba, and Vietnam. The eight elements, still relevant in today's world, are: the strength of the intervening country's motivation, an asymmetry of motivation favoring the intervener, clarity of intervention policy objectives, a sense of urgency to achieve these goals, adequate domestic political support for the intervention policy, usable military options, opponents' fear of unacceptable escalation, and clarity concerning the precise terms of settlement.

These evaluation points have enlivened the contentious atmosphere in discussions about American foreign policy direction (or drift) by gearing the focus of interpretation of particular cases of intervention and the lessons and guidelines to be extracted from them. At a general level, there are other factors important to shaping the unipolar, Post–Cold War, international system beyond global structure that fuel the spirited debate, including: (1) world perspectives: different sweeping historical interpretations of recent world events, from optimistic and pessimistic viewpoints, combined with images and expectations of the United States within this context; (2) policy perspectives: alternative philosophical orientations appealing to America's role in the universe of nation-states; (3) foreign policy doctrine: proposals to establish different national interest parameters as the substantive basis for U.S. intervention; (4) historic patterns of intervention opportunity—instances of civil conflict and international crises—occurring across the globe; and (5) historical trends of U.S. intervention practice. Each element is examined more closely in subsequent chapters.

The shaping process may be approached from two perspectives: empirically, describing how the United States has structured its responsibilities through intervention action; or normatively, recommending how the United States *should* structure its responsibilities through intervention choice. This study emphasizes descriptive features of U.S. intervention choice in order to understand intervention practice in the post–Cold War era as a preliminary step to formulating reasonable policy recommendations. The objective is to look through an empirical lens, examining roughly the first decade of the post–Cold War era with respect to what has happened in order to discern if a pattern of events over time—crises and U.S. reactions to them—points to a clear policy direction or shows confusion and randomness in setting the foreign policy stage for the future. The significance of the task is obvious: without a new doctrine statement defining the international terrain and the role of the United States within it—American policy goals and principles, perceived threats, and national interest, to replace the definitive guidance developed in the early Cold War years—a thematic mission for the post–Cold War is likely to be shaped by evolving experiences gathered from these first cases, that is, intervention situations confronted by the United States during the first dozen years of the new age.

Eight conflict cases selected for this purpose include the major American intervention decisions between 1989 and 2001: the Persian Gulf War, Panama and Haiti, Somalia and Rwanda, Bosnia and Kosovo, and the war in Afghanistan. Three cases fall within conventional national interest parameters reflecting perceived levels of threats to the United States and involved traditional military combat operations: participation in the Persian Gulf conflict and the interventions into Panama and Afghanistan. Four cases form part of the experiment with humanitarian-based intervention arguments, namely the introduction of military ground troops into situations of civil unrest in Somalia, Rwanda, Haiti, and Bosnia, for purposes of peace enforcement or peacekeeping. One case, Kosovo, is unique: the U.S. intervention rationale was humanitarian need, American military air power engaged in combat operations through NATO (North Atlantic Treaty Organization); no ground troops were involved. At the conclusion of battle, America send a peacekeeping force contingent.

Various levels of comparisons of American intervention have been incorporated to see how the activities in this era depart from the past or reflect a continuing policy trend: a general analysis of American intervention experience—when, where, why, and how often military contingents were sent abroad throughout the entire twentieth century; a timeline of intervention opportunities—defined here as domestic unrest and civil uprising in countries around the world—over the past 50 years; and a comparison among intervention opportunity, action, and U.S. policy doctrine during the first decade of the Cold War and first decade of the post–Cold War.

THEORETICAL PERSPECTIVE

The analysis is guided by a structural orientation, for the objective is to examine how the United States contributes to the evolving form of the international system through its intervention policies. According to Kenneth Waltz (1979:

80), a structure is defined by the arrangement of its parts and by the principle of that arrangement. Structures shape processes. For the international system, the essential rules of operation which describe general relationships between the actors, expectations for stability or parameters for system transformation, or which assign definite systemic role functions to actors characterizing behavior, are important, says Morton Kaplan (1964: 9). All systems have regulatory, integrative and disintegrative processes that maintain or preserve a system's identity over time and information flows of norms and expectations, of aspirations, and estimates of capabilities; together these form an equilibrium. The logic of power politics assumes that states observe and monitor the changing distribution of power, assess that distribution in terms of the threats it generates to their own interests and survival, and make policy within the limits of their resources and options so as to minimize their vulnerabilities and maximize their opportunities. Agents who do not behave this way risk elimination and replacement. Thus, rationality is a behaviorally engineered quality of actors within an anarchic political system (Buzan, 1996: 55). The structure of the system acts as a constraining and disposing force.

Is it possible for structures to have effects apart from the attributes and interactions of agents? The challenge of systemic theory is not to show that structure has more explanatory power than agents—as if the two were separate—but to show how agents are differently structured by the system so as to produce different effects, says Alexander Wendt (1999: 12). The debate is not between systemic theories that focus on structure and reductionist theories that focus on agents, but between different theories of system structure and how structure relates to agents. Two different forms of structural international relations exist: materialists believe power and interests are juxtaposed against ideas, as causes of outcome, whereas idealists see the meaning of power and interests and their effects depend on actors' ideas. "Materialists privilege causal relationships, effects and questions; idealists privilege constitutive relationships, effects and questions," states Wendt (1999: 25), who views causal and constitutive effects as different but not mutually exclusive. In a causal relationship, an antecedent condition generates an effect and assumes an independence between them. In a constitutive relationship a condition exists in virtue of its relation to other conditions or effects; things are contingent.

In theoretical language: do structures "construct" agents? Does this mean the international system "creates" U.S. intervention policy? To say that a structure "constrains" actors is to say that it has only behavioral effects. To say that a structure "constructs" actors is to say that it has property effects, defining identities and interests. Both property and behavioral effects can be either caused or constituted by structures, argues Wendt (1999: 26–27). Individualism is compatible with a theory of how structures cause agents' properties but rules out the possibility that social structures have constitutive effects on agents, since this would mean that structures cannot be reduced to the properties or interactions of existing agents. Waltz looks only at causal, not constitutive, systemic arrangement, while Wendt looks at both.

The approach of Wendt, that agency and structure are mutually constitutive and codetermined, is more compelling. The structure of any social system contains three elements: material conditions, interests, and ideas. Without ideas there are no interests, without interests there are no meaningful material conditions, without material conditions there is no reality at all. Structure exists, has effects, and evolves only because of agents and their practices; structure is instantiated only in process (Wendt, 1999: 139, 185). Structure confronts actors as an objective social fact that constrains and enables action in systematic ways. The distribution of capabilities has effects on international politics only because the desiring and believing state agents give it meaning. Therefore, the dependence of structure on agency and the social process is both constitutive and causal: operating norms in a system exist only in virtue of actors' desires and beliefs; yet, social structures also depend on agents and practices in a causal sense. Constitutive analysis indicates what structures are made of and how they can have certain effects, but not about the processes by which they move through time. In both a causal and constitutive sense, structure is an ongoing effect of process; at the same time, that process is an effect of structure. Social processes are always structured, and social structures are always in process.

These conditions describe the post–Cold War international environment: the United States tries to shape the new order through its intervention policies, and simultaneously is shaped by the existing and evolving structural arrangement. While modern states share some beliefs about the rules of the international game—who its players are, what their interests are, and what constitutes rational behavior—there is no settlement about the extent to which a new system structure has been grounded or how much it matters. The new international system is evolving. The process is directed, though not completely controlled, by American policies and practice. The United States is shaping itself, and shaping the structure *and* the global structure is having causal effects on the identity and interests of the United States. Thus, the unipolar international system consists of agents and structure, mutually constituted, socially constructed. This deeply embedded relationship is shaping the new global order: the United States is the agent shaping the structure and the post–Cold War environment is the structure shaping the United States. The United States and the current structural setting are mutually instantiated, coexisting in symbiotic arrangement.

One comprehensive, recent work, *System Effects: Complexity in Political and Social Life* (Jervis, 1997), celebrates the systems perspective, providing hundreds of examples of interaction and linkages and structural impact in international politics. Consistent with Wendt, Jervis argues that systemic structure may be treated as either the independent or dependent variable; systems have indirect and delayed effects; outcomes do not always follow from intentions; and systems often display nonlinear relationships—results cannot be understood by adding together the units or their relations. A systems approach shows how individual actors, following simple and uncoordinated strategies, can produce aggregate behavior that is complex and ordered, although not necessarily predictable and stable. Testing the validity of propositions is difficult in a system because we cannot readily hold all other factors constant when the variable of focus influences the composition of the set of cases we are studying. "Few miracles will follow from thinking systematically because the interactive, strategic, and contingent nature of systems limits the extent to which complete and deterministic theories are possible," warns Jervis (1997: 81). Yet, very little in social and political life makes sense except in the light of systemic processes; exploring them gives an opportunity for new insight to understand and formulate effective action.

Various theoretic arguments explain the relationship between international system structure—based on an analysis of power distribution among states—and the level of stability and conflict in the world. It is not clear, though, precisely the number of poles or power centers, or the distribution of capabilities among them, that determines the amount and types of conflict. What level of power concentration controlled by how many states yields stability? Is it power parity, when major states are in equilibrium, or disparity, when states are not in equilibrium in status and capability hierarchy, that makes for peace? Theoretical guidelines for multipolar and bipolar balance of power systems exist, as do proposals for collective security systems and for world government. None of them quite fits with the existing (and evolving) constellation of global forces of the post–Cold War order.

We currently lack a developed, systematic, integrated theory about rules, operations, expectations, and predictions of a unipolar international system. Advocates for stabilizing the present environment with the United States as a "sole standing superpower" are not hard to find, but their positions combine policy preferences with logical analysis rather than resting on logic alone. Hegemonic stability theory—that order depends on a single dominant state or consolidated power group—constructed from international political economy processes, not from intervention behavior, comes closest to addressing the contemporary scene. Hegemony is defined as a situation in which one state is powerful enough to maintain the essential rules governing interstate relations and willing to do so; decisions to exercise leadership are necessary to activate the posited relationship between power capabilities and outcomes. This means that states with preponderant resources will be hegemonic except when they decide not to commit the necessary effort to leadership. As a causal theory, this is not helpful; whether a hegemon chooses to maintain a set of rules to keep a system intact or to change it remains indeterminate. While there is a distinctive role for a hegemon, providing its partners with leadership in return for deference, it cannot make and enforce rules without a certain degree of consent from other sovereign states. Robert O. Keohane (1984: 46) writes that material predominance alone cannot guarantee either stability or effective leadership. A hegemon may have to invest resources in institutions in order to ensure that its preferred rules will guide the behavior of other countries.

Hegemony is a unipolar configuration of political, economic, and military capability with a structure of influence to match it. Unipolarity without hegemony is a configuration where the preponderant capability of a single state is not matched by a corresponding predominant influence, states David Wilkinson (1999: 143). Even though the strongest, it is never sufficiently powerful to maintain its master role consistently. As evidence in favor of U.S. hegemony, Wilkinson cites the removals and installations of governments in Panama and Haiti, restoration of order in Bosnia, and consensual command in the Persian Gulf War and the Kosovo operations. He believes collective military action by the great powers is impossible in most places and impractical generally without U.S. participation and leadership (Wilkinson, 1999: 144). As evidence against U.S. hegemony Wilkinson mentions a series of U.S. foreign policy failures: from the inability to restore order in Somalia, to deterring or punishing massacres in Rwanda, to removing the Iraqi regime from power, and to extraditing persons accused of terrorism against the United States.

It seems clear, weighing the balance of evidence, that the United States is currently in a position of unipolarity without hegemony. The unipolar power configuration, "neither inherently durable and reliable, nor unstable and fleeting," will continue for a decade, a generation, or longer, Wilkinson (1999: 166) predicts. This structure is not informed by theoretical guidance, nor does it have historical precedent, further underlining the importance of evaluating interrelationships among structure, process, and agency, within the conceptualization outlined by Wendt, to understand how these forces are shaping the future. Because of the limits of causal explanation in hegemonic theory—the mechanism activating both "will power" and "capability application" in decisions to intervene is lacking—prediction precision will never emerge.

What are the behavioral implications of unipolarity? Michael Mastanduno (1999: 141) searched for propositions in Waltz's (1979) "balance of power" theory and Stephen Walt's (1987) "balance of terror" theory to examine this question. In a unipolar structure, the top state is in an enviable position. It is significantly unconstrained and enjoys wide discretion in its statecraft. It is helpless, however, to perpetuate this attractive state of affairs. For Waltz, preponderance of power in the hands of a single state will stimulate the rise of new great powers. Efforts to preserve unipolarity are bound to be futile and likely to be counterproductive. The more rational strategy is for the dominant state to accept the inevitability of multipolarity and maneuver to take advantage of it.

There is support for Waltz's expectation in U.S. intervention policy patterns, states Mastanduno (1999: 143–144). Significant differences in the pattern of intervention as the international structure changes from bipolarity to unipolarity will be evident: a consistent pattern will appear under a bipolarity system, while intervention will be haphazard and episodic under unipolarity. Mastanduno cites the breakup of Yugoslavia: if it had happened in the Cold War, it would have been an overwhelming priority for U.S. foreign policy. But in the early 1990s, the United States was left with considerably more room to maneuver, taking time to redefine the problem over several years. Was it a problem of vital interest or not, was it a European problem, a humanitarian problem, as a war of aggression and genocide, or a civil war requiring an honest broker to make peace? After the Cold War, U.S. officials seem far less concerned about less than successful interventions—for example, Somalia and Haiti, where they backed down. And the role of the United States? Global policeman in Persian Gulf intervention, but reluctant to intervene in Bosnia; intervention in Somalia for humanitarian purposes, but not in Rwanda where it was also desperately needed.

Walt's theory says the United States will attempt to prolong the unipolar moment and will rely on multilateralism in its international undertakings. While less efficient, the superpower will function to reassure other states and help to convince them that their preferences matter and that they are not simply being coerced or directed to follow the dictates of the dominant state (Mastanduno, 1999: 143–144). Thus, America will adopt policies of reassurance toward status quo states, policies of confrontation toward revisionist states, and policies of engagement or integration toward undecided states. Mastanduno, citing support for Walt's argument, says the United States orchestrated military coalitions for several interventions to exercise its dominant power with legitimacy, (1999: 167–169).

Both realist theories would predict U.S. strategy has been responsive to the constraints and opportunities of the international structures and to America's position within it. Ultimately, duration of the unipolar period will depend on the U.S. reaction to several challenges, most importantly, the contradiction between the persisting desire to remain in the premier global spot and reluctance to bear the costs associated with this position. The pursuit of primacy will induce the United States to be the stabilizer of last resort in regional crises. Mastanduno believes U.S. officials have responded to the domestic constraint by emphasizing pragmatism in interventions, avoiding excessive commitments, minimizing casualties, and emphasizing exit strategies. That adds up to selective engagement—a case-by-case, nondoctrinal, nontemplate approach.

To explain structural change, complexity theory, an offshoot of the basic systems framework, offers an approach to the study of many actors and their simultaneous interactions, specifying how the agents interact, and, as a consequence, what properties occur at the level of the whole society (Axelrod, 1997; Cederman, 1997). Among the questions raised in this framework are these: With given rules or operating norms about such behaving units, do some strategies dominate the population? Do clear patterns of behavior develop? How can we know a complex agent-structure system is working, that is, adapting? The answer lies in achieving a measure of fitness—a midpoint between ordered hierarchy (ultrastability) and chaos, which depends on the capacity of America to convert hard and soft power into influence to shape the global order, says Clemens (2000: 9, 223). Thus, if the ability of the United States to cope with complex challenges and opportunities presented by intervention issues yields an emergent phenomenon without central direction or planning bringing a new system based on cooperation for mutual gain, then the post–Cold War system meets the test of fitness and adaptability.

This study explores the implications of U.S. intervention in the remodeled structure of the international system, the unipolar post–Cold War framework and American actions and reactions within it, by examining the interplay among intervention policy choices, resultant success or failure of implementation methods, and cumulative foreign policy learning experience expressed through proposed foreign policy and military doctrines of intervention and alternative definitions of national interest. To that end, the picture of intervention is analyzed from varying perspectives: the early chapters analyze aspects of the current global structure, various interpretations of it, and intervention policy alternatives; later chapters focus on post–Cold War intervention cases, historical trends in U.S. intervention practice, and developing world conditions that offer intervention opportunity. At the close, intervention lessons and impact are brought together through the lens of fitness and adaptability.

1

Global Structure and American Intervention

INTRODUCTION

Global structure helps shape a superpower's response to world problems once its form is clear, widely accepted, and firmly set. In times of transition, however, leading powers assume a premier role in shaping a new international system by virtue of their dominant position. The United States as sole superpower occupies a special place: its influence will be determined by the degree of power concentration and superiority it holds in relation to other units and the way it chooses to activate such capability. Existing conditions within and among countries throughout the world provide fodder for a superpower to construct new rules and policies of involvement, determining when, where, why, and how to intervene. The most important feature of this process, which becomes more significant over time, is reflected through the intervention actions taken in response to opportunity. This was true during the Cold War era and it is true today. Internal problems of states often become international concerns, and decisions to intervene in these situations reflect a powerful linkage between domestic and international politics, showing first, the way domestic unrest in countries around the world is perceived to be tied to the security of the international system, and second, how the structure of the system dictates norms of intervention policy and practice in particular cases.

Intervention events essentially defined the historical moments delineating the beginning, midpoint, and end of the Cold War: from the American intervention in the Greek civil war to the Soviet Union's intervention in Hungary and Czechoslovakia, from the U.S. long-term involvement in Vietnam to the Soviet parallel experience in Afghanistan, and from the installation of communist regimes in Eastern Europe to the collapse of this political order in 1989—made possible by the Soviet decision not to intervene to maintain the status quo. When the Cold War ended, the elegant simplicity of bipolar conceptualizations that had explained intervention activity in international relations for nearly 50 years became obsolete. Today, the status of state sovereignty is changing and restrictions on intervention no longer exist. The growing significance of indigenous ethnic groups and transnational movements, both claiming popular loyalty, presents challenges for national governments, particularly when coupled with a plethora of social grievances and economic hardship. Problems of civil strife frequently develop out of such situations, exacerbating already intolerable living conditions for substantial segments of the population, and of necessity leading to pleas of assistance from the outside. The scene creates a ripe moment: an intervention opportunity. Forms of civil tension and instability—standard fare in the mosaic of contemporary politics—continue to appear in the current age, from extreme repression in Afghanistan, to anarchy in Somalia, to self-determination, secession movements in ex-Yugoslavia. Throughout the international community, discussion of these conflicts focuses more and more on the need to render assistance, with the burden for this task falling to the United States, and to international organizations. The call to intervene is loud and clear.

Changing world conditions and expanded requests for intervention have led to a serious dilemma of the post–Cold War era: the disappearance of bipolar hostility between the United States and the Soviet Union relaxed important guidelines that previously dictated superpower intervention choices. The concept of sphere of influence, widely accepted implicitly and explicitly as a legitimate operating rule during the Cold War, allowed the United States and Soviet Union to extend their foreign policy domain over designated geographical regions and groups of states, making it extremely easy or extraordinarily difficult for each side to intervene in situations of domestic instability in given countries. Today, it is far easier and more acceptable for great powers and international organizations to intervene in all kinds of conflicts abroad, but harder to decide where and when such intervention is warranted; the contemplation and evaluation of a range of intervention activity in the modern world is both complicated and confusing. What is the rationale justifying intervention decisions in the new world order?

What is the global structure of the post–Cold War and how is intervention related to it? This question will be addressed by discussing (1) intervention logic and theoretical expectations in a unipolar and/or hegemonic international system; (2) dominant features of the contemporary global environment: domestic instability challenges, superpower intervention challenges, and global leadership issues; (3) global system-intervention linkages; and (4) assessments of contemporary world order.

INTERVENTION LOGIC AND EXPECTATIONS

What logical basis informs American intervention decisions? During the Cold War, the policy argument was constructed in accordance with the bipolar division, in defensive language: intervention was designed as competition with an enemy, a fight to be won. Justifications for intervention included: to protect the free world, to maintain balance of power predominance over the Russians, to contain Soviet geographic expansion and advantage (keep sea lane access to other territories open), prevent the spread of communism, and keep the Western Hemisphere under U.S. sphere of influence. The logic undermining intervention in the post–Cold War period, when this long-held and amply applied reasoning fell apart, derives from a different set of premises, reflecting positive, offensive strategic thinking designed to shape the new environment: create internal order, build civil society in failed states, neutralize rogue states and/or their leaders, alleviate human suffering in refugee populations. The goals extend into social concerns; the shift in competition from power balances between superpowers moves to control over local disturbances, and the enemy concept is less specifically defined. These new directives plague policy-makers because it is usually easier to follow a defensive directive—for example, damage control (prevent communism and Russians from expansion designs) defined Cold War mentality—than to implement an offensive goal (help the suffering through humanitarian gestures, expand civil society) used to structure post–Cold War policy thinking.

The new slogans have not led to a focused simple guideline or clarifying momentum achieved during the Cold War years. As a result, public debate on American foreign policy doctrine proceeds along three dimensions: (1) why a new doctrine does not exist (lack of long-term vision and persistence of short-term planning are the major reasons); (2) why a new doctrine is necessary (general guidelines are necessary to make rational policy responses); and (3) what the doctrine should be (suggestions range from isolationism to multilateral engagement; from narrow definitions of national interest to broad conceptualizations of humanitarian concerns).

In the first decade of the post–Cold War era, over the course of *two* presidents, the United States participated in *six* major interventions—Panama, the Persian Gulf, Somalia, Haiti, Bosnia, and Kosovo. At least *six* foreign policy doctrinal themes and presentations have surfaced, though not one has assumed permanence. The four themes include: the new world order, assertive multilateralism, selective engagement, and preventive defense; major proposals include: the U.S. Commission on National Security/21st Century (2000) and the Commission on America's National Interests (2000).

By contrast, during a similar time frame marking the start of the Cold War: under the watch of a *single* president, Harry Truman, American policy coalesced around a *single* doctrine governing its global actions: a National Security Council Report (NSC-68) which outlined a world view and U.S. policy goals within it. This document essentially established policy guidelines for the entire Cold War period, although precise application of particulars changed over time. The United States intervened in *two* civil conflicts, in Greece and in Korea, during those early years, actions that largely defined parameters for future involvements, linked doctrine with practice, and established rules of engagement between the superpowers structuring the environment of international politics that operated for more than 40 years. The rules placed limits on what either could do, or what they were willing to do.

Ironically, the fast-paced activity characterizing the contemporary age has not produced a quick-serve fresh foreign policy plan. For various reasons, ranging from theoretical arguments to policy hopes to cynical perspectives, the degree of intervention and its motivating causes were expected to change after the Cold War was over. Some suggested there would be a reduction in superpower intervention levels, others suggested an increase, still others predicted no changes at all. The theoretical argument projecting expansion of intervention in a single-superpower international system is basically correct, although the nature and purpose of intervention called for in the post–Cold War environment was not anticipated.

A Reduction of Superpower Intervention Levels

As Richard N. Haass (1994: 2) stated, there were grounds for supposing that the end of the Cold War would usher in a period of international relations in which political and military competition would diminish and the need to use force abroad would decline. As the 1990s began, it looked as though a world was emerging in which democratic and market-oriented governments would dominate, old conflicts were being solved, and the United Nations was starting to resemble the institution originally created by its founders—as peace and conflict manager for the international system. The Soviet Union and later Russia were working with the United States to resolve conflicts, "gone were the days when Moscow provided material and diplomatic backing for its clients while casting vetoes in the Security Council to frustrate Western initiatives" (Haass, 1994: 2). Neither Russia nor anyone else was able or willing to compete with the United States in the political-military realm on a global scale. In this environment, it became possible for the Bush administration to speak of building a new world order in which states did not threaten or use force to settle disputes and governments embraced democracy, human rights, or liberal economic policies. As Haass indicated, though, things have turned out differently. There have been many undesirable developments, including war in the Persian Gulf, violence in Bosnia, a variety of humanitarian nightmares in Africa. On balance, says Haass (1994: 2), the post–Cold War world promises to be a messy one where violence is common, where conflicts within and between nation-states abound, and where the question of U.S. military intervention becomes more rather than less commonplace and more rather than less complicated.

Continuity of Superpower Intervention Levels

Walter LaFeber (1998: 38–39) has suggested that the Cold War and post–Cold War areas represent a continuous pattern defined by the root of American foreign policy as the determination for control over order as the stabilizing factor. The basis of U.S. policy in the Cold War was designed to take advantage of imperial ambition opportunities for business, cultural, and political interests. Expansion or enlargement of U.S. market and political principles produced not stability but discontent. This led America to step in to create order and stability not realizing how their interests and power had contributed to disorder and instability initially. Americans have pushed for self-determination in Latin America in recent years because it reflects what they like to think are their historic values, and because U.S. officials have believed that they can control the rate of change in the hemisphere, according to LaFeber (1998: 39). Now, foreign policy decision-makers have finally concluded that favoring electoral processes is preferable to the damage done by aligning the nation's interests with military rulers with whom Americans have historically cohabited. Still, Americans have used force even after the Cold War because they continue to see its use justified by traditional American principles even when they embark on their own contradictory course of seeking both opportunity and stability (LaFeber, 1998: 40).

An Increase in Superpower Intervention Levels

In a prophetic statement published in 1968, Oran R. Young (178–180) argued that intervention would expand in the future. Defining intervention as "organized and systematic activities across recognized boundaries aimed at affecting the political authority structures of the target—designed either to replace existing structures or to shore up structures thought to be in danger of collapse," Young views it as a variable, recurrent feature of the history of international politics though not of equal importance in every region of the world. Several factors determine the opportunities for intervention in international politics. First are disparities in effective power among the actors in an international system: the more extensive the disparities in power, the greater the opportunities for intervention among the actors in the system, for the ability of the weaker actors to fend off outside intervention is likely to be sharply limited. Second is the structure of an international system: in a system clearly dominated by a single actor there is little lesser powers can do to prevent intervention by that actor. Third is the relative internal viability of the actors in an international system: the less viable an actor is, the more susceptible it will be to intervention by outside powers. During periods of extended civil strife, the ability of an actor to resist external incursions tends to decline. Fourth is the level of interdependence (as opposed to autonomy) among the actors in an international system: the higher the level of interdependence, the greater the opportunities for intervention in international politics. The growth of interdependence among actors increases both the volume and the functional significance of interactions among them. While this may produce opportunities and incentives for the expansion of political community, it also enlarges the scope for interventions on the part of any given actor in the affairs of other actors. In the contemporary international system, opportunities are particularly marked since the level of interdependence among the actors in the system is both high and rising.

The implications of these systemic determinants indicate that intervention will continue to be an important feature of the international system for the foreseeable future and that existing norms of nonintervention in international politics will be ineffective and unacceptable in the foreseeable future, says

Young (1968: 184). Norms of nonintervention are particularly characteristic of state systems in which the boundaries between actors are clear and the ability of individual actors to operate autonomously is great. Young suggests that new questions will arise in place of discussions of nonintervention. One focuses on the purposes or objectives for which intervention is to be considered legitimate (for example, in the interests of encouraging democracy or free enterprise). Is intervention an acceptable means of altering the highly asymmetrical distribution of welfare values in the contemporary system? Despite the prevalence of intervention, a notable lack of consensus appears on these normative problems, Young notes, and he declines to forecast any confident conclusions concerning such trends.

Why might we expect more intervention during the current age? Richard Smoke (1977: 27–28), also in a prophetic statement, describes the world at the end of the twentieth century with a vastly greater number of independent and semi-independent centers of decision-making, including some players who are not organized governments all coming to possess a wide range of advanced, very destructive military capabilities. Conflict may occur on a greater number of layers in the world social system—economic, political, ideological, territorial, tribal—Smoke asserts, and he suggests if the analysis proves accurate, a fresh look of the problem of military intervention is necessary. The world he imagines is likely to be highly intervention prone. It is more intervention prone than a bipolar (or tripolar) world system, in which conflict runs mainly along one or two layers and most actions of global significance are taken by, or at the instigation of, the two or three polar powers. In a world of military plenty and a substantial number of independent or semi-independent actors, there is considerably higher probability that a minor conflict may seem to threaten the interests of—or present opportunities to—regional powers who are prepared to intervene largely on their own and who have the capability to do so, according to Smoke. Moreover, this kind of world constellation is intervention prone owing to increasing instabilities in local situations that often tend to create conditions inviting more and larger interventions. The consequences of local instability include the fact and threat of much greater intervention.

Smoke (1977: 31) points to a paradox of the logic of military intervention in that early recognition by decision-makers of the escalation-prone character of a local conflict can generate an antidote to it in the form of greater caution in policy-making. Their comprehension of the hazards which the political complexity and military plenty of the coming world may create could lead them to accept the danger as a real limitation upon the feasibility of intervention strategies—even in specific situations where the exact route by which the hazards could materialize might not be clear.

Changing Intervention Demands

The post–Cold War world has created significant expectations with respect to the type of intervention demands. Today, greater attention is given to planning scenarios of peacekeeping, preventive deployment, and selective enforcement, concepts not linked to traditional ideas of threats or enemies. This complicates military planning and also constrains efforts to develop public support. The peacekeeping and preventive deployment missions are devoid of such thinking of deterrence and defeating an enemy. The American military emphasis on heavy forces as a means of winning wars was appropriate to the primary Cold War missions, and remains essential to enforcement operations, but does not suffice for the wider range of peace operations, states Robert B. McCalla (1998: 105). The perception of threats affects how the overall mission of the armed forces is conceptualized and how success in carrying out those missions is measured. This influences strategy and force structure, a major challenge in the twenty-first century. The United States continues to be well prepared to deal with traditional military threats to interests and allies, but it is less prepared politically and militarily to deal with contingencies that involve low intensity conflict or are essentially noncombatant in nature. McCalla's comparison of Cold War missions of the U.S. armed forces with some of the missions proposed for the post–Cold War period is shown in Table 1.1. In the post-Cold War world, a known and agreed upon enemy no longer exists; policing activity plays a far stronger role than before. Intervention today demands constabulary training beyond traditional skills of the professional soldier, a clear change.

GLOBAL STRUCTURE FEATURES

The changes in superpower intervention levels—increased demands for humanitarian tasks, peacekeeping, and peace building—develop from three interrelated features of the modern international system: (1) the degree of domestic instability within countries around the world, taking account of two recently developing phenomena: ethnic conflict and nation-state breakdown; (2) the degree of international stability defined by changing threats and interests, derived in significant measure from assessments of civil unrest, and norms of intervention strategy toward suffering states viewed as legitimate within the international community; and (3) the nature of global leadership exercised by the United States. Together, the challenges and policies affiliated with them determine structural evolution of the global system.

Domestic Instability Challenges

Since the end of the Cold War, conflicts between communal groups and states have been recognized as a major challenge to domestic and international security in most parts of the world. Minority peoples are the principal victims of gross human rights violations (Gurr, 1995: 212). Communal conflict has devastated the former Yugoslavia and East-Central Africa and threatens the stability in former republics of the Soviet Union: protracted conflicts are being

Table 1.1
U.S. Armed Service Roles and Participation in Different Missions

Cold War Mission: To deter and defeat enemies; offense strategy preferred. Primarily interstate conflicts, military means dominate.

Army:	Heavy forces; armor and artillery dominant; equipment in key locations; forces in place with reserves to follow.
Air Force:	Long-range bombing and fighters; transport secondary. Army troops and reserves moved to meet equipment.
Navy:	Power projection and sea control; aircraft carriers and submarines; transport secondary.
Marines:	Limited amphibious and low-intensity conflict operations.

Post–Cold War Peacekeeping Mission: To engage in conflict resolution; armed defensive force; inter- and intra-state conflicts; noncombat operations.

Army:	Lightly armed forces, mobility important, support units greater role, no combat role.
Air Force:	Primarily transport and logistical role, surveillance.
Navy:	Primarily transport and logistics for Army and Marines.
Marines:	Noncombat roles, patrol and evacuations.

Post–Cold War Preventive Deployment Mission: To deter potential combatants from fighting. To avoid combat but be prepared for it if needed.

Army:	Latent combat role but mostly a presence "just in case."
Air Force:	Latent combat role; if extended stay, transport and logistical role becomes more important.
Navy:	Latent combat role; if extended stay, transport and logistical role becomes more important.
Marines:	Noncombat roles intended.

Source: Adapted from McCalla (1998: 108).

fought over ethnic and national issues in the Middle East and Southeast Asia. The Minorities at Risk project, directed by Ted Gurr, an ongoing study of the status, demands, and conflicts of 292 groups throughout the world (virtually all active organizations during the 1980s and 1990s), discovered that:

- Of 190 countries in the world, 120 have politically significant minorities.
- Indigenous peoples, strongly motivated by a desire to protect and assert group identity, form the basis of contemporary movements for secession or regional autonomy.
- Communal contenders who have experienced discrimination demand greater rights within societies, not a desire to exit from them.
- About 30 countries in parts of Eurasia and Africa are at serious risk of violent conflict and instability for the foreseeable future.

"Ethnopolitical" conflict increased sharply from the 1950s through the early 1990s. Most communal conflicts begin with acts of protest that escalate into violent conflict, often escalating very quickly, in part because official responses are likely to be repressive. "Ethnonationalist" civil wars are the longest, most deadly conflicts of recent decades. They are fought with great intensity because communal demands for independence imply the breakup of existing states. The potential for this type of conflict remains high in many parts of the world because organized, assertive minorities want access to social, political, and economic opportunities and protection of their rights in existing societies and states. One radical proposal for resolving conflicts of this nature is to redraw territorial boundaries of states to correspond more closely to the social and cultural boundaries among ethnic groups, states Gurr (1995: 217). But such a strategy would leave the aspirations of many nonterritorial communal groups unsatisfied, and even if political reconstruction is achieved peacefully, it may create or intensify new communal conflicts.

The array of ethnic unrest illustrates how the feature of the post–Cold War world that is most troubling is hatred that divides people by race, creed, and national origin. The explosion of communal violence is the paramount issue facing the human rights movement today, and containing the abuses committed in the name of ethnic or religious groups will be a continuing challenge for the future. Charles King (2001: 168), however, cautions that ethnic conflict can be a misleading label, for it mistakes the causes of hatred for the causes of violence. Since communist doctrine began unraveling in 1989, conventional wisdom has linked the psychology and politics of hatred to the end of totalitarian rule that repressed ancient rivalries. The passions have been produced by a confluence of diverse factors ranging from modernization and migration to democratization and limited resources. They flourish on fear and uncertainty. But the proliferation of hatreds is not emerging out of nowhere; it is shaped and given form. What is assumed to be historic and ancient is often modern and of recent origin. The proliferation of minority consciousness has created a new set of incentives for conflicts: rising ethnic tension over minorities is built around traditional differences that, except for nationalist appeals of opportunistic leaders, would not have been transformed into hostility or violence. Rather, contemporary leaders use the accumulated historical animosity for their own political and economic gains through deliberate manipulation of long-standing fears and passions. As King (2001: 167) writes, "(N)o one would deny that all civil conflicts have a volatile mix at their core: myths that can be mustered into service, politicians willing to use those myths, and a state apparatus too weak to ensure basic civil order."

Finally, transitions to democracy can create uncertainty that fuels passions and rivalry. The problem is not democracy, but the turbulent transition to democracy; the psychological pressure on populations undergoing political change creates a sense of anxiety that frequently makes people seek refuge in belief systems that involve definitions of membership and belonging. This is especially true when economic conditions limit the resources. The more limited the resources the greater the danger of communal strife. Conflicts over self-determination are being settled usually when ethnic groups gain greater autonomy and power-sharing within existing states, notes Gurr (2001: 1). Moreover, democratic governments continue to be more successful in resolving violent social conflicts than autocratic ones.

Apart from communal violence, a second problem facing countries these days is nation-state breakdown. Robert Kaplan (1994: 44) describes conditions in West Africa arising from coalescence of ethnic, economic, and political issues as an archtypical situation that will spread and soon confront civilization, remapping the political world. Kaplan sees worldwide demographic, environmental, and societal stress, in which criminal anarchy emerges as the real "strategic" danger. "Diseases, overpopulation, unprovoked crime, scarcity of resources, refugee migrations, the increasing erosion of nation-states and international borders, and the empowerment of private armies, security firms, and international drug cartels are now most tellingly demonstrated through a West African prism." Much of the underdeveloped world, he asserts, is experiencing the withering away of central government, the rise of tribal domains, and the growing pervasiveness of violence.

The gloomy historical analogy Kaplan draws is instructive. "Africa may be as relevant to the future character of world politics as the Balkans were a hundred years ago, prior to the two Balkan wars and the First World War. Then the threat was the collapse of empires and the birth of nations based solely on tribe. Now the threat is more elemental: nature unchecked" (Kaplan, 1994: 76). The coming upheaval, in which states collapse and contact with the outside world takes place through dangerous coastal trading posts, will loom large in the twenty-first century.

Precisely because much of Africa is in duress at a time when the Cold War has ended, when environmental and demographic stress in the world is becoming critical, and when the ability of nation-states to survive is receding, African politics suggests what war, borders, and ethnic politics will be like in the future. The central proposition is that some of the greatest threats to international security in the future will result from the absence of legitimate sovereignty, manifested in collapsing central governments and accompanied by the rise of new forces in politics, such as religion and ethnicity. Overwhelmed by the burden of their financial commitments and debt, governments have been forced to withdraw from their standard political, economic, and social roles they had once played. Relinquishment of authority has created a vacuum in social services, now being filled by previously rejected socioeconomic forces—religion, ethnic associations, and privately organized economic interests—that have succeeded in capitalizing on the failure of the state.

The real political threat to stability lies in the structural detachment of populations from their traditional dependency on government and the attendant increases in various kinds of nongovernmental or private initiative that can prove disruptive to social cohesion. According to Alex Rondos (1994: 485), any government in need of such managerial correction is likely to be quite unpopular and surviving on little political support. Economic survival for most of the population will be largely unrelated to any government initiative. Survival sought by autonomous means invariably entails alternative political and social organization that is usually provided by religious, ethnic, or private economic interest groups. To date, the social impact of economic reforms and the retreating state has been insufficiently understood. The explosion of nongovernmental initiatives, bringing communities together to achieve a particular social or economic purpose, is one of the unheralded documented developments of the last decade, states Rondos (1994: 487). This poses real danger for future international peace and stability because of the magnitude of the mental leap from comprehensive social security to comprehensive insecurity that may ultimately cause the greatest threats to international security. A serious reality faces the current world in which both the infrastructure of society and the superstructure of a belief in a social contract have disappeared. These conditions engender uncertainty for political and economic futures.

Do these countries represent a threat of imminent disorder that can be averted by international acts of intervention? The West's failure to develop a successful approach to deal with political disintegration stems from the inability of leaders to operate in a secular state-based system of developing relief policies appropriate for political systems in the midst of chaos and collapse, argues Rondos (1994: 488). Whether countries in the midst of transition from highly centralized economic systems and authoritarian political regimes to deregulated and demilitarized democratic pluralism will achieve this goal will rest on the willingness of the international system to move forward such a complex process. Ethnic and religious tensions require solutions designed for a specific context that maximize the influence of local regimes. Problems, while localized, will demand internationalized organized help.

International Stability Challenges

How serious is this international call for aid? How should threat and national interests be determined in the new age? Stanley Hoffman, a leading American scholar and critic of the U.S. role in the Vietnam War, warned in the 1960s that it was important to distinguish between two kinds of threats to international stability and the attendant implications for intervention. First are threats that caution against intervention. There will arise in scores of countries risks of internal disruption that may be helped from abroad yet correspond to domestic realities. "We must learn to live with such perils and to accept violent social and political change—even if private American interests happen to be the targets, even if communists should occasionally be the local beneficiaries and communist powers the likely allies of the local winners," he said. Yet, some threats are more serious and intervention may be appropriate as a means to reestablish international stability. On the other hand, warned Hoffman, the United States should be concerned with the external implications of internal changes, and "especially interested in preventing domestic disruptions from engulfing the major powers and domestic revolutionary regimes from exporting their recipes by force" (quoted in Pfeffer, 1968: 198).

With the Cold War over, the United States retains more traditional resources of power than any other country. It also has the ideological and institutional resources to retain its leadership in the new domains of transnational interdependence. In the decades immediately ahead, America will be the world's leading nation—militarily and politically, and to a large extent economically. It may consent to leadership only reluctantly, but it cannot escape its destiny. Hoffman's distinction between real and marginal global stability threats, therefore, is particularly critical for the United States at this juncture.

How are U.S. leaders to learn to distinguish between vital and peripheral security interests? Ted Galen Carpenter (1991) proposes a rigid set of criteria to evaluate threats to vital interests: country crises should have a direct, immediate, and substantial connection with America's physical survival, its political independence, or the preservation of its domestic freedoms. Such threats, to truly vital interests are relatively rare, and may be even rarer in the post–Cold War setting where no potential adversary is capable of making a bid for global domination. The pursuit of stability thus is an elusive goal, since most solutions to complex political, social, and economic problems are merely temporary. New opposition forces invariably arise, and maneuvering for advantage on the part of rival parties within states continues unabated. If the United States links domestic instability issues with the achievement of global stability, and thereby injects itself into a host of regional quarrels, it will need military forces that are larger, more diverse, and more expensive than those maintained to wage the Cold War, Carpenter predicts. It was one thing to undertake such expensive and risky obligations to prevent Soviet global domination, but is quite another to perpetuate those obligations merely to prevent vaguely defined instability or discourage the outbreak of local quarrels that have little or no relevance to America's security interests.

Rondos (1994: 488–489) offers a counter perspective, identifying civil violence as an international security threat. Civil conflicts, the collapse of civil order, represent a particular challenge in the post–Cold War era. The images of starvation and torture provoke international outcry that plays an integral part in the course of a conflict. An outpouring of public opinion has come to influence the course of civil conflicts and elevate them to the international level. A related problem concerns the plight of refugees. Populations crossing frontiers to establish temporary residence and prepare or arm themselves for a return to their homeland have become a singular characteristic of the regional insecurity generated by these civil conflicts. By crossing a frontier, they are classified as refugees requiring protection and either resettlement or repatriation. The security dilemma created by migration is the following: refugee programs attract more refugees, and in the context of war, these programs can suit the purpose of the aggressor. This dilemma forces the question whether the cause of human rights, international security, and the interests of refugees are served by providing victims with mere protection upon escape.

The conflict in the former Yugoslavia during the 1990s is perhaps the primary reason that the international community began to recognize civil disorder as a potential international security challenge. But this realization left important policy questions unanswered: To what degree does any interventionary measure in a civil conflict (such as humanitarian efforts) become the first step in a long chain leading to protracted military commitment? What are the costs and benefits of this type of commitment? Should intervention initiatives be directed unilaterally by the United States through multilateral coalitions, or by the United Nations, the major international body chartered to deal with peace and security problems in the global arena? The warring leaders in Bosnia manipulated divisions over ethnic and religious identity that perpetuated the crisis. For the international community to take action that would have legitimacy in the eyes of the parties to the conflict, an intervention would have to be justified by standards immune from the prevailing sentiments of local nationalism. But when a government no longer guarantees basic services for its population, it has abdicated the right to sovereignty. The tasks, first to disarm and then to maintain civil order until authority is regained by local authorities and sovereignty is reconstituted, involves significant levels of intervention with a broad mission: to create conditions that enable the restitution of a legal system, the re-establishment of economic activity and regulations, the fostering of political parties. This is a tall order.

During the Cold War, it would have been unthinkable for outside governments to seriously consider the dispatch of military forces to protect the delivery of humanitarian supplies to a country undergoing civil strife. Yet this situation occurred in Iraq, Somalia, and Bosnia. Although the dissolution of the U.S.-Soviet rivalry has removed political impediments to such forms of intervention, new obstacles to such engagements are emerging at the multilateral level. A better understanding of what constitutes elements of potential insecurity in the post–Cold War era is an essential prerequisite to proposing ideas for reconstruction packages for states experiencing massive civil unrest. Although domestic instability is a reality, the influence it has on the level of international security remains interpretative. Investigating problems of social collapse and their attendant effects on the climate of international peace and stability requires fresh thinking about local-global linkages and revised perspectives in anticipation of what post–Cold War crisis might bring.

A second issue of relevance to the international community is the evolution of international norms. Ian Forbes and Mark Hoffman (1993: 13) remind us that the principle of nonintervention is firmly and formally embedded in the normative conventions governing international relations. In contemporary international law, states are clearly proscribed from intervening in the domestic affairs of other states because such intervention violates sovereignty. In the United Nations, severe restrictions are placed on the right to intervene in the domestic jurisdiction of states. Article 2 (7) states: "Nothing contained in the present Charter shall authorize the United Nations to intervene in matters which are essentially within the domestic jurisdiction of any state or shall require Members to submit such matters to settlement under the present Charter; but this principle shall not prejudice the application of enforcement measures under Chapter VII." In December 1965, the General Assembly adopted a "Declaration on the Inadmissibility of Intervention in the Domestic Affairs of States and the Protection of their Independence and Sovereignty," according to which "no state has the right to intervene, director or indirectly, for any reason whatever, in the internal or external affairs of any other state" And "no state shall organize, assist, foment, finance, incite or tolerate subversive, terrorist or armed activities directed toward the violent overthrow of another state, or interfere in civil strife in another state." It was strengthened in General Assembly Resolution 2625, unanimously passed in 1970. Here nonintervention is depicted as one of the "Principles of International Law Concerning Friendly Relations among States." The prohibition was reconfirmed in the judgment reached by the International Court of Justice in 1986, which examined the merits in military and paramilitary activities in and against Nicaragua. The principle of nonintervention, therefore, has played a central role in the evolution of the international order, which now exists. Both legal commitments against intervention and the practice of intervention serve the political purposes of particular nations.

There is disagreement, though, about the basis on which the principle of nonintervention should be established. For some theorists, the principle rests on the inherent right of states to claim sovereignty and independence; others argue, however, that the principle must be grounded on the rights of individuals to self-determination. The controversy between these theorists, therefore, revolves around the question of whether rights in the international system inhere in individuals or states. If we are going to have a principle of nonintervention, then we need to know exactly what the principle protects, say R.J. Vincent and Peter Wilson (1993: 127–128). A simple notion of domestic jurisdiction or political space is hardly adequate. The argument, if it is to be morally convincing, needs to be about the precise nature and content of that space. The difficulty with the principle of nonintervention in this regard relates to the initial allocation of that political space we now call the state. Was it allocated according to some just principle? This requires that the meaning of self-determination and legitimacy needs to be examined. It seems no longer relevant in an age in which several "self-determining" and therefore "legitimate" states have committed, and continue to commit, gross violations of the basic rights of their citizens. In the face of these various difficulties, we have to engage with an emerging notion of international legitimacy, which opens up the state to scrutiny from outsiders and propels us beyond nonintervention.

N.J. Rengger (1993: 179) says that a system of states based on territorial integrity and political sovereignty must view the possibility of legitimate intervention as, at least potentially, one of the most fundamental challenges possible to its ruling features. When is it legitimate for one state to intervene in the affairs of another? If the ethical state of the contemporary international system is a fragmented one, then it is possible under certain circumstances to make statements such as "this is a justified intervention" but that no "set of rules" with universal applicability could be drawn up to tell us what those circumstances might be. Judgments about particular cases of intervention would need to be sensitive to the compelling levels of ethical considerations at work in such instances, but simple judgments in general will not be possible, states Rengger (1993: 189). Further, if the notion of a list of conditions for "just" intervention and a list of prohibitions for "unjust" is abandoned, new questions about the ethics of intervention arise. These questions can be answered only contextually, in judgment about a given case. In effect, traditional approaches to ethical and explanatory questions involved in assessing instances of intervention no longer work.

There may be no simple panacea, no ready remedy to apply to the problem of intervention in the international system. A shift in the nature of the analysis away from legal interpretation means leaving aside old, established assumptions about statehood and sovereignty in favor of a practice that recognizes the relational character of power and the significance of subjective judgment (Forbes, 1993: 227). Classic international law treatises speak of intervention as "dictatorial interference" resulting in the "subordination of the will" of one sovereign to that of another. Intervention is an influencing force designed to modify, settle, or hinder some action. In the field of international law, "intervention" generally indicates an external power's unlawful interference with the territorial integrity or political independence of a state such as by means of invasion, intimidation, or subversion.

To what extent is the international community prepared to treat certain internal problems as warranting a collective response, whether or not a specific threat to international peace can be demonstrated? asks Lori Fisler Damrosch (1993: 5). Internal conflict includes ethnic strife, overthrow of an established government, disintegration of civil order, interference with humanitarian relief efforts, and other violence occurring within a state. The phenomenon of fragmentation of existing nation-states has transformed some internal conflicts into interstate ones. Here, the Yugoslav crisis is illustrative. When the crisis began, the Serbian-dominated federal government contended that boundaries between Yugoslav republics had no significance in the eyes of international law, and that its own actions to prevent secession fell within exclusive domestic jurisdiction. With the disintegration of the federation and eventual international recognition of most of the republics as separate states, the conflict was transformed to an international rather than predominantly internal set of crises. The overlapping issues of self-determination, secession, and the contested legal significance of internal borders have emerged vividly in other parts of the world as well.

The international system is going through a period of change, but the essential features of a structure of independent states are likely to remain relatively stable. The UN charter reflects two clusters of values, says Damrosch (1993: 8), which intersect with each other and may sometimes work at cross-purposes. In one cluster are state system values, including sovereign equality. In another cluster are human rights values, principles relating to fundamental rights and freedoms of individuals. These two value schemes interrelate with two types of objectives relevant to international legal rules on intervention: objectives of conflict prevention or containment and objectives of realization of autonomy. They are at the core of the legal system's commitment to a norm against external involvement in internal affairs. As to whether a normative consensus is emerging under which international involvement in an internal crisis is justified, a significant majority in the international community has been willing to endorse collective action over situations including: (1) genocide, ethnic cleansing, war crimes, crimes against humanity, and similar atrocities entailing loss of life on a mass scale; (2) interference with the delivery of humanitarian relief to endangered civilian populations; (3) violations of cease-fire agreements; (4) collapse of civil order, entailing substantial loss of life and precluding the possibility of identifying any authority capable of granting or withholding consent to international involvement; and (5) irregular interruption of democratic governance.

Global Leadership Challenges

Three main strategy and policy issues face the United States in the post–Cold War environment: first, deciding and designing effective perceptions of its power; second, formulating templates to make appropriate policy choices; and third, setting meaningful parameters for peace and security that shape the global order toward a desirable end. Though separate problems, they are linked. How American leadership and power will be managed and perceived in the international community is a function of its policy choices. The collection of intervention policy choices over time and across situations will influence the expectations for future involvement with states in the international community. In turn, the predictions and accompanying role of U.S. intervention will shape the environment for global security and for peace.

International politics may be conceptualized as the process of acquiring, shaping, distributing, and exercising power and influence. Randall L. Schweller and David Priess (1997: 14–15) outline a model for governance involving three interrelated processes: the exercise of power, the rules of order, and the level of institutionalization. With respect to the first process, power may be exercised in three ways: naked power relies on brute force or coercion, with threats of severe sanctions for noncompliance; influence rests on legitimacy, authority, and socialization; management is centered on administrative capacity, skill, and directorship. The second process focuses on the rules of order. Three generic mechanisms regulate which social order can arise: negotiation, imposition, and spontaneous, uncoordinated action. The first case involves voluntary bargaining among roughly equal actors. Imposed orders are intended to advance the interests of dominant actors and do not require the explicit consent of subordinates. Spontaneous orders arise without deliberate purpose and do not involve explicit consent of subjects; they are consequences of the behavior of actors seeking their own interests. The third process revolves around the degree of institutionalization (low, moderate, or high) that characterizes the system. Institutions can be formal or informal; they are the sets of rights and rules governing interstate behavior and world politics. A highly institutionalized system has formal organizations with the capacity, skill, and authority for management, with explicit rules and rights based on shared understandings among the major actors.

From this typology, Schweller and Priess predict that the exercise of naked power is likely to create an imposed order characterized by low institutionalization, as in malevolent hegemony and imperialism. Influence as a means of governing often combines aspects of negotiated and spontaneously generated orders and tends to require a moderate to high level of institutionalization, as in benevolent hegemony, bipolar condominium, Great Power spheres of influence, and balance of power politics. Management is the product of negotiated orders and usually entails a high level of formal or informal institutionalization, illustrated by collective security and the Concert system (Schweller and Priess, 1997: 15–16).

When the international system is ruled by a hegemon, governance is probably accomplished through naked power and the imposition of rules or by means of a negotiated order. Which order arises and how it is maintained will depend primarily on whether the hegemon assumes the role of a liberal leader or a nonliberal despot. Whether the hegemon imposes or negotiates the institutional arrangements governing the international system, it will attempt to establish its dominance in several issue areas and to set up a world order based on global rules and rights conducive to its interests. The hegemon provides leadership because it has an overriding interest in the creation of such a system and because it is the only state with enough power to do so. Schweller and Priess (1997: 17–18) assert the hegemons that have most successfully navigated their rise to power and established an order consistent with their objectives have been those that most clearly recognized the limits of power as a basis of rule. Diplomacy is dictated by prudence and expediency—knowing what is possible and acting in accordance with the particular situation. The ideal is the prudent, benevolent hegemon that understands the limits of coercive power and so promotes legitimacy and emulation of its values while tolerating pluralism and diversity.

Where is the United States headed? There no longer exists a shared overarching vision of the U.S. place and purpose in the world. There is no American consensus on the desirable degree of unilateralism versus multilateralism of U.S. foreign policy, or on the extent to which the United States should be engaged in the use of force for less than vital interests. François Heisbourg (1999–2000) describes contemporary perceptions of U.S. power against which to appraise the governance models. In rough composites, two particular images are popular. One characterization is of a harmless, safe leader, a benign hegemon; the other portrays a risky, unpredictable one, the trigger-happy sheriff.

The Benign Hegemon Image. The United States has no countervailing force to balance it. The absence of balancing forces concerns most of international life: unparalleled military force, unrivaled strategic strength through a global network of U.S.-led alliances, close to absolute dominance of information technology, and unsurpassed cultural penetration. The world cannot ignore it, but America is basically attempting to focus on what it sees as its own affairs, with no malign intentions. "Strong rather than brutal, candid and possibly naïve, rather than sly or crafty" are images associated with this perspective. A political mindset favors unilateralism. Given its incomparable range of means of power and influence, though, the United States today has a capability to orient multilateral decision-making notably in the United Nations. Yet, even if UN Security Council endorsement of U.S. actions is still valued, there is clearly no appetite for involving the Security Council in any systematic manner. The complexities of diplomacy and particularly multilateral diplomacy are seen as inevitable but secondary at best, needlessly burdensome and constraining at worst. Yet, American institutions tend to make it difficult for the United States to act in an unrestrained manner. The benign hegemon can and should be accommodated.

However reluctant some of America's allies may be to trumpet the fact, leaders and public opinion in many countries have a fairly clear perception of America's role as a key element in what measure of international order may exist, and that the United States remains the only credible ultimate guarantor of that order. The United States is the guarantor of last resort, the only global-scale exporter of security. Europeans are well aware that the world would be a much more dangerous place without the structuring framework provided by global American alliance commitments, be they multilateral or bilateral, and the military means to sustain them. As was demonstrated in the Kosovo intervention, Europeans also understand that preserving a modicum of order in a disorderly world implies a rewriting of some of the traditional rules of the international system. During the Cold War, such American participation in the international security architecture was a given. Now, it is the result of America's own perception and choices. The United States is the great stabilizer.

The Trigger-Happy Sheriff Image. The United States is widely perceived as emphasizing military power as a tool of foreign policy, at the expense of the complexities of diplomacy and other forms of soft power. It uses that power frequently—since the 1990s, countries as different as Panama and Somalia, Haiti and Bosnia, Serbia and Iraq have been the theatre of significant U.S.-led military operations. A second perception is that the sheriff is fickle, not necessarily there when you actually need him. The Dayton Peace Accords ending the Bosnian conflict in 1995 could have been brought about several years earlier. Another perception is that the United States is a paper tiger: not ready to accept pain in the pursuit of less-than-vital interests. Some dictators know that they can hunker down and survive any attack: the Saddam Hussein strategy worked for more than a decade. President Clinton's reluctance to put ground forces in Kosovo during the first two months of the bombing provided a signal as to the limits of U.S. commitment in certain types of crisis, where less-than-vital interests are at stake. The paper-tiger perception leads to the dangerous miscalculation that the polycentric, affluent, and apparently heterogeneous nature of American society makes it impossible for the United States to rise to sustained and painful challenges. Why does the United States rely primarily on military tools, and comparatively little on soft-power assets in which it is also dominant? The United States hardly uses its financial power as a geopolitical tool; foreign aid is not popular, leading to another perception: a penny-wise, pound-foolish sheriff. The costs of military intervention vastly exceed the amount of seed-money that could help preempt crises. For example, providing significant aid to Yugoslavia and continuing the aid package to Somalia in 1990 might have forestalled the disintegration and violence levels later experienced in these regions.

Foreign perceptions of the United States are unlikely to remain static. Several factors could exacerbate the already troublesome trends generated by some of the current perceptions. The shifts since the end of the Cold War indicate a wider gap between the United States and other industrialized states. Also, resentment and feelings of victimization could grow against a globalization process, a process essentially seen as reaping benefits in the United States. There is the greater risk of growing inconsistency in the making of U.S. foreign and security policy and possibilities that the importance of local politics across America will increasingly determine security. Complex pressures may increase the unpredictability of future commitments. The danger posed by these changes is this, according to (Heisbourg, 1999–2000: 16–17): there is no existing institution or paradigm that could handle the consequences of a perceived reduction of the United States' commitment without a heightened risk of destabilization in the international system. The end of the Cold War left America in a position of preponderance. As former Secretary of State Madeleine Albright put it, the United States is "the one indispensable power." This position, though, has not guaranteed that the United States can achieve its foreign policy objectives. There is clear evidence of interventionary limits and obstacles. In Iraq, for more than a decade, neither economic sanctions nor a series of U.S. air strikes could remove Saddam Hussein; in Bosnia, the peace agreement negotiated by the United States failed to resolve the conflict and reduce ethnic tension—only the presence of NATO troops prevents further eruption. Walt (1999: 44) asks what the combination of omniscience and impotence means for the United States as superpower. Is it explained by pursuing the wrong goals at the wrong time with the wrong strategy? Is it explained by a failure of will?

"Americans would like to coerce others to do what they want, but they aren't willing to risk much blood or treasure to make sure they do," says Walt (1999: 46). This tendency is not caused by a lack of vision, leadership, or courage within the U.S. government; rather, it is a direct result of the favorable international position that the country now occupies. The reluctance to "bear any burden" also reveals the tacit recognition that the problems the United States is trying to solve may not be worth an extraordinary level of effort. When other states care more about an issue than the Americans, Washington won't use all its power to press its case; consequently, it will be less likely to determine the outcome to get what it wants.

Another reason reflects the nature of the goals that American leaders have chosen to pursue. The euphoria that accompanied the end of the Cold War encouraged them to adopt an ambitious set of international objectives, from expanding NATO membership to reducing the Russian nuclear arsenal, brokering peace efforts in the Middle East to reconstituting a stable, multiethnic society in war-torn Bosnia, while trying to foster a solution to the simmering conflict between Serbs and ethnic Albanians over Kosovo. This is a breathtaking array of foreign goals. The world is a complicated, chaotic place; trying to run it is costly and difficult. International influence cannot be had on the cheap, and those who want to use U.S. power to deter aggression, halt genocide, or discourage proliferation will have to provide leaders with the means to ensure that their voice is heard and their actions felt.

As an economic power, the post–Cold War United States weighs just about what it did during the previous quarter of a century—a bit less than one-fourth of the world's gross domestic product. The United States represents approximately one-third of the world's military spending, though expenditure has dropped by 25% from the 1986 peak (Heisbourg, 1999–2000: 5). The number of American Army personnel stationed abroad has dropped significantly from Cold War levels, as shown in Table 1.2, changing the intervention occupation profile significantly. New figures reflecting enhancement of Homeland security commitments put spending on the rise. America's economic heft and military strength are currently not much different from what they were during the Cold War, yet the assumption is that the might of this superpower represents a fundamentally new force.

GLOBAL STRUCTURE AND INTERVENTION

In the post–Cold War world, the United States is dominant and is pressured to intervene abroad to remain actively involved in the world in support of its general and central security interests. Given America's preponderance, all crises around the world will require some level of America's attention and often a level of intervention—diplomacy, humanitarian aid, logistical support for other nations' military efforts, and so on. Yet, a strong argument against major and sustained U.S. intervention in certain areas of the world can be made. The case against substantial intervention in conflicts and crises that are peripheral to America's long-term strategic interests is that by focusing on the periphery America will lose the core, states Fareed Zakaria (1994: 180–181), who takes the position that U.S. core strategic interests lie in the preservation of peace and prosperity between the great powers, most of which are clustered around Western Europe and East Asia (with Russia astride both). Some areas are connected to this central goal, "but with one exception—stability in the Middle East is vital to the peace and prosperity of the great powers—these connections often tend to be greatly exaggerated."

Table 1.2
Deployment of U.S. Army Personnel by Geographic Region and Selected Countries: 1967–2000 (September 30 each year)

Year	1967	1970	1973	1977	1980	1983	1987	1990	1993	1997	2000
Latin America	**9,194**	**n.a.**	**196**	**131**	**6,884**	**9,431**	**7,656**	**8,828**	**8,318**	**3,657**	**427**
Panama	8,236	6	7	6	6,771	6,628	6,813	7,608	7,550	2,853	8
Honduras	13		8	4	2	2,592	534	863	626	339	156
Europe (no USSR)	**214,383**	**175,899**	**198,504**	**199,910**	**217,550**	**223,124**	**218,194**	**205,191**	**92,766**	**62,811**	**70,251**
Germany	206,659	169,386	191,448	192,060	207,898	214,825	209,583	197,245	87,030	44,394	53,995
Asia	**376,759**	**364,281**	**49,995**	**35,373**	**32,395**	**29,949**	**34,010**	**35,577**	**27,392**	**28,524**	**29,368**
Japan	7,224	5,917	2,037	2,903	2,423	2,489	2,145	2,030	1,961	1,817	1,787
Korea	50,946	42,629	34,258	32,024	29,647	27,304	31,567	30,150	25,316	26,576	27,481
Thailand	9,328	9,055	4,745	80	49	65	114	122	45	48	39
Vietnam	294,962	294,088	31						2	3	5
Middle East*	**2,564**	**n.a.**	**512**	**731**	**386**	**1,678**	**1,556**	**2,851**	**1,444**	**9,012**	**3,477**
Egypt		31		2	5	1,180	1,258	1,043	493	5,716	354
Saudi Arabia *	58	56	71	218	284	243	150	1,644	655	1,429	770
Kuwait									211	1,605	2,235
Africa	**1,693**	**n.a.**	**270**	**45**	**69**	**117**	**82**	**72**	**6,068**	**40**	**42**
Ethiopia	1,457	1,426	225								
Somalia					3	26	28	6	6,017	2	2

*Categorized as North Africa, Near East, and South Asia in reports.
*May be inaccurate given Operation Desert Shield buildup in 1990. 80% total troop strength is Air Force.

Source: Department of Defense, Washington Headquarters Services, Directorate for Information Operations and Reports.

The "Lippmann foreign policy test" should be applied by the United States when it comes to intervention choices, Zakaria argues (1994: 179–180): a nation should not take on commitments that exceed its power and it should always balance commitments and power so as to leave itself "a comfortable surplus of power in reserve." The stability and prosperity of the world depend in some large measure on America's solvency and credibility, which means it must retain the resources, influence, energy, and domestic support to engage itself on a sustained basis. The strategic impetus during the Cold War urged intervention, the humanitarian one urged caution and noninvolvement. Today the roles are reversed: strategists have become cautious about far-flung ventures, and those who used to be anti-interventionists now urge "humanitarian interventions." Indeed, the new interventionists urge involvement precisely in those areas where the United States has no interests—for only if America has no interests in the area can its motives be pure. Almost all crises in the world merit some U.S. intervention. How one ranks the event or the interest or the crisis, however, will determine how sustained and significant this intervention should be, thus linking it to the question of how America should intervene.

Prophetically, Abolfathi, Hayes, and Hayes (1979), examining trends in U.S. crisis behavior by comparing the 1956–1965 decade with 1966–1976, discovered the set of actions taken by the United States during a crisis was much more likely to include military involvement when there was no communist adversary. They also noticed an increasing variety in the set of actors with whom the United States experienced international crisis, and a tendency for American crisis management objectives to shift away from the containment of communism focus toward a more general desire for global stability in the later period. The United States used military assistance less frequently and used military deployments and repositioning more frequently in the latter decade. Abolfathi, Hayes, and Hayes speculated global stability would be a goal that placed the United States toward involvement in crises with a greater variety of countries, particularly smaller powers, and that because the United States would be increasingly involved in crises with lesser powers over issues of stability, options to use military force would be limited—the country would have to choose between impotence and military involvement (Aboulfathi, Hayes and Hayes, 1979: 79). New instruments of diplomacy should be developed, they advised, that avoid the need for military exposure and are relatively free from the risks and consequences of endless involvement.

The United States is moving into a period in the post–Cold War environment in which intervention questions are more central to foreign policy than in the past. More incidents of intervention will probably arise, and the situations will be highly varied in their participants and contexts. The United States will need to be more deeply involved or interested in the internal activities of nations. Often such actions will be multinational, confronting America with challenges to control the limits of its commitments in the face of subtle influences that may alter the actions of such coalitions.

Intervention has traditionally been viewed as an off-shoot of power theory and regarded as the process by which great powers exercise influence over the internal affairs of weak states, either to defend their interests in the latter or because they happen to possess the capability for intervention. With this approach, intervention is seen as the result of a "push" by an external party defending its own interest. Thus, the causes of intervention are to be found either within the structure of the intervening state or in the nature of the surrounding international system. Alternatively, recognizing that a lot of intervention takes place as a result of the existing involvement of external socioeconomic, religious, ethnic, or political groups within the boundaries of the disrupted state, such prior external connections of various types and different levels involve postulating a complementary spill-over or "pull" theory of internal initiative, or appeal for aid. Such an approach may help to explain situations where a superpower becomes involved in domestic conflict, although its direct interests are minor and the official desire to intervene minimal, says C. R. Mitchell (1970: 191).

The twin concepts, push and pull, reflect, respectively, a willingness to intervene and an opportunity for intervention. Separately, they imply reversible theoretical perspectives to explain how domestic instability is linked to the global political system. One perspective emphasizes "willingness to intervene" and assumes that the international system structure defines foreign policy goals and pushes great powers' involvement into internal affairs of other nation-states. Thus, global conditions determine intervention patterns. The opposite perspective, emphasizing opportunities for intervention assumes that the sum of domestic conflict defines the chance for great power intervention response alternatives, in essence pulling outside help inside and eventually reinforcing or reshaping the international system structure. Hence, local conditions determine intervention patterns. Both arguments are probably valid, although the latter is easier to test because it works directly from an observable, inductive base where variation can be readily identified. It also reflects the increasingly dominant selective engagement grand design thinking. It is most suitable for analysis when the system structure is changing. Roughly, the progression of steps outlining the relationships between the key concepts and the components, from domestic instability to intervention to doctrine development to a global system structure, has two patterns: a deductive model that applies when the international system has a fixed structure, as in the Cold War; and an inductive model that fits a fluid international system, such as the post–Cold War world in its first decade. In a transitional system, a selective engagement strategy encourages both continuance of political fluidity and movement toward defining structural rules—it will depend entirely on the consistency of the intervention policies and their implementation. Two schemes outline the steps in this process: how intervention shapes the global structure, the post–Cold War condition, and how the global structure shapes intervention, the Cold War condition.

How Global Structure Shapes Intervention: The Cold War Era

1. An intervention opportunity created from domestic instability challenges
depends on
- *Fixed* U.S. national identity in foreign policy
- *Fixed* U.S. national interests in foreign policy

2. An intervention decision created from superpower intervention challenges
depends on
- *Established* U.S. foreign policy doctrine
- U.S. intervention trends and lessons from past experience
- *Established* international community norms
- International community trends and lessons from past
  experience

3. An intervention strategy created from global leadership challenges
depends on
- U.S. intervention lessons from past experience
- International community lessons from past experience

4. Patterns of intervention strategy *reinforce* rules of international engagement

5. Rules of engagement *reinforce* global system structure

How Intervention Shapes Global Structure: The Post–Cold War Era

1. An intervention opportunity created from domestic instability challenges
depends on
- *Changing* U.S. national identity in foreign policy
- *Alternative* U.S. images of major world issues

2. An intervention decision created from superpower intervention challenges
depends on
- *Changing* U.S. foreign policy doctrine
- U.S. intervention trends and lessons from past experience
- *Changing* international community norms
- International community lessons from past experience

3. An intervention strategy created from global leadership challenges
depends on
- U.S. intervention lessons from past experience
- International community lessons from past experience

4. Patterns of Intervention strategy *create* rules of international engagement

5. Rules of engagement *create* global system structure

To create a new, fixed international system of intervention rules and guidelines to replace the old, two paths are possible: creation by vision, or policy plan, for example, the new world order (what we will do and what we should do); or creation by experience (what we have learned). In a fluid environment, policy-makers try to persuade others through visionary plans or a focus on foreign policy principles. The beauty of these arrangements is that if the United States is able to come to policy agreement on a world vision or set of foreign policy principles to be consistently applied in the future, then the system rules revert back to a deductive argument drawing the connection of domestic instability to intervention practice. Deductive logic simplifies decision-making. If the new course has wide agreement and is designed to promote values and objectives dear to American ideas of governance, security, and peace, then it will be powerful.

Yet, in the post–Cold War period, the latter way to reach policy clarity, that is, fixing intervention standards through *experience,* seems to be catching on. Although visionary plans, moral principles, and national interest priorities have been debated, lack of consensus prevents the emergence of a single theme or clear direction. By default, the collective picture of U.S. interventions, the inductive route, is implicitly setting a new foundation of American foreign policy. Its formation is gradual, subtle, drawn from accumulated experience. This applies whether a U.S. military mission is engaged for international reasons—to retaliate against terrorism on American soil (Afghanistan), or to control resource flow (Persian Gulf oil, drug trafficking by Panama's Noriega), or guided by domestic instability and humanitarian concerns within a country (Somalia's famine and lawlessness, Haiti's antidemocratic coup, Bosnia's and Kosovo's ethnic cleansing, Rwanda's genocide). The great variety of operations and multiple purposes indicates no single reason governing these foreign policy choices.

The receding ability of a visionary or principled approach to establish new intervention rules and doctrinal mission is a result of different forces. It is due in part to the increasingly participatory environment in policy-making; today, more actors are involved in forming more complex patterns with a greater number of states. Problems are complicated, not simple; there are more states, more issues of interconnectedness. The chance for a single perspective gaining wide acceptance is slim. It also results from a considerably developed analytic atmosphere in policy-making circles which benefits from hindsight: the United States was victorious in the Cold War but a loser in the Vietnam conflict—a mixed picture suggesting deeper deliberation of new doctrinal policy proposals. It also reflects changes in the world environment—colonialism is no longer a major fixture of international relations, a shift that occurred throughout the Cold War. This puts greater pressure on the United States in its global leadership position.

Since the end of World War II, during the Cold War and beyond, the overwhelming majority of conflicts have been some form of internal war. Most wars are fought within the territory of a single state. Domestic threats increasingly appear to result from internal, tribal, or ethnic cleavages, noted

Harvey Starr and Benjamin Most (1985: 39). Questions about the recognition and legitimacy of governments, identifying parties to the conflict and their standing as official actors, have to be addressed in the context of norms against intervention in domestic affairs of sovereign states and the equally explicit norms regarding rights of self-determination and autonomy. Domestic instability, usually arising out of dissatisfaction with local conditions and internal politics, presents the occasion for an intervention choice—intrusion by the international community. When multiplied throughout the global universe, collected instances of internal unrest create a substantial complete realm of intervention opportunities.

In general, intervention is the process of overt or covert involvement by an outsider in the internal economic, social, or political processes of another society with the aim of determining the direction of trends in the target country's policies, institutions, or policies. Strategies used to exercise leverage in these situations include a range of assistance through military instruments (supplying combat troops or peacekeeping observers, weaponry, advisors), economic support or sanctions (financial aid, embargo), and political and diplomatic initiatives (mediation offices, nonrecognition, refugee policies). The intervention approach may be passive, providing little beyond words of support or condemnation to the parties in conflict; or active, with physical movement of troops and supplies. Together, policy deliberation—discussion and decision whether or not to intervene—combined with policy implementation yields a profile of intervention patterns. The picture is important: short of doctrinal definition, it is the foundation for a new global order.

WORLD ORDER OR DISORDER

Three visions of world order have emerged to describe the post–Cold War early years: one of disorder and danger, one of greater stability and calm, one of interregnum transition.

The Disordered World

Stanley Hoffman (1998: 1–2) sees the combinations of human passions, state struggles for power, modern technological advances into the hands of leaders and followers with extraordinarily large capacity for destruction; social democratic synthesis of liberal and social values of individual freedoms and welfare, but with very high costs and an insatiable demand for rights and countless battles of entitlements; alongside a great movement for emancipation from traditional hierarchies: the liberation of colonized peoples, the transformation of the conditions for discriminated groups, and the successive revolutions in communications have shrunk the world. Societies that suddenly face increasingly inequalities, rising corruption, and much diminished protection provide little support for their political system resulting in a number of failed and troubled murderous states.

The system of sovereign states has been undermined: from below, the collapse of states whose claims to sovereignty are untenable, and from above, by the revolution of globalization and interdependence (Hoffman, 1998: 3). It is still a world of states, yet many of its problems cannot be solved unilaterally by them. Many of its inhabitants live in the age of traditional interstate conflicts and rivalries, where national histories, myths, and prejudices flourish, and where force and heroism, rather than rational calculations and efficiency, remain essential. The state is no longer a very effective agent, often under attack even when it is solid, and certainly it is not solid everywhere. The only remaining superpower, the United States, may be indispensable, but it acts fitfully and does not see as far as its leaders think.

If we want a world that is both peaceful and fair, Hoffman offers a list of suggestions: (a) develop more global norms by consensus with respect to criteria for intervention, human rights, and obligations of assistance to states and people in need; (b) find the right balance between the indispensable and still weak institutions of global governance and the desire of people to preserve their distinctive identities and cultures; (c) redefine security to take into account not only security against physical threats to states but also the various insecurities international relations inflict on states and on people. Hoffman concludes (p. 157) that issues of military intervention in the international relations of states is central in a post–Cold War international system characterized by the presence of many dangerous and troubled states.

The Stable World

John Mueller (1994) presents an alternative view. He believes that major problems that have bedeviled the world over the last half century have been resolved. Yet, the notion has taken hold that international affairs have somehow how become especially tumultuous, unstable, and complex, where turbulence and violence are widespread, where global change is out of control, which implies there was a time when it was notably in control. Commentators regularly judge the many states of the world that have suddenly become democratic and capitalist and bemoan the corruption that is accompanying the process. Problems related to the proliferation of weapons of mass destruction, ethnic and national hatreds, terrorism, and economic and environmental challenges were all part of the Cold War setting; none is actually new, and some of them are less urgent than they were earlier. Mueller (1994: 355) says the past has been simplified; a Eurocentric bias has been introduced; standards have been raised, and problems previously considered minor have been elevated in perceived importance.

The Cold War often seemed intractable; Soviet strength and the U.S.-USSR conflict were viewed as near permanent fixtures of international relations. Yet the international communist threat was overcome, extinguished. In a short time virtually all major problems that tormented superpower foreign policy for nearly half a century were resolved, "the unpopular and often brutal Soviet occupation of East Europe; the artificial and deeply troubling division of Germany; the expensive, virulent, crisis-prone and apparently dangerous military contest between East and West; and the ideological struggle between authoritarian, expansionist, violence-encouraging communism and reactive, sometimes panicky capitalist democracy" (Mueller, 1994: 356).

However, although we are now free to use capital, skill, and science to do away with poverty and human misery, it does not feel too much like a golden age; rather, the idea that the contemporary world is especially unstable has become quite popular. President Clinton in his presidential address in 1993 proclaimed the new world is more free but less stable. The metaphor was that the large dragon had been slain, but now we lived in a jungle filled with poisonous snakes. Conclusions about the comparative complexity of the world in the wake of the Cold War stem in part from a simplified recollection of what went on during the Cold War. This phenomenon is related to the tendency to look backward and to see the past as more benign and innocent than it really was. No matter how much better the present gets, the past gets better faster in reflection. The remembered past of the Cold War period is represented as a world in which the threat was singular, precise and succinct, and universally understood (Mueller, 1994: 357). In fact, the communist threat was shifting, multifaceted, and extremely complicated. The policy of containment may have been a generally useful guide, but how to deal with the universally understood threat did not translate easily into policy.

On nationalism, and local war, Mueller states that conflict arising from ethnic and national hatreds is certainly not new. Nationalism played a key role in the decolonization process, fueling both revolutionary and inter-state wars. New concerns about this are focused in Europe, from the civil wars that have erupted in the former Yugoslavia to political and economic chaos, some of it violent, that has accompanied the disintegration of the Soviet Union. These problems are very real, but not worldwide. If post–Cold War Europe now has more armed conflict than it experienced during the Cold War, much of the rest of the world is suffering *less* warfare than earlier. Latin America underwent a series of civil wars inspired or exacerbated by the Cold War; now this area has become far freer of conflict. In East and Southeast Asia, the Cold War led to or exacerbated costly wars—Korea, Malaysia, Thailand, China, Vietnam, Cambodia. Thus, in a global context it is simply not true that conflicts among nations and ethnic groups are escalating or engulfing the world (Mueller, 1994: 360).

Finally, several important developments may act to reduce the frequency and intensity of at least some local wars in Europe and elsewhere, says Mueller. First, as communism died, so did many romantic myths about revolution (Mueller, p. 361). As violent revolution became discredited, peaceful democratic reform began to look pretty good—the democratic idea has flared up throughout the world. Democracy is an imperfect but often effective method for resolving local conflicts peacefully. Although few local wars were directly initiated by the superpowers in the Cold War, a number were aggravated by their interference. At times they tried to restrain their smaller client, but more often they jumped in. According to Mueller (1994: 362), in addition to Korea, Vietnam, the Dominican Republic, Lebanon, India, Afghanistan, and Granada, where troops from the United States, the Soviet Union, and/or China became directly involved, the Cold War can be said to have exacerbated violent conflict within Thailand, Burma, Guatemala, Nicaragua, El Salvador, Venezuela, Cuba, Greece, Peru, Uruguay, Argentina, Bolivia, Cambodia, Laos, Angola, India, Mozambique, Chile, Congo, Brazil, Ethiopia, Algeria, Iraq, various Yemens, Hungary, Zanzibar, South Africa, Guyana, French Indochina, Malaysia, Iran, Indonesia, and the Philippines.

With the demise of the Cold War, it is to be expected that such exacerbation will not take place—fewer foreign arms and less aid will now be infiltrated to the local contenders, thus violence will be lower. Lastly today there exists a strong incentive, an international norm, to cooperate to generate peace and stability. According to Mueller, patient police work probably saved thousands of lives over the years, but it tends to be a thankless job because the people whose lives have been saved do not know who they are; in fact, they may be critical or contemptuous of their saviors. The mission to Somalia in 1992–1993 helped to reduce considerably the number of deaths of citizens in the country from thousands of people per day down to two or three per day. Unlike the Gulf War, which *cost* lives, this military mission brought no calls for celebratory parades. "The American troops who helped pull it off remember it for the teenagers who cursed them and pelted them with stones and fruit. Asked if the mission was worth it, one Army specialist responded, 'How many Americans did we lose? Seven? Well, not one of those lives was worth it' " (Mueller, 1994: 363).

Mueller predicts the great powers will send their troops into harm's way only in those areas where national interests are importantly engaged. For the most part, the United Nations will be encouraged to take over, in peacekeeping and peace enforcing operations in peripheral areas. Indeed, of the 26 peacekeeping missions the United Nations undertook between 1945 and 1992, fully 12 were begun after 1988 in the wake of the Cold War. In addition, with the application of economic sanctions to Iraq in 1990, to Haiti in 1991, and to Serbia in 1992, the big countries may be honing a credible, inexpensive, and potentially potent new weapon for use against small and medium-size aggressors and troublemakers.

The Interregnum World

In the modern era, the old form of rule is dying but a new one has not yet been born. Sovereignty is under challenge, yet the institution of the state remains more or less intact in spite of various predictions about its decline and imminent demise in a world without major wars or borders. Unimaginable events and developments have occurred: Iraq went to war with the United States, a European state engaged in ethnic cleansing, NATO was used as an instrument of military humanitarianism. The vision of a better world depends on the exercise of a great deal of power by the United States, assert Cox, Booth, and Dunne (1999: 12). Yet, there remains the accusation that U.S. foreign policy of the nineties reflected an unwillingness or inability on the part of American presidents to place U.S. soldiers in harm's way, placing a serious constraint on the use of force whether in defense of the national interest or in situations where threats to liberal values would seem to demand a military response. In practice, this meant a great reluctance to commit ground, combat units into conflicts, and instead to rely on missile technology and air power to fulfill military intervention missions.

There is an irony to this situation: the state with the strongest military establishment, and as with any military organization, must operate under a "prepare to kill" mission but is not prepared to risk the lives of its soldiers; consequently, its power is weakened through moral compromise and its vulnerability is heightened because other political leaders are not so constrained, states Chris Brown (1999: 40). The unfolding events in the Balkans in 1999 put these points into perspective: NATO's war with Yugoslavia over the fate of Kosovo, a war fought predominantly in response to gross human rights violations and threats of genocide, meant expecting to fight a war without sustaining casualties; the apparent belief that *inflicting* casualties is morally unacceptable, irrespective of the overall justice of the action or the intentions of the participants (Brown, 1999: 49).

The celebration of unipolar preeminence and comprehensive economic advantage that the United States now enjoys still means that American pundits confuse a comprehensive paralleled hegemony with omnipotence, with America's ability to get its way on any issue: there is no such power in the world, and there never was, says Bruce Cumings (1999: 274, 286), who sees hegemony as most effective when it is indirect, inclusive, plural, heterogeneous, and consensual—less a form of domination than a form of legitimate global leadership. Liberalism inspires a call to action; by declaring its principles, it calls forth a commitment. One example is humanitarian intervention. "Often derided by realists as an idealism equating the conduct of foreign policy with choices between good and evil, or that intervention in defense of liberal values equals foreign policy as social work, this new phenomenon also is an outcome of the mutability and therefore the attractiveness of liberalism," states Cumings (1999: 287). This liberal form of hegemony has a message: capitalism, pluralist democracy, and self-determination. Whether the liberal world order will continuously unfold or whether it remains merely a partial and limited world view unavailable to the continuing plight of the world's majority peoples will become clearer in the future and will depend on U.S. intervention attitudes and policies.

Whether the world is dangerous, safe, or merely changing, commentators agree that American intervention will be a primary factor shaping its future.

2

World Perspectives and American Intervention

INTRODUCTION

In January 1992, UN Secretary-General Boutros Boutros-Ghali was invited to prepare an analysis and set of recommendations for strengthening the capacity of the United Nations to engage in preventive diplomacy, peacemaking, and peacekeeping. The result was a blueprint, *An Agenda for Peace,* in which the Secretary-General said the future aim of the United Nations should be to concentrate on conflict resolution efforts under the following guidelines:

- Identify at the earliest possible stage situations that could produce conflict: try through diplomacy to remove the sources of danger before violence results.

- Where conflict erupts: engage in peacemaking aimed at resolving the issues that have led to conflict.

- Through peacekeeping: work to preserve peace, however fragile, where fighting has been halted, and assist in implementing agreements achieved by the peacemakers.

- Stand ready to assist in peace building in its differing contexts: rebuilding the institutions and infrastructures of nations torn by civil war and strife; and building bonds of peaceful mutual benefit among nations formerly at war.

- Address the deepest causes of conflict: economic despair, social injustice, and political oppression. (Boutros-Ghali, 1992: 1–7).

The foundation stone of this work is the state, declared the Secretary-General; respect for its fundamental sovereignty and integrity are critical to common international progress, and it is the responsibility of leaders to find a balance between the needs of good internal governance and the requirements of an ever more interdependent world. Sovereignty, territorial integrity and independence of states within the established international system, and the principle of self-determination for peoples should not be permitted to work against each other. Altogether, the outlined program, though it has a great deal of merit and puts forth enlightened international norms, is a complicated task to carry out in the context of intervention. As Gidon Gottlieb (1993: 88) writes: "The issue of intervention in foreign conflicts—whether ethnic or otherwise—is obscured by a tangle of legal doctrines and intense ideological expectations. The principle of nonintervention, doctrines of collective intervention and multilateralism, collective self-defense, collective security and humanitarian intervention, arguments about the scope of authority of the Security Council and of regional organizations—these are all snagged in a web of legal and policy considerations." Thus, legitimacy, justification and rationale, collective reaction, and humanitarian need are among the items to be considered and wrapped into policy choice.

Intervention is generally seen to be an illegal act, a violation of sovereignty. Intervention beyond the boundaries of the state identifies an activity that is not socially approved in the modern international community (Little, 1993: 13). The principle of nonintervention is embodied in the Charter of the United Nations, which severely restricts the right to intervene in the domestic jurisdiction of states. Further, attempts by the United Nations to establish a more absolute principle of nonintervention have not been endorsed by state practice. This does not disturb the general proposition that there is a reluctance to intervene militarily in others states, and particularly into civil wars.

Intervention may proceed quietly or with dramatic visible flair depending on the systematic or haphazard method by which it is introduced—gradually or suddenly; overt and legitimate, or covert and sinister; active and physical, backed by military troops and economic consequences, or passive, limited to diplomatic maneuvering and declaratory statements. It has no fixed boundary of intrusion. But it is a constant in the politics of nations: there will always be states in need, whether endemic social problems, humanitarian emergencies, government instability, growing domestic dissatisfaction and anger, or civil wars provide the rallying call to define their cause; and there will always be other states—theoretically and potentially—on standby to help alleviate such problems. For states in need, the major questions are how to get top priority to be served by the international community or by a single donor-state and how to be given the best care under acceptable and satisfying conditions. For states who help, and for help offered through the United Nations, the main concerns are how to prioritize calls for assistance and how to deliver appropriate care in a just and efficient manner. For the needy, the focus is on "getting attention" while for the helpers it is on "defining reasons to act and what to do." In the post–Cold War world, priority setting is neither agreed nor fixed. Which situation requires quicker, more extended, and compassionate reaction by the international community: massive starvation or violent protests within a state? If several states suffer similar fates of duress, who shall be treated first? In the operating political reality, states are not equal. The best interventionary care has no conventional formula; no template; no clear compass, principally, though not exclusively, because the relationship between means and ends is uncertain and sometimes unknown.

Debate over the use and value of intervention strategies revolves around these issues muddied by the fact that changes in the world state system are occurring, raising new theoretical, legal, practical, and moral issues in international politics that touch on the intervention concept in major ways. The "state" is no longer the autonomous, authority-organizing unit in the global arena. Forces of integration and disintegration pull it in opposite directions. Extensive analysis of this phenomenon has developed in two principal forms: first, as distressing commentary about future world order and disarray, and second, as a theoretical puzzle calling for new paradigms in international relations. Just as a glean of light emerged in the post–Cold War world occasioning fresh, freer thinking and rational discussion of states-in-need and states-meeting-needs relationships in order to redefine "getting attention" guidelines and the search for new, meaningful doctrines, the world seemed to become more turbulent, shaking the groundwork of intervention thinking.

The challenges to consider are these: the role of the third world in the new international system, the rise of ethnic conflicts and their projected role in international stability, and the development of an international ethical standard to promote human justice in all countries; U.S. perspectives on multilateralism, unipolarity, and global leadership; and the perceived benefits and negative consequences of applying coercive strategies to treat far off domestic disorders. The development of policies and range of debate will depend on a basic set of attitudes toward American military intervention in the post–Cold War era grounded in assumptions and understandings about the United States and the world, in at least these areas: (a) U.S. self-image: how America sees the world and its role within it; (b) world visions: how global developments are interpreted (optimistically or pessimistically) with respect to overall conditions in the system and future security; (c) U.S. leadership expectations: how the world sees the United States' role in meeting its needs and desires; and (d) Intervention and world perspectives.

U. S. SELF-IMAGE

If a single theme pervades the history of American thinking about the world, it is that the United States has a peculiar obligation to better the lot of humanity, states H.W. Brands (1998: vi). "From the moment John Winthrop planted his 'city on a hill' as a self-conscious example for the whole world to see; through the era when the American revolutionaries cast their conflict against Britain as a blow for the unalienable rights of *all* men; (sic) to the day when Abraham Lincoln defended the war for the Union as a struggle to guarantee that government of the people, by the people, and for the people not perish from the (entire) earth, to the day when Woodrow Wilson called for a crusade to make the world safe for democracy; to Franklin Roosevelt's extrapolation of the Atlantic Charter to the Pacific and Indian oceans; to John Kennedy's pledge to pay any price and bear any burden in the defense of the liberty of Berlin and other Cold War hot spots; to George Bush's assertion of the need for Americans to secure a 'new world order'; to Bill Clinton's dispatch of troops to Bosnia to enforce an American-brokered peace in that broken and bleeding land—which is to say, from the beginning of American history to the present—this sense of obligation to suffering humankind has been a persistent theme in American thought, speech, and writing about the world."

Yet there has been decided disagreement regarding the precise nature of this obligation. Brands highlights the two opposite poles: on one side are the *exemplarists*, who believe the United States owes the world merely the example of a humane, democratic, and prosperous society, arguing that perfecting American institutions and practices at home is a full-time job. Meddling in the affairs of other nations would not only fail to benefit those states, since societies have to solve their problems themselves, but could jeopardize American values. "In attempting to save the world, and probably failing, America would risk losing its democratic soul" (Brands, 1998: viii). On the other side of the debate have been those who contend that America must move beyond example and undertake active measures to vindicate the right. In a nasty world, say these *vindicators*, evil goes armed, and so must good. "Human nature is too recalcitrant for mere example to have much lasting effect, and until human nature changes...military might, even if it doesn't necessarily make right, certainly can restrain wrong" (Brands, 1998: viii).

Under both exemplarist and vindicator visions, America's national interest is a critical factor in shaping relations with the world. The two sides have commonly agreed on the nature of the long-term American interest—they desire to see other regions of the world become more like America. The idealism of the exemplarists consists of thinking evil abroad would succumb to the American example; the idealism of the vindicators meant thinking modest and intermittent efforts by American intervention usually would help. Each party is also grounded in realism: exemplarists assert that people have to save themselves, vindicators assert that they needed help to do so.

In the post–Cold War decade, intervention debate surfaced along this division. The vindicators of the 1990s, says Brands (1998: 316), seeking historical support for intervention in Somalia, Haiti, and Bosnia could recall the arguments of "Daniel Webster on behalf of Greek freedom fighters; of Josiah Strong and Albert Beveridge on Americans' ordained obligation to share American values with such heretofore unfavored places as the Philippines; of the young Walter Lippmann on the need to cease drifting and master the opportunity to stand up to German aggression; of the young Kennan on America's unique capacity to contain totalitarianism in Eastern Europe; of Kirkpatrick on how if Americans didn't resist evil overseas, no one would."

The exemplarists of the 1990s, who held that American troops could deliver food to Somalia but nothing approaching lasting peace, that they could deliver a president to Haiti but not the values prerequisite to democracy and development, that they might momentarily stop the killings in Bosnia but not eradicate hatred, likewise had precedents for their arguments, says Brands (1998: 316). They could remember George Washington's farewell address to cultivate peace and harmony with all nations, mindful that benefits would accrue only if the United States remained distant from the affairs of foreign countries; or John Quincy Adams, who argued that once America assumed responsibility for the welfare of others, she would endanger the interests of her own people—"She might become the dictatress of the world. She would no longer be the ruler of her own spirit"; or Charles Beard, on the eve of the onset who argued the United States should stay out of the war in Europe, for the burden would be too great for the American people; or William Appleman Williams asking whether America needed a frontier in the form of an informal empire in order to have democracy and prosperity at home, criticizing U.S.-Cuban relations and predicting a debacle in South East Asia if the United States did not mend its ways.

History had proven both parties to the debate partially right. Anticommunist containment may have made sense in Europe after World War II as Cold War vindicators contended, but it proved a disaster extended to Vietnam, as the exemplarists warned. The debate between exemplarists and vindicators demonstrates that neither approach to the world suits all situations; neither an intervention nor a nonintervention stand can be a permanent solution (Brands, 1998: 318–319). There is an element of moral self-assuredness that the examplarist and vindicationist positions reflect which pushes the American desire to improve the world.

The United States is a world power and has worldwide interests. It is blessed by geographical isolation and an abundance of natural wealth. A multilateral world order vision is singularly compatible with America's own collective self-concept, says John Gerard Ruggie (1994: 565); the vision taps into the essence of America with its community orientation and universal openness to everyone. Multilateralism is likely to figure prominently in American foreign policy for the foreseeable future. The evolving American sense of community—Congress is more decentralized and more actively involved in the foreign policy process, grassroots involvement in foreign policy issues has expanded, and a general fragmenting tendency for American domestic society (Ruggie, 1994: 568). America enjoys the luxury of defining the content of its interests and deciding how best to pursue them. In the post–Cold War era, Americans' sense of who they are and what kind of work they aspire to will shape the choice of ends and means.

Global leadership has also gained increasing prominence as a guiding principle for American foreign policy, though the vagueness of the term allows policy-makers to rationalize dramatically different initiatives and makes defining policy difficult. "Taken to an extreme, global leadership implies U.S. interest in and responsibility for virtually anything, anywhere," states Barbara Conry (1997: 1). Billions of dollars in defense budgeting are spent to support US aspirations to lead the world, not to defend the United States. It is risky in that it forces U.S. involvement in numerous situations unrelated to American national security.

Former secretary of state Warren Christopher has said, "America must lead...American leadership is our first principle and a central lesson of this century. The simple fact is that if we do not lead, no one else will"

(Christopher, 1995: 8). Former House leader Newt Gingrich echoed the theme: "We have to lead the world. If we don't we have a continuing decay into anarchy, more violence around the planet, and it is highly unlikely anybody will replace us in leadership roles in the next 30 years." Nearly everyone agrees on the undiminished need for American leadership, although the world is used to mask profoundly different views of America's role in the world.

Conflicts are going to continue. The world is going to look to the United States for leadership. It is in American interests to lead, but we should not and cannot bear the full burden alone. "Doing something, doing it alone, or doing nothing—these are false choices," says Conry (1997: 4). Global social worker or global cop? The answer is both and neither. In proper dosages.

John Muravchik, in *The Imperative of American Leadership* (1996: 1), argues in favor of an expansive and costly version of global leadership that encompasses both humanitarian and realist objectives: a foreign policy that is engaged, proactive, interventionist, and expensive, for in the community of nations there is no authority higher than America. America is the wealthiest, mightiest, and most respected nation. At times it must be the "policeman or head of the posse—at others, the mediator, teacher or benefactor." In short, America must accept the role of world leader. Still, the proponents of leadership cannot agree on the proper criteria for making such decisions, about when and where to exercise American leadership, given the impossibility of applying it everywhere American values are offended. If we decide to confront evil, ethnic cleansing, and aggression on a highly selective basis, will our actions more closely resemble bullying than leadership? asks Conry (1997: 6).

Global leadership demands U.S. involvement in many issues that have little or no impact on American vital interests and doing whatever is necessary in order to prevail to preserve U.S. credibility. If leadership is the raison d'être of American foreign policy, and especially if it is the primary rationale for a U.S. military operation, then the country must always succeed, even at heavy cost, for the preservation of American credibility is of paramount importance (Conry, p. 8). The difficulty of pursuing a policy that not only demands involvement in numerous affairs that are not firmly tied to American security but also requires a successful outcome in all diplomatic and military missions is obvious.

Global leadership is tremendously costly. The question of what military, economic, and human resources Americans are willing to devote to ensuring that the United States remains the world's only superpower is important. One alleged benefit of United States leadership is burden sharing and diplomatic achievements. By taking the lead, the United States can persuade the rest of the world to pay for and accept some of the risks of its foreign policy initiatives. The preeminent post–Cold War example is the Gulf War. The United States would have gone to war over the matter with or without assistance from others. But because of President George H. W. Bush's display of leadership, it gained the cooperation and financial support of numerous other countries, and by internationalizing the opposition to Iraq, the UN Security Council legitimized American policy, states Conry (p. 11). But the strategy carried costs: giving economic aid to the Soviet Union, forgiving Egypt's debt, ignoring human rights abuses in China, Ethiopia, and Syria. Some countries could be accused of "free riding" on American efforts in order to preserve their own security and interests.

Do the nebulous benefits of U.S. global leadership justify its immense costs? Instead of trying to lead the world, the United States could concentrate on the protection of its vital national security interests and behave as the "first among equals" in the community of great powers, rather than insisting that as the world's only superpower it should take responsibility for events all over the globe, declares Conry, (pp. 14–15), who asks, if Washington renounces world leadership, is the United States condemned to stand idly by while villains and irredentists around the world terrorize helpless populations? Nasty parochial wars cannot be settled by outside powers at an acceptable cost to the intervener, whether or not the United States claims the mantle of world leadership.

As the system leader, the United States has the means and motive to maintain key security institutions in order to ease local security conflicts and limit expensive competition among the other major powers. Unipolarity means stability for the world, and the chief threat is U.S. failure to do enough to maintain it. The more efficiently Washington responds to these incentives and provides order, the more long-lived and peaceful the system: it is safer and cheaper than bipolarity or multipolarity; it pays to invest in its prolongation, argues William Wohlforth (1999: 8–9). Pax Americana reflects reality and focuses attention on the stakes involved in U.S. grand strategy. Doing too little is a greater danger than doing too much. In many cases, U.S. involvement has been demand driven; engagement seems to be essential for the proper functioning of the system. If the United States fails to translate its potential into the capabilities necessary to provide order, then greater power struggles for power and security will reappear soon. The world could become more dangerous as a result.

We should not exaggerate the costs, asserts Wohlforth (1999: 39). Because the current concentration of power in the United States is unprecedentedly clear and comprehensive, states are likely to share the expectation that counterbalancing would be a costly, probably doomed, venture. Unipolarity can be made to seem expensive and dangerous if it is equated with hegemonic behavior, a global empire demanding U.S. involvement in all issues everywhere. Maintaining unipolarity does not require limitless commitments. The United States can assume the role of "global security manager" and "indispensable nation" in all matters of importance, says Wohlforth (1999: 40), concluding that the current world order is characterized not by the U.S. superpower threat that drives other powers toward multipolar counterbalancing, but by a material structure that presupposes and demands U.S. preponderance coupled with policies and rhetoric that deny its existence or refuse to face its modest costs. These alternative views on American leadership reflect updated versions of the continual, historical division in U.S. identity between visions preferred by exemplarists and vindicators.

WORLD VISIONS

Perspectives on leadership join with opinions on what type of world the United States is (or should be) trying to lead. Two contrasting orientations are quite popular; one sees the world as more enlightened, the other as more threatening.

The Optimistic View

Francis Fukuyama (1989) celebrated the end of the Cold War by proclaiming the progression of events an "unabashed victory of economic and political liberalism," in "The End of History?" published in *The National Interest*. Liberal democracy was the best social-political system for fostering freedom; it would not be superseded by a higher form of government. Fukuyama does not hesitate to identify liberal democracy with capitalist democracy. The appeal of capitalist democracy lies in the convergence of two connected but distinct sequences. First, capitalism is allegedly the most efficient of economic systems, and since states depend on economic efficiency for the military power enabling them to survive, history has moved in the direction of capitalism. Second, democracy is portrayed as the natural outcome of a struggle by humans for recognition of their dignity by others. Capitalist democracy accords mutual recognition to the equal persons living within it. Fukuyama thinks capitalism and democracy satisfy the deepest urges of humanity—the urges for goods and for recognition, so when joined, they provide an optimal mechanism for humanity. Capitalist democracy can only spread; it cannot be superseded.

With respect to international stability, Fukuyama argues that the world is moving toward a state of peace. To the charge that nationalism seems incompatible with this new age of peace, he sees it as part of a transition away from the great collapsing empires, such as the Soviet Union. In the established democracies, nationalism has been turned into a private matter, much the way that religion became a private matter in the original capitalist democracies.

In *The End of History and the Last Man*, Fukuyama (1992: vii) sees a coherent, directional history of mankind that will eventually lead the greater part of humanity to liberal democracy. He has revealed the enormous weaknesses at the core of the world's strongest dictatorships, from Latin America to Eastern Europe, from the Soviet Union to Asia. Such strong governments have been failing over the last two decades. Many have given way to stable liberal democracies, liberal democracy being the only coherent political aspiration that spans different regions and cultures (Fukuyama, 1992: xiii). The current crisis of authoritarianism started with the fall of a series of right-wing authoritarian governments in Southern Europe in the 1970s, in Portugal, in Greece, in Spain, in Turkey. Since then, all of these countries have held regular, free multiparty elections (Fukuyama, 1992: 13). The transformation that occurred in less than a decade was remarkable: these countries had earlier been condemned by their religious and authoritarian traditions to reside outside the mainstream of democratic Western European development. A similar set of democratic transitions took place in Latin America. Among the major milestones marking the Cold War's end, says Fukuyama, are calls for democracy: in China, protesters want an end to corruption and the establishment of democracy; in Hungary, reformers call for free, multiparty elections; in Poland, the solidarity trade union government came to power; in East Germany, Czechoslovakia, Bulgaria, and Romania, communist governments fell. By 1991, free elections were held in all formerly communist states in Eastern and Central Europe. Freely elected parliaments in every constituent republic of the former Soviet Union declared their sovereignty as independent units (Fukuyama, pp. 26–27).

The liberal revolution has left certain areas such as the Middle East relatively untouched, but the fact that there will be setbacks and disappointments in the process of democratization, or that not every market economy will prosper, should not distract us from the larger pattern that is emerging in world history, writes Fukuyama (1992: 45).

There is no ideology with pretensions to universality that is in a position to challenge liberal democracy, and no universal principle of legitimacy other than the sovereignty of the people, although the growth has not been continuous or unidirectional. Periods of democratic upsurge are interrupted by radical discontinuities and setbacks, yet all of these reverses tended to be themselves reversed eventually, leading over time to an impressive overall growth in the number of democracies around the world. There are numerous examples of countries that do not meet a number of so-called cultural preconditions for democracy and that nonetheless have managed to achieve a surprisingly high level of democratic stability. The chief example of this is India, which is neither rich and highly industrialized nor nationally integrated. At other times in the past, entire peoples have been written off as culturally unqualified for stable democracy: The Germans and Japanese were said to be hobbled by their authoritarian traditions; Catholicism was held to be an insuperable obstacle to democracy in Spain, Portugal, and any number of Latin American countries, as was Orthodoxy in Greece and Russia. Many of the peoples of Eastern Europe were held to be either incapable of or uninterested in the liberal democratic traditions of Western Europe. And the degree to which democratic ideas have taken root among the broader population in Russia was evident in the widespread resistance to the hard-line coup attempt in August 1991 (Fukuyama, 1992: 221).

And nationalism? Common wisdom has it that once awakened, nationalism represents such an elemental force in history that it is unstoppable. The view of nationalism as permanent and all-conquering is parochial and untrue, for it does not have very deep roots in the human psyche (Fukuyama, 1992: 268). Nations have not been permanent or natural sources of attachment for people throughout the ages. Nationalism grows most intense just at or past the point of transition to industrial society and becomes particularly exacerbated when a people, having gone through the first phases of economic modernization, is denied both national identity and political freedom. For national groups whose identity is more secure and of longer standing, the nation as a source of identification appears to decline. To the extent that nationalism can be modernized like religion (a separate but equal status), its basis will weaken (Fukuyama, 1992: 270). There is no reason to believe such a recent development as nationalism to be a permanent feature of the social landscape. Economic forces are now encouraging the breakdown of national barriers through the creation of a single, integrated world market. The fact that the final political neutralization of nationalism may not occur in this generation or the next does not affect the prospect of its ultimately taking place (Fukuyama, 1992: 275).

At the end of the turbulent 1990s, nothing that had happened in world politics or the global economy in the past decade challenged Fukuyama's view that liberal democracy and a market-oriented economic order are the only viable options for modern societies. Fukuyama (1999: 18–19) stated that research shows liberal democracies do not fight each other, and thus existing democracies could improve their security by enlarging a democratic zone of peace. The best means of promoting democracy is through economic development, and the best way to promote economic growth is to inaugurate a country fully into the liberal capitalist trade and investment world.

The essence of Fukuyama's position is that history is shaped not by interests, passions, or ideas but by inanimate forces and deeper realities, writes Himmelfarb (1999: 37). Fukuyama sees as the directionality and progressive character of history driving toward a modern, market-oriented society, and a struggle for recognition culminating in the equal dignity or universal rights of all humans and the establishment of liberal, capitalist democracy. As a guide for the future or a roadmap for policy, Fukuyama's perspective may not be very useful. The Cold War imposed a framework on American thinking, providing a threat and a moral purpose. The post–Cold War quest has been to discover some similar formula to fuse national interests and ideals aimed to fill the void. Fukuyama argues that what we wanted to happen has become inevitable!

The implication for intervention policy is that the United States should use its immense power to hasten the process and the world will grow more peaceful and stable. The theory is a reaffirmation of the righteous path of American foreign policy, and reflective of the idealism of both the exemplarists and the vindicators.

The Pessimistic View

In contrast to Fukuyama's argument, Robert D. Kaplan (1994) warned of an anarchistic future in the world. In his essay "The Coming Anarchy," published in *The Atlantic Monthly*, Kaplan challenged the assumption that ideals of democracy always give people a better alternative than any form of authoritarianism. In regions such as West Africa or South Asia, economic misery and environmental degradation promote trends of fragmentation, he said, and the state ceases to function. War becomes the normal condition of certain places on the periphery of the rich world where urban overcrowding and disease, tribal warfare, the breakdown of central government operations, and a concomitant rise in crime characterize these seething underdeveloped areas. Kaplan sees a world without order, a hostile world. He warns of a bifurcated universe divided between the Western, industrialized sector and those mired in various forms of chaos. His vision of the future is bleak, full of ethnic conflict and gangster mentality. Kaplan's thesis, an anti-utopian vision of the twenty-first century throughout many regions of the globe, is a major alternative for understanding the post–Cold War world.

In a later publication, *The Coming Anarchy: Shattering the Dreams of the Post Cold War* (2000), Kaplan elaborates this theme: part of the globe is healthy, well fed, and pampered by technology; the other, larger part condemned to a life that is "poor, nasty, brutish, and short." (Kaplan, 2000: 24). The rosy world view that usually accompanies the end of a turbulent era is often unfounded: "The years that follow an epochal military and political victory such as the fall of the Berlin Wall are lonely times for realists. The victors naturally assume that their struggle carries deep significance, of a kind that cannot fail to redeem the world. Indeed, the harder and longer the struggle, the greater is its meaning in the mind of the winning side, and the greater the benefits it sees for humanity. Victory in World War I saw a burst of such idealism under the banner of 'Wilsonianism,' a notion that took little account of the real goals of America's European allies and even less account of the realities in the Balkans and the Near East, where democracy and freedom meant heightened ethnic awareness. The same pattern followed the West's victory in the Cold War, which many believed would bring simple freedom and prosperity under the banner of 'democracy' and 'free markets.' But just as after World War I and World War II, our victory has ushered in the next struggle for survival in which evil wears new masks" (Kaplan, 2000: xi).

The coming anarchy, a paradigm for the post–Cold War era, is a concrete reality: the division is not only between the north and south, but within countries and regions themselves, says Kaplan. In Africa many wars are in progress, and the criminalization of regimes involved in money laundering and drug smuggling proceeds apace. Africa suggests what war, borders, and ethnic politics will be like a few decades hence. To understand the events of the next 50 years, then, one must understand environmental scarcity, cultural and racial clash, geographic destiny, and the transformation of war (Kaplan 2000: 9, 18–19). The national security issue of the early twenty-first century is the political and strategic impact of surging populations, spreading disease, deforestation and soil erosion, water depletion, air pollution, overcrowded regions that will prompt mass migrations and incite group conflicts, which will be the core foreign policy challenge for the United States in considering intervention. As state control mechanisms wither in the face of environmental and demographic stress, "hard" Islamic city-states or shantytown-states are likely to emerge (Kaplan, 2000: 42).

To appreciate fully the political implications, Kaplan considers the question of war, suggesting the intense savagery of the fighting in such diverse cultural settings as Liberia, Bosnia, the Caucasus, and Sri Lanka is not a means but an end. In places where there has always been mass poverty, people find liberation in violence; physical aggression is a part of being human. Trust is narrowed to one's immediate family and fighting comrades. The legality breaks down, crime is rampant, as in the case of Lebanon, El Salvador, Peru, and Columbia. Private security will be taken up as a way to provide physical protection to local inhabitants (Kaplan, 2000: 44–47). The future wars will be about communal survival-caused anarchy, Kaplan predicts (2000:49).

The collapse of communism from internal stress says little about the long-term viability of Western democracy. We have no guarantee that subtler tyrannies may develop. "To think that democracy as we know it will triumph— or is even here to stay—is itself a form of determinism, driven by our own ethnocentricity," states Kaplan (2000: 60), who argues that democracies do not always make societies more civil. To illustrate, Kaplan offers the case of Sudan, where in April 1985, crowds overthrew a military regime and replaced it with a new government which the following year held free and fair elections. The newly elected democracy "led immediately to anarchy, which in turn led to the most brutal tyranny in Sudan's postcolonial history: a military regime that broadened the scope of executions, persecuted women, starved non-Muslims to death, sold kidnapped non-Muslim children back to their parents for $200, and made Khartoum the terrorism capital of the Arab world" (Kaplan, 2000: 62). Similarly, in Afghanistan: A fragile tribal society in which the United States encouraged democracy in the 1990s, the security vacuums that followed the failed attempts at institutionalizing pluralism were filled by Islamic tyranny. In Bosnia: Democracy legitimized the worst war crimes in Europe since the Nazi era (Kaplan, 2000, 62–63). In Russia: Because both a middle class and civil institutions are necessary for successful democracy, the country, which inherited neither from the Soviet regime, remains violent, unstable, and poor despite its high literacy rate.

The lesson to be drawn, states Kaplan (2000: 67) is that democracy emerges successfully only as a capstone to other social and economic achievements; evolving as an organic outgrowth of development, not through a moral fiat imposed by outside forces. Politics today may depend more on power relationships and the demeanor of society than on whether we continue to hold elections (Kaplan, 96–97). To force elections may give us some instant gratification, but after a few months or years, a group of soldiers with grenades will get bored and greedy, and will easily topple their fledgling democracy. "As likely as not, the democratic government will be composed of corrupt, bickering, ineffectual politicians whose weak rule never had an institutional base to start with modern bureaucracies generally require higher literacy rates over several generations," writes Kaplan (2000: 71). While we must accept a certain amount of evil in order to pursue an attainable good, and we must stay engaged, it should be within strict limits, seems to be his principle.

The implication for intervention policy is that the United States should be very careful to use its power when becoming involved in anarchy settings, for the actions may have little effect in pacifying the violent forces. Unlike Fukuyama's idealism emphasis, Kaplan's philosophy represents the realism of both exemplarists and vindicators.

U.S. LEADERSHIP EXPECTATION

To assert that U.S. leadership can stave off otherwise inevitable global chaos vastly overestimates the power of any single country to influence world events. The greatest fear of most states is not external aggression but internal disorder. The United States can do little about the latter, whereas it used to be able to do a great deal about the former. Among the basic problems dominating expectations about the role of the global leader in the post–Cold War age, one concerns the type of attention that will be given to problems of the third world, another emphasizes the role that should be given to ethnical standards in foreign relations in a world transformed.

Third World Attention

Decidedly different points of view from two third world leaders, Nelson Mandela and Muammar Khadafi, on the evolving global structure and attendant intervention pressures show up on these statements about the future world system:

Nelson Mandela, president of South Africa: "But the nation-state still remains as the focus of loyalty for millions and is seen as the appropriate arena for the defense of people's interests.... As they witness these events, people and nations are increasingly anxious about their individual and collective futures. If governments respond to these insecurities with indecision and vacillation, the world will become a dangerous place in which the opportunism of the day will triumph over the necessity to make far-reaching choices. This is not the time for indecision. What governments do today will influence that future, but the key to action lies—as it has done across the ages—in an understanding of the past" (Mandela 1997: 4–5).

Muammar Khadafi, leader of Libya: "America wants to rearrange the situation in the world in a manner that would definitively safeguard its interests in all regions: in Central America, Europe, Asia, and the Arab region, even at the expense of millions of people and through the creation of an illusion of a false world peace. More dangerous still, America is seeking to impose its own concepts and understanding of peace and security, terrorism, human rights, development, and social peace on all countries and peoples.... There is stability according to the American definition and its equivalent, which is the people's rejection of American hegemony and its wild behavior.... We believe that this situation, in which America has become a policeman citing people for infringements, confiscating peoples' wills and property, and using international organizations in implementing its policies, will create accumulated layers of hatred and resentment against America and hostility toward its people" (Khadafi, 1997: 244–245).

Did the Cold War's end made a difference to third world security? One argument implied the Cold War increased third world country conflicts as the superpowers diverted their systemic competition from more dangerous to less dangerous theatres in accordance with the geopolitical dictates of their competition. Yet, as S. Neil MacFarlane notes (1999: 21), this is difficult to demonstrate since we cannot know what the level of conflict in the third world would have been in the absence of the Cold War. The post–Cold War era should bring greater security to the third world and less conflict: peacekeeping, mediation activities, and democratic institution building through humanitarian intervention could be handled by the United Nations, as outlined in *An Agenda for Peace*.

Another argument suggested the Cold War constrained conflict and enhanced stability in the third world. As the United States and Soviet Union sought influence with established states, and ruling regimes had a vested interest to remain in power, superpower diplomacy also tended to sustain them. Since each engaged in balancing behavior, they tended to support opposite sides in regional conflicts, contributing to an equilibrium and hence to stability.

A third position suggested the Cold War was largely irrelevant to third world conflicts—emphasis on superpower competition ignored poverty conditions, the most important source of third world instability. Preconditions at Cold War onset are not sufficient to conclude that bipolar competition was unrelated; it may have acted as a constraining or a permissive play in its politics, argues MacFarlane (1999: 23).

The Cold War may have been stabilizing in much of the third world; its end may be destabilizing. Resources from the superpowers allowed client regimes to control internal processes of disintegration; hence, the end of the Cold War resulted in disorder in such states as Somalia. With regard to the new world order, initial optimism concerning the capacity of the United Nations to adopt a more ambitious global role in the management of security has weakened. The promise of the Gulf War and intervention in Somalia by the United States led to unipolar visions of a new world system based on hegemonic stability ideas that has been largely unmet. The ability of the Security Council to agree on common action in the face of crises in the third world was dramatically enhanced by the end of the Cold War (judged from the flood of resolutions on peacekeeping since 1990); however, other constraints on UN activities (e.g., the lack of a standing force and the dependence of the United Nations on state contributions of military personnel and financial resources) remained. The failure or mixed results of UN involvements in regional crises (Iraq, Somalia, Yugoslavia) and the hazardous nature of activities of peacekeeping have dampened enthusiasm for providing personnel for such ventures.

The impact of global structural change in terms of the specific nature of the linkages between the regions of the third world and the international system as a whole have been limited (MacFarlane, 1999: 31). Some civil conflicts related to the Cold War have persisted even when two superpower adversaries had previously attempted to resolve them (Angola, Horn of Africa, Afghanistan); others, not part of the Cold War ideology split (Cambodia, Sudan), continue, and exacerbation of conflict in areas where the superpowers had avoided involvement (Rwanda) suggests that analysts overestimated the global systemic determinants of security and insecurity in the third world (MacFarlane, 1999:32). The systemic factor in fact varied in relation to both the perceived strategic significance, and the internal characteristics of the particular states in conflict.

Ethical Attention

Can intervention be ethically required to prevent suffering when it is readily within our power to do so? It may be temping to suppose that foreign atrocities can be kept at a safe distance by this distinction: that whereas we have a clear moral duty not to take the life of another person (an act) we have no such duty to prevent a life from being taken by someone else (an omission) particularly when the lives are at risk as a result of a quarrel in a far away country between people of whom we know nothing. The problem is to clarify the act/omission distinction sufficiently. Perhaps a moral distinction can be drawn between what we intend and what we merely foresee. "We may foresee that our failure to act will lead to many deaths, but those deaths are hardly intended and hence not our moral responsibility," states David Fisher (1994: 56). The moral dividing line may be drawn between those consequences that are within our control, and consented to by us, and those that are not. Is it possible to be held responsible when we have knowledge of something but no control over what is happening? Only when the consequences are in our control, and when by persisting with an action the consequences, even if not intended, are to that extent consented to by use, can we be regarded as morally responsible, says Fisher (1994: 57). The moral argument, framed this way is that humanitarian interventions are justified. If we are aware, under the glare of the television camera, of atrocities happening within our own continent, and it is within our power to stop genocide, if we fail to act, in a sense we are consenting to what is happening. We may have a duty to prevent the suffering. In such circumstances, there appears to be a prima facie case to intervene (Fisher, 1994: 57). The best case that can be made in support of humanitarian intervention is that it cannot be said to be unambiguously illegal, argues Fisher (1994: 52). With a bipolar nuclear stalemate, the demands of prudence, morality, and law appeared to coincide: it was dangerous to intervene and intervention would in any case breach the sanctity of the state. With the ending of the Cold War, the clamoring for intervention can no longer be dismissed quite so easily.

Military intervention can take several forms: support for one state against external aggression by another, support for one or another side in a civil war, peace enforcement or peacekeeping operations, and humanitarian interventions to prevent genocide or assist in bringing aid to war-torn people. To appraise such demands, an ethical framework is needed. The just war tradition provides a conceptual basis for evaluating military intervention. What are some of the just war conditions and how may they apply to military intervention? Fisher (1994: 54–58) proposes the following:

1. Military interventions should be undertaken only as a last resort. It does not follow, however, that the use of military force in a limited mode (for example, to assist a humanitarian, food distribution operation) should never be undertaken in preference to other measures, because economic sanctions, for example, can sometimes be a greater

threat to human life than limited military force. It may be morally preferable to use limited military force against carefully targeted military objectives *before* applying such an indiscriminate weapon as general economic sanctions.

2. There should be a just cause for the use of force, namely "an injury received." Until recently, interpreters of the just war tradition tended to restrict this to individual or collective self-defense against aggression as provided for by Article 51 of the UN charter. On the basis of such a restrictive interpretation, the coalition operations to eject Iraq from Kuwait would have been justified, but subsequent allied operations to protect the Kurds in northern Iraq, the Shi'ite Muslims in southern Iraq, and current allied operations in the former Yugoslavia would not. International opinion now considers such actions to be justified.

3. The aim of bringing peace by using superior force to separate belligerent parties could constitute a just cause for intervention, depending on whether there is a reasonable prospect of achieving such an objective at a proportionate cost. A frequent pretext for intervention has been to support one side in a civil war. This does not on its own, however, constitute a just cause, because interference is designed to turn the balance, which gives superiority to the side which would not have been uppermost without it. If the interference does not achieve this end, it misses the point, it fails. Yet, there are times when intervention in a civil was is an option not to assure victory to one side or the other but to try to prevent further bloodshed by keeping the warring factions apart and so impose a peace, that is, *peacemaking*. It is on these grounds that peacemaking operations have often been resisted based on the fear that the intervening party may be drawn into the civil war without achieving peace. Both conditions are more easily satisfied when the issue is *peacekeeping*, that is, the use of military force to enforce a peace settlement or truce that has already been agreed. Peacekeeping certainly constitutes a just cause.

4. Humanitarian interventions, undertaken not to achieve a particular political objective but to prevent suffering, constitute a just cause for intervention though it requires a degree of caution: The burden of proof for any intervention must rest with its advocate because it is a regrettable breach of the integrity of a sovereign state with potentially harmful consequences. When human rights are at risk on a limited scale or where redress is available within the legal system of the state concerned, external interference would not be warranted. When people are threatened with large-scale torture, massacre, or even genocide, however, the prevention of such suffering would constitute a just cause for humanitarian intervention.

5. That the harm likely to result from war must not be disproportionate to the likely good to be achieved, taking into account the probability of success. This condition is important: many who demand military action have no clear idea what the objective that they wish to achieve, by what means, at what cause, and with what likelihood of success. Make a careful assessment of the likely consequences of one's actions before military force is applied and ensure that the good to be achieved will outweigh the harm (often unintended) that may result. "Hastily prepared and ill-conceived interventions, however worthy their motives may be, would not, therefore, be sanctioned by the just war tradition."

The just war tradition with modifications provides a helpful guide through the maze of issues raised by the question of whether to intervene, militarily or otherwise. The moral presumption should be against intervention, yet on occasion, it is ethically permissible, and may even be required. Indeed, morality may require more intervention rather than less action to prevent certain barbarities.

WORLD PERSPECTIVES AND INTERVENTION

When is it legitimate for one state to intervene in the affairs of another? The answer becomes an investigation into the contextual setting of a particular instance of conflict, its relation to other instances, and our own understanding of the appropriate ethical response, according to Rengger (1993: 189–190). Does this imply the key principle of order based upon sovereignty will largely be ignored? As a result, will the possibility and the permissibility of conflict increase? What kind of problem is intervention? What is at stake is not simply "political space" or the agents by which that political space is transgressed, but how that political space is constructed and the nature of the identities which follow from it. It brings into play the tensions between constructions of self and other, of insider and outsider, and of particularism and universalism in both theory and practice, says Hoffman (1993: 194). The nature of political space and the nature of responsibility and obligations between "insiders" and "outsiders" in terms of relations between states, between the state and citizens, either its own or those of other states, or between citizens of different states all become part of the intervention equation.

Beyond the realm of the state, a shift in the nature of the analysis away from legal interpretations has significant implications for the study of intervention. Wendt (1999: 193–245) says sovereignty is a social construction, not a given. Sovereign identities are socially learned through interaction with other states, and sovereignty is both a practice and an institution. It is the practice of political communities that generated the idea of the sovereign state, it is an institution because these practices instantiate relatively stable rules regarding the nature of states, their interactions, and the nature and functioning of international society. Sovereign states are thus inherently social actors whose identities are articulated within the confines of an international society which they instantiate.

The nature of the international system depends on the practices of its members, not objective features. The structure of a states system is constituted as anarchic by member states having and acting on the identity of juridical independence and self-governance. Structures do not exist except by virtue of the agent—or unit—level properties and relations by which they are instantiated. Hence, as these practices change, so does the problem of intervention. The key issue is a proper conceptualization of the relationship between state agents and systemic structures in terms of the concept, "supervenience," which Wendt (1999: 156) defines as a nonreductive relationship of dependency, in which properties at one level are fixed or constituted by those at another, but are not reducible to them. The structure of the states system is supervenient on the properties of states, and the properties of states—including state identities—are, to a significant but lesser extent, dependent on properties of the states system. This partial mutual constitution enables analysis of structural change in terms of identity change.

The givens of sovereignty of state boundaries, and the location and nature of political community is particularly called into question by acts of intervention. Interventionary activity does not necessarily constitute a form of "closure" sustaining existing sovereign identities, but also opens up the possibility of questioning existing boundaries and of constructing alternative identities, according to Mark Hoffman (1993: 202). Sovereignty, the absolute, independent, and recognized authority a state holds over a territory and people, serves as a fundamental point of reference for international relations, stabilized historically through the practices of political intervention. Thus, intervention discourse begins by positing a sovereign state with boundaries that might be violated and then regards transgressions of these boundaries as a problem (Weber, 1995: 1–3). For a state to have a voice in global politics, it must speak for its domestic constituency, and this constituency must already be organized into a community, differentiated both from the realm of global politics and from other domestic communities. The permeability of state authority in economics and security matters makes it difficult to imagine these boundaries and also boundary transgressions dividing domestic space. Intervention is regarded as an essentially uncontested concept, which has to do with its coupling with sovereignty. The sovereignty/intervention boundary where authority relations are contested would help give an account of how sovereign states are constituted in practice. Weber (1995: 11) suggests that the meanings of sovereignty and intervention are inscribed, contested, erased, and reinscribed through historical practices.

World politics is driven by the interaction of international politics, factional politics within national and transnational policy coalitions, and constituency politics, states Lamborn (1997:196), who views the three arenas as interdependent and mutually constituted. Although the principal sources of variation are sometimes international and sometimes domestic, the effects are driven by how the three arenas interrelate. For example, the strategic situation in each arena will depend on the ways actors' preferences, power positions, beliefs about legitimate relationships, and expectations about the future are linked across the three levels. Accordingly, policy choices that states make will vary with the mix of international and domestic incentives attached to different options, and the outcomes will vary with how successfully those choices bridge international, factional, and constituency politics, Lamborn (1997: 200) asserts, suggesting that international relations and domestic politics are so interrelated that they should be analyzed simultaneously as wholes. This is the environment of the modern intervention phenomena: the world operates in a constrained model in which domestic imperatives interact with international structural forces to shape foreign policy outcomes.

Benjamin Barber (1996), in *Jihad vs. McWorld: How Globalism and Tribalism Are Reshaping the World,* echoes the argument and, in his view, only dangers lie ahead in this intermeshed environment. The clash of Jihad and McWorld will not develop into some overriding good, for the tendencies of the two sets of forces appear so intractably antithetical, "one driven by parochial hatreds, the other by universalizing markets, the one recreating ancient subnational and ethnic borders from within, the other making national borders porous from without. Yet Jihad and McWorld have this in common: they both make war on the sovereign nation-state and thus undermine the nation-state's democratic institutions" (Barber, 1996: 6). In the confrontation between global commerce and ethnicity and identity, the virtues of the democratic nation are lost. Jihad may begin as a simple search for a local grounding to ward against the uniformity of modernization and globalization. Even the nations of the developed world are affected by globalization trends. A new class of institutions that extend global reach have developed—in commerce and communications that lack distinctive national identities and neither reflect nor respect nationhood as an organizing or regularizing principle. "If McWorld in its most elemental negative form is a kind of animal greed, one that is achieved by an aggressive and irresistible energy, Jihad in its most elemental negative form is a kind of animal fear, propelled by anxiety in the face of uncertainty and relieved by self-sacrificing zealotry," asserts Barber (1996: 215). His solution is to lay a foundation for civil society and civic culture in traditional societies, to allow citizens to take control of governments and markets. Civil society is a key element in local democracy, and global, strong democracy depends on the internationalization of civil society. He concludes that peace and stabilization achieved through military intervention are unlikely to contain the spread of Jihad. The misconceived challenge for outsiders seeking to assist citizens in Bosnia, Rwanda, and Haiti was how to divide and pacify these disintegrating countries while the real and continuing challenge is how to make them democratic (Barber, 1996: 291). Yet if the process is to be hastened, it needs to come from the outside arena, hence setting up a situation of intervention. With a host of new problems demanding global attention, and Nongovernmental Organizations (NGOs) with energy and ideas call for a larger role, the world is moving toward a different future.

The United Nations declared itself in favor of humanitarian intervention without the request or consent of the state involved, and a concern with the plight of citizen populations in dangerous territories occasionally overrides the primacy of state interests. Many of the Security Council resolutions since the end of the Cold War authorizing forceful intervention concerned domestic situations that involved awful human suffering but posed little direct threat to international peace. Election monitoring has become popular in many emerging democracies, with a large foreign presence dispensing advice and recommending standards for voter registration, campaign law, and campaign practices, to some extent addressing Barber's concern.

If current trends continue, the international system 50 years ahead will be profoundly different. During the transition, the state system and an evolving one will exist side by side. States will set the rules by which all other actors operate, but outside forces will increasingly make decisions for them. Intervention is at the center of this plan. How the United States exercises its intervention discretionary power as recognized global leader whether through exerting influence in the United Nations to encourage or discourage collective action, or by operating independently using its own military intervention tools to solve problems—will profoundly shape this future world.

3

Policy Perspectives on
American Intervention

NATIONAL INTERESTS

Two dominant themes have long provided explanations for U.S. intervention strategy and justified American foreign policy and national security behavior. One set of ideas is based on spreading economic, political, and social values— America intervenes to promote liberalism, democracy, and capitalism. Another rationale derives from power politics—America intervenes to maintain or expand its hegemonic ambitions to ensure its strength and influence in the world. These activization mechanisms do not stand apart; they connect contextually within and across crises and cases and reflect policy-maker priorities in particular environments, to configure the national interest. Debates over the direction and purpose of American foreign policy emerging at each instance of an intervention opportunity are structured around these general motivational pressures.

Proponents of military intervention argue troops should be introduced to (a) maintain world order (to prevent a slippery slope toward a lawless universe); (b) contain threats to international peace (to prevent local disturbances from expanding across territorial borders); (c) respond to the moral imperative (we should not stand by while gross violations of human rights are taking place); and (d) deliver a message to bad leaders in repressive countries (to show rogue behavior will not be tolerated). Yet there remains the issue of the utility of military intervention. No decisive argument has demonstrated that military intervention provides a satisfactory answer to important policy questions related to conflict solution and operational support. By committing foreign troops into a civil conflict, is it reasonable to expect to achieve a political settlement? (It is always easier to send troops in than to get them out, leaving the country concerned in good political shape.) Is it reasonable to expect dependable public support for maintaining troops abroad? (Ground forces inserted to fight and then manage postwar reconstruction are there for the long haul requiring steady, indefinite support.) Any intervention discussion inevitably addresses the national interest concept and its relation to policy objectives.

Definitions of national interest provide limited guidance for actual security policy. What matters is the price the United States will pay to secure them, yet interests remain central to explaining security policies. Debates about whether to intervene emphasize discrete U.S. interests and systemic interests—that is, the norms of state behavior shared generally by the international community. It is always easier to justify military intervention when clear, demonstrable, and discrete national interests are threatened. Theoretically, behind every decision is an identifiable balance: a specific national interest evaluation and a fair price to pay in order to protect it, yielding a calculation which explains how a particular policy is promoted. The calculation derives from an assessment of a moral urge to intervene versus a rational temptation to keep out; knowing only a serious application of military force will provide effective influence is weighed against a promise not to introduce any ground troops. Consequently, policies on intervention tend to gravitate toward arguments about what can be achieved by a method of low risk: follow the moral urge to do something but bring the least harm to intervening, fighting forces. The general formula seems to be this: specify clear goals with measures to meet them, including reasonable deadlines and an exit strategy; rely on power by air rather than on the ground (preference for high technology weapons over combat troops); seek policy support through Congressional approval, public opinion, and UN authority.

There is no political consensus capable of sustaining a military intervention or peacekeeping operation involving a significant human and material cost; loss of confidence in an operation comes easily and quickly. While solutions require patience and long-term commitments, intervention demands a short duration and quick, recognizable results. The two are incompatible. Were it reversed— solution come quickly, intervention is patient—there would be no problem, nor a debate. Generic national interests in any civil-based conflict seem to be these: prevent conflict spread outside national borders, minimize violence and relieve the suffering, and encourage peaceful settlement.

National interest debate tends to proceed from two perspectives. One is policy oriented, the other ethically oriented. Exactly where the boundary line runs between them, and precisely what programs are to be pursued within its limits, are matters of constant discussion, since security and survival (vital interest) are not fixed points: their precise importance and relation to one another depend on one's perspective of the world and the role of the United States within it, states Robert C. Good (1965: 271). The national interest as a problem in political ethics is reconciling necessity and principle: protecting group interests and dedication to values such as justice and equality for everyone. There are two dangers in giving attention to the fact of national self-interest: the danger of giving too little, and the danger of giving too much, says Good (1965: 274). "Between the sentimental illusion that nations can pursue moral crusades without reference to interest and the cynicism that believes the nation in practice has no obligations beyond interest, there is the possibility of limited 'moral transcendence' or 'wise self interest' capable of finding the point of concurrence between the interests of the self and the general welfare," is the way Good (1965: 274) summarizes the position of Reinhold Niebuhr (1950: 5–7), a central figure in early Cold War debates.

What is the relevance of norms that transcend interest to behavior that is limited primarily to interest? Are principles separable from interests? Are interests actually values? "If a statesman decides that the dangers to the security of his country are so great as to make necessary a course of action that may lead to war, he has placed an exceedingly high value on an increment of national security," says Good (1965: 283). The relationship between national interest and principles transcending the nation remains problematic. Although the national interest is said to be a more reliable guide to intelligent policy than principle, the relation of principle to interest is not easy to evaluate.

The interest of a nation is to satisfy national needs. Is the national interest objective? Some regard national interests as permanent, unchanging, and related to power, while those who treat national interest as a subjective idea include values beyond power. According to Morton Kaplan (1964: 165) the self-centered interests of the national actor in "balance of power" and "bipolar" international systems are in part the product of the social structure of those systems. However, even in those international systems different national actors have different national interests which function with their values and internal system needs as well as their international needs. Some national actors place greater value upon supranational and international interests in the "balance of power" and bipolar systems than other actors. Moreover, in other international system structure configurations the international interest becomes an autonomous and intrinsic value for the actors within the system. In a hierarchical system, for example, national actors, and consequently national interest, cease to function (M. Kaplan, 1964: 165). When political formulas such as national interest or national security gain popularity, they need to be carefully evaluated. While appearing to offer guidance and a basis for broad consensus, they may be simply a preferred policy hidden behind a broadly accepted concept. When the United States can afford to be concerned mainly with extensive interests, beyond its core values then military bases, security zones, and special regions of interests may be acquired. They then become new national values requiring protection. Pushed to its logical extreme, spatial extension of this nature would not stop short of world domination.

National interest definitions and interpretations, however vague, are part of mental maps—an ordered but continually adapting structure of the mind, alternatively conceived as a process, by reference to which one acquires, codes, stores, recalls, reorganizes, and applies in thought or in action, information about the larger scale geographic environment and orientation in the world (Henrikson, 1991: 177). Mental maps often are latent; triggered into use whenever a person is required to make a spatial decision. Moreover, mental maps tend to be somewhat narrowly thematic; that is, pertinent to specific kinds of spatial problems, such as military, economic, or political challenges. In 1985, *The National Interest*, a quarterly magazine devoted to American foreign policy and world politics was founded, because, in the words of the editor, "In the post Cold-war era, America finds itself without a clear set of governing assumptions about either one. A principal aim of the journal is to stimulate and focus discussion about just what those assumptions should be." This theme echoes in Samuel Huntington's article, "The Erosion of American National Interests," published in *Foreign Affairs* in 1997, where he makes the point that national interest derives from national identity. "We have to know who we are before we can know what our interests are" (Huntington, 1997: 1).

Historically, American identity has had two primary components, culture and creed: the values and institutions of traditions including the place of the individual in society and universal ideas and principles articulated in the founding documents by American leaders—liberty, equality, democracy, constitutionalism, liberalism, limited government, private enterprise. With the end of the Cold War and social, intellectual, and demographic changes in American society, the validity and relevance of both components of American identity have been brought into question. "Americans have become unable to define their national interests, and as a result sub national commercial interests and transnational and nonnational ethnic interests have come to dominate foreign policy" (Huntington, 1997: 1). The common goal, focus, and enemies to structure national security are hard to discern, and America needs a continuing consensus on political ideology to support national strength, argues Huntington (p. 4). A national interest is a public good of concern to all or most Americans; a vital national interest is one which they are willing to expend blood and treasure to defend, argues Huntington, who conceptualizes national interests as a combination of security and material concerns with moral and ethical ones. In the Cold War, the Soviet Union and communism were perceived as threats to both American security and American values, an ideal linkage between the demands of power politics and the demands of morality. In the post—Cold War setting, the need is not to find the power to serve American purposes, but rather to find purposes for the use of American power (Huntington, 1997: 5). He suggests a policy of restraint and reconstruction aimed at limiting the diversion of American resources to the service of particularistic interests which he views as the promotion abroad of highly specific commercial and ethnic interests—protecting small nations against aggression, promoting human rights and democracy, or economic and social development in the Third World. At some point, the combination of security threat and moral challenge will require Americans once again to commit major resources to the defense of national interest, but a more restrained role now could facilitate America's assumption of a more positive role in the future when the times for it to renew its national identity and to pursue national purposes for which Americans are willing to pledge their lives, their fortunes and their national honor, Huntington (p. 11) recommends.

An alternative position is advocated by Joseph Nye (1999: 22), who asserts that moral values are simply intangible interests; the United States has interests—in the broadest sense—in maintaining international order, which requires a significant investment, for "it is difficult to be a superpower on the cheap." If the largest beneficiary of a public good (such as international order) does not provide disproportionate resources toward its maintenance, then the smaller beneficiaries are unlikely to do so. Thus, the United States should make sure that top priority is given to those aspects of the international system that, if not attended to properly, would have profound effects on the basic international order and therefore on the lives and welfare of Americans. We need to continue to "shape the environment," and that is why we keep 100,000 troops based in Europe, another 100,000 in Asia, and some 20,000 near the Persian Gulf, says Nye (1999: 24). Our role is as a stabilizer and reassurance against the rise of hostile hegemons.

What should be done about the humanitarian concerns and strong moral preferences in the American larger national interest framework? There are tradeoffs. Certain rules of prudence may help the integration of such issues into the larger strategy for advancing the national interest. We should save violent options for the most egregious cases, Nye advises, and when we do use force, it is worth remembering some principles of the "just war" doctrine; having a just cause in the eyes of others, not unduly punishing the innocent, setting proportionality of means to ends, and having a high probability of good consequences, rather than wishful thinking. We should generally avoid the use of force except in cases where our humanitarian interests are reinforced by the existence of other strong national interests. This was the case in the Gulf War, says Nye, but not the case in Somalia. In Bosnia and Kosovo our interests combined both humanitarian values and the strategic concerns of European allies and NATO. Prudence alone cannot determine the national interests in the information age. Better consequences will flow if American values and goals are related to American power and interests are rationally pursued within prudent limits. Determining the national interest has always been contentious. But the debate about the American national interest in the information age, says Nye, should pay more attention to the peculiar nature of American power today. It should establish strategic priorities accordingly, and it should develop prudent rules that allow the United States to meld its strategic, economic, and humanitarian interests into an effective foreign policy. Therein lie the temptations and dilemmas of intervention.

POLICY ALTERNATIVES

America has global power, but does it have global leadership ambition? If America has the ambition, will it be able to sustain the passion to maintain it? If Americans enjoy the role as leader, will they accept the sacrifices that such a role inevitably requires? Three different approaches to the issue of America's place in the world and the future of its foreign policy have emerged in the post–Cold War debate. Charles William Maynes (2001: 50) categorized each school in terms of the scope and level of engagement recommended as appropriate for U.S. policy commitments abroad, labeling them the controllers, the shapers, and the abstainers. The controllers are the hegemonists, who argue the best strategy for U.S. interests is to ensure American leadership in the international system by dominating the plans for the new international order, making commitments and choices that allow U.S. power and influence to last as long as possible. The shapers believe that "a quest for leadership is more realistic than a quest for domination." As powerful as America may be today, it cannot prevail without the help of others. The goal should be to shape the changing international environment into more permanent patterns that will benefit U.S. interests over the long run. The abstainers focus on the economic issues and structures facing global politics: believing the country can comfortably scale down its active role in the world, trusting to natural balances the task of keeping the peace.

Despite their differences, all three schools are attempting to confront the fundamental problem of national interest: how can American security be guaranteed? The controllers believe the international system must be determined and directed by American foreign policy. The shapers believe the international system is best influenced and molded by America with the participation and cooperation of others. The abstainers believe that the international system is less threatening than it was during the Cold War and that America should not seek to control or mold it (Maynes, 2001: 51). The hegemonists and the isolationists share a common vision. They argue that U.S. foreign policy should focus on the protection of core values such as the lives and prosperity of American citizens, the United States' territorial integrity, and the autonomy of its political process. These objectives should be achieved not by multilateral policies, but by maintaining the military balance of power and abandoning objectives such as the promotion of democracy and human rights. Each group wants to make sure that America remains the sole arbiter of its own fate, either by keeping others subservient or by staying out of their quarrels. The shapers, both conservatives and liberals, do not believe that U.S. power is sufficient for America to ignore or reject the need for allies and friends.

The controllers advocate that America should exploit its dominance, following a strategy that maintains security dependence among client states. Make the bid for world hegemony. After all, no state can be trusted over the long run. The logic is basically this: America's unparalleled power should be used to hold down others as long as possible, because other states will eventually attempt to exert power and seek domination if the United States does not assume the strong leadership role. An anarchic international system needs someone in control, and the United States will be a better hegemon for his benign and beneficent character. America will exercise its power with some restraint. And whoever dominates the international system will be able to dictate to it politically and economically (Maynes, 2001: 52). Some states are still governed by evil people; human suffering and repressive governments continue to exist. Hence, why not use American power to eradicate evil and to do good? Imposing order over current uncivilized powers is urged as an American duty. The controllers maintain that it would be a dereliction of national interest or moral duty not to do so (Maynes, 2001:52).

The shapers warn that America should not be mesmerized by its own power. In humanitarian interventions that would require taking over the powers of other governments to the point of engaging in a form of neocolonialism, that would not be successful (Maynes, 2001: 53). Shapers are global internationalists who say that America should work with others to try to create an international environment in a manner that serves not only the U.S. national interest, but that of other states too. America's goal should be to persuade other centers of power—states and international organizations—to support constructive solutions to the world's problems and create an international order based on resolving international disputes without military force, reducing the number of weapons of mass destruction in the world, working toward a limited doctrine of humanitarian intervention, and maximizing global economic openness. Shapers presume a more benign world and operate on more optimistic premises than controllers.

With respect to the abstainers, the end of the Cold War and globalization has rendered the call for American isolation as a credible foreign policy alternative. The United States is no longer forced to pursue an internationalist strategy. Moreover, it is dangerous to do so. An excessive concern with control is misplaced and pointless. What are called for are modest, occasional efforts of involvement. Maynes (2001: 56) divides the abstainers into two groups: the liberal abstainer, for whom economics is more important than politics; and the conservative abstainer, the traditional isolationist, who values politics over economics. The liberal abstainer believes the nation's highest priority is to open markets among economies and communications among cultures; the conservative abstainer is worried that global forces will constrict political choices in the United States and erode national sovereignty. The goal is to keep America out of conflict and the best way to do this to disengage and pull back.

U.S. post–Cold War foreign policy organizing principles, from the new world order to assertive multilateralism to selective engagement, attempt to explain U.S. policy in specific cases, though principles articulated in one scheme were never consistently applied. By default, "selective engagement," although it has become an identified policy strategy, actually describes the real basis of intervention choices. The United States decides to do what it decides to do, not deductively, by determining action from principles, but inductively, by contextual-based choices, with post hoc justification for intervention direction (including choices not to intervene). This stand reveals the apparent drift and lack of consensus in foreign policy circles while maintaining the different presumptions of national interest. It keeps the debate alive too. Realists denounce those who urge humanitarian interventions. The more idealistic-minded ask if a world leader can maintain respect from others if it remains quite indifferent to what is happening within the system, even at the periphery.

HISTORICAL PRACTICE

The Monroe Doctrine of 1823 announced three imperatives for American foreign policy: The American continents would be closed to further colonialization by European powers; the United States must not involve itself in the wars of Europe; and the United States would view any attempt by a European power to extend its political system to the Western Hemisphere as a peace and security threat (Gaddis Smith, 1994: 3). The Monroe Doctrine's warning against foreign intrusion in the Americas remains alive and vigorous in

U.S. policy orientation, but during World War II the old prohibition against American entanglement in the political affairs of Europe was abandoned.

Europe in the 1930s was the site of significant political tension, violence, and intervention, from the Spanish Civil War to Germany's seizure of Austria and Czechoslovakia and invasion into Poland in 1939. In April 1940 Hitler's forces overwhelmed Denmark and Norway; in May, the German armies drove into the Netherlands, Belgium, and Luxembourg, and France. During the summer, the battle of Britain was underway. The outlook for the Western democracies in Europe was dismal in September 1940. If Great Britain fell, would the United States be next to feel Hitler's power? Americans overwhelmingly considered Germany the aggressor and hoped for an Allied victory, yet most hoped the United States would not be drawn into the conflict. As a consequence of conflicting desires of the American people with regard to the European war, states Wayne Cole (1953: 6-9), vocal elements in the American public divided into two highly heterogeneous groups. The interventionists in the foreign policy debate were those who believed that it was more important for the United States to assure a British victory over the Axis than for the United States to keep out of the European war. The isolationists or noninterventionists were those who believed it was more important for the United States to keep out of the war than to assure a British victory over the Axis.

Both sides in the foreign policy debate in 1941 claimed to represent a majority of the American people. The interventionists cited the re-election of Roosevelt for a third term in 1940 as evidence of popular approval of the president's policies. They could point to public opinion polls that indicated that a majority of Americans had approved each major proposal advanced by the Administration to aid the British, short of war. Since 1940, a clear majority had believed it more important to aid Britain in her effort to defeat Germany than for the United States to keep out of the war. The noninterventionists argued the "short of war" phrase merely masked the real intentions of the pro-war faction, who advocated direct entry by the United States into the conflict in Europe. This position lacked public support—an interventionist minority was attempting to drag the unwilling majority into war by deceitfully misleading the public— only one-fifth of the American people supported an interventionist position, asserted Cole (1953: 52–55). The debate ended in December 1941 with the Japanese attack at Pearl Harbor, putting the country into an interventionist mode.

American foreign policy activism and intervention practice continued from the moment of entry into World War II through the Cold War into the post–Cold War period. The end of the communist threat did not necessarily mean a downturn in U.S. interventionist practices. In fact, the proclamation of a new world order by President Bush implied a continuation of the previous direction. Interestingly, legacies of both American foreign policy choice and debate are evident in the deliberations and decisions in the early post–Cold War years. Intervention into the Persian Gulf in 1990 leading to war in 1991 was the first major test of the new world order theme, largely representing a continuation of U.S. global activism and involvement set in stone during World War II. The unwillingness to intervene in Bosnia until 1995, also representing a consistent strand in U.S. thinking, was a replay, in some respects, of the foreign policy intervention debate in America more than 50 years earlier.

How did the public react to intervention decisions in the 1990s? After some experience as a leading nation in international affairs throughout the Cold War decades, one might anticipate that the contours of U.S. popular attitudes would change, at least in a general way, to reflect a more globalist outlook and greater willingness to take on a strong, forceful role in international affairs. Did Americans support involvement in the Persian Gulf and the Bosnian conflicts? Surprisingly, American public opinion on these issues mirrored divisions evident in the intervention debates of 1940–1941. Kurt Taylor Gaubatz (1995: 542) reported that the public response in different polls taken in 1990 toward the use of military force to reverse the Iraqi invasion of Kuwait varied widely from 32% to 70% of the public agreeing with the position; in 1992 and 1993, polls showed as little as 12% and as much as 94% of the population supportive of American military action in Bosnia or similar situations (Gaubatz, 1995: 534). Beyond the technical difficulties of comparing poll results across somewhat differently stated questions, problems emerge from aggregating individual preferences owing to differing perceptions of the seriousness of a given threat to national interest, the expected costs of intervention, and the willingness to use force to deal with international conflicts. (Gaubatz, 1995: 535). "The higher the costs of intervention, the more effective a case for intervention leaders will have to make. An intervention that is supported because of an expectation of low costs will quickly lose its public support if it turns out to involve very high costs," states Gaubatz (1995: 541), who concludes that military intervention requires a sizable rather than a simple majority, a situation most likely when leaders feel confident in either the prospects for a quick victory or the intensity of their support.

Cost-benefit assessments of intervention choices are influenced by underlying beliefs on three dimensions: the role of force in international politics, support for international involvement, and preference for unilateral or multilateral action, discovered Ronald Hinckley (1988), in reviewing poll data and literature on public opinion on foreign policy. He concluded that any intervention debate would focus on evaluations of whether "the particular issue involves the United States in international affairs, how it involves America in those affairs, and what the military implications of that involvement are, regardless of the real objective of the particular policy" (Hinckley 1988: 316). He formulated a typology of six attitude profiles along with their relative weight projections in the public mind: those advocating force include slightly more than half; hardliners (representing 18% of public opinion), internationalists (26%), and forceful isolationists (13%); and those who do not support use of force abroad—slightly less than half— include soft unilateralists (7%); accommodationists (19%), and restrained isolationists (17%). (Hinckley, 1988: 301). Such distribution promises a continuing debate on U.S. foreign intervention policy and its application.

INTERVENTION TEMPTATIONS

There are at least four reasons why the United States may be increasingly tempted to intervene, according to Arnold Kantor and Linton F. Brooks (1994: 15–16): first, the end of the Cold War, which removed many constraints on U.S. action; second, increasing predominance of economic considerations in U.S. foreign policy; third, renewed American emphasis on democracy and human rights as foreign policy goals; and fourth, that U.S. leaders will face intervention decisions simply because the post–Cold War world is disorderly and full of dangers. Ethnic, religious, and sectarian conflicts threaten to erupt around the globe; internal anarchy prevails, terrorism threatens.

Increased opportunities for intervention—and even increased ability to intervene—do not necessarily mean that intervention has become either more desirable or more effective. With intervention no longer tied to superpower rivalry, the benefits of intervention may have actually decreased. Such benefits become harder to see and easier to argue about; hence, attention has focused on the real-term costs of intervention. Have the frequency and intensity of conflict increased since the Cold War ended, or do we simply pay more attention to organized violence than before? Given that some degree of turmoil in the international system is inescapable, where are the most serious challenges to global peace and security likely to arise, and how, by reference to what set of standards, should the United States respond? Demands for resources to help prevent conflicts and to manage those that do erupt will far exceed the supply, making difficult choices for U.S. policy-makers inevitable. Governments in the periphery must also contend with a long list of problems. Foremost among these is the persistently high level of civil strife that can be traced either to the unfinished business of the national struggle or to the process of state formation exacerbated by disparities in wealth between contending groups. Blacker (1994: 60–61) concludes that most of the root causes of instability that existed during the Cold War are also present in today's world, and several new sources of conflict have been added.

In developing a new template to guide U.S. action in the post–Cold War era, enlargement of democracy through development of free markets and support for democratic processes contains within it the seeds of new, limitless intervention in the affairs of countries. These countries have little history or experience of power-sharing or representative government. Corr D. Blacker (1994: 65) asks: Is the rhetoric of enlargement of democracy and support for human rights real or is it a smokescreen behind which a policy of disengagement and neoisolationism is being implemented? Further, the explosion in the field of UN peace operations in the first half-decade of the post Cold War, with the promise of continuing requirements in the peacemaking, peacekeeping, humanitarian assistance, and peace-building areas, puts the issue squarely on American policy-makers wrestling with intervention criteria—whether to become involved, and if so, how, when, and under what conditions.

Does the international community have a moral responsibility to intervene to stop a sovereign nation from taking international law into its own hands and behaving irresponsibly toward other nations? Some believe that if the principle of humanitarian intervention is entrenched further, it will lead to the development of democratization processes, assist the human rights cause and bring a stronger sense of responsibility to many nations around the world for their international obligations and commitments. If the goal of the intervention is well defined and the participants establish a clear mandate, then open-ended involvement will be prevented. It is also important to supplement the deployment of military forces or peacekeeping missions with sanctions, political isolation, and other diplomatic means, since the root causes of many humanitarian crises are political. A central problem of recent experience in the name of humanitarian intervention is that the results of foreign military involvement do not endure and fail to provide a framework for security. The idea is that a military intervention in another country can be humanitarian in its original motives, in its stated purposes, in its methods of operation, and in its actual results. The problem of *any* military intervention in another state to protect the lives of its inhabitants is complex, though, and politically sensitive. In recent years, grim details of civil conflicts and effects on the local population were reported on television. This led to calls for action that were expressed both in U.S. circles and within the UN Security Council. Such discussion and media portrayals of world disasters appeared often, and might have led to interventions, the imperative to "do something" that might otherwise have been hotly contested.

Possibilities for developing a coherent notion of humanitarian intervention involve crucial questions about the authorization of such action. The possibility that the society of states as a whole might somehow authorize particular acts of intervention significantly weakens the traditional objection to it, though. Still, the issue of authorization is significant, because the main foundations of the nonintervention rule in the international law of states have been concerns about states' acting unilaterally, pursuing their own interests, dominating others, and engaging in conflicts with others. If an intervention is authorized by an international body and has specific stated purposes, these concerns are far less relevant. Yet the real difficulties in the contemporary practice of humanitarian intervention concern its purpose and consequences, both of which reflect a certain degree of uncertainty. What is the relationship among humanitarian intervention motives, political motives, and desires to transform a situation of conflict (often anarchy) into one of peace? Does it make sense to call an intervention in a country "humanitarian" when troops committed may have to fight and kill those who obstruct them, as happened in Somalia? Or, if troops involved fail to protect the inhabitants from hostile forces, as happened in Bosnia? The absence of any precise idea as to what kind of state or political structures might resolve the crises in these situations is the reason why the humanitarian impulse for intervention is challenged. Recent practice involving elements of humanitarian intervention has reflected real and urgent problems.

Another dilemma of current intervention thinking relates to the idea of its limited and presumed impartiality. Richard Betts (1994: 21–28) argues that limited and impartial intervention is impossible: Limited intervention may end a war if the intervener takes sides, tilts the local balance of power, and helps one of the rivals to win—in other words, if it is not impartial. Impartial intervention may end a war if the outsiders take complete command of the situation, take over all the local competitors, and impose a peace settlement—an unlimited intervention. Other strategies indicating less involvement, less commitment—a smaller mission, without real attempts to finish a conflict—usually block peace. Such intervention may do enough to keep either belligerent from defeating the other but not enough to make them stop trying. A war does not begin, says Betts, unless both sides in a dispute would rather fight than concede. It is not hard to avert war if either one cares primarily about peace—all it has to do is let the other side have what it claims is its due. A war will not end until both sides agree who will control whatever is in dispute. Betts (1994: 28) presents it this way: "Impartiality works best where intervention is needed least: where wars have played themselves out and the fighting factions need only the good offices of mediators to lay down their arms. Impartiality is likely to work against peace in the more challenging cases—where intervention must make the peace, rather than just preside over it—because it reflects deeper confusion over what war is about."

If outsiders such as the United States face demands for peace in wars where passions have not burned out, they can avoid the costs and risks that go with entanglement by staying away, letting the locals fight alone. Or they can jump in and help one of the contenders defeat the other. But can they bring peace sooner if they remain impartial? Not with a gentle, restrained impartiality, but with an active, harsh impartiality that overpowers both sides: a high level of commitment, a dedicated strategy, and a set of plans to handle all forms of contingency making it possible. This is a tall order, seldom with many supporters, and it is hard to think of instances where it has been invoked.

Most international interventions of the post Cold War were not driven by the material, power-based interests of outside parties, but by their moral concerns: securing peace and justice. In Betts' view, peace and justice are not natural allies, unless right just happens to coincide with might. Outside intervention in a civil war usually becomes an issue when the sides are closely enough matched that neither can defeat the other quickly. When traditional national interests are not involved, neither the United States nor the United Nations will expend their resources for an overwhelming and decisive military action. Betts' guidelines for involvement include: (1) recognize that to make peace is to decide who rules; (2) avoid half-measures; (3) do not confuse peace with justice; (4) do not confuse balance with peace or justice; and (5) make humanitarian intervention militarily rational.

An alternative view is presented by Tony Smith (1994: 46), who believes the United States must recognize the limits on its power and cooperate with peoples whose political systems are not like its own. Smith argues that American policy is conditioned by the geographical recognition that resolving local questions has a bearing on the global structure of U.S. interests and obligations. But, "the seemingly compelling logic of the geopolitical vision" began to override "any reading of the logic of local developments." This caused problems, for there is no threshold between involvement and intervention in situations of entangling patron-client relations with governments around the world for a great power state. The United States should do what it can to foster human rights and democracy in Latin America and Eastern Europe and Russia, but it should be far more reserved on these matters with respect to China, the Muslim world, and Africa. But the criticism that fostering human rights and democratic government abroad is idealistic, utopian, or moralistic, and hence unsuited to furthering American interests, needs to be confronted. The establishment of democratic governments holds the best promise of stability and the emergence of states feeling a community of interests with the West. A forward-looking policy in defense of human rights and democracy in these circumstances is not only morally appealing, but also is in the security interests of the United States.

What is the current picture of U.S. intervention? At least five factors can be identified: a preference of multilateralism, an intolerance for U.S. casualties, an aversion to enemy civilian suffering, a reliance on high-technology options, and a commitment to international norms, state Daniel Byman and Matthew Waxman (1999: 108). None is present in every instance of coercive diplomacy undertaken by the United States, yet together they create a reputation for American credibility abroad. Preference for multilateralism derives from several factors—sometimes coalition partners provide the bulk of ground troops, in other instances its value is political cooperation and international legitimacy. While the United States often asserts its right and willingness to act unilaterally when threats demand it or when wider participation conflicts with domestic political or operational priorities, lone coercive operations remain the exception rather than the rule.

While the United States opts sometimes for an overwhelming application of force, in other situations limited application of military force is the strategy, and it has not always influenced the outcome toward peace or a political settlement desired by the Americans. Even when threats are carried out, adversary resistance may actually increase rather than decrease: Saddam Hussein's decision to continue marching Iraqi troops into Kuwait in the wake of U.S. actions, which led the United Nations to impose sanctions and create a multinational military force for deployment in Saudi Arabia is an example. The uneven record is partially explained by the common axioms of coercive diplomacy. According to Byman and Waxman (1999: 107), coercion generally requires a credible threat of pain beyond the benefits an adversary may anticipate through resistance. However, the United States often imposes constraints on its own use of force and therefore on the level of pain that it can realistically deliver. Adversaries can capitalize on such constraints and win a coercive contest despite being militarily, politically, and economically inferior. Whether a reactive, adaptive foe will yield does not depend solely on the levels of threat or motivation present at the time U.S. demands are issued; it also depends on self-imposed limits the United States places on the use of force and understanding how adversaries can manipulate key features of U.S. strategy.

The United States' use of military force is currently dictated by policy-maker sensitivity to the potential casualties among U.S. servicemen designated to participate in an intervention mission. The relatively low American death total in the 1991 Gulf War raised public expectations that intervention would be safe and low in casualties, now that high technology weaponry had taken over, restricting the use of ground forces. A primary feature of the American approach to military engagement has been a reliance on high technology over low-technology force. Such high-tech instruments provide the necessary target discrimination to satisfy the public's demand for minimizing civilian suffering and do not place significant numbers of U.S. personnel in danger (Byman and Waxman 1999: 109–110). When 18 soldiers were killed in Somalia in 1993, public support for the humanitarian intervention there was cut short, which emphasizes the low tolerance for casualties and the implicit calculation to evaluate an intervention mission in terms of its costs and benefits. Sensitivity to casualties and suffering among the enemy civilian population also shapes the application of U.S. force. Air strikes, for the most part, are designed to avoid collateral damage and population centers. In the war in Afghanistan, both bombs and food packages were dropped from the sky—many of each.

Related to civilian casualties aversion is a commitment to achieve or maintain perceived legitimacy of an intervention operation—both at home and abroad. Most U.S. military adventures are justified in terms of international principles and international legal obligations. Such concerns mean careful crafting of the rules of engagement, usually limiting action. Together these characteristics restrict the range of intervention strategies and turn the United States from a hegemonic power (will and capability matched and applied at necessary levels to achieve desired ends) into a unipolar entity, with its reduced ability to dictate world affairs. Byman and Waxman (1999: 112) believe states can exploit this picture when they assert the most common counter-coercive strategy to take advantage of American intervention sensitivities is for adversaries to use human shields to deter U.S. strikes. This was used in Kosovo, making it almost impossible for personnel to target enemy forces without risking civilian bloodshed. These strategies are effective because dictatorial regimes do not depend on popular support, and the tight control of media and their internal propaganda machines allow for such leadership to exploit inaccurate accounts of incidents. In effect, U.S. sensitivity may urge such adversary practices and, ironically, the U.S. response is usually to reduce its level of commitment, to restrict threats on its own deployed forces, undermining the entire effort.

If the United States decides to intervene, it means some level of recognition that their soldiers may die; the intervention means human sacrifice. If this is not acceptable in terms of costs to benefits, then the decision is clear: stay home. This is the real problem. Byman and Waxman (1999: 118) believe that U.S. interests might be better served by refraining from military action altogether rather than working from a restricted format. The balance between political demands and military needs, between perception of national interest and national identity and commitments on the line, have to be determined beforehand. Policy-makers often view limited air strikes as compromise solutions, satisfying demands for military action while avoiding the need to put U.S. personnel in danger. This type of thinking makes sense politically, but from a strategic point of view it both undermines coercive strategies in a given crisis and decreases U.S. credibility in the long term, thereby inviting future challenges.

CHOOSING TO INTERVENE

The United States can protect itself from national security threats in two ways: either by taking proactive measures to ameliorate potential threats, usually requiring substantial commitment and sustained attention, which may be politically difficult; or by relying on a reactive approach—waiting for threats to materialize. It is far less costly, at least in the short term, but lacks vision. Neither of these approaches will work—the first is unrealistic, the second, inadequate. An optimal strategy needs to strike the right balance between the two of them. A major factor is available resources and deciding where and how they should be expended. The choices are fundamentally, profoundly, important: ignoring homeland security (and its relation to intervention impact) carried an extremely heavy casualty toll in civilian deaths with the attacks of September 11, 2001, far exceeding the combined casualty list for those participating in American military interventions throughout the post Cold War.

Among the issues in deciding this balance, is figuring out what causes domestic discontent abroad, how it swells into a popular movement, and at what point international threats arise, including specific national security problems for the United States. This suggests that great attention needs to be given to regime rule in various countries throughout the world. But which ones matter? When should intervention be considered, and at what strategic level, in order to reduce local discontent and minimize security threats to the international community? Most civil wars do not directly threaten the United States or its allies, but internal war has emerged as a principal threat to security in the post–Cold War world. Conflicts fought within the borders of a single state may send shock waves far beyond their frontiers. As Steven R. David (1999: 103–104) hypothesizes: were the Persian Gulf oil fields destroyed in a Saudi civil war, the American economy (and those of the rest of the developed world) would suffer severely. Internal wars can also unleash threats that stable governments formerly held in check. As central governments weaken and fall, weapons of mass destruction may fall into the hands of rogue leaders or anti-American factions. And when internal wars erupt on U.S. borders, they threaten to destabilize America itself. All of these dangers are grave enough to warrant consideration. What makes them even more serious is the fact that their impact on America is largely unintended. Being unintended, the spill-off effects of civil wars are not easily deterred, which creates unique challenges to American interests.

Where are these new threats likely to crop up? Two criteria must guide policy-makers in formulating assessments: the actual likelihood of civil war in any particular state, and the impact of a civil war on the United States with respect to threatening its security and economic concerns. David (1999: 105–106), for example, speculates that civil conflict in Mexico would produce waves of disorder that would spill into the United States, endangering the lives of thousands of Americans, destroying a valuable export market, and sending a torrent of refugees northward. A rebellion in Saudi Arabia could destroy that country's ability to export oil on which the world depends. Internal war in Russia could devastate Europe and trigger the use of nuclear weapons. David urges more proactive strategies—American policy-makers should work with governments of threatened states to prevent domestic conflict from erupting, which may require generous American support for a regime under assault. In some instances, Washington may be required to replace these regimes. Either way, the difficulties of preventing internal war pale in comparison to the problems of coping with its effects, David argues, and the United States should prepare itself for these eventualities. Civil wars could inadvertently unleash catastrophic harms. Because these risks are so hard to prevent, they must now get the attention they so urgently deserve.

Pressing for an open world and enforcing its rules will generate new military requirements for interventions and emergency deployments, with complex tasks. Andrew Bacevich (1999: 12) describes the Pentagon blueprint for the future (a document known as joint Vision 2010) with its singular, broad goal: the ability to win quickly and overwhelmingly across the entire range of operations, or in other words, Full Spectrum Dominance. Particular attention is given to security under asymmetric threats, threats coming from "terrorists, criminals, religious crazies, too-big strongmen with big ambitions, anarchy-minded hackers and unscrupulous scientists peddling weapons secrets to make a buck." Eagerness to use the military does not imply eagerness for war. On the contrary, it may mean a devotion to peace. No longer permitted the luxury of concentrating on a single powerful threat, as during the Cold War, the United States today must arm itself, in Albright's words, "against a viper's nest of perils." Those perils run from terror and international organized crime to genocidal violence fueled by ethnic hatred. In short, having prevailed in the Cold War, the United States finds itself not more secure, but less. "American prosperity and well-being are now more precarious, held hostage to a world order that is susceptible to attack from any quarter at any time" states Bachevich (1999: 11). That is the logic of globalization. That is the peace dividend. American soldiers have a mission that is primarily a constabulary one, in that if U.S. military power is removed, the system will break down and globalization will fail. The struggle for U.S. foreign policy, and intervention in particular, is to create a peaceful equilibrium between the forces of integration and the forces of disintegration. Globalization and continued American military supremacy share a common assumption, that the United States can achieve its aspirations painlessly and without hard choices.

The UN Charter set its limits on state power, recognizing all states as sovereign equals, prohibiting interference in their internal affairs and permitting the use of force only when authorized by the UN Security Council. At the time, in 1945, just after World War II, the main problems were thought to be interstate conflict. But the far more common problem today is conflict within states, which is hardly addressed by the charter. The charter regards internal violence as a question of "domestic jurisdiction," that is, beyond official international concern, says Michael Glennon (1999: 3). The new system of world politics means that major threats to stability and well-being arise from internal violence. While domestic order is the primary and initial responsibility of the state, the difference now is that intervention is regarded as appropriate when the humanitarian costs of failing to respond to situations of mass suffering are too high. In general, multilateral intervention is favored over unilateral action, with the hope that this approach minimizes the extreme forms of national self-interest that alter the purpose of such actions.

No one has devised safeguards sufficient to guarantee that power will not be abused by the strong, that coercion will not be misdirected to undermine the values that it was established to protect, says Glennon (1999: 5). But what of justice? International justice can be pursued ad hoc, without a fully functioning legal system. This is what NATO and the United States set out to do in Kosovo. A child saved from ethnic cleansing in Kosovo by NATO's intervention is no less alive because the intervention was impromptu rather than part of a formal system, states Glennon. Yet it is dangerous for NATO to unilaterally rewrite the rules by intervening in domestic conflicts on an irregular, case-by-case basis. The real test is whether the community of nations, not simply the United States, believes intervention in this form is just. "Justice requires legitimacy; without widespread acceptance of intervention as part of a formal justice system, the new interventionism will appear to be built on neither law nor justice, but on power alone. It will then be only a matter of time before the meddling of the illegitimate interventionist regime is rejected just as roundly as was the one it replaced," asserts Glennon (1999: 7). The ideal of justice backed by power should not be abandoned so easily. Glennon believes that if power is used to do justice, law will follow.

The cause of justice calls liberal states to intervene in response to humanitarian crises, human rights violations, and political tyranny in civil conflict situations where concrete national interests may be lacking. At the same time, argues Mark Peceny (2000), the political constraints imposed by liberal institutions of governance make these states reluctant to use force or to pay high costs to achieve liberal goals. Liberal values and liberal political institutions have somewhat contradictory impacts, which may explain the confusing pattern of contemporary, post–Cold War military interventions and its accompanying critique, says Peceny (2000: 1). U.S. intervention policies have been criticized in two directions: first, that the government has been too *eager* to launch military actions and second, that it has been too *weak and indecisive* in its use of force abroad. These faults were levied against President George H.W. Bush in the Persian Gulf War, and against President William Clinton in former Yugoslavia. Those who support intervention on behalf of ideological or humanitarian causes wish that President Clinton had done more to achieve these goals; those more reluctant to support these interventions criticized him for launching limited interventions of incremental escalation rather than the application of overwhelming and decisive force or stepping into territories without strong U.S. national interests at stake.

Why has the United States committed to use American military might to resolve a variety of crises, as with the constant threats to launch air strikes against the Bosnian Serbs from 1993 to mid-1995, only to back off at the last minute, damaging U.S. prestige and the credibility of American commitments?

Why does it send troops only when it is relatively certain those troops will not face combat, as in its permissive occupation of Haiti in 1994? Why has it consistently done less than the minimum necessary to achieve its goals in these conflicts, as the failure of nation-building efforts in Somalia illustrate? Presidents must respond in a manner consistent with liberal values to the political and humanitarian crises that reach the consciousness of the American people. Yet, presidents who send troops into combat make themselves vulnerable to political charges that they have needlessly sacrificed the lives of U.S. soldiers (Peceny, 2000: 2–3). Suboptimal intervention outcomes are produced from this policy tension. A logical decision is to carry out any actions that do not involve ground troop commitment to demonstrate a credible crisis response. But the greater the extent of U.S. resources and prestige dedicated to achieving a solution—measured through political and diplomatic efforts, economic and military aid (excluding direct involvement of soldiers)—the more difficult and costly it becomes to disengage from a situation if it appears substantial *military* power will be necessary to end the conflict and bring resolution. The following decision steps in intervention policy and action derive from Peceny's argument to account for the confusing picture of post–Cold War U.S. interventions: first, a president may choose to take limited, humanitarian action to demonstrate commitment to a liberal cause because it may be less costly than inaction; second, a president may expand non-military commitments in an ongoing, escalating conflict, because it may be less costly than continuing a smaller commitment; third, if military intervention becomes necessary, when the political costs of suffering casualties are greater than the costs of violating liberal principles, then presidents are likely to withdraw the troops before solving the conflict. Thus, gradually escalating involvement in crises will be expected, and when military force is introduced it will often be used in a limited and vacillating manner leading to ineffective results.

In a critique of the Vietnam War policy, "To Intervene or Not to Intervene," Hans. J. Morganthau (1967) pointed to this problem precisely, arguing that the United States had failed to act wisely. Intervening in the political, military, and economic affairs of other countries in excess of $100 billion, and involvement in a costly, risky war in order to build a nation in South Vietnam, shows little wisdom, he said. "Have the commitments made and risks taken been commensurate with the results to be expected and actually achieved? The answer must be in the negative. Our economic aid has been successful in supporting economies, which were already in the process of development; it has been by and large unsuccessful in creating economic development where none existed before, largely because the moral and rational preconditions for such development were lacking. Learning from this failure, we have established the theoretical principle of concentrating aid upon the few nations which can use it rather than giving it to the many who need it" (Morganthau, 1967: 435–436). While this principle of selectivity is sound in theory, Morganthau asserted, its consistent practical application has been thwarted by the harsh political and military realities, which may require economic aid, which is economically not justified, as well as by political and military considerations.

Morganthau urged that the principle of selectivity should be extended to the political and military spheres. "We have come to overrate enormously what a nation can do for another nation by intervening in its affairs—even with the latter's consent. This overestimation of our power to intervene is a corollary of our ideological commitment, which by its very nature has no limit….But in truth, both the need for intervention and the chances for successful intervention are much more limited than we have been led to believe. Intervene we must where our national interest requires it and where our power gives us a chance to succeed" (Morganthau 1967: 436). The choice of these occasions will be determined not by blind reliance on American power but by a careful calculation of the interests involved and the power available. If the United States applies this standard it will intervene less and succeed more, he predicted.

Interestingly, post–Cold War military intervention choices came to be defined by both Presidents George H. W. Bush and Clinton as selective engagement, that is, each emphasized selectivity, a case-by-case approach (Haass 1994: 16). President Bush articulated his views on the use of military force with the announcement of his decision to intervene militarily in Somalia in December 1992, and at the same time, to avoid intervention in Bosnia. He argued against using interests as an absolute guide, noting that military force may not be the best way of safeguarding something vital, while using force might be the best way to protect an interest that qualifies as important but less than vital. Five requirements for military intervention were outlined: force should be used only where the stakes warrant it, where and when it can be effective, where no other policies are likely to prove effective, where it can be limited in scope and time, and where the potential benefits justify the costs and sacrifice. A clear, achievable mission, a realistic plan for accomplishing the tasks, and pragmatic criteria for withdrawal of troops are essential.

Clinton administration pronouncements on the use of force were concerned with U.S. involvement in multilateral military efforts, specifically UN peacekeeping operations: Is there a real threat to peace and security? Does the proposed mission have clear objectives and can its scope be clearly defined? Is a cease-fire in place, and have the parties to the conflict agreed to a UN presence? Are the financial resources needed to accomplish the mission available? These questions formed the essence of President Clinton's address to the UN General Assembly, making clear that his purpose was to make it harder for the world body to launch such efforts. "The United Nations simply cannot become engaged in every one of the world's conflicts. If the American people are to say yes to UN peacekeeping, the UN must know when to say no" (reported in Haass 1994: 17). The number of criteria that had to be met or considered had expanded in order for U.S. combat troops to become involved. These pronouncements affected current thinking about the use of military force, shaped in part by recent or ongoing conflicts and political contexts in which policy-makers sought to justify policies of intervention and nonintervention.

SELECTIVE ENGAGEMENT

The selectivity principle continues to dominate intervention policy. Former Secretary of State James Baker in a speech delivered in 1994, "Selective Engagement," expounded on the theme (Baker 1997). He said the United States is moving into its third great period in foreign policy. The first lasted until 1941, with a brief interregnum during World War I. During this period, U.S. foreign policy was guided by the "principle of disengagement." The second period began with America's entry into World War II when foreign policy was driven by what he calls "compulsory engagement." With the end of the Cold War, says Baker, we are entering a third distinct era of foreign policy which should be guided by the principle of "selective engagement"—a principle that embraces the freedom of action but recognizes the imperatives of U.S. leadership in the global arena. Such a strategy depends on a careful assessment of U.S. interests: preventing, containing, and where possible resolving regional conflict.

"America's specific interest in avoiding conflict on the Korean peninsula differs in type and magnitude from our interest, for example, in promoting a peaceful settlement in Angola. War in Korea would immediately involve thousands of U.S. troops and, given North Korea's dangerous game of nuclear hide-and-seek, the potential use of atomic weapons. In short, all interests are not equal. Specific policies must be reflecting this fact. Above all, they must be proportionate to the American interests involved. . . . Clearly the United States does have an interest in encouraging democracy in Haiti, just as we do in averting human suffering in Somalia. But those interests are not of sufficient importance to squander American lives or fritter away American prestige. Only a sense of proportion, I believe, permits us to craft appropriate policies. We cannot solve every one of the world's problems. What we can and must do is focus our attention and resources on the key challenges to our real vital interests" (Baker, 1995: 202–203).

Assessing national interests and balancing objectives are not enough, Baker said. There must be a firm understanding of the nature and exercise of U.S. power, and empty threats to use force in Bosnia, missteps in Haiti, and the tragedy in Somalia raised doubts about American resolve. When the United States acts or fails to act, no matter where, the whole world watches and draws lessons. In the end, any U.S. action or inaction may either enhance or diminish the reputation of American power in the world. Comfort with U.S. power is a precondition to its competent exercise, argues Baker. Selective engagement recognizes the idea of the United States actively engaged in international affairs; it stresses that U.S. engagement means making choices—that is, selecting how, when. and where we will engage. Today's world allows unprecedented freedom of action, making it imperative that leaders set clear, coherent, and comprehensive criteria for making these important decisions. Above all, concludes Baker, "selective engagement stresses that American engagement means making choices—that is, selecting how, when and where we will engage. . . .[W]e need to act in proportion to our interests, see balance in our objectives, and remain credible in the exercise of our policies" (Baker, 1995: 205–206). He makes no grand claims for selective engagement, but recommends less focus on grand theory and more on conceptual tools of solving problems.

Echoing Baker's advocacy for selected engagement, Robert Art (2000: 141) recommends that the concept should be elevated into a viable grand strategy in American foreign policy, because it is balanced, flexible and reflective of America's national interests and offers efficient choices of appropriate means to protect them. Art puts forth a list of six national interests grouped in two categories: (1) vital interests: those whose costs to the nation are between severe to catastrophic if not protected and whose benefits are large when protected include preventing an attack on the American homeland, keeping weapons of mass destructions out of the wrong hands; preventing great power wars and security competition among Eurasian great powers and maintaining secure oil supplies, keeping Persian Gulf reserves divided among oil-rich Gulf States; and (2) desirable interests: those which contribute to America's prosperity making its external environment more congenial, but do not have the same magnitude of potential costs and benefits to the nation as the vital ones, preserving an open international economic order; fostering the spread of democracy and respect for human rights and preventing mass murder and genocide; and protecting the global environment from adverse effects (Art, 2000: 141–142, 145).

Selective engagement steers the middle course between an isolationist, unilateralist policy and a world-policeman, highly interventionist role. It is neither overly restrictive nor overly expansive of America's interests, striking a balance between doing too much and too little militarily. "It allocates political attention and material resources to the vital interests first, but holds out hope that the desirable interests can be partially realized," states Art (2000: 142–143). Selective engagement holds that military power remains a useful and fungible instrument of statecraft; that military power is useful for producing results, and therefore the United States can use its military forces to help shape the international environment so as to make it more congenial to America's political and economic interests.

America's military power is best used indirectly to support the achievement of its three desirable interests, says Art (2000: 161–162). In general, the United States should not wage war to make states democratic, nor intervene militarily in their internal affairs to protect human rights. Military intervention for either purpose is a risky and costly proposition, one that usually requires a long-term presence to create the basis for success. The commitment of American military power to Eurasia and the Gulf plays a clear and direct role in retarding the spread of weapons of mass destruction, helping to maintain a deep peace among the great powers, and keeping Persian Gulf oil reserves divided. The link between America's military power and its desirable interests is more diffuse. There are two clear exceptions to the injunction that the United States should refrain from forceful intervention to create democracy or to protect human rights, and neither type of intervention will be short-term, in-and-out affairs, but will require both a long-term military presence and considerable economic assistance. The United States should eschew going it alone and organize international coalitions of the willing if military intervention can make the difference in restoring or creating democracy. Such occasions will generally involve small states with weak militaries, an ongoing political crisis, and a suitable political base on which to build democratic institutions, a willingness on the part of a large segment of the population to welcome an American military presence. It must also serve other important American interests to justify intervention. If military intervention can prevent genocidal mass murder.

There are some dangers of a selective engagement strategy; that is, risks that would make it too expensive to implement and thus infeasible, Art admits (2000: 169). One is the loss of selectivity, where commitments become open ended, due largely to decision-makers who have underestimated the difficulty of the initial task—which may result from bad planning or legitimate miscalculation—or to domestic political considerations that cause leaders to undertake additional obligations (that a foreign policy success will consolidate their home support, or that they face irresistible domestic forces). Second is an increased risk that the United States will become embroiled in unnecessary wars. This depends on how America's interests and the threats to them are defined. Selective engagement is more likely to prevent wars in regions where the United States has important interests that could be harmed by the outbreak of hostilities. Should its approach fail to prevent war, however, then war will have to be waged because America's interests require it. Whether the net result of this position is greater risk of embroilment in war is not easy to say.

Is selective engagement the best grand strategy for the United States? By its conceptual basis, it is not a priori a doctrinal statement, but rather a flexible, pragmatic foreign policy slogan, and one not committed to a particular set of guiding principles. Short of greatly expanded criteria for selectivity, and considerable consensus around those criteria, its usefulness is likely to be quite limited in times of crises beyond ex post facto justifications for policy choice. Selective engagement fails to provide a deep basis or principled understanding for intervention decisions.

4

Foreign Policy Doctrines
on American Intervention

INTRODUCTION

The United States has been searching for a new foreign policy theme to prioritize its national interests: a sharp and simple yet sophisticated and persuasive statement, to replace its well-worn Cold War premise, the policy of communist containment. The search is elusive; neither a vision nor an elegant idea has taken hold; the country has not embraced a specific plan of mission and goals at a level to rival the earlier concept. To be sure, contenders have proposed ideas to redefine America's purpose, and the quest for a new theme seems quite important to everyone; the lack of a unifying doctrine has spawned an important debate.

In January 1994—about halfway through the first decade of the post–Cold War period—*Harper's Magazine*, in a topical forum, "Is There a Doctrine in the House," published a transcript of conversations between experts who were trying simultaneously to understand the current world and to set fresh standards for the course of U.S. foreign policy within it. Two central questions guided their discussion: first, whether global events had evolved sufficiently and into stabilized form so that a doctrinal statement could be created in the existing environment, and second, whether America should be guided by Wilsonian moral imperatives emphasizing democracy, human rights, and self-determination or stand by a strict and traditional realist calculation of interests, derived from power assessments and goals. The humanitarian concerns and national interests are two polar points, often confused, and hard to navigate. Among the ideas aired in the search for anchoring motives to guide U.S. policy, the following composite quotes are representative:

A doctrine must reflect the national interest; to pretend that foreign policy can operate without regard for our self-interest is a breach of the social contract between the U.S. government and the American people.

No doctrine can encapsulate all of the diverse problems in the world. We must be content with setting priorities among our interests and stating which regions of the world are important to us and which are not.

It's a huge mistake to divorce considerations of national self-interest from ethical imperatives. Ethical imperatives historically have been a part of our national interest. A policy of pure interest severed from ethics gets brutal and opportunistic too easily. A policy that's too idealistic and severed from interests becomes naïve and Utopian rather quickly. To bring these together in a fruitful mix—that's our challenge.

We need a foreign policy based not on national interests but on a minimum articulation of principles. There is no fixed set of national interests.

The problem with elevating any humanitarian principle to a foreign-policy goal is this: as soon as you state it, you have to start issuing exceptions. In foreign policy, you have to abandon the world of pure moral ideas, where consistency is effortless, for the practical world of international relations, where hypocrisy comes easy. The difference between what we say and what we do is that the former is unlimited and the latter is not.

I don't rule out intervention for humanitarian reasons, if that's what the American people decide to do. I don't insist on some narrowly defined national interest as a criterion. In fact, I think this choice between interests and principles is a false one.

If you want to build a consensus for internationalism, you must ground your foreign policy in the sentiments of the public. There's no reason why you can't have national distinctiveness within an increasingly liberal and democratic framework. The end of the Cold War means that our democratic convictions and our interests are more likely to converge than ever. (*Harper's Magazine* 1994: 57–64)

There is no defining, guiding, official American foreign policy doctrine for the post–Cold War age. And, in the foreseeable future, asserts Haass (1994: 6–7), "no single overarching foreign policy doctrine or touchstone is likely to command widespread popular and elite support." This is not for lack of imagination, but a reflection of a more complicated world of economic, political, and military power and relationships. In such a world, no simple, clear concept is likely to emerge to suggest how specific local events are to be viewed and what the United States should do about them. Decision-making on a case-by-case basis is all but unavoidable.

The international system structure is fluid, as is the role of the United States within it, in part because of doctrinal absence. A successful foreign policy requires "an intellectual underpinning or mooring in a vision of the country's mission in the world," states Jonathan Clarke (1993: 1), who advocates the concept of American interests as the only way to provide a sure compass in the foreign policy decision-making process to protect its national security and project its principal values. Should the United States remain active and prepare to intervene to help solve conflicts as they arise around the globe? This depends on the changing perception of global threats, the role of U.S. power, and the importance of moral responsibility in foreign policy conduct.

What are the new threats? Nuclear proliferation, antidemocratic movements, Islamic fundamentalism, narcotics, ethnic tumult, international terrorism. Yet not one of them carries the immediate physical threat of annihilation of the United States in a way that was present every second of the Cold War. There is a discretionary quality to these threats: deciding to act, crafting an appropriate response, and timing the action are quite different in the current age according to Clarke (1993: 5).

What is the responsibility of the sole-remaining superpower to solve the world's problems? Is mere identification of problems sufficient to trigger U.S. involvement, with the implicit assumption that some form of military intervention is the preferred pathway toward resolution? "Even if for argument's sake one concedes the United States has vital interests in every corner of the globe, today's problems are still far less susceptible to military solutions than the earlier ones were. The reason for the lack of consensus on Bosnia was not that the U.S. military could not do the job of repelling Serbian aggression, but that this was only part of the job. We wanted also to persuade Serbs, Croats, and Muslims to live side by side in peace. For this purpose high-level bombing seems (as) inappropriate across the Atlantic," writes Clarke (1993: 10). Foreign nations are happy to see the United States as the protector of last resort, but an undifferentiated list of the world's problems is hardly a valid basis for creating a hearty foreign policy doctrine and national security program. And, before active engagement is justified, a clear demonstration is needed that the problems could usefully be addressed by the U.S. military.

What is the moral challenge to American foreign policy? To what extent should the United States commit humanitarian relief, resistance to genocide, human rights, and support for democracy? The question is not whether morality belongs in the foreign policy realm, but the practical choices that derive from its presence there, argues Clarke (1993: 15), putting it this way: "Alas, unless morality is anchored in some coherent concept of national interest, it is likely to prove an erratic compass. The reasons are familiar: morality is indivisible. It does not apply selectively. If it is right to support democracy in the former soviet republics, then it must be wrong to neglect encroachments on it in Algeria and Peru. If we demand that Hong Kong accept Vietnamese boat people, we ourselves must do the same for Haitian ones. If it was our duty to provide succor to Somalia, we should do likewise for Sudan. Morality demands total commitment. Half measures are not allowed. If we are called upon to counter genocide in Bosnia, we must deliver, even if that means ground troops, casualties, and tremendous expenditures." Morality points the way to areas where American values and public opinion demand activity. Yet, when morality appears to make an overwhelming case for activism, it needs to be balanced by considerations of effectiveness. Resolving conflict by introducing armed forces may not constitute appropriate action or touch core, underlying issues.

Throughout any consideration of a military intervention solution to handle problems in global politics, the concept of American interest—what constitutes the national interests in the current age—looms large in an imprecise, often implicit, formula; it has different faces, different theories, different concerns.

National interest is contested, the content is constructed. It is at the center of American foreign policy doctrine discussion. How did intervention doctrinal policy develop at the end of World War II to set the operating rules for the Cold War international system? How was national interest configured? What doctrinal thinking seems to be defining national interest and national security to influence policies in the post–Cold War period?

COLD WAR DOCTRINE

The Cold War conflict characteristically has been taken to be a competition between free and totalitarian political systems, differing forms of economic organization—capitalism versus communism, West and East, and a conflict between two power blocs, America and Russia, arising from particular interest considerations. The United States' Cold War conception of conflict specified principal values and interests crafted from two primary U.S. sources—(1) a presidential statement, the Truman Doctrine, issued in 1947, and (2) a National Security Council Report NSC-68, issued in 1950. It is interesting to note the principal directives of these official positions were tested in civil war conflict theatres, one in Europe—Greece, the other in Asia—Korea. Although each conflict had become internationalized, with great power support committed to opposing sides, they were essentially domestic-based issues about internal governance. The net result of the two doctrinal configurations and their application in two conflicts, all carried out within a five-year period immediately following the end of World War II, came to define Cold War essence: operating rules for American foreign policy and the new bipolar international system structure, which were in effect for the next four decades.

At the beginning of 1947 the United States had almost completed the most rapid demobilization in the history of the world. The Army had been cut from 8 million to 1 million men, the Navy from 3.5 million to less than 1 million, the Air Force from over 200 to less than 50 effective combat groups (Stephen E. Ambrose, 1985: 80). Foreign policy and military policy were moving in different directions. President Truman and his advisors wanted to meet the communist challenge whenever it appeared. While military force was decreasing, there was a growing fear in Washington of the Soviet threat. The final aim of Russia came to be seen as world conquest that would be achieved not through large-scale war but through internal subversion. The challenge was worldwide; it would have to be met everywhere. Communism thrived on chaos and poverty, and thus the way to respond to it was to promote stability and prosperity through economic aid (Ambrose, 1985: 81). But to obtain the economic and military resources to carry out a globalist, proactive foreign policy, Truman had to convince Congress and the bulk of the voters of the reality and magnitude of the Soviet threat. He needed a dramatic issue. Greece stood near the top of the list of potential trouble spots.

The Truman Doctrine

The Greek civil war started in 1944 between communists and royalist Greek guerrillas. Upon the withdrawal of Nazi Germany's troops in October, the two sides were brought together under British auspices in an uneasy coalition government in Athens. A civil war broke out in Athens in December, which the British military forces managed to suppress with great difficulty after the communist forces had overrun virtually all of Greece except Athens and Salonika. A general election was held in March 1946, but the communists and their followers abstained from the voting. A royalist majority was returned and a plebiscite in September restored the Greek king to the throne. During 1946 a full-scale war reopened. The Greek government had already complained in the United Nations that the insurgents were receiving outside assistance and a UN mission had gone to Greece to investigate. In February 1947, the British informed the United States that it could no longer provide aid to Greece and would pull out by the end of March. President Truman, Undersecretary of State Dean Acheson, and Secretary of State George Marshall met to discuss the issue. Acheson made the presentation: if Greece were lost, Turkey would be untenable. Russia would move in and take control of the Dardanelles with the clearest implication for the Middle East. Morale would sink in Italy, Germany, and France (Ambrose, 1985: 83; Acheson, 1969: 198). Truman called in congressional leaders to describe the Greek situation in dark terms and presented his plans for requesting substantial foreign aid, and he met with his Cabinet where the main concern was the way the public would receive such a sharp break with America's historical foreign policy, especially as the aid plan promised to be so expensive.

On March 12, 1947, Truman presented his plan to a joint session of Congress. There was no hedging in the speech; it was America's answer to the surge of expansion of communist tyranny. The strategy was to explain aid to Greece not in terms of supporting monarchy, but rather as part of a worldwide program for freedom. Truman seized the opportunity to declare an open-ended doctrine when what was called for was a simple declaration of aid to a single nation. He described the situation in universal terms, good versus evil, to get support for containment. Truman asked for immediate aid for Greece and Turkey, then explained his reasoning: "I believe it must be the policy of the United States to support free peoples who are resisting attempted subjugation by armed minorities or by outside pressures." Whenever and wherever an anti-communist government was threatened by indigenous insurgents, or foreign invasion, the United States would supply economic and military aid. The terms "free peoples" and "anti-communist" were thought to be synonymous. On May 15, 1947, Congress appropriated $400 million for Greece and Turkey. By later standards the sum was small, but for the first time in its history, the United States had chosen to intervene during a period of general peace in the affairs of people outside the Western Hemisphere. The Truman Doctrine had cleared the way for a massive American aid program to Europe, the Marshall Plan. At this moment, according to Cumings (1999: 285), the United States became the power with all the burdens-of-last-resort in the world system. Excerpts from Truman's speech to Congress:

Greece must have assistance if it is to become a self-supporting and self-respecting democracy. The United States must supply that assistance. We have already extended to Greece certain types of relief and economic aid but these are inadequate. There is no other country to which democratic Greece can turn. No other nation is willing and able to provide the necessary support for a democratic Greek government. . . .

We have considered how the United Nations might assist in this crisis. But the situation is an urgent one requiring immediate action and the United Nations and its related organizations are not in a position to extend help of the kind that is required. It is important to note that the Greek Government has asked for our aid in utilizing effectively the financial and other assistance we may give to Greece, and in improving its public administration. It is of the utmost importance that we supervise the use of any funds made available to Greece; in such a manner that each dollar spent will count toward making Greece self-supporting, and will help to build an economy in which a healthy democracy can flourish. . . .

To ensure the peaceful development of nations, free from coercion, the United States has taken a leading part in establishing the United Nations. The United Nations is designed to make possible lasting freedom and independence for all its members. We shall not realize our objectives, however, unless we are willing to help free peoples to maintain their free institutions and their national integrity against aggressive movements that seek to impose upon them totalitarian regimes. This is no more than a frank recognition that totalitarian regimes imposed on free peoples, by direct or indirect aggression, undermine the foundations of international peace and hence the security of the United States. . . .

I believe that it must be the policy of the United States to support free peoples who are resisting attempted subjugation by armed minorities or by outside pressures. I believe that we must assist free peoples to work out their own destinies in their own way. I believe that our help should be primarily through economic and financial aid, which is essential to economic stability and orderly political processes. . . .

Discouragement and possibly failure would quickly be the lot of neighboring peoples striving to maintain their freedom and independence. Should we fail to aid Greece and Turkey in this fateful hour, the effect will be far reaching to the West as well as to the East. We must take immediate and resolute action. I therefore ask the Congress to provide authority for assistance to Greece and Turkey in the amount of $400,000,000 for the period ending June 30, 1948. . . .

The seeds of totalitarian regimes are nurtured by misery and want. They spread and grow in the evil soil of poverty and strife. They reach their full growth when the hope of a people for a better life has died. We must keep that hope alive. The free peoples of the world look to us for support in maintaining their freedoms. If we falter in our leadership, we may endanger the peace of the world—and we shall surely endanger the welfare of our own nation. Great responsibilities have been placed upon us by the swift movement of events. I am confident that the Congress will face these responsibilities squarely. (President Truman, Speech to Congress, March 12, 1947)

The doctrine set off a process of official policy development leading to worldwide programs to help build up the economic, social, political, and military strength of free nations. The request for Greek aid was modest, but the occasion was promoted as a fundamental shift toward worldwide responsibilities of great power. According to Michael Klare (1989: 32–33), the Greek civil war played an especially pivotal role in the evolution of U.S. policy. The American public was weary of war by 1946 and leery of involvement in what was essentially viewed as an internal third world conflict. Truman encountered domestic resistance to his plans for aiding the conservative forces in Greece, and because this resistance was seen as a significant obstacle to the emerging policy of containment—which envisioned active U.S. military efforts to prevent further communist gains on the Soviet periphery—President Truman was determined to use the Greek affair to mobilize public support for a policy of global intervention. Congress approved the president's request. In succeeding years, U.S. policy-makers sought to amend the doctrine to allow for the *direct use* of U.S. forces (as distinct from the provision of military aid) in resisting Soviet/communist gains abroad. Such a policy was explicitly proposed in National Security Memorandum No. 68 (NSC-68). Most Americans, though, continued to oppose the direct use of U.S. troops in third world conflicts (Klare, 1989: 33).

The Greece experiment, successful in its immediate outcome, revealed a series of questions later to plague American policy-makers in widely dispersed areas such as the Middle East, Central America, South America, and Southeast Asia. The necessities of power arising for American policy-makers in the Soviet-American confrontation were not identical with the necessities of freedom as described by Truman. As Paul Seabury stated (1967: 48), the danger was that freedom risked being sacrificed to the presumed requirements of power, or that power might be withheld in the presumed interests of freedom. While the Cold War conflict could be reduced and made to appear simply as a contest between America and Russia, "As this competitive dialectic was acted out during the 1950s and 1960s, there came a point where paradoxically, each contestant tacitly or explicitly accepted complex sets of understandings about the limits of permissible action, each acquiring vested interests as to see these not infrequently threatened, not by the old adversary but by complex new forces which the encounter itself had helped bring into being" (Seabury, 1967: 68).

The dangers of adopting and applying the Truman doctrine worldwide were made clear during U.S. Senate deliberations in 1947. The containment principle and intervention justification would be extended beyond the European theatre. Senator Walter George (D-Georgia) was prophetic in his remarks about the line drawn in the Truman Doctrine too:

I know very well that this is simply the beginning of a program the end of which no man can foresee at the moment....Call it communism, totalitarianism, or whatever you want to call it, it is there. If we are going to stand on that line, so far as this issue is concerned, I think your United Nations is simply short circuited and out....Nobody thinks Russia is going to attack us. Nobody thinks Russia is to make any war now on anybody. Certainly not. That she will keep up the same aggravating aggressiveness that she has had in the past, and infiltrations and the pressures and war of nerves, I guess few of us doubt, few of us question....But I know that when we make a policy of this kind we are irrevocably committing ourselves to a course of action, and there is no way to get out of it next week or next year. You go down to the end of the road. (U.S. Congressional Hearings 80th Congress, 1st Session: p. 198, quoted in Gardner, 1991: 134–135).

Congressional support for the Truman Doctrine was substantial. The vote on requested aid for Greece and Turkey was approved 67 to 23 in the Senate, and 281 to 107 in the House in May 1947 (Graber, 1958: 323). The public was less supportive. That March, a Gallup poll found approval of Truman's Greek aid program at 56%; a Roper poll put it at about 52%. Other opinion surveys reported a majority of Americans were critical of circumventing the United Nations and of sending U.S. military assistance to Greece (Wittner, 1982: 81). The impact of the Truman Doctrine was expected to be felt everywhere to be useful. Containment was a generalized commitment and a prescription for action: a proposal for encirclement serving Russian fears chasing in all directions. It seemed indiscriminate—simply to check Soviet outward thrusts wherever they occurred and to blur the crucial distinction between primary and secondary objects of Soviet attack, and risky—American policy would be dependent on weak, unstable agent states. By this policy, moreover, the United Nations as an effective instrument for solving global issues of peace and security was marginalized, and collective security under international control would not be the operating norm. The choice of economic assistance was significant for several reasons: it linked the whole structure of relief, reconstruction, grants, and loans that had been developed by the United States during and after World War II and extended past practices, modified by the containment concept; it played down political action and thus avoided questions of interference with domestic affairs of other states; and there was no mention of military intervention.

American military and economic aid was provided to the Greek royalists. The initial outlay was $250,000, and by the 1960s it had reached nearly three billion dollars (Couloumbis, 1983: 14). U.S. military personnel took over command of the Greek military, effectively determining policy and strategy for them. American advisors controlled the national budget, taxation, price and wage policies, state economic planning and imports and exports, and the direction of military reconstruction and relief expenditures (Memo from American Mission to Aid Greece [in Athens] to State Department in Washington, November 17, 1947). On October 16, 1949, hostilities ended. It was estimated that more than 50,000 combatants died in the conflict, and more than 500,000 Greeks were temporarily displaced from their homes by the fighting. As part of the European Recovery Program (Marshall Plan), an American Mission of Aid to Greece (AMAG) was established to assist and oversee the nation's economic recovery. As part of the agreement between Greece and the United States, members of AMAG were given wide-ranging supervisory powers that quickly led to the formation of parallel administrations—one Greek and one American. Greece had become a client to the United States. Initially, the bulk of foreign aid went into military expenditures, but with the cessation of the civil war in 1949, the focus of aid spending shifted to civilian priorities.

As an intervention statement, the Truman Doctrine was pivotal. This sweeping declaration was intended primarily as a warning to the Soviet Union that the United States was prepared to intervene in the relations between communist and noncommunist states on behalf of any noncommunist country which was being attacked, overtly or covertly, by communist forces. The doctrine claimed a broad right to intervene. It was a declaration of intention and of implication everywhere, though everyone knew the United States lacked the power to enforce the doctrine to the fullest; the United States would have to pick and choose those against which it would intervene (Graber, 1958: 331). The shaping of U.S. grand strategy was set.

NSC-68

While the Truman Doctrine announced the American intervention plan to the world in 1947, inside official documents were significant as well in structuring the political orientation and objectives of U.S. policy-makers, including the "National Security Memorandum No. 68" (NSC-68: United States Objectives and Programs for National Security), a secret document of January 31, 1950, declassified in 1975, prepared by a joint State-Defense department committee under the supervision of Paul Nitze. NSC-68, intended to elaborate the overriding objectives of the U.S. national security policy, regarded that the principal task of U.S. policy should be the assurance of the integrity and vitality of its society and containment of the Soviet system. Given that American integrity was in greater jeopardy than ever before, the document rejected explicitly the preceding policy of isolationism and called for a positive participation in the world community. The containment strategy meant standing up to further expansion of Soviet power, retracting the Kremlin's control and influence through a rapid buildup of political, economic, and military power of the free world.

The following are excerpts from NSC-68:

Objectives: We must make ourselves strong, both in the way in which we affirm our values in the conduct of our national life, and in the development of our military and economic strength. We must lead in building a successfully functioning political and economic system in the free world. It is only by practical affirmation, abroad as well as at home, of our essential values, that we can preserve our own integrity, in which lies the real frustration of the Kremlin design. . . .

Means: Practical and ideological considerations therefore both impel us to the conclusion that we have no choice but to demonstrate the superiority of the idea of freedom by its constructive application, and to attempt to change the world situation by means short of war in such a way as to frustrate the Kremlin design and hasten the decay of the Soviet system. . . .

Intentions and Capabilities: As for the policy of "containment" it is one which seeks by all means short of war to (1) block further expansion of Soviet power, (2) expose the falsities of Soviet pretensions, (3) induce a retraction of the Kremlin's control and influence, and (4) in general, so foster the seeds of destruction within the Soviet system that the Kremlin is brought at least to the point of modifying its behavior to conform to generally accepted international standards. . . .

Course of Action: A comprehensive and decisive program to win the peace and frustrate the Kremlin design should be so designed that it can be sustained for as long as necessary to achieve our national objectives. It would probably involve: ...substantial increase in military assistance programs designed to foster cooperative efforts; some increase in economic assistance programs, development of programs designed to build and maintain confidence among other peoples in our strength and resolution and to wage overt psychological warfare calculated to encourage mass defections from Soviet allegiance and to frustrate the Kremlin design in other ways; intensification of affirmative and timely measures and operations by covert means in the fields of economic warfare and political and psychological warfare with a view to fomenting and supporting unrest and revolt in selected strategic satellite countries. . . .

The gravest threat to the security of the United States within the foreseeable future stems from the hostile designs and formidable power of the USSR and from the nature of the Soviet system. . . .

Soviet domination of the potential power of Eurasia, whether achieved by armed aggression or by political and subversive means, would be strategically and politically unacceptable to the United States. (NSC-68, 1975: 51–108)

The document recommends helping nations who are willing and able to make an important contribution to U.S. security, to increase their economic and political stability and their military capability. The concept of containment provided some reference points for when force should be used. NSC-68 proposed significant changes in national strategy, namely, developing a logic to remove deep American psychological and historical prejudices against maintaining and funding a large military ground force during peacetime, and provided the rationale for U.S. national security for much of the Cold War (Fautua, 1997: 2). The argument went as follows: America was not operating in a period of total peace, but a tense cold war with the Soviet Union, the threat was both ideological as well as military, the risk was of a new order and magnitude, and the clear implications were that "the Kremlin seeks to bring the free world under its domination by the methods of the cold war." The U.S.-USSR confrontations would not be through general war, but most likely in limited war settings and "the U.S. and other free countries do not now have the forces in being and readily available to defeat local Soviet moves with local actions." The drafters argued for a new military structure that could address the various threats along a spectrum of war that now included subversion and limited war. This Cold War army had to support national policies that now covered the globe where Soviet moves were most likely to occur at the "local" level.

In June 1950, conflict erupted in Korea, setting the stage for a direct application of the Truman Doctrine and NSC-68. Acheson stated, "The attack upon Korea makes it plain beyond all doubt that communism has passed beyond subversion to conquer independent nations and will now use armed invasion and war" (Gardner, 1991: 141). The distinction between communist and Russian threats blurred. Paradoxically, Korea's very remoteness and apparent strategic unimportance (Korea was placed outside the U.S. defense perimeters) magnified its consequences for future occurrences (probes) and options. In terms of a geopolitical explanation, the adopted logic ran as follows: The United States had to take a firm stance somewhere in Asia in order to demonstrate that communism could be stopped, that it would not spread uncontrollably. In a famous remark, President Truman said, "Korea is the Greece of the Far East. If we are tough enough now, there won't be any next step" (Gardner, 1991: 143). The linkage had been forged.

Korea was occupied by Japan from 1910 until the end of World War II, when Allied forces took over: Russian troops replaced the Japanese in the northern part of the country and American troops landed and took the southern half. Elections were held under UN auspices in 1948 and Syngman Rhee was proclaimed to be the president of the provisional Republic of Korea but Kim Il Sung, a communist leader of the north, along with the Russians, denounced Rhee's victory. In June 1949, the United States withdrew all but a small contingent of advisors. In January 1950, the U.S. Senate foreign relations committee had said that U.S. defense interests ran from the Sea of Japan and the Strait of Taiwan down through the China Sea to Malaya. The defense line excluded Korea.

North Korean armed forces crossed the border into the south in June 1950. The United States brought the North Korean attack on South Korea to the notice of the United Nations. The UN Security Council passed a resolution on June 25, 1950, condemning the attack and calling on all members of the UN organization to assist in implementing the resolution and giving such assistance to the Republic of Korea as may be necessary to repel the armed attack. (The resolution escaped a Soviet veto because the Soviet Union was boycotting the council in protest against the organization to seat the delegate of the People's Republic of China.) The U.S. action was taken for several reasons: the Americans were convinced, or decided, that the attack was ordered by Moscow and reasoned that if the North Koreans succeeded, the whole of Indochina would fall under communist control with similar domino-theory consequences for Malaya, the Philippines, and even Japan. The administration was under increasing domestic criticism for failing to enforce the Truman Doctrine against the People's Republic of China, a country embroiled in a long, intense civil war. U.S. intervention in Korea seemed one way to save the complete failure of the doctrine in Asia. Thus, American resolve to fight in Korea was the fear of the Soviet-inspired spread of communism, which, after China's entry into the war, was called "international communism." Fighting continued until October 1953, when the long-standing dividing line between north and south stabilized around the 38th parallel, effectively creating two countries. The war of 1950–1953 killed more than two million people, military and civilian, and injured three million more. The cost exceeded $20 billion (Dunnigan and Ray, 1985: 197). America committed more than two million troops throughout the course of the conflict; 300,000 were stationed in the field at the high point (Grimmett, 1999: 16) and around 54,000 troops lost their lives (Singer and Small, 1972: 68). Around 50,000 U.S. troops were deployed in Korea throughout the Cold War following the war, and after 10 years into the post–Cold War era, at least 35,000 remained.

The coexistence of the two ideological powers, the United States and Soviet Union, became de facto and permanent as of the time in the 1950s that the two sides became able to maintain rough parity, as patterns of relationships emerged through crises involving extraterritorial intervention. Guidelines developed to identify the policy considerations underpinning further U.S. intervention seem to point to the following general conclusions: (1) the principle of nonintervention becomes inapplicable if any event in any part of the world threatens either the existing superpower balance or their vested interests; (2) in the event of such a threat, the threatened state has a "right" to intervene in another country with armed force that is proportional to the threat; and (3) the degree of force must not go beyond the minimum necessary to neutralize the threat and must not threaten the interests, goals, and security of the rival party (Dore, 1984: 40).

The Korean War took place on the periphery, and was being fought for limited political gains. This fact showed that atomic superiority proved unable to deter the invasion and useless to recoup the lost territory; ground troops were needed. As a result, NSC-68 recommendations for U.S. military buildup were adopted and funds made available for the significant buildup of conventional forces—the best forces were sent to Europe to fight the Cold War against communism (Fautua 1997: 9–10). The move fundamentally meant that the United States now had a different type of military power more appropriate to the demands of the Cold War, that is, dealing with "local" actions. The myth of unpreparedness in 1950 became part of the new ideology to dominate the national security discourse. It became the common currency of most policy-makers. According to Michael Hogan (1998: 20), the great budget debates of the early Cold War squared off the traditional commitment to a balanced budget with the burgeoning price of national security, including expensive foreign assistance programs and the more imposing cost of a large military establishment. The debates indicated how difficult it was to disentangle the defense budget from ongoing arguments over military strategy and unification. The new theme of American national security ideas was set: America's political identity was bound in freedom, an indivisible concept, for the United States had to cast off old isolationist habits and accept their new role as the champion of freedom everywhere. The survival of democracy at home was intricately tied to its defense and expansion abroad (Hogan, 1998: 296–297).

In its socially constructed format, Hogan (1998: 17) describes the national security ideology of the Cold War discourse in a system of symbolic representation that defined American national identity by reference to un-American "other," usually the Soviet Union. The Soviets were hostile and active (part of communism), while the Americans were friendly, reactive, and usually reluctant. The Soviet Union was animated by a doctrinaire rightness, the United States behaved like a pragmatic nation-state. The Soviets were equated with aggression and domination, while the Americans were equated with peace and cooperation. The Soviet system was unnatural and ungodly, while the American system "dovetailed with natural law and divine Providence." An ideal American identity cast it against a demonized Soviet other with powerful rhetorical symbols: freedom versus slavery, tolerance versus coercive force. America was the new global defender of democracy everywhere. "Instead of identifying minimum interests it embraced maximalist claims by stressing the need for United States involvement beyond it shores, envisioning freedom for all of 'the victims of the Kremlin' as a global mission."

In less than a decade following World War II, a new, somewhat inexperienced, hegemonic power had been designated, the parameters of its role defined, setting the stage for the rules of global order and instability. Henceforth, international politics could be understood largely through the lens of intervention opportunity, strategy and success determined through American perceptions of national security threat presented, in part, by instances of civil unrest in countries around the world. Intervention shaped the Cold War order.

The Doctrine Challenge

The American foreign policy doctrine defining the Cold War, while dominating U.S. reaction to world events, was not invincible. As Alexander L. George (1955: 209) wrote, "The Korean War represented the first American experience with the problem of meeting local Communist aggression by means of limited, if costly, warfare. But despite the revulsion with that experience, and the 'new look' at military strategy and foreign policy, it may not be the last." The most significant, major test of the Truman Doctrine and NSC-68 directives was the American intervention into the conflict in Vietnam. In 1954, Vietnam had been partitioned into north and south sectors following a war with the French colonialists. U.S. assistance to South Vietnam increased after that point, and from 1961 through 1973, U.S. forces participated directly in attempts to stop communist-based insurgencies into South Vietnam through neighboring Laos and Cambodia, which were supported by the People's Republic of China and the Soviet Union. American ground troops engaged actively in combat from 1965 through 1972. At the peak of involvement, more than 546,000 U.S. military personnel from all services were committed to Vietnam. Some 59,000 died in combat (Serafino, 1999: 9). The United States had little support from other countries for its efforts; there were no UN Security Council resolutions on the issue.

Shortly after his inauguration, President Kennedy assigned Vice President Lyndon Johnson to conduct a mission to Southeast Asia, India, and Pakistan. Following the trip, in a memorandum of May 23, 1961, Johnson summarized points that would be of value as guidance for those responsible in formulating policy, among them, that "The battle against Communism must be joined in Southeast Asia with strength and determination to achieve success there—or the United States, inevitably, must surrender the Pacific and take up our defenses on our own shores. Asian Communism is compromised and contained by the maintenance of free nations on the subcontinent....There is no alternative to United States leadership in Southeast Asia. Leadership in individual countries— or the regional leadership and cooperation so appealing to Asians—rests on the knowledge and faith in United States power, will and understanding" (*The Pentagon Papers*, 1971: 128).

Johnson argued that the fundamental decision required of the United States was "whether we are to attempt to meet the challenge of Communist expansion now in Southeast Asia by a major effort in support of the forces of freedom in the area or throw in the towel. This decision must be made in a full realization of the very heavy and continuing costs involved in terms of money, of effort and of United States prestige. It must be made with the knowledge that at some point we may be faced with the further decision of whether we commit major United States forces to the area or cut our losses and withdraw should our other efforts fail (*The Pentagon Papers,* 1971: 130). When American involvement ended with a humiliating defeat for a policy based on preventing communist success in Vietnam, this produced searching policy reflection, and the basic premise of U.S. involvement and intervention was under close, critical scrutiny.

The purpose and national interest justifications for intervening in South Vietnam were ideological and geopolitical—to save South Vietnam from the spread of communism and preserve its pro-Western government; to protect nearby countries who were in danger of falling to communism, and prevent Soviet and Chinese expansion in the region which would impede U.S. ability to defend its interests in the Pacific. Michael Lind (1999: 256) argues that the United States could not afford to do too little in Indochina, for fear of a disastrous setback in the Cold War—a struggle that was as much a test of nerve as a test of strength. At the same time, the United States could not afford to do too much in Indochina, for fear of undermining American pubic support, first for the defense of the Indochina front, and then for U.S. Cold War strategy in general.

Declining public support, increasingly vocal and active opposition that became broader and deeper, to continued intervention in Vietnam exposed preexisting divisions in American attitudes about foreign policy. In World War II, the Korean and Vietnam wars, the balance of power between interventionists and isolationists in the U.S. Congress and the public was held by a swing vote sensitive to casualties, says Lind (1999: xv): the choice between global credibility and domestic consensus was forced on American leaders. It was necessary for America to escalate the war in the mid-1960s to defend the country's credibility as a superpower, and it became "necessary to forfeit the war after 1968 to preserve the American domestic political consensus in favor of the Cold War on other fronts." Lind argues that the Vietnam War was neither a mistake nor a betrayal, nor a crime, but a military defeat (p. 284).

Indochina was strategic because it *was* peripheral, states Lind (1999: 5, 31). Like the Korean War, the Afghan war, the Greek civil war, the Taiwan crises, and a number of other conflicts, during the Cold War, Indochina mattered to the Soviet Union and China and to the United States; beyond the sphere of influence into sphere of competition geographic theatres. It fit the containment directive. American leaders had feared that a U.S. abandonment of Indochina would convince America's communist-bloc adversaries of America's military inability or political willingness to fight limited proxy wars in the third world, and thus encourage them to be bolder and more assertive elsewhere, perhaps to the point of risking a direct superpower confrontation. Lind (1999: 72) justifies American involvement in this way: Great military powers are reluctant to cede territories to their adversaries; withdrawal from conflict will be interpreted as evidence of military weakness or lack of political resolve. It means a loss of prestige and reputation for strength, and thus the need to preserve a surplus of American credibility required the United States to escalate its involvement in Indochina by going to war.

Within two years after the U.S. troop withdrawal and cut-off of military aid, the South Vietnamese government collapsed in 1975. Major critiques of U.S. policy and action during the war, from those who attributed U.S. difficulties to a failure to commit sufficient force to the operation, from those who believed the United States should withdraw because the South Vietnamese regime did not enjoy the popular support to prevail, and from those who believe the containment doctrine seemed outdated or inapplicable in this setting—the national interest threat remote, hard to justify—influenced the introspective thinking and lessons drawn from the experience. Caspar Weinberger (1986), applying extracted lessons from the Vietnam experience, proposed a set of criteria to justify any future American military intervention. These criteria were produced under the influence of the Vietnam syndrome, a set of attitudes reflecting American timidity and/or disinclination to engage in military interventions in internal conflicts in third world countries, a restraint on U.S. capability to protect critical national interests abroad, and a reluctance to operate as world policeman or meddler. The syndrome in effect altered the psychological stance of the United States as global leader; it created a paralysis, a tendency toward inaction and nonintervention. In spite of U.S.-perceived interventionary activism in the 1990s, it is Weinberger's set of recommendations of caution (outlined below) that have taken on significance in the post–Cold War era.

In the early 1980s, under the Reagan presidency, the first major intervention of U.S. ground troops following the Vietnam withdrawal was the deployment of 1,200 Marines sent to Lebanon as part of a 4,000-strong multinational force (Italy, France, and Britain filled out the unit) on September 29, 1982. Their mission, extended by Congress for 18 months, was to facilitate the restoration of the Lebanese government's sovereignty and stabilize conditions in Beirut, the capital city, following a civil war with Israeli and Syrian intervention. It was not linked with a communist containment threat; it was not part of the East-West bipolar conflict. Thirteen months later, on October 23, 1983, a suicide bomber entered the American Marines' headquarters, killing about 240 soldiers. With the situation deteriorating further, the Marines were moved to warships offshore in February 1984. Many critiques of the Lebanon losses cited problems such as the vagueness of the objective and the lack of a clear concept as to when the mission would be accomplished, a lack of political consensus and conflicting expectations among the contributing nations, lack of appreciation of the complexity of the situation and the lack of a sense of realism about events on the ground, a failure to anticipate local reactions, and ineffective diplomacy. Finally, part of the failure was due to an insufficient, inflexible unrealistic mandate that tied the peacekeepers to one side on the conflict, making them appear biased toward the factions controlling the Lebanese government, and was not adjusted when it became apparent that circumstances warranted a change.

On October 25, 1983, just two days after the Marine bombing in Beirut, the U.S. military forces—about 1,800 Marines and up to 2,300 from the Army— intervened in Grenada, a small Caribbean country, to restore law and order, following the death of its Marxist President Maurice Bishop a few days earlier in a violent intraparty coup. Some 8,800 American troops were involved at the peak period (Serafino, 199: 9). The reasons for the stated mission included concern for the safety of American citizens on the island, among whom were 600 students and faculty at a medical school, and a classical Cold War justification: to prevent projection of Soviet power into the region—Cuba, a Soviet ally, was assisting with the construction of an airfield, naval base, munitions storage area, and barracks and military training on the island. Hostilities involving American soldiers, Cubans, and forces of Grenada ended on November 2, a week after they began. Nineteen U.S. soldiers were killed. Most of the troops withdrew within two months, while a small training and advisory group remained for more than a year. The Grenada operation was counted as a success in achieving its stated objectives. The U.S. decision to intervene was accepted by the local constituency because it deposed de facto leaders who had seized power by force from a popular president. The United States provided substantial assistance to compensate for damages to help rebuild the country. The next president elected was decidedly pro-American. As Reagan's Secretary of State George Shultz proclaimed a year later: "If we had not shown the will to use our strength to liberate Grenada, its people would yet be under the tyrant's boot, and freedom would be merely a dream....What we did was liberate a country, turn it back to its own people and withdraw our forces.... Grenada was a tiny island and relatively easy to save. But what would it have meant for this country—or for our security commitments to other countries—if we were afraid to do *even that?*" (Shultz, address at Yeshiva University, December 9, 1984).

POST–COLD WAR DOCTRINES

U.S. intervention experience in Vietnam, Lebanon, and Grenada through the 1970s and 1980s inspired Caspar Weinberger, defense secretary under Reagan, to craft a set of conditions governing the future use of American military power, which he presented on November, 28, 1984, and published in *Foreign Affairs* in 1986. Significant sections of the doctrine have been integrated into recent proposals and policies.

The Weinberger Doctrine

1. The United States should not commit forces to combat unless our vital interests are at stake.

2. Should the United States decide that it is necessary to commit its forces to combat, we must commit them in sufficient numbers and with sufficient support to win. If

we are unwilling to commit the forces or resources necessary to achieve our objectives, or if the objective is not important enough so that we must achieve it, we should not commit our forces.

3. If we decide to commit forces to combat, we must have clearly defined political and military objectives. Unless we know precisely what we intend to achieve by fighting, and how our forces can accomplish those clearly defined objectives, we cannot formulate or determine the size of forces properly, and therefore we should not commit our forces at all.

4. The relationship between our objectives and the size, composition and disposition of our forces must be continually reassessed and adjusted as necessary.

5. Before the United States commits combat forces abroad, the U.S. government should have some reasonable assurance of the support of the American people and their elected representatives in the Congress.... The president and the leadership of the Congress must build the public consensus necessary to protect our vital interests. Sustainability of public support cannot be achieved unless the government is candid in making clear why our vital interests are threatened, and how, by the use, and only by the use of American military forces, we can achieve a clear, worthy, goal.

6. The commitment of U.S. forces to combat should be a last resort—only after diplomatic, political, economic and other efforts have been made to protect our vital interests (Weinberger, 1986: 686–687).

On vital interests, Weinberger (1986: 687, 689) had this to say: judgments about American vital interests will sometimes depend on circumstances of the case; they are subjective, determined by ourselves and our definition of the threat. And, although he recognizes the circumstances that endanger the safety of nations are infinite, "We cannot never say never, we can never *think* never." At the same time, he argued that fighting where our vital interests are not at stake, and without continuing public support, invites domestic opposition similar to that experienced during the Vietnam War. The caution sounded by the six tests was intentional. "The belief that the mere presence of U.S. troops in Lebanon, or Central America or Africa or elsewhere could be useful in some way is not sufficient for our government to ask our troops to risk their lives. We remain ready to commit our lives, fortunes and sacred honor when the cause warrants it. But the hope that a limited U.S. presence might provide diplomatic leverage is not sufficient." Overwhelming force commitment was the answer to the failure to prevail in Vietnam and the cause for success in Grenada. Clarity of objectives fit success in Granada, while lack of specificity drew from Vietnam, and especially experience in Lebanon.

On August 2, 1990, Iraqi forces invaded Kuwait and occupied the country. Within a month, an overwhelming number of U.S. troops were dispatched to Saudi Arabia as a protection against outside invasion, in line with the Weinberger doctrine. This conflict in the Middle East coupled with the historic creation of a coalition military group composed of more than 25 nations, combining the old east and west Cold War blocs to join forces in the fight against Iraq, gave a momentous occasion for President George H.W. Bush to present to an open, sympathetic community—both here and abroad—a recast foreign policy doctrine for the United States, one that suited the changing post–Cold War setting. On September 11, Bush delivered a message to a joint session of Congress on the Persian Gulf Crisis where he introduced the "new world order" concept: "Out of these troubled times, a new world order can emerge; a new era—freer from the threat of terror, stronger in the pursuit of justice, and more secure in the quest for peace." He repeated the theme, elaborating its context, when addressing the nation on allied military action in the Gulf, January 16, 1991: "We have before us the opportunity to forge for ourselves and for future generations a new world order—a world where the rule of law not the law of the jungle, governs the conduct of nations. When we are successful—and we will be—we have a real chance at this new world order, an order in which a credible United Nations can use its peacekeeping role to fulfill the promise and vision of the U.N.'s founders."

Iraqi forces were defeated; the Gulf War was a success. Colin Powell, chairman of the Joint Chiefs of Staff (who had been Weinberger's military assistant in 1984) was arguing that successful cases of U.S. military intervention in the post Cold War were drawn from applications of the Weinberger doctrine. "When the political objective is important, clearly defined and understood, when the risks are acceptable, and when the use of force can be effectively combined with diplomatic and economic policies, then clear and unambiguous objectives must be given to the armed forces. These objectives must be firmly linked with the political objectives" (Powell, 1992–93: 39). Citing a number of successes—in Panama, a dictator was removed from power; in the Persian Gulf conflict, a country was liberated—Powell explained the twofold reason for the victory is clarity of mission purpose coupled with a careful match of the use of military force to political goals. "There have been no Bay of Pigs, failed desert raids, Beirut bombings, or Vietnams." The policy was the right answer to the Vietnam syndrome—apply overwhelming force quickly, without hesitation in situations where victory is near certain and the exit strategy clear, he said, advising that ground troops serve American purposes better than gradual escalation and air power alone. The United States should not enter conflicts without strong public support, according to Powell. He predicted future missions would likely focus on peacekeeping and humanitarian operations, and thus, that the new armed forces would be redesigned to be "*capabilities* oriented as well as *threat* oriented" (Powell, 1992–93: 41), that is, able to meet a host of challenging situations.

The first instance of a humanitarian operation came at the tail end of President Bush's term in December 1992, when the United States decided to participate in a major humanitarian intervention in Somalia. This was a new step: a humanitarian intervention task, not linked to other categories of national interests or threats to international peace. The program was undertaken in response to a request from the United Nations who had encountered difficulties in the delivery of food supplies within the country. U.S. acquiescence showed the new world order idea was working: a peaceful mission, a task to ensure the law of the jungle did not prevail, and a close U.S.-UN cooperative arrangement. The President delivered an address to the nation on December 5, 1992, in which he discussed the rationale for his policy, and made it very explicit: this action was not to be generalized to other cases, it carried no weight of doctrine, it did not set a new course for American foreign policy thinking. It was rather, and simply, the right thing to do at the right time. The Somalia speech made no mention of the new world order theme. Bush's statement differed from the Truman Doctrine decades earlier in that it sent no key message, no phrase that would fit a variety of circumstances that might justify future interventions, although sections of the public who had encouraged reconsideration of national interests to a broader notion that would highlight humanitarian obligations interpreted the act as a positive sign. The President said, "In taking this action I want to emphasize that I understand the United States alone cannot right the world's wrongs, but we also know that some crises in the world cannot be resolved without American involvement, that American action is often necessary as a catalyst for broader involvement in the community of nations. Only the United States has the global reach to place a large security force on the ground in such a distant place quickly and efficiently and, thus, save thousands of innocents." And, "Once we have created that security environment, we will withdraw our troops, handing the security mission back to a regular U.N. peace-keeping force." Rather than emphasizing a change of foreign policy direction toward an application of the new world order, the message focused instead on American leadership and American indispensability. Less than two months later, Bush's term expired.

Presidential Decision Directive   PDD-25

When President Clinton assumed office in 1993, he ordered a review of U.S. peacekeeping policies and programs in order to develop a comprehensive policy framework suitable to the post–Cold War period. On May 5, 1994, he signed a Presidential Decision Directive (PDD-25) which sets forth American policy on multilateral peace operations, including criteria for U.S. support or participation in these missions. The directive reflected the later unfortunate experience in Somalia under his term and rationales for reluctance to help the grave, genocidal scene in Rwanda. Evidence of the Weinberger and Powell doctrines—public support, mission clarity, sufficient force commitments, and appropriate adjustments—are written into the policy. The world order theme is not mentioned. Instead, the set of guidelines for making coherent choices in the Security Council for UN peace operations, and when participating includes U.S. troops, put forth rigorous standards with the most stringent applying to U.S. troops in missions that may involve combat. The spirit of the new world order idea was taking a different turn in the policy directive: PDD-25 recognizes that peacekeeping can be a useful tool for advancing U.S. national security interests in some circumstances, but that both U.S. and UN involvement in peacekeeping must be selective and more effective, and that U.S. authority should not be compromised in any operation. The full statement of PDD-25 is not available to the public. What has been released, however, includes these points:

1. The U.S. will support well-defined peace operations, generally, as a tool to provide finite windows of opportunity to allow combatants to resolve their differences and failed societies to begin to reconstitute themselves. Peace operations should not be open-ended commitments but instead linked to concrete political solutions; otherwise, they normally should not be undertaken.

2. To the greatest extent possible, each UN peace operation should have a specified timeframe tied to intermediate or final objectives, an integrated political-military strategy well-coordinated with humanitarian assistance efforts, specified troop levels, and a firm budget estimate. The U.S. will continue to urge the UN Secretariat and Security Council members to engage in rigorous, standard evaluations of all proposed new peace operations.

3. The Administration will consider several factors when deciding whether to vote for a proposed new UN peace operation or to support a regionally-sponsored peace operation: UN involvement advances U.S. interests, a threat to peace exists (international aggression, urgent humanitarian disaster coupled with violence, sudden interruption of established democracy etc), the means to accomplish the mission are available, including the forces, financing and a mandate appropriate to the mission, the operation's anticipated duration is tied to clear objectives and realistic criteria for ending the operation.

4. For U.S. personnel to participate in a given peace operation: the participation should advance U.S. interests, U.S. participation is necessary for operational success, the role of U.S. forces must be tied to clear objectives and an end point for U.S. participation must be identified. Domestic and Congressional support should already exist or can be marshaled.

5. For situations of U.S. participation involving likely combat there must exist a determination to commit   sufficient forces to achieve clearly defined objectives, a plan to achieve those objectives decisively, and a commitment to reassess   and adjust, as necessary, the size, composition and disposition of our forces to achieve our objectives.

6. The Command and control arrangements are acceptable.

    •   The President as Commander-in-Chief will never relinquish command of U.S. forces, though he has authority to place U.S. forces under the operational control of a foreign commander when doing so serves American security interests. The greater the anticipated U.S. military role, the less likely it will be that the U.S. will agree to have a UN commander exercise overall operational control over U.S. forces. Any large scale participation of U.S. forces in a major peace enforcement operation that is likely to involve combat should ordinarily be conducted under U.S. command and operational control or through competent regional organizations such as NATO or ad hoc coalitions.

    •   When interests dictate, the U.S. must be willing and able to fight and win wars unilaterally whenever necessary. To do so, we must create the required capabilities and maintain them ready to use. UN peace operations cannot substitute for this requirement. Circumstances will arise, however, when multilateral action best serves U.S. interests in preserving or restoring peace. In such cases, the UN can be an important instrument for collective action.

7. The U.S. does not support a standing UN army, nor will we earmark specific U.S. military units for participation in UN operations.

8. It is not U.S. policy to seek to expand either the number of UN peace operations or U.S. involvement in such operations. Instead, this policy...aims to ensure that our use of peacekeeping is selective and more effective (PDD-25).

Presidential Decision Directive PDD-56

In May 1997, PDD-56 presented the master plan for guiding the process to ensure that PDD-25 could be put to maximum use. It reflected a set of integrated steps for the conduct of complex contingency operations, much of it correcting the poor planning and ad hoc organizational issues which plagued the operations in Somalia and Bosnia, and mirrored the success of the Haiti intervention experience. Civil-military joint planning and coordination improvements are prominent   (Bowker, 1998: 61). When the U.S. government contemplates undertaking a complex contingency operation, according to PDD-56, a Deputies Committee is tasked to develop a political military implementation plan. The specifics include:

Political Military Implementation Plan for Complex Contingency Operations

1. A situation assessment.

2. Statement of U.S. interests.

3. Statement of strategic purpose or mission.

4. Key civil-military objectives.

5. Desired political-military end states including specifying the conditions for exit.

6. Organizational responsibilities—identification of lead agencies, an organizational chart of structures in Washington and in the field.

7. Preparatory tasks.

8. Functional or mission area tasks.

9. Evaluation: demonstrable milestones, measures of success and transition arrangements. Updates: lessons learned about planning and implementing such operations regularly incorporated into new situations.

Two tests of PDD-25 have occurred. The first, in May 1994, shortly after the President signed the order, concerned the American position on the violent, ethnic-based conflict that erupted in Rwanda the previous month. The UN

Security Council adopted no peace enforcement plan to stop the massacre, an outcome occurring largely because of the United States' PDD-25 policy which argued for narrowly defined American national interests (that excluded this African country) and a belief that the UN effort would fail (funds insufficient, objectives not achievable) drawing again on PDD-25 criteria language for voting yes to a peace enforcement operation. National interest won over humanitarian obligations.

Another test of the new American policies on complex operations came in Kosovo, in spring 1999. In what sense did U.S. intervention fit the Weinberger guidelines for involvement specified 15 years earlier? Writing in *The New York Times* on April 12, 1999, Weinberger said it met the doctrinal directives to some extent in that "the United States should enter a conflict only if it was vital to our national interest. That is the case here. The Balkans have been at the heart of two world wars in this century so stability of the region is important." Moreover, he said, "the United States cannot ignore an assault in Europe against all our values by a thug who has directed brutal atrocities in Kosovo and Bosnia."

The Clinton Doctrine

In the immediate aftermath of the Kosovo war, President Clinton indicated that the conflict established a new precedent for future U.S. response to similar crises. His remarks, delivered to the military troops in Macedonia, on June 22, 1999, became known as the Clinton Doctrine on humanitarian intervention against genocide. With respect to U.S. hesitation to intervene in Bosnia he said: "we watched for four years while reasoned diplomacy tried to save lives, and a quarter of a million people died and two and a half million refugees were created before NATO and our friends on the ground in Croatia and Bosnia forced a settlement there and ended the horror there. This time, we didn't wait. And it took 79 days, but that's a lot better than four years." On the values and principles governing intervention in Kosovo he said that "people should not be killed, uprooted or destroyed because of their race, their ethnic background or the way they worship God." The key passage focused on a new policy of humanitarianism: "Whether you live in Africa, or Central Europe, or any other place, if somebody comes after innocent civilians and tries to kill them en masse because of their race, their ethnic background or their religion, and it's within our power to stop it, we will stop it."

Clinton's new doctrine—not tested—was incorporated into his State of the Union Address on January 27, 2000, when he spoke of intervention in this way: "A second challenge we've got is to protect our own security from conflicts that pose the risk or wider war and threaten our common humanity. We can't prevent every conflict or stop every outrage. But where our interests are at stake and we can make a difference, we should be, and we must be, peacemakers." It was a reiteration of PDD-25.

The war in Kosovo additionally illustrated another perspective on U.S. intervention that sought a middle course between the slippery slope of Vietnam and the harsh, cautionary criteria spelled out by Weinberger and advocated by

Powell. Critical of Powell's reluctance to use force, Secretary of State Madeleine Albright once stated, "What's the point of having this superb military you're always talking about if we can't use it?" The "diplomacy backed by the threat of force" idea was borne of her intervention strategy crafted to confront Milosevic over Kosovo, to confront him, to confront the root of his power, to find a new role for NATO in the post–Cold War world (Hirsh, 1999: 64–65). Will the multiple effects of the Kosovo intervention translate into long-term policies—the fight against genocide, supporting diplomacy with armed force, moving more toward a middle ground on military engagements abroad? It is perhaps too soon to tell, although this experience, like all intervention involvement, will undoubtedly have an impact on future U.S. policy.

TWENTY-FIRST-CENTURY DOCTRINE PROPOSALS

In the year 2000, several efforts were launched to structure clarity in the U.S. national interest and its role in future foreign policy choices, especially those pertaining to military intervention. Among the various ideas, four specific plans are described here, two with ties to government policy-making although their reports are not official positions, and two especially commissioned by the U.S. government. The nonofficial proposals have been presented under these themes, "Preventive Defense" and "America's National Interests." Two official reports, based on a Defense Department reorganization law passed in 1986, were constructed on American national interests and security—one prepared by the White House issued in December 1999, the other a product of a bipartisan group, released in three sections between September 1999 and March 2001.

Preventive Defense

The concept Preventive Defense, formulated by Aston Carter and former Secretary of Defense William Perry, specifies a hierarchy from the most dangerous to least dangerous group of threats—an A and B list of problems, and a C list of countries—as criteria for guiding national involvement and intervention urgency. The A-list refers to potential future problems that could threaten U.S. survival, way of life, and position in the world. They identify five: (1) a rising China that spawns hostility, (2) the danger that Russia might descend into chaos, (3) the danger that Russia and other Soviet successor states might lose control of the nuclear, chemical, and biological weapons legacy of the former Soviet Union, (4) proliferation of weapons of mass destruction, and (5) catastrophic terrorism. On the B-list are the actual threats to vital U.S. interests, deterrable through ready forces, including major theatre wars in Northeast or Southwest Asia. The C-list covers important problems that do not threaten vital U.S. interests: Kosovo, Bosnia, East Timor, Rwanda, Somalia, and Haiti are mentioned (Carter, 1999–2000: 104).

The reason for preoccupation of American strategy with problems on the C-list, state Carter and Perry (1999: 13), is due to the absence of an A-list threat to the United States. They call for a refocus on A-level threats to fill out comprehensive strategic thinking for American security, for problems on the C-list do not threaten America's vital security interests, and dealing with them individually or as classes—peacekeeping, peacemaking, humanitarian operations, and the like—cannot make up the core national security strategy of the United States. The attack on American territory September 11, 2001, surely fulfills that function. As a result, it is possible that the C-list emphasis will receive far, far less attention in designing new intervention doctrine.

America's National Interests

The proposal entitled *America's National Interests* (2000) constitutes another serious attempt to clarify what features should guide U.S. foreign policy and intervention in the twenty-first century. The report by a group of concerned Americans who believe "the US is in danger of losing its way," was produced under the auspices of the Harvard Belfer Center for Science and International Affairs, the Nixon Center, and the RAND Corporation. Condoleezza Rice, National Security Advisor under President George W. Bush, was a commission member. They identify a hierarchy of U.S. national interests into four categories beginning with those that are vital, followed by the extremely important, important, and less important or secondary. They strongly urge that American foreign policy focus on the five *vital* national interests: (1) prevent, deter, and reduce the threat of nuclear, biological, and chemical weapons attacks on the United States or its military forces abroad; (2) ensure U.S. allies' survival and their active cooperation with the United States in shaping an international system in which we can thrive; (3) prevent the emergency of hostile major powers or failed states on U.S. borders; (4) ensure the viability and stability of major global systems (trade, financial markets, supplies of energy, and the environment); and (5) establish productive relations, consistent with American national interests, with nations that could become strategic adversaries, China and Russia. At the second level, they identify *extremely important* national interests: (1) prevent, deter, and reduce the threat of nuclear, biological, or chemical weapons *anywhere;* (2) prevent the regional proliferation of weapons of mass destruction; (3) promote the acceptance of international rules of law and mechanisms for resolving or managing disputes peacefully; (4) prevent the emergency of a regional hegemon in the Persian Gulf; (5) promote well-being of U.S. allies and protect them from external aggression; (6) promote democracy, prosperity, and stability in the Western Hemisphere; (7) prevent, manage, and if possible at reasonable cost, end major conflicts in important geographic regions; (8) maintain a lead in key military-related, strategic technologies; (9) prevent massive, uncontrolled immigration across U.S. borders; (10) suppress terrorism, transnational crime, and drug trafficking; and (11) prevent genocide. At the third level, they identify four *important* national interests explicitly related to conflict: (1) discourage massive human rights violations; (2) promote pluralism freedom and democracy in strategically important states as much as is feasible without destabilization; (3) prevent, and if possible at low cost, end conflicts in strategically less significant geographic regions; and (4) protect the lives and well-being of American citizens targeted by terrorist organizations. Other important national interests listed relate mainly to business and economic foreign policy goals. At the fourth level, *less important or secondary* national interests, they list (1) enlarging democracy everywhere for its own sake and (2) preserving the territorial integrity or particular political constitution of other states everywhere, as intervention- related items within a group of four goals.

A National Security Strategy for a New Century

The report, *A National Security Strategy for a New Century* (2000), issued by the White House, set forth three core objectives: to enhance America's security, to bolster America's economic prosperity, and to promote democracy and human rights abroad. It categorizes national interests into three categories: vital, important, and humanitarian and other interests. Vital national interests are those of broad, overriding importance to the survival, safety, and vitality of our nation. Among these are the physical security of our territory and that of our allies, the safety of our citizens, the economic well-being of our society, and the protection of our critical infrastructures—including energy, banking and finance, telecommunications, transportation, water systems and emergency services— from paralyzing attacks. We will do what we must to defend these interests, including, when necessary and appropriate, using our military might unilaterally and decisively.

Important national interests include regions where the United States has a sizable economic stake or commitment to allies, protecting the global environment from severe harm, and crises with a potential to generate substantial and highly destabilizing refugee flows. "Our efforts to halt the flow of refugees from Haiti and restore democracy in that country, our participation in NATO operations to end the brutal conflicts and restore peace in Bosnia and Kosovo, and our assistance to Asian allies and friends supporting the transition in East Timor are examples."

The third category is humanitarian and other interests. "In some circumstances our nation may act because our values demand it. Examples include responding to natural and manmade disasters; promoting human rights and seeking to halt gross violations of those rights; supporting democratization, adherence to the rule of law and civilian control of the military; assisting humanitarian demining; and promoting sustainable development and environmental protection. The spread of democracy and respect for the rule of law helps to create a world community that is more hospitable to U.S. values and interests. Whenever possible, we seek to avert humanitarian disasters and conflict through diplomacy and cooperation with a wide range of partners, including other governments, international institutions and non-governmental organizations."

With respect to a strategy of engagement, the report stresses selectivity, focusing on the threats and opportunities most relevant to U.S. national interests, and applying resources where they can make the greatest difference (p. 16). The United States must be prepared, states the report, to respond to the full range of threats to our interests abroad, including participation in peace operations, and humanitarian assistance. It must be prepared to do so in the face of challenges such as terrorism, information operations, and the threat or use of weapons of mass destruction. U.S. forces must also remain prepared to withdraw from contingency operations if needed to deploy to a major theatre war (p. 24).

The decision to employ military forces, the report states, for vital interests will be decisive and if necessary, unilateral. For important national interests, "military forces should only be used if they advance U.S. interests, they are likely to accomplish their objectives, the costs and risks of their employment are commensurate with the interests at stake, and other non-military means are incapable of achieving our objectives. Such uses of military forces should be selective and limited, reflecting the importance of the interests at stake" (p. 25).

On the decision to use military forces to support humanitarian and other interests, a variety of conditions are specified: "when the scale of a humanitarian catastrophe dwarfs the ability of civilian relief agencies to respond, when the need for relief is urgent and only the military has the ability to provide an immediate response, when the military is needed to establish the preconditions necessary for effective application of other instruments of national power, when a humanitarian crisis could affect U.S. combat operations, or when a response otherwise requires unique military resources" (p. 26).

Does a military intervention advance the interests of the American people? Is there public support for the operation? These factors, too, are important.

Seeking a National Strategy

Produced by a bipartisan commission chaired by former Senators Gary Hart and Warren Rudman, the report *Seeking a National Strategy: A Concert for Preserving Security and Promotion Freedom* (2000: 6–9) combined aspects of realism and idealism, putting forth six precepts to guide formulation of national strategy: (1) Strategy and policy must be grounded in the national interests. The national interest has many strands—political, economic, security, and humanitarian. National interests are nevertheless the most durable basis for assuring policy consistency. (2) The maintenance of America's strength is a long-term commitment and cannot be assured without conscious, dedicated effort. (3) The United States faces unprecedented opportunities as well as dangers in the new era. (4) The United States must find new ways to join with other capable and like-minded nations. (5) This nation must set priorities and apply them consistently. (6) America must never forget that it stands for certain principles, most importantly freedom under the rule of law.

The first precept addressing national interest is the most crucial of all, states the commission report. Interests must be protect *and advanced* (italics in original). The commission divided layers of national interest into three categories: survival interests, critical interests, and significant interests. Survival interests include America's safety from direct attack, by states or terrorists, preservation of the country's constitutional order and core strengths—educational, industrial, scientific-technological—that underlie America's political, economic, and military position in the world.

Critical U.S. interests include "the continuity and security of those key international systems—energy, economic, communications, transportation, and public health (including food and water supplies)." It is a critical national interest that no hostile power establish itself on U.S. borders, or in control of critical land, air, and sea lines of communications, or in cyberspace; that no hostile hegemon arise in any of the globe's major regions, nor a hostile global peer rival or hostile coalition.

At the third level, interests identified as significant include advancing constitutional democracy and market-based economies worldwide, fighting international terrorism, criminality, and violations of human rights—including genocide. The commission had trouble defining the U.S. attitude toward incidents of genocide in areas of the world not of particular strategic significance for the United States, but decided that genocide can be a sufficient cause, in and of itself, for U.S. military action abroad, said Charles Boyd, executive director of the commission (Boyd, 2000: 6). He added that certain values are becoming geographically indivisible and that the divide between interests and values has an artificial nature to it.

To fulfill strategic goals, one of the six main objectives of U.S. policy identified in the report calls for helping the international community take the disintegrative forces spawned by an era of change: "To address these spreading phenomena of weak and failed states, ethnic separatism and violence, and the crises they breed, the United States needs first to establish priorities. Not every such problem must be primarily a U.S. responsibility....There are countries whose domestic stability is, for differing reasons, of major importance to U.S. interests (such as Mexico, Colombia, Russia, and Saudi Arabia)" (U.S. commission on National Security/21st Century, 2000: 13). These countries should be a priority focus of U.S. planning, the report recommends, while for other cases, the U.S. should help the international community develop innovative mechanisms to manage the problem—they propose standing procedures to facilitate organizing peacekeeping operations and UN "conservatorships." Yet the United States should be prepared to act militarily (in conjunction with other nations) in situations where: U.S. allies or friends are imperiled, the prospect of weapons of mass destruction portends harm to civilian populations, access to resources critical to the global economic system is imperiled, a regime has demonstrated intent to do serious harm to U.S. interests or genocide is occurring. While arguing that if most of these conditions are present, the case for multilateral military action is strong, *any one* of these criteria is serious enough, however, the case for military action may also be strong (p. 13).

CONCLUSION

The changes intrinsic to the post–Cold War world have created new, intense conflicts that complicate any use of force by the United States. Some political and technological developments enhance opportunities for the United States to use its military might effectively. There is little fear of direct conflict with another superpower growing out of a local confrontation with a third state, and less danger that a great power rival will furnish political, economic, and military support to a client embroiled with the United States, states Haass (1994: 5). But with new opportunities for the United States to use force, the proposals and guidelines for when and how to do it vary. Moreover, only the United States possesses the means to intervene decisively in many situations, in particular those that are more demanding militarily. Yet, U.S. means are necessarily limited; there will always be more interests to protect than resources to protect them. Choosing is critical, and that means evaluating the national interest role in any situation and selecting wisely. Setting the bar either too high or too low for intervention choices carries costs: defining interests too narrowly or setting rigid prerequisites for employing force would mean isolationism; applying all-encompassing, loose criteria to intervene would wear out resources and defeat effectiveness.

The U.S. response to these issues in PDD-25 was designed to ensure that America supported the right operations, developed rigorous standards to determine when peace operations should be undertaken, and when, specifically, American troops should take part. It addressed various ways to improve UN peacekeeping capabilities, and in essence was designed to be a discriminating document in future interventions. It dealt with detail.

The post–Cold War foreign policy doctrinal proposals described here all try to answer the one critical question: when should the United States intervene? The arguments draw from at least three sources: (1) the morality premise: participation should be undertaken for just and worthy cause, humanitarian intervention to help peoples vis-à-vis their own governments or one another, reflects American values and principles; (2) the cost-benefit premise: participation should be undertaken when the objectives are clear and attainable, when realistic political goals are matched with military missions, and contingencies are short-term with clear exit points; and (3) the political premise: participation should be undertaken when threats to national interest are the highest. The first two issues are relatively easy to address; they have direct answers. The third, the political aspect of choosing to intervene, is subjective, changeable, and contentious. This is a problem both of theory and policy: no substantive linkage unites local conflict in countries around the world into a broader, systemic perception of international, structural threat. The Cold War architects solved this theoretic puzzle by uniting "communism" and "Soviet power" into a single hostile force, forming a conspiracy; local disturbances were "communist inspired" and therefore linked to global designs of the Soviet Union and thus threatening to the balance of power in the universe. The assumption was reverberations, dangerous and destabilizing, could be felt throughout the system if the balance were to change. While sweepingly simple and most likely wrong, it provided intervention policy guidance by treating situations of civil disturbance at the highest levels of threat to national interest. The choice to intervene was less complicated, less conditional, less nuanced. National interest was not at all a hierarchy-based concept in the older time. This theoretical simplicity eventually led to its policy downfall. In the evolving global environment, the doctrinal policy began to show wear in the Vietnam intervention: the conflict of Indochina gradually seemed remote and peripheral to an American foreign policy based on national interest, and at the same time, American victory seemed to be fading (maybe all policy-makers knew this investment was not high priority in national interest). The theoretic doctrine application was harder to sell to the public. Interestingly, public support for the withdrawal from Vietnam was based in part on the decline in national interest value of involvement—challenging the theoretical linkage concept—but it did not disturb the fundamental bipolar superpower global structure governing U.S.-USSR relations and its consequences for world order—only half of the equation was removed, the local-to-global concept, which was insufficient to force a downfall of the entire Cold War system. Bipolarism continued to set the rules.

The modern, post–Cold War architects are trying to work both within and around the national interest theme. All proposals reaffirm the centrality of national interest for policy guidance, but diverge in the way problems, issues, and countries are evaluated. No overarching linkage theme equivalent to the communism-cum-Russian idea shows up in any new doctrinal concept. The enemy is elusive, either untrackable or unknowable. What is clear, though, is attention to *criteria* of choice, and a range of considerations—national interest aspects, ethical concerns, costs and benefits—where American intervention may be appropriate. Mostly, the proposals pay attention to morality and efficiency standards which serve, in the final analysis, as rhetorical principles and technical aspects in doctrinal perspectives but are not sufficiently discriminating, selective, or directional for the substantive content base pointing to overwhelming agreement on policy arguments. The net effect is floundering policy, or contentious policy, which shows few signs of transformation into singular, universally conventional agreement. The split is deep, and broad in application. Thus the empirical picture, one intervention experience and its evaluation and the next intervention and its assessment, by default continue to dominate the perspectives on intervention, the debates and the choices to shape the global order, short of a persuasive single world-purpose theme, a U.S. mission. The mission is still under construction. It is appearing only gradually, less by design than by evolving, almost unseen threads.

5

American Intervention:
Post–Cold War Cases

OVERVIEW

American military forces engaged in a number of significant intervention operations from December 1989 through October 2001. Ground troops, dispatched for combat or on peacekeeping missions, participated in eight conflicts spread over four continents. In Central America, troops were sent to Panama in December 1989 and to Haiti in September 1994. In Europe, peacekeeping troops arrived in Bosnia in December 1995, and in Kosovo, Yugoslavia, NATO attacks led by the United States started in March 1999; peacekeeping troops were introduced in the summer. In Africa, the United States contributed to peacekeeping missions in Somalia between December 1992 and March 1994, and a limited intervention relief operation was carried out in Rwanda from July to September 1994. In the Muslim world—the Middle East/Southwest Asia geographic sector—troops were dispatched to Saudi Arabia during the Gulf crisis of 1990 to participate in military operations against Iraq in 1991, and sent to Afghanistan in October 2001.

The ultimate decision, to introduce American ground forces into an ongoing conflict or into an unstable post-conflict environment, carries great risks and thus represents a critical feature of any modern intervention policy. Sending members of the armed forces into harm's way is a serious matter. Instituting economic embargoes, imposing sanctions, or conducting air strikes, all punitive intervention efforts by a state to alter the course of a conflict, are strategies carrying different levels of risks, but because they are less costly in potential human sacrifice, they imply a smaller shade of commitment to bring about cessation of violence or create a secure environment for peace. While such measures were introduced by the international community in some cases, the truly notable distinction in all of these interventions is ground troop commitment to the effort.

The decisions reflected in these policies were crafted from diverse political pressures coming from two primary sources: concerns of the foreign policy community (within the United States and abroad), and varying opinion filtered through the American domestic politics environment. The somewhat inherent, ongoing tension between advocates pushing for expanded or reduced U.S. military commitments abroad—by those who believe the country must exercise global leadership through greater involvement, against champions of disengagement and a more narrowly circumscribed foreign policy agenda—was a constant theme throughout this period. Scattered, far-flung arguments in favor of or against sending military troops abroad to handle problems of civil unrest or international conflict were debated in different ways. Heated, extensive discussion about American foreign policy principles, namely the appropriate commitment to national interests and moral obligation guiding intervention choices, characterized discussion in some cases (Bosnia), but not others (Rwanda). Even in situations with a perceived high level of national interest, the pattern of intervention support differs: committing troops for war against Iraq in January 1991 was not strongly backed by Congress (the Senate voted 52 in favor, a bare majority), but nearly unanimous (just one dissention) in favor of sending forces to Afghanistan following terrorist attacks on American soil.

Despite the relatively large number of interventions conducted by U.S. forces in this twelve-year time frame, the nature and form of each intervention operation bears a distinctive stamp. A general pattern is hard to discern. The case of Panama appears to reflect (or was later rationalized as) a decision outcome culminating out of gradual, calculated escalating responses to an increasingly hostile situation, where intervention is regarded as "a policy of last resort." In the case of Bosnia, intervention into an active battle theatre was discussed often but ultimately resisted. The United States was not willing to commit ground troops into the conflict in spite of the morally reprehensive, continuing genocidal operation of "ethnic cleansing"; the war dragged on for three years before the United States introduced decisive efforts to stop it (through a combination of intensive bombing and intensive negotiations) and broker an agreement. Only afterward was the country willing to send troops—in peacekeeping roles, not as combat participants. The story of Rwanda (where genocide was being committed and intervening to stop it was never seriously considered) is similar: a small, short-term "disaster relief" force arrived as violence subsided. The case of Saudi Arabia may be considered a third intervention strategy, "a policy of first-resort," illustrated by the quick decision to amass a large contingent of troops in the country to pose as a credible deterrent to an Iraqi attack. Sometimes intervention policy resulted from a strong, decisive push by the U.S. administration—the case of Kosovo seems apt. On other occasions the United States seemed to be pulled into action from outside pressures, for example, assisting the United Nations in its efforts to provide humanitarian assistance in the case of Somalia.

To a great extent, U.S. intervention policy worked in a multilateral framework, although American leadership and command dominated in most instances; only Panama was conducted unilaterally. The United States chose to work with the United Nations by seeking policy support in some cases—arguing for intervention in the Persian Gulf, Haiti, and Somalia, and arguing strongly against intervention in Rwanda—while bypassing institutional involvement or approval in others—Panama, Kosovo. In some instances, American intervention came *after* UN peacekeeping efforts (Somalia, Bosnia); in other situations, American intervention came *before* UN peacekeeping was installed—in addition to U.S. peacekeeping operations outside of the United Nations' jurisdiction (Haiti, Iraq-Kuwait). Extracting from these cases, from consideration and debate, to decision and implementation, U.S. intervention policy in the post–Cold War age shows little evidence of a clear, consistent plan.

The reasons governing post–Cold War American intervention decisions vary. In two cases, the United States sent military troops into Islamic territory in response to major violations of international law and threats to world peace and security—the Iraqi invasion and occupation of Kuwait, home of extensive oil reserves, was the catalyst leading to the Gulf war; the terrorist attacks on American soil by the Al Qaida group, whose leader, Osama bin Laden, conducted training camps in the Afghan mountains, triggered retaliatory action leading to the war in Afghanistan. The other interventions occurred largely as a result of civil conflicts within states, although the background situation and purpose of American action differed from case to case. In Panama and Haiti, the issue of local leadership was seen as a contributing source to sensitive social problems in the United States, namely, the flow of drugs and boatloads of refugees arriving on American shores. In each instance, the United States decided to solve the problem by replacing the head of state. Noriega was forcibly removed from Panama; Aristide was peacefully restored to power in Haiti. In Somalia and Rwanda, intervention goals emphasized humanitarian assistance. Objectives in the Somali case changed over time, starting initially with efforts to alleviate human suffering from starvation and later moved toward nation-building attempts. In Rwanda, a mass genocide campaign in the spring of 1994 failed to draw in either the United States or other members of the international community to stop it. By mid-summer, after the period of major violence was over, a small American contingent arrived to help relief workers. In Bosnia and Kosovo, where ethnic-based conflicts in the former Yugoslavian provinces included genocidal violence, mission goals were broader: humanitarian aid to help thousands of refugees, weakening Serbian leadership power, and establishing a framework to build civil society in the region. In the first case, the intervention came after more than three years of fighting and a U.S.-brokered accord was signed promising a peacekeeping mission; in the second instance, NATO forces intervened at a far earlier stage in the conflict, when the internal violence was at a lower level.

U.S. intervention included military force combat participation in half the cases: Panama, the Persian Gulf, Somalia, and Afghanistan. For the other half, troops arrived as peacekeepers after the most violent stage of conflict had finished its course: Rwanda, Haiti, Bosnia, and Kosovo. The latter was unique in that military personnel participated solely in remote, high-tech air-based bombing campaigns without direct battle engagement while the conflict raged, and afterward, ground troops were brought in to monitor a peace. The United States proceeded unilaterally in Panama (with condemnation by the UN General Assembly for its actions) and in Afghanistan (with international community support; in some cases countries contributed small assisting forces). In the remaining interventions, the United States participated within a multilateral arrangement, though the details varied from one situation to another. In the Gulf conflict and also in Haiti, the United States led a twenty-odd coalition of countries who committed various levels of military or financial support to the effort. The U.S. contribution, though, constituted an overwhelming proportion of troops and weapons. In Kosovo, NATO was ultimately responsible for the intervention, but the United States, by its alliance obligations, was by far the greatest contributor. In Somalia under UNOSOM II, and in Rwanda, U.S. forces stood apart yet embedded with larger multinational humanitarian operations.

The interregnum U.S. interventions fall into three categories varied by purpose, force application, and strategy, arranged in chronological sequence under three American Presidents: George H. W. Bush led the United States into Panama, the Persian Gulf, and Somalia; Bill Clinton led the United States into Rwanda, Haiti, Bosnia, and Kosovo; George W. Bush led the United States into Afghanistan.

The first phase of post–Cold War interventions occurred during the presidency of George H. W. Bush when the U.S. military stormed into Panama in 1989 in a surprise attack and in the Persian Gulf crisis during 1990, leading to the war against Iraq in 1991. Both interventions applied some of the Weinberger doctrine guidelines: the introduction of massive force to achieve quick victory and clear mission objectives. In each instance, mission objectives were fulfilled. The timing of these events was critical to their success. The Cold War era was coming to a close, meaning American-Soviet rivalry was obsolete—a new role and corresponding set of demands would be placed on U.S. foreign policy. The international community looked to America for global structural leadership; U. S. military force needed an update in its composition and purpose of defense objectives to justify its role in preserving security in the new world order. These crises provided convenient opportunities for the United States to address both problems: the interventions demonstrated American power to the world and simultaneously showed how U.S. defense forces quickly adapted to the new, unfolding constellation of international structural conflict. While neither intervention was *necessary* for the United States to shape a global order to its liking, these decisions conveyed a message about its preferred role in the post–Cold War international system.

The next phase in U.S. intervention strategy in the interregnum was the introduction of military troops into Somalia in December 1992, a decision made by President George H. W. Bush although the operation continued and changed under President Clinton. This was a genuine experiment, a different kind of intervention policy test, for several reasons: first, the United States had decided to participate in an internationally sanctioned peacekeeping operation; second, U.S. troops were part of a multinational, UN-supported activity; and third, perhaps most significantly, the mission was based on a nonpolitical objective—

to provide humanitarian aid in a region not regarded as a vital national interest. Other humanitarian interventions followed: Rwanda (1994), Haiti (1994), and Bosnia (1995) fall into this category and represent a phase or focus of American foreign policy identified with the Clinton administration.

A third phase of intervention strategy, the intervention in Kosovo in 1999, also promoted by the Clinton administration, demonstrated another new strand in the evolving American foreign policy framework: a military mission that depended exclusively on weapons of high technology to achieve objectives; no ground troops participated in combat. By one interpretation, this might be regarded as an application of the Weinberger doctrine of overwhelming force, which was now measured by units of technological capability, not in quantities of human labor. The operation lasted far longer than had been anticipated, most likely due to unforeseen strategic designs introduced by the opposition. The intervention in Afghanistan in 2001, under George W. Bush, shares similar features—extensive use of highly sophisticated weaponry—and although the mission also includes ground troops, force levels are minimal, far, far below commitments in the Persian Gulf, and significantly smaller than committed strength in the Panama, Haiti, and early Somali operations.

A final characteristic of these American intervention cases in the post–Cold War is their geographic location. The settings were quite spread out. Historically territorial positioning has been an important determinant in U.S. intervention decisions. The Western Hemisphere was (and still is) designated as the American sphere of influence; stronger moves would be undertaken to keep other great power contenders out of the area and to build strong relations with the governments of these societies. American involvement in this region has been constant, heavy, unchanging. By contract, U.S. intervention into countries in Africa has been rare, owing in part to the special distance from U.S. shores, the colonial attachments linking specific African regions and countries with specific European states, and the seeming absence of centrality of any of these states to the determining features of international relations, either because of scarce, desirable resources or unique waterway access to points beyond. The legacy of Europe-U.S. relations is yet another story. Strong relations were cemented with various west European states following World War II, and the American involvement with domestic politics in Greece has a long history dating from that time. For the Islamic Middle East, a limited military intervention pattern began in the 1980s, but post–Cold War involvement is certainly more extensive. A brief synopsis of each case follows, arranged by geographic region.

INTERVENTION IN CENTRAL AMERICA

Panama

Triggering Event. Fraudulent national elections in Panama, May 7, 1989, and killing of an American Marine by Panamanian forces on December, 16, 1989.
UN Peacekeeping forces. None.

U.S. Intervention. Unilateral action, surprise attack, 27,000 U.S. troops committed; combat forces entered Panama on December 20, 1989.

Mission Objective. To capture Manual Noriega, head of state, and bring him to trial in the United States on charges of drug trafficking.

Domestic Situation. General Noriega, a former intelligence officer, became commander of the newly created Panamanian Defense forces (PDF) in 1983. In 1984, Panama held a national election. The voting was considered fraudulent because results were altered to produce a victory for Noriega's candidate, Nicolas Barletta. In September 1985, Dr. Hugo Spadafora confronted Noriega accusing him of illegal activities and announced he would expose Noriega's involvement in drug trafficking and arms smuggling. Before the public exposure, he was captured and murdered. Noriega and the PDF were prime suspects. President Barletta insisted on an investigation, but Noriega forced him to resign.

Noriega was to retire in 1987 when his deputy Colonel Roberto Diaz Herrera was to replace him, but on June 5, 1987, he announced that he would remain PDF commander for another five years. Diaz Herrera retaliated by publicly revealing details about Noriega's crimes—murdering Spadafore and rigging the 1984 elections. His charges inspired massive protests against the government: on June 8, nearly 100,000 people in Panama City demonstrated against Noriega demanding his resignation, and demonstrations and strikes continued for several weeks in cities and rural areas. Noriega responded by destroying and damaging property belonging to political opponents and shutting down the media.

Panamanian national elections were scheduled for May 7, 1989. Noriega was persecuting the opposition, restricting the press and observers, and manipulating the electoral council. The vote showed Noriega's candidate lost by a three-to-one margin. Former President Carter, who observed the elections, tried to meet with Noriega to convince him to accept the results. Regional foreign ministers came to Panama to try to negotiate a peaceful transfer of power. Noriega was unresponsive, blamed the United States, replaced valid votes with fraudulent ones, and appointed one of his friends to serve as provisional president. This led to further mass protests, which were violently put down by Noriega's paramilitary squads. In October 1989, a nonviolent coup attempt failed (U.S. assistance has been sought). Noriega murdered the coup plotters, purged the PDF of dissident elements, and cracked down harder on civilian dissent. On December 15, the Panama National Assembly, with the urging of Noriega, declared a state of war against the United States.

U.S. Policy. The United States maintained a contingent of military troops in the country to protect the Panama Canal, which it had built and operated since it opened in 1914. It is one of the world's greatest engineering achievements, a fifty-mile waterway linking the Caribbean Sea with the Pacific oceans. The United States is the largest user in terms of cargo tonnage. While its strategic importance has diminished over time, the Panama Canal "endures as an icon of the American experience, built by American sweat and ingenuity and whose security remains in the national interest" (Baker, 1995: 193). Under treaty arrangements of 1903, signed by the United States and Panama (a newly independent state), the canal and Canal Zone, a ten-mile strip of land around it, were designed as American territory with full sovereignty. In exchange, the United States paid, beyond $10 million at the start, an annuity of $250,000, which each year increased at a rate far beyond inflation. In 1977, President Carter signed a treaty to transfer full control of the canal to Panama on December 31, 1999. A number of steps were to be taken during the twenty-year transition period. Under the treaty terms, the nationalities of the Administrator and Deputy Administrator of the Panama Canal Commission were to be reversed on January 1, 1990. Until that date, the chief administrator had been an American; the deputy was Panamanian. This changeover would be in effect for the final decade of the transition period. The idea that the Canal official would be appointed by and responsible to Noriega was not attractive to the United States.

Noriega had been a close ally of the American government, cooperating with the Drug Enforcement Administration (DEA), and with the CIA as early as 1971, a source of intelligence and a communication channel between the United States and Cuba, and during the civil war in Nicaragua in the 1980s provided access and assistance to the Contra campaign (supported by the United States) against the Sandinistas. Beginning in 1987, the U.S. government began to seek Noriega's removal from power; in June, the Senate approved a nonbonding resolution calling upon Noriega and his principal officers to step down pending a public accounting of Herrera's charges. Noriega sent government workers to demonstrate near the American embassy, which turned into a rock throwing and window-smashing event. The State department suspended military and economic assistance to Panama (the Department of Defense reduced military contacts between the U.S. Southern Command and the PDF, and the CIA removed Noriega from its payroll). Economic sanctions were imposed. In December 1987, the United States conditioned resumption of such aid on democratic reforms in the country. In February 1988, Noriega was indicted by two federal grand juries in Miami and Tampa, Florida, which included 12 counts of racketeering, drug trafficking, and money laundering, and accused Noriega of assisting the Colombian Medellin cartel in transporting cocaine to the United States via Panama in return for a $4.5 million payment. The U.S. used several negotiating channels to present Noriega with plans and deals for his resignation. He rejected them all.

Panamanian troops had been harassing American servicemen and their families for some time—in January 1989 alone, according to former U.S. Secretary of State James Baker, 87 incidents were reported (Baker, 1995: 188). In May 1989, President George H. W. Bush made a major statement on the situation in Panama, announcing a plan designed to remove Noriega; at the same time, the United States increased its troop levels in the canal area after the fraudulent elections. In September, he delivered a major address to the nation declaring the war on drugs as a central policy issue. The failure to sequester Noriega during the PDF coup attempt in October narrowed U.S. options. Beginning in November, American troops and military equipment were gradually and secretly moved into Panama for possible use. A blunt message was delivered to the Panamanian President: if any Americans were harmed or harassed in any way, President Bush would hold Noriega personally responsible. Incidents against U.S. nationals stopped until December 16, when Panama-U.S. shots were exchanged and an American Marine was killed, a U.S. Navy officer was beaten, and his wife was threatened. This was a turning point in U.S. policy. "There would be no internal debate over our course this time," said Baker (1995: 189). "The death of one of its own had finally brought the military around. After years of reluctance the Pentagon was ready to fight." This intervention would be the dividing line between the Cold War agenda toward Central America pursued by Reagan in the 1980s and a new post–Cold War program to be followed by George H. W. Bush, in which ideological intensity was no longer relevant.

Intervention Action. On December 17, 1989, President Bush approved a plan for large-scale military intervention in Panama. Three days later, on December 20, military forces invaded Panama to safeguard the lives of Americans, defend democracy in Panama, combat drug trafficking, and protect the integrity of the Panama Canal treaty. Ten thousand U.S. troops backed by helicopter gunships and fighter-bombers flew into Panama and joined about 13,000 others who were already based in the canal area. They secured control of the country within five days.

Intervention Outcome. Within two days, U.S. forces had largely eliminated the resistance of the Panamanian Defense Forces, and on January 4, 1990, General Noriega, who had been seeking asylum at the Papal Nuncio, surrendered to the U.S. military and was flown to the United States to await trial on criminal drug operations. "Noriega believed up until the night we came in that he'd stared us down. Another dictator had underestimated the resolve of the United States to protect its vital interests. He thought he could weather the storm," wrote Baker (1995:193).

The invasion was criticized throughout the world, but judged a success in Panama and the United States (see Table 5.1). On December 29, 1989, the UN General Assembly passed a resolution condemning the intervention, strongly deploring the U.S. actions as flagrant violation of international law, of independence, sovereignty, and territorial integrity of states, demanding immediate withdrawal of American forces. The vote was 75 in favor, 20 against, 40 abstaining. Panama has had no army since the 1989 removal of Noriega from office, leaving police forces to secure its borders. The transfer of the Panama Canal from American to local control occurred on schedule, on December 31, 1999, marking withdrawal of the U.S. military presence and full relinquishment of U.S. sovereignty in the area.

Haiti

Triggering Event. A violent military coup ousted the president of Haiti on September 29, 1991.

UN Peacekeeping Forces. United Nations Mission in Haiti (UNMIH) created on September 23, 1993, with about 1,850 troops to implement Governors Island Agreement (although it was not deployed until October 15, 1994) to assist in

Table 5.1
Panama Intervention Summary

Cause of the conflict	International Issue. Regime leadership in Panama.
Level of U.S. national interest	High (historic U.S. involvement in Panama Canal, sphere of influence location, U.S. war on drugs policy significance).
Intervention characteristics	Overwhelming force, clear objectives, unilateral, quick exit.
Public Opinion	Congress passed a bill in May 1989 condemning Noriega and supporting the president in handling the crisis. Bill supporting Operation Just Cause presented in Congress, January 30, 1990.
Role of United Nations	No intervention role. U.S. intervention condemned by UN General Assembly Resolution on December 29.
Intervention outcome	Successful, mission achieved.

modernizing the armed forces of Haiti and establishing a new police force, help sustain a secure, stable environment for free elections in the country. Security Council authorized expansion of UNMIH in July 1994 to 6,000 troops.

U.S. Intervention. Multilateral action (U.S. led 20+ countries in a coalition); 21,000 U.S. troops, committed in a 23,250-force contingent in a unified multinational force (MNF), entered Haiti on September 19, 1994.

Mission Objective. To return Jean-Bertrand Aristide, the country's democratically elected ousted president, to control the government under a safe and secure environment.

Domestic Situation. A coup in 1986 ending Jean Claude "Baby Doc" Duvalier's rule in Haiti ended nearly three decades of family rule. General Henri Namphy assumed control of the government through a civilian-military junta, the National Council of Government. A new constitution was approved in 1987 but not put into effect until 1990. It included provisions for the election of a parliament, mayors, and a president. Elections set for November 29, 1987, were marred by violence, leading to the suspension of the process after only three hours. With U.S. help, on December 16, 1990, the first free, fair election was held in Haiti. Voters elected Aristide by a 67% margin. A popular priest who had been dismissed from the Silesian order in 1988 for his vocal political stand and opposition to the government, he had been given a clear mandate for political change. However, the main victors in legislative elections were supporters of the economic and military elite, holdovers from the previous regime. The Aristide government took office on February 7, 1991.

Haitian history has been a record of short presidencies, failed reform, corruption, violence, and poverty. A French-speaking mulatto elite has dominated the nation, while a black, Creole-speaking majority remained poor. By the 1990s, GDP per capita had been declining annually; by one estimate, at least three-fourths of the population lived in absolute poverty; life expectancy was 54 years; just 47% of the population could read; malnutrition among children was widespread; underemployment and declining standards of living in the rural areas, coupled with rapid population growth, created mass urban migration leading to slums and violence. AIDS became a widespread disease. Haiti is the poorest country in the Western Hemisphere.

As the new government took power, there was little hope for economic improvement. Although international lending institutions provided $511 million in grants and loans, this failed to translate into clear social betterment: few reforms were initiated, few new jobs were created, foreign investment did not increase. Aristide was accused of cronyism by placing associates in positions of authority, his attempts to end corruption were unsuccessful, and he was unable to discipline the military for its repressive role or break the power of paramilitary supporters of the old regime. The middle-class and wealthy Haitians and the military were completely dissatisfied with the new regime. Aristide addressed the United Nations on September 27, 1991, calling for Haitians and the international community to join him in the struggle against corruption and rule to maintain rule of law. Two days later, on September 29, military forces led by General Raoul Cédras, Chief of Staff of the Army, overthrew Aristide in a violent coup. Human rights violations following the coup were widespread; scores of Aristide's supporters were reportedly killed. Methods included brutal beatings, torture, execution without trial, and gang rape. Thousands of residents fled the capital for the safety of the countryside; about 25,000 refugees went to the Dominican Republic. Aristide escaped to Venezuela, and eventually lived in New York. An economic trade embargo was introduced, further depressing conditions for average Haitians; the small, wealthy elite did not suffer much.

In February 1992, Aristide and members of the Haitian Senate and Chamber of Deputies along with representatives from the Organization of American States (OAS) signed the Protocol of Washington. The goal of the protocol was Aristide's return. It was denounced by the de facto government as unconstitutional. By the end of that year, Aristide's request to the OAS and the United Nations for an International Civilian Mission in Haiti to monitor human rights abuses was granted. Still, oppressive practices in the Cédras regime increased through 1993. An estimated 3,000 Haitians had been killed, about 300,000 were internally displaced, and between 60,000 and 100,000 refugees fled Haiti by small boats bound for Florida and the Dominican Republic between 1991 and 1994. In July 1993, the Governor's Island Accord, created under UN and OAS sponsorship, was signed by Aristide and Cédras in New

York. It called for parliamentary, police, and military reforms under UN oversight, the quiet retirement of Cédras, and the restoration of Aristide to power, but it was clear by September that the agreement would not be implemented. The promised amnesty degree was repeatedly delayed, and the military and its allied thugs increased their violence against Aristide supporters. Parliament couldn't meet as the cabinet members dared not go to their offices; violence was rampant. As a result of growing instability, the International Commission monitoring abuses was evacuated in October. Economic sanctions tightened. Human Rights violations increased.

United States Policy. Throughout the Cold War, Washington had good relations with Haitian leaders, who supported U.S. policy to prevent the spread of communism and Cuban isolation; U.S. foreign assistance was a constant, although it had been decreasing. During the Duvaliers' reign human rights were violated and residents attempted to flee. As a result of illegal migration by Haitian poor, a joint 1981 Haitian Interdiction Agreement allowed the U.S. Coast Guard to intercept and repatriate all refugees and to screen them to ensure they were not moving for political purposes. (The 1980 U.S. Refugee Act reiterates distinctions between economic and political refugees. Haitians were normally characterized as economic refugees, Cubans as political refugees.) More than 27,000 Haitians were returned to their homeland between 1981 and 1991. Following Aristide's ouster, thousands of Haitian refugees attempted to enter the United States. The Bush administration summarily returned them. Presidential candidate Clinton promised to revoke Bush's order and grant asylum to Haitian refugees, but in January 1993 he announced he would continue the Bush policy, now supported by a U.S. Supreme Court decision. About 50,000 refugees were interdicted and returned. A hunger strike by African American activist Randall Robinson and efforts by the Congressional Black Caucus eventually pressured President Clinton to eliminate the policy of forced repatriation. He replaced it with a program that brought the refugees to Jamaica to determine whether they were political or economic migrants, leading to a "safe haven" policy bringing refugees to Guantanamo Bay.

The United States seemed in no hurry to restore the Aristide presidency. Although the coup was condemned, officials noted that arrangement needed to be reached among Haitians and reconciliation takes time. Following Clinton's inauguration, though, the United States seemed more concerned to return Aristide to power. A plan was presented to Haitian authorities but rejected. The United States, supported by three other "Friends of the Secretary-General" (Canada, France, and Venezuela), had participated in the Governor's Island agreement.

On October 11, 1993, the USS *Harlan County*, carrying a contingent of 200 U.S. military advisors and trainers (along with some Canadians), docked in Port-au-Prince, as part of the Governor's Island agreement, where an angry mob of anti-Aristide forces was demonstrating. Fearing it was too dangerous for personnel to disembark, U.S. authorities ordered the ship to sail away. Further attempts made by the United States to negotiate a compromise agreement failed.

In May 1994, the United Nations called for the resignation of the coup perpetrators, and tighter embargo conditions were threatened. Clinton demanded the immediate removal of Cédras. The United States deployed additional ships to enforce the blockade; the Clinton administration produced Presidential Decision Directive 25, which included participation in international forces to restore democracy as a justifiable use of force. The United States began sounding out allies about their possible participation in a Haitian peacekeeping force.

Intervention Action. On July 31, 1994, the UN Security Council adopted a resolution authorizing member states to form a multinational force (MNF) under unified command and to use all necessary means to bring about an end to the illegal regime in Haiti and prompt return of the legitimate president. On September 10, the order was issued and the Defense department began final intervention preparations. On September 15, President Clinton stated that 20 countries had offered to participate in an American-led intervention. On September 17, a last-effort negotiation team consisting of former President Jimmy Carter, General Colin Powell, and U.S. Senator Sam Nunn arrived in Port-au-Prince to talk with the junta leaders. A deal was worked out when the Haitian military became convinced that U.S. threats were credible, that force would be used if negotiations failed, and that U.S. troops were already on their way to Haiti. The military leaders agreed not to oppose the intervention and to resign in return for a general amnesty.

Intervention Outcome. On September 19, U.S. forces began landing in Haiti, encountering no opposition. By October 10, General Cédras and other coup leaders had left Haiti for exile. On October 15, Aristide returned to Haiti; the United Nations lifted economic sanctions and the embargo the next day. Order was restored, but economic prosperity did not follow. The United Nations took over peacekeeping functions from the multinational force on March 31, 1995 (see Table 5.2).

INTERVENTION IN AFRICA

Somalia

Triggering Event. No single event; conflict escalating since uprising in May 1988, overthrow of military dictator Siad Barre in January 1991, situation exacerbated by drought resulted in massive starvation, conditions of anarchy.

UN Peacekeeping Forces: (1) United Nations Operations in Somalia (UNOSOM I) created April 24, 1992, with 500 troops to protect aid workers and supplies and escort convoys; (2) UNOSOM II created March 26, 1993, with 21,500 troops for comprehensive peacekeeping and disarming faction groups and local militia.

U.S. Intervention. (1) Unified Task Force (UNITAF) approved by the United Nations on December 3, 1992, for 37,000 multilateral troops to use all necessary force to establish a secure environment for humanitarian relief operations; peacekeeping troops entered on December 9, 1992, under UNITAF, commanded by the United States, 26,000 U.S. troops committed (of 37,000 total); (2) peace-

Table 5.2
Haiti Intervention Summary

Cause of the conflict	Civil conflict issue. Social structure and regime leadership in Haiti.
Level of U.S. national interest	Medium (historic U.S. involvement, sphere of influence location, domestic refugee impact).
Intervention characteristics	Overwhelming force, clear objectives, multilateral.
Public Opinion	Administration did not seek Congressional approval. Majority of Americans opposed the intervention.
Role of United Nations	Intervention approval granted by the UN Security Council.
Intervention outcome	Successful, mission achieved.

keeping troops under UN command, on May 5, 1993, as part of UNOSOM II, multilateral action, about 5,000 U.S. troops committed (of 21,500 total force).

Mission Objective. (1) UNITAF: to deliver food supplies safely to starving civilians in the country in order to stop the famine caused by drought, disease, and civil war. (2) UNOSOM II mandate: to break the power of Somalia's warlords and their armed militias and to rebuild the country by disarming the factions and restoring destroyed institutions ranging from banking and finance to health, education, sanitation, and communications.

Domestic Situation. The termination of economic and military aid and the decline in world prices of Somalia's main export, livestock, in the late 1980s led to the fall of the government and state collapse. Somali dependence on foreign aid began in 1969 after a military coup brought Mohamed Siad Barre to power. He populated his government with members of the Marahan, his clan, favoring them with economic benefits. Until 1977, his main outside donor was the Soviet Union, but this role shifted to the United States following the coup in Ethiopia, when the Soviet Union built a stronger relationship with that country's new government. Military, economic, and food aid to Somalia kept the nation propped up: 57% of its GNP in 1987, all of its development budget, and half of its annual budget came from international assistance. Corruption and informal or illegal activities became the primary method of augmenting income because actual state wages were insufficient for survival. Massive influx of military equipment, especially small arms, contributed to the insecurity that became prevalent in the late 1980s. The sudden and total absence of economic aid in 1988 led to economic collapse, producing an internal conflict. The government's inability to provide food due to a drought and general political ineffectiveness resulted in mass migration, a devolution of power to the clans, and starvation. No faction had the strength to hold an economically viable area; clan power resulted in extreme fragmentation of Somali society. By 1990, Barre's sole support was confined to the Marahan, his own clan.

The Somali National Movement began an armed revolt in the north against Barre, whose forces responded with brutal attacks leaving between 15,000 and 60,000 killed, and nearly half a million refugees fled into Ethiopia. Another 600,000 were displaced. In June 1990, a group of faction leaders known as the "Manifesto Group" gathered in Mogadishu, where they agreed that Barre should be overthrown. In November, fighting broke out in the capital, Mogadishu, with Barre fighting the United Somali Congress and a coalition of rival factions led by General Mohammed Aideed who defeated Barre some four months later. Aideed expected to become the leader of the organization; however, Ali Mahdi was elected interim president. Over the next few months, conflicts escalated among factions, particularly between Aideed and Ali Mahdi that split Mogadishu into two heavily armed camps. Various international conferences to negotiate peace between rival forces were unsuccessful.

There was no central government to administer food aid, distribute medical supplies, or maintain power or roads. Lack of electricity, fuel, and sanitation idled plants. Portable items were looted by clans. In April 1992, the UN Security Council established the United Nations Operation in Somalia (UNOSOM I) to consist of 500 troops to protect aid workers and supplies and escort aid convoys into the countryside. An agreement with the clans fighting over Mogadishu was required before the troops could be deployed; as a result cease-fire monitors arrived in July; the infantry unit was not sent until mid-September 1992. It was estimated that as early as July, drought and disease had pushed nearly two-thirds of the Somali population to the brink of starvation. Fighting continued. No seaborne relief supplies were unloaded because rival factions shelled ships in the Mogadishu port. Prompted by the United Nations, relief supplies and logistical support were provided by member countries, but raids on these supplies continued. The United Nations proposed in August 1992 that 3,000 additional troops be joined to UNOSOM, but Somali faction leaders refused to give their consent. Instead, they became more resistant to UN requests for security forces to protect humanitarian supplies and workers. In October, General Aideed, the most powerful man in Mogadishu, demanded they be removed.

UN forces and relief workers were continuously threatened by Somali warlords. In June 1993, a Pakistani force of UN peacekeepers was ambushed by Aideed's forces. Twenty-four troops were killed. UN efforts to punish those responsible were unsuccessful. Coordination problems between contingents from different nations and definition of mission goals remained unclear. Anarchy continued.

U.S. Policy. Somalia became a U.S. ally in 1977. American involvement increased and included substantial cash payments, food and agricultural programs, health services, and economic advice. From 1985 to 1989, the United States provided $300 million in economic aid; from 1980 to 1989, $33.5 million in military aid. The Barre regime cooperated with American military units in the area, the U.S. Air Force had landing rights at Somali airports, one of which maintained the longest runway in Africa (built by the USSR) and the U.S. Navy had port-of-call privileges. Washington signed an arms-for-bases agreement with Somalia in August 1980. In return for U.S. military aid, the United States was given access to the former Berbera bases, which along with similar facilities in Oman, Kenya, Egypt, and Sudan would make possible U.S. power projection in the Middle East by President Jimmy Carter's Rapid Deployment Force. In 1988, in the wake of a Barre offensive in northern Somalia, the United States delivered $1.4 million worth of rifles and grenade launchers to Barre's armed forces. In Congress, the House Subcommittee on Africa threatened to cut off all aid to Somalia due to human rights abuses, and the State Department placed a hold on further lethal aid to Barre. In July 1989, civil war was spreading and the Bush administration asked for $20 million in economic support for security assistance in Somalia. Congress blocked it. In February 1990, General Norman Schwarzkopf, head of the U.S. Central Command, went before the Senate Committee on Appropriations to request continuing military aid to Somalia, arguing that the country's geographical location had strategic importance to the United States. It was situated along the Red Sea, a vital sea lane of communication between Europe and Asia, with the Suez Canal in the north and the Bab-el-Mandeb in the south. Congress blocked it. By December 1990, the U.S. base in Berabera had been abandoned, and all U.S. development assistance was cut off because Somalia had gone into debt arrears.

In the spring of 1991, Senator Nancy Kassenbaum called on the president of the United States to lead a worldwide humanitarian effort in Somalia to relieve the suffering and for the United Nations to make the humanitarian crisis in Somalia an item of high priority, and the Congressional Black Caucus asked the Bush administration to take the initiative in the United Nations in forcefully advocating a high-level UN presence in Somalia. Andrew Natsios, the head of the U.S. Agency for International Development (AID) office of Foreign Disaster Assistance, testified before Congress in January 1992 that Somalia was the greatest humanitarian emergency in the world. On July 27, 1992, the U.S. State Department made an announcement that supported the sending of armed UN security personnel to Somalia. A U.S. airlift of food relief began on August 14, but due to distribution difficulties, it was not working. Seven Congressional hearings on Somalia were held during 1992.

Intervention Action. On November 21, 1992, the Deputies' Committee of the U.S. National Security Council considered the options on Somalia and decided in favor of intervention. Their decision was presented to President Bush, who accepted it. There was wide support for the policy. On December 3, 1992, the UN Security Council approved a military intervention in Somalia authorizing member states to use all necessary force. The U.S. intervention plan began on December 9, in combination with a UN mission, the Unified Task Force (UNITAF). The Americans commanded UNITAF, a 37,000-member force, and provided the largest contingent of troops. Because of the fears of "mission creep," the Unified Task Force mission was mandated to last just five months; its main aim was to protect food relief delivered to the country. In this setting, a transition into another peace operation, UNSOM II, a multinational operation with a broader agenda in nation-building, was arranged for May 1993. The mission was to monitor all factions with respect to cessation of hostilities, prevent resumption of violence, maintain control of heavy weapons and seize the small arms of all unauthorized armed elements, secure ports and lines of communication, and repatriate refugees. The United States provided some troops, though far fewer than under UNITAF; these forces served within the operational control set by the United Nations, unlike the UNITAF structure.

The operation was complicated in a situation of prolonged state collapse, warlord feuding, and chaos. Limited UN efforts increased American actions to disarm the factions. In August 1993, four American soldiers were killed when a land mine blasted apart their Humvee in Mogadishu, marking the biggest single loss of American life since the intervention began. Later that month, 400 elite U.S. troops from Delta Force and the U.S. Rangers arrived on a mission to capture Aideed. By the end of September, President Clinton, facing a questioning Congress who wanted a justification for the role of U.S. forces in Somalia, said he wanted from the United Nations a fixed date when American troops would be replaced by forces from other nationals in the peacekeeping operation. The United States wanted to deemphasize the search for Aideed. UN officials worried that slowing down the hunt for him would erode UN credibility in protecting its forces and undermine the attempt at political stability in Somalia. On October 3, 18 U.S. soldiers were killed and 84 wounded along with approximately 1,000 Somalis during an assault on Mogadishu's Olympia Hotel in search of Aideed. The battle lasted 17 hours—the most violent U.S. combat firefight since Vietnam. President Clinton announced on October 7 that he would dispatch 1,500 more U.S. troops to the region to strengthen the operation and that all American combat forces and most logistical units would leave Somalia by the end of March 1994. Other nations followed suit.

Intervention Outcome. (1) Under UNITAF, humanitarian efforts achieved their maximum effect. The famine was finally confined to a few small areas, and most Somalis were receiving food aid. Medical care was increasingly available, supplies entered various Somali ports without resistance. The United Nations began programs to restore agricultural and livestock production. (2) Under UNOSOM II, mass starvation had been averted, no new national government was installed, factional violence continued. The UN mission officially ended in March 1995, failing to settle an ongoing internal conflict (see Table 5.3).

Rwanda

Triggering Event. Rwandan president's plane shot down, Hutu extremist groups began immediately massacring all Tutsi and also Hutu opposition leaders in Rwanda on April 6, 1994, conducting a genocide.

UN Peacekeeping Forces. United Nations Assistance Mission in Rwanda (UNAMIR) established October 5, 1993, with about 2,500 troops to help implement the Arusha Peace Agreement (signed by Rwandese parties in August) with mandate to monitor the cease-fire agreement and security situation.

Table 5.3
Somalia Intervention Summary

Cause of the conflict	Civil conflict issue. Social structure, weak government,criminal anarchy elements in Somalia.
Level of U.S. national interest	Medium (foreign aid program during the 1980s, strategic sea lane location).
Intervention characteristic	UNITAF: overwhelming force, clear objectives. UNOSOM II: minimal force, vague objectives.
Public opinion	UNITAF: public and congressional support. UNOSOM II: little public or Congressional support.
Role of United Nations	Intervention approved by the United Nations as a peacekeeping and peace enforcement operation.
Intervention Outcome	UNITAF: Successful, mission achieved. UNOSOM II: Failure, mission not achieved.

UNAMIR strength cut to 270 troops on April 21, 1994, and expanded to 5,500 from May 17, 1994 to June 8, 1995, to contribute to security and protection of refugees and civilians, establishing humanitarian areas, providing support for humanitarian assistance operations inside Rwanda.

U.S. Intervention. Multilateral, 3,000 U.S. troops committed; peacekeeping troops entered on July 22, 1994, part of the UN Rwanda Emergency Office (UNREO), but under U.S. command.

Mission Objective. Following the genocide, to help improve conditions for refugees by carrying out water purification and distribution in Goma, site of a major refugee camp, to improve airfield services in Goma and Kigali, the capital city, and to organize cargo distribution from the airport in Entebbe, Uganda.

Domestic Situation. Ethnic conflict has been a part of Rwandan politics since its drive to independence. About 85% of the population are Hutu; some 14% are Tutsi, who were favored in the educational system and civil administration under Belgian colonial rule. Between 1959 and 1961, Hutu staged a revolution that abolished the monarchy and ended Tutsi domination; in September 1961, elections gave 80% of the legislative seats to Hutu-led parties, and the exodus of more than 100,000 Tutsi into neighboring states started a cycle of violence between the two groups. The Tutsi refugees living outside Rwandan borders began organizing and staging military attacks against Hutu and the government, leading to retaliatory attacks, which created more refugees. Ethnic divisions were reinforced when President Habyarimana, a Hutu, seized power in 1973 and established a single-party state and a quota system for jobs and resource allocations where the Tutsi minority received a 10% allotment. By the end of the 1980s, about half of the Tutsi population had become refugees. The president allowed their return only if they would be self-supporting. At this point, Rwanda, a small, densely populated country, of little intrinsic strategic value to outsiders, had economic problems as well: a sharp decline in coffee prices, the country's leading export, combined with population growth, a World Bank structural adjustment program forcing currency devaluation, and a drought that diminished food supplies, resulted in a serious situation that continued despite substantial foreign aid.

In 1988, Tutsi refugees in Uganda along with some moderate Hutu founded the Rwandan Patriotic Front (RPF) dedicated to returning refugees to their homeland and reforming the government to allow ethnic power-sharing. President Habyarimana was pressured to change government policy and agreed in July 1990 to accept multiparty rule. That October, the RPF, composed of civilian militias, launched an attack from Uganda with 7,000 troops. The government and RPF began peace talks in 1992; the Arusha accords were signed in January 1993, committing the parties to a cease-fire, power-sharing, and the rule of law. Still, fighting continued. In August 1993, a comprehensive peace agreement was signed by the parties calling for a democratically elected government, repatriation of refugees, a broadly inclusive transnational government, and a neutral internal force to help implement and monitor the agreement. The UN Assistance Mission in Rwanda (UNAMIR) was established for this purpose and began service in October.

Government militants, fearful of losing their jobs, were not eager to join a power-sharing arrangement and frequently expressed ethnic hatred toward the Tutsis. To complicate matters, on October 21, 1993, a military coup in neighboring Burundi drove 375,000 Hutu refugees into Rwanda, exploding the regional refugee problem: Hutu fled to Rwanda from Tutsi-led Burundi; Tutsi fled to Burundi from Hutu-led Rwanda. President Habyarimana was sworn into office in January 1994, but no agreement on cabinet ministries or the National Assembly had been reached. Arms and ammunition continued to be imported in contradiction of the Arusha Accords, and the UNAMIR commander, upon hearing reports of a Hutu militia stockpiling of weapons and plots to kill large numbers of Tutsi in Kigali, passed on the information to the UN Department of Peacekeeping Operations. In February violence continued, and an RPF convoy accompanied by UNAMIR forces was ambushed; repeated attempts to install the new government failed. On April 5, the UN Security Council renewed the UNAMIR mandate for four months, contingent upon a transitional government installed within six weeks.

In an attempt to rescue the Arusha Accords, President Habyarimana met with RPF representatives and President Ntaryamira of Burundi in Tanzania. While returning on April 6, 1994, their plane was shot down by a rocket, crashing into Kigali airport. The act, believed to be an act of sabotage of the Presidential Guard, who was most threatened by any reconciliation efforts, led to full-scale civil war between the Hutu-dominated government and Tutsi (RPF) forces. Immediately following the crash, Hutu extremist groups began to massacre all Tutsi and Hutu opposition leaders; it became evident this was not spontaneous violence but a preplanned assault, genocide. Traditional sanctuary centers— churches, hospitals—became the site of massacres. Ten Belgian peacekeepers, part of the UNAMIR force assigned to guard the prime minister, laid down their arms but nonetheless were slaughtered. Massacres were carried out by torturing, maiming, rapes; the aggressors used machetes, axes, and clubs. Within one week, over 20,000 had been killed; by the end of April, an estimated 200,000 were dead. By midsummer, the end of July 1994, around 800,000 people has lost their lives because of genocide or general civil violence. At the end of the conflict, more than 2.25 million refugees (of a total population numbering about 7.7 million) had fled to neighboring Burundi, Tanzania, and Zaire.

U.S. Policy. The record of United States–Rwandan relations before 1994 is rather sparse—coffee was exported to the United States and America contributed to the country's foreign aid package, albeit in modest amounts. In Congressional testimony, it was reported that about 9% of all foreign assistance to Rwanda between 1971 and 1994 came from the United States. (By contrast, 22% of Somali aid was provided by the United States, and America contributed more than 45% of Haiti's total assistance for the same period.) There are few historical ties with the political leadership, and the country has not played a role in U.S. security policy, either during the Cold War or after.

On April, 21, 1994, the UN Security Council voted to reduce the UNAMIR force from 2,500 down to 270, after Belgium decided to withdraw its contingent in light of the volatile situation and violent death to its peacekeepers. The UN Secretary-General called for a decision reversal and expansion of UNAMIR. Shortly thereafter, debate developed between UN officials and the United States over Rwandan intervention, with the United Nations urging greater commitment of troops and the United States proposing safe areas in the neighboring countries, and no troop commitment. Furthermore, Washington did not wish to pay for a peacekeeping mission it believed would inevitably fail, and the recently approved PDD-25, with guidelines on U.S. peacekeeping participation, argued against intervention in areas and countries outside America's strategic interest. During the debate no mention was made of genocide. The White House and State Department realized such language would require a stronger military intervention based on the international agreement to act under the terms of the 1951 Convention on Genocide. Officials referred to "acts of genocide" instead. Within Congress, the House African Affairs committee urged an active role for the United States to respond to the crisis but were opposed to sending U.S. troops. The Black Caucus showed no strong interests in the Rwandan issue.

On May 17, 1994, the Security Council authorized an expanded UNAMIR II to consist of 5,500 personnel, although logistical and bureaucratic difficulties delayed its deployment. Meanwhile, the French decided to organize a unilateral intervention and eventually 3,000 troops composed of a coalition of forces—without any U.S. contribution—were dispatched to Rwanda. France made Goma, Zaire, its support center for the operation. As a result, many refugees fled there with the promise of security. The airport was capable of handling a large number of flights per day—somewhere between 500,000 to 800,000 refugees arrived in Goma on July 14 and 15. The basic needs of the great number of refugees in Goma could not met. Lack of clean water and grossly inadequate sanitation facilitated rapid spread of disease, dehydration, and exhaustion. For the remainder of the month, it was estimated that one refugee was dying per minute; in fact, more than 50,000 lost their lives in Goma, by far the highest mortality rate ever recorded in a refugee population. The Goma humanitarian crisis triggered a U.S. intervention response.

Intervention Action. The United States began a humanitarian assistance operation (called "disaster response," rather than peacekeeping), and the U.S. military command assumed a subordinate role within the UN relief operations rather than taking on any leadership. Through its efforts, within a few weeks, sufficient amounts of clean water were being produced, sanitation tasks were carried out at the Goma refugee camp (building latrines, digging mass graves), airport operations expanded at Goma and Kigali, and massive convoys delivered food and other relief supplies throughout Rwanda. The force left Goma on August 28 and withdrew from the area entirely on September 29, 1994.

Intervention Outcome. The death rate in the Goma refugee camp was reduced, due to sanitation efforts of the U.S. military force in water purification and construction of sanitation facilities. A secure environment was created for humanitarian organizations to move effectively into the region. Airport efficiency increased which facilitated coordination among agencies to deliver humanitarian assistance (see Table 5.4).

INTERVENTION IN EUROPE

Bosnia

Triggering Event. A referendum in favor of Bosnian independence from the Federal Republic of Yugoslavia passed on February 29, 1992; Bosnia declared itself an independent nation March 3, 1992. International recognition followed on April 5, 1992. Intense fighting among Bosnian Serbs, Croats, and Muslims began.

UN Peacekeeping Forces. United Nations Protection Force (UNPROFOR) created on February 21, 1992, to monitor a cease-fire agreement and help establish conditions of security for Croatia, with 14,000 troops. It was extended to Bosnia on June 5, 1992. About 1,100 troops were to provide humanitarian assistance and secure functioning of Sarajevo airport. Later expanded to protect convoys of civilian detainees, monitor the "no-fly" zone "safe areas," and cease-fire agreements. By March 1995, near the end of the mission's operation, force strength was about 38,600 military personnel. On December 21, 1995, the Security Council created the United Nations International Police Task Force

Table 5.4
Rwanda Intervention Summary

Cause of the conflict	Civil conflict issue. Social structure and ethnicity conflict in Rwanda.
Level of U.S. national interest	Low (no historic U.S. involvement, no issue linkage, no strategic linkage).
Intervention characteristics	Phase I: no intervention during the genocide. Phase II: limited force, clear objective, quick exit.
Public opinion	No intervention support to stop genocide. Phase II emergency support not sought beforehand.
Role of United Nations	Very limited intervention approved and carried out within UN mandate.
Intervention outcome	Phase I: failure to act on genocide. Phase II: mission achieved, success.

(IPTF) with a troop strength of about 2,000, in accordance with the Dayton Peace Accords. Its operations have come to be known as the United Nations Mission in Bosnia and Herzegovina (UNMIBH).

U.S. Intervention. Multilateral action through the NATO Implementation Force (IFOR). Peacekeeping troops entered on December 20, 1995. U.S. contribution up to 20,000 of a full 60,000 total troop contingent. Tasked to maintain cessation of hostilities, separate the armed forces, patrol the demilitarized line, repair and replace roads, bridges and other structures.

Domestic Situation. In the 1980s, after the death of Tito and changing world economic conditions, Yugoslavia faced rapidly accelerated trends in unemployment and inflation. The collapse of communism eliminated many importers of Yugoslavian exports, increasing dependence on local resources; the country was no longer important with the end of the Cold War: aid decreased, loan requirements became increasingly harsh. The dissolution of the state economy was accompanied by an increase in banditry, organized crime, and black market activity. Yugoslavian republics each began to look inward and to rely increasingly on their own, largely ethnic, leadership. One region hit hard by the economic decline was Serbia, home of the federal republic. Slobodan Milosevic, leader of the Serbian party, sought to consolidate a hold on the central state, and to incorporate his ethnic brethren into a unified greater Serbia, and he began encouraging Serb solidarity, focusing on ethnic identity, which increased discrimination against and maltreatment of Serbs in other republics in response to his rhetoric. Leaders in Slovenia and Croatia, two economically richer republics, responded by portraying Serbia as the enemy of republican democracy, and their own republics as the guarantors of individual rights. The controversy shifted from economic issues to the rhetoric of national exploitation and ethnic rights. Demographically, the Yugoslav federation in 1991, a population of 23.5 million, was about 36% Serbian, about 20% Croat, and 10% Muslim. The rest were smaller percentages of various nationalities. Although Serbs were the largest group, they were also geographically the most diffused, with significant proportions residing in Croatia and Bosnia. In Slovenia, Serbs composed less than 3% of the population.

Slovenia and Croatia each declared independence in June 1991. Immediately, the Yugoslavian national army (JNA), composed primarily of Serbs, attacked Slovenia. Fighting ended about 10 days later, when the JNA withdrew forces. Fighting turned to Croatia. Multiparty elections and the rise to power of Croatian nationalists in 1990 had increased the fear of Serbs living there that they would become victims (as they had been during the Nazi period) in an independent Croatia. They held a referendum in the late summer leading them to declare a Serb Autonomous Region of Krajina and a declaration of secession and desire to join with Serbia. By August 1991, the JNA and Croatian-Serb forces had gained control over one-third of Croatia. By the end of the year, between 6,000 and 10,000 people had been killed, and about 250,000 Serbs and 100,000 Croats had been displaced by the round of fighting, fleeing to other areas and creating a substantial voice for revenge. A cease-fire, but no comprehensive political settlement, was negotiated by the end of 1991.

The issue of independence was introduced in the Bosnian parliament after Slovenian and Croatian independence was recognized by the European Community in December 1991. Bosnia was a democratic, ethnically mixed republic: 44% Muslim, 31% Serb, and 17% Croat, with a high degree of intermarriage. Both Croatians and Muslims felt threatened by the prospect of a nationalist state ruled by Serbia. In the debate, the Bosnian Serbs walked out, and formed their own parliament, declaring an intention to annex territory rather than cede to an independent Bosnia and to remain within a unified Yugoslavia. Bosnian Croats in the western part of the republic also declared autonomy; their region was incorporated into the Croatian economy. A Bosnian referendum on independence passed overwhelmingly in February 1992 (boycotted by the Bosnian Serbs). International recognition was granted in April. Radovan Karadzic, leader of the Bosnian Serbs, declared an independent Serb republic that same day. War broke out. Serbian forces quickly secured control over about 70% of Bosnia, which remained fixed for the next three years. The conflict led to a massive refugee crisis and widely documented genocide resulting from the "ethnic cleansing" policy: 250,000 killed, some 50,000 tortured, 20,000–50,000 raped, more than two million persons displaced.

In 1992, the United Nations imposed economic sanctions against Serbia, and sent a peacekeeping force to Bosnia to facilitate humanitarian relief. The Secretary-General estimated that 40,000 peacekeepers were needed fully to protect humanitarian convoys and Bosnians in "safe areas," and 17,000 were required minimally to carry out these mandates. In early 1994, however, only about 14,000 UNPROFOR troops were in Bosnia. NATO agreed to provide

UNPROFOR with close air support to defend UN troops and to carry out air strikes consistent with UN mandates. (Before NATO could act, however, the call for strikes would have to originate with the United Nations, and it was only when the Special Representative arrived that those calls could originate in Bosnia.) UNPROFOR's goal in Bosnia was to provide humanitarian assistance and try to contain the fighting. The approach to protecting "safe areas" approved by the UN Security Council in June 1993 aimed at preventing the destruction of Muslim cities and their populations. It failed. UN forces had neither the resources nor the will to put up an adequate defense or respond to aggressive actions by the combatants. In July 1995, the Serbs overran Srebrenica with only slight resistance from the United Nations, creating 40,000 refugees and casting doubt on the continued UN presence in the former Yugoslavia.

The international presence restrained Serb behavior and bought time that allowed Bosnia to develop its forces and augment its firepower. But the international presence was also used by the French and British as a justification for not undertaking bombing or other major military actions, either because of the likelihood of UN troops being hit by friendly fire or because of the fear that such action would spark retaliation against troops by the Serbs. At a low cost to the providers, therefore, the troops supplied a modest amount of humanitarian and peacekeeping assistance, but with the consequence of preventing more aggressive action by the West that might have deterred Serb behavior.

In 1994, NATO began air strikes against Bosnian Serb forces to halt Serb attacks on Muslim enclaves that had been declared "safe areas" by the United Nations. This escalation did not deter the violence and aggression within the country, and UNPROFOR was considering withdrawal of their forces.

U.S. Policy. In June 1991, Secretary of State James Baker visited Belgrade urging the republics to remain united into the Federal Republic of Yugoslavia. The country broke apart a few days later, and the first of the Balkan wars began. The United States remained interested but aloof in the course of the conflict, Baker declaring it was time for the Europeans to show they could manage problems in their neighborhood now that the Cold War was over. It was a European problem. The Bush administration refrained from the use of force and avoided any statement of actions that would suggest that they might use force. "We don't have a dog in that fight," Baker said. During the U.S. presidential campaign, candidate Bill Clinton promised change in the Bosnia policy and was critical of Bush's policy of inaction. The Clinton position advocated bombing the Serbs if necessary to ensure that relief supplies went through and to open up the camps, said lifting the arms embargo should be considered, and condemned the Bush approach as immoral and out of step with American values. Once in office, President Clinton discovered the Bosnia problem to be both more complex and more difficult than it had appeared. Both force and diplomacy were needed if meaningful results were to be achieved. Clinton's position promised much that his policies could not deliver. On January 13, 1993, as the Clinton administration was about to take power, Richard Holbrooke, chief negotiator of the Dayton Accords, wrote, "Bosnia will be the key test of American policy in Europe. We must therefore succeed in whatever we attempt. The administration

cannot afford to begin with either an international disaster or a quagmire."
(Holbrooke, 1998: 51). He advocated the United States should act in concert
with other nations, even in some military coalition, but avoid getting dragged
into a ground war in the region.

There were six stages in U.S. policy toward Bosnia as identified by Wayne
Bert (1997: 129): (1) until July 1991, keep Yugoslavia together, maintain the
status quo via diplomatic efforts (failure); (2) from July 1991 to April 1992,
allow border adjustments in a framework of intact Yugoslavia, with a ceasefire
in Croatia (failure); (3) from April 1992 to February 1993, support the
independent republics (war in Bosnia resulted); (4) between February 1993 and
June 1994, advocate an end to the conflict through negotiation (the conflict
continued); (5) from June 1994 to August 1995, pressure parties to stop fighting
(failure); and (6) from August 1995, strike with military air power and negotiate
with leaders to stop fighting and negotiate a peace treaty (success).

The question of intervening to prevent atrocities formed a continuing debate
within the United States about what appropriate action to take in Bosnia. There
was a humanitarian interest in minimizing ethnically based violence and a
security interest in preventing atrocities which could encourage such behavior
elsewhere and could seriously threaten world order. Stopping the buildup of
large numbers of refugees had both a humanitarian and security dimension:
refugees could affect adversely the countries that accepted them and constitute a
group that could later disrupt the status quo in order to gain acceptable status.
Where the potential costs of pursuing humanitarian interests were considered to
be high, both the Bush and Clinton administrations declined opportunities to
intervene.

Few people believed that vital U.S. security interests existed in Bosnia to
justify substantial human sacrifice and other costs related to an intervention
effort. Instead, all options presented were low risk/low cost policies appropriated
to the limited security stakes or the humanitarian goals. Events were judged not
significant enough to merit a major involvement but too important to be ignored
completely. Some argued that the prospect of expansion could drive intervention
to stop the conflict, yet neither the United States nor any large European power
was prepared to send in the required number of troops to do it. American
prescriptions for less drastic measures such as air strikes and a lifting of the arms
embargo were opposed by Europeans, in part because the Europeans feared a
widening of the war would result.

Another concern was the effect of a weak Western response in Bosnia on the
coherence and credibility of NATO. Disagreement over the proper NATO
strategy in Bosnia was preventing action and hurting the organization. If NATO
were not up to the challenge of an appropriate response to the Yugoslav crisis,
then what would be its future as a military organization? Concern about the
effect of Bosnia on NATO itself, however, was not sufficient to convince the
NATO countries of the need for intervention.

The Western argument over the Yugoslav situation was not over whether
Western values were at stake, whether the public would like to do something to
remedy the situation, or whether the West could do something to further

humanitarian values, but over the cost of intervention to influence the situation, the perseverance needed to complete the job once it was started, the nature of the conflict, and what could be done to stop it. Hard choices needed to be made on Bosnia policy. President Clinton's instincts were to intervene and help halt Serb military actions in Bosnia, but there was a domestic political price to be paid for that. Was the intervention worth that price?

Air strikes were the weapon of choice for those favoring a more aggressive stance in Bosnia: low-cost in terms of casualties and moderately effective in slowing down the Serbs. Others doubted the efficacy of air strikes. Heavily wooded areas would make it easy to hide weapons, the fog and precipitation would hinder visibility and make it difficult to find targets, and the Europeans worried about the risk to their troops if air power was used on Serbian troops. Many in the Pentagon opposed the use of air power in the Yugoslav terrain— forests make it far more complicated than deserts. Those who opposed the use of air power tended to believe having troops on the ground would be the only way to effectively control Serbian aggression. In addition, some policy-makers worried that any solution that did not entail a massive use of force would fail to stop ethnic cleansing.

Clinton's preferred policy combined the use of air strikes with lifting the embargo on arms going into Bosnia (lift and strike). It would allow the Bosnians to acquire arms to defend themselves, permitting them to meet the Serbs on a more equal basis. The British were opposed. They feared the introduction of more arms would only escalate the capabilities on all sides, raising the level of violence, threatening peace talks, and threatening the expansion of the war to other parts of Yugoslavia. President Clinton's proposed policy was rejected. Leaks in the embargo, though, that assisted both the Croats and the Bosnians in strengthening their forces, combined with the NATO bombing campaign, brought about changes in the Bosnian situation.

Negotiators representing the United Nations and European community proposed de facto partitioning of Bosnia, the Vance-Owen plan. This plan generated controversy for advocating partitioning along ethnic lines, though some thought it was the best that could be done under the circumstances and better than continued fighting. The Clinton administration provided little support for it and promoted another plan, the Contact Group plan which required the Serbs to withdraw from less territory than was required by the Vance-Owen proposal.

Refusing for a year to take part in negotiations on the war, the United States told the allies it would press the Bosnian government to accept a peace plan that partitioned the country along ethnic lines. The negotiating strategy that was emerging was to use force if necessary, but to be willing to impose a peace plan while rewarding a cooperative Milosevic with loosened sanctions. This new direction would produce the peace plan fashioned by the Contact Group. Although it would not achieve a settlement, it was forerunner of the Dayton agreement, negotiated by the United States.

The Dayton agreement recognized Bosnia as a sovereign state with its present internationally recognized boundaries and within it, two entities, the Federation of Bosnia and Herzegovina (Federation) and the Serb Republic (Republica Srpska). Bosnian territory was split into 51% for the Federation and 49% for Bosnian Serbs. Sarajevo would be governed as single entity. The agreement obligated the parties to withdraw their forces behind agreed-upon cease-fire lines, engage in confidence-building measures to promote peace, and impose arms limits for heavy weapons. The arms embargo and economic embargo on Serbia were lifted. A NATO troop force of 60,000 would serve as enforcer, compelling adherence to the agreement and defending itself. Americans committed troops.

The American involvement, seen as a welcome step to end the long, tragic conflict was regarded as coming three years too late, meaning the potential results for peace would be considerably less than they might have been and purchased at a higher price in democracy and ethnic tolerance than was necessary. Yet, as Ignatieff (1996: ix) stated, "throughout the Yugoslav conflict, the demand for intervention has come from intellectual and cultural figures who, in the nature of things, could not either 'intervene' themselves, or directly order intervention. The political leaders who hesitated to intervene did so because they would have had to bear the political costs of failure more directly than most of those counseling intervention."

Intervention Action. Several factors impelled the Clinton administration to act more decisively in Bosnia. The most important factor was that the outbreak of fighting and its continued escalation raised the real prospect that UN forces would have to be withdrawn from the area. The UN Secretary-General raised the idea of UNPROFOR withdrawal in March 1995. This decision would require the United States to commit substantial ground forces and logistical support to Bosnia in an effort to protect allied troops as they were removed, which Clinton had acknowledged in a speech on May 31, 1995, stating the United States has a long-standing commitment to help NATO allies and to take part in a NATO operation to assist them in a withdrawal if that should become necessary. Clinton had pledged troops would be used to help the withdrawal and the United States would be expected to provide between 20,000 and 25,000 troops to assist in the safety of the troops withdrawing.

On July 15, 1995, a decision was made by the United States to use force in Bosnia to end the conflict when the administration realized that their commitment to support a NATO withdrawal made U.S. involvement on the ground inevitable. If the United Nations withdrew, once NATO gave the order to assist with the withdrawal it would trigger immediate deployment of 20,000 American troops to Bosnia. The Clinton administration embarked on a concerted effort of intensive bombings and cease-fire negotiation attempts between late August and October 1995. The parties finally agreed to negotiate peace, reached through intensive sessions in Dayton, Ohio, during November. Peace accords were signed in Paris on December 14, 1995. A critical factor in the agreement was the U.S. commitment of over 20,000 ground troops in Bosnia as part of a year-long NATO peacekeeping operation. Troops arrived on December 20, 1995, committed after the fighting, not during it.

Those supporting deployment believed that U.S. leadership was as crucial to implementing the peace agreements as it was in negotiating it; that the peacekeeping operation was a test of NATO's ability to deal with post–Cold War security threats, and that it is in America's national interest for the mission to succeed. Those opposed to troop deployment argued that the deeply rooted, centuries-old strife among the Balkan peoples could be erased in a year by military peacekeepers. Nor did they think the Bosnian conflict represented a direct threat to European security or to vital U.S. interests. President Clinton's address "U.S. Role in Bosnian Peacekeeping" on November 27, 1995, justified American action this way:

Tonight I want to speak with you about implementing the Bosnian peace agreement, and why our values and interests as Americans require that we participate.... Our mission will be limited, focused, and under the command of an American general. . . .

There are times and places where our leadership can mean the difference between peace and war, and where we can defend our fundamental values and serve our most basic, strategic interests.... Nowhere today is the need for American leadership more stark or more immediate than in Bosnia. . . .

Just three weeks ago, the Muslims, Croats and Serbs came to Dayton, Ohio, in America's heartland, to negotiate a settlement. There, exhausted by war, they made a commitment to peace. The agreed to put down their guns; to preserve Bosnia as a single state; to investigate and prosecute war criminals; to protect the human rights of all citizens; to try to build a peaceful, democratic future. And they asked for America's help as they implement this peace agreement.

America has a responsibility to answer that request, to help to turn this moment of hope into an enduring reality. To do that, troops from our country and around the world would go into Bosnia to give the confidence and support they need to implement their peace plan. . . .

The only force capable of getting this job done is NATO, the powerful military alliance of democracies that has guaranteed our security for half a century now. And as NATO's leader and the primary broker of the peace agreement, the United States must be an essential part of the mission. If we're not there, NATO will not be there. The peace will collapse.

And America's commitment to leadership will be questioned if we refuse to participate in implementing a peace agreement we brokered right here in the United States, especially since the presidents of Bosnia, Croatia and Serbia all asked us to participate and all pledged their best efforts to the security of our troops.

NATO is completing its planning for IFOR, an international force for peace in Bosnia of about 60,000 troops. Already, more than 25 other nations, including our major NATO allies, have pledged to take part. They will contribute two-thirds of the total implementation force, some 40,000 troops. The United States would contribute the rest, about 20,000 soldiers....The mission will be precisely defined with clear, realistic goals that can be achieved in a definite period of time.... Second, the risks to our troops will be minimized. American troops will take their orders from the American general who commands NATO. (President Clinton, speech to the nation, November 27, 1995)

In the U.S. Congress, the senate debated the deployment of American troops in Bosnia on December 13, 1995. Among the opposition views, Senator Daniel R. Coats' (Indiana, Republican) statement is representative:

We have two burdens in this debate: One is to exercise American leadership and the second is to justify American sacrifice.... Why Bosnia? Why this region? Why this moment? It is said we have a moral responsibility to end the bloodshed. But I think that goal is too broad to be useful. Bosnia, unfortunately, is not unique when it comes to undeserved suffering. . . .so how do we choose where American troops are used to end the world's civil wars? . . . The Balkan war has not been expanding but contracted.

It is said that our vital national interests are challenged by a Balkan civil war, but this is simply not credible. What resources are threatened? What trade route is interrupted? What strategic military threat to the United States has developed? What American citizens are being placed in danger?

.... A third question: What exactly is our mission and how will we define success?... The most clear portion of the proposed mission is keeping the warring factions separated. That will not be easy, but at least its effectiveness can be measured. But the second component of the President's mission statement, that of "giving the parties the confidence that each side will live up to their agreements" is dangerously unclear.

These confidence building measures include establishing the foundation for economic, social and political reconstruction in the region. But, it is the stated mission of arming and training one side in what I believe to be a civil war that is most disturbing.... I am convinced that this Bosnian crisis is a symptom of a deeper foreign policy crisis, the evidence of a basic misunderstanding of what it means to be a superpower. The will to intervene, to spend lives and money, is a limited resource of any nation. It must be carefully preserved for essential missions that concern our vital interest and maintain stability in the world. Endless and pointless interventions squander that limited resource of national will. It is precisely because we cannot be isolationists that we must be deliberate and realistic in our actions. It is because intervention must remain an option of American policy that our interventions must be wise. In Bosnia, discretion is wisdom." (Coats 1996: 43-47)

Intervention Outcome. Mission completed, the military annexes of the General Framework Agreement for Peace were implemented within one year. The force was reduced to about 18,000 and the name changed to SFOR (stabilization force) to provide a secure environment, and the United States contributes (see Table 5.5).

Kosovo

Triggering Event. March 18, 1999, Kosovar Albanians sign Rambouillet Accords, Serbian-Yugoslav Federal Republic of Yugoslavic (FRY) delegation refuses.

Table 5.5
Bosnia Intervention Summary

Cause of the conflict	Civil conflict issue. Social structure, weak government in Bosnia, regime leadership in Yugoslavia.
Level of U.S. national interest	Low (no historic level of U.S. involvement).
Intervention characteristics	No intervention during "ethnic cleansing." Phase II: after Dayton Peace Accords, substantial force contribution.
Public opinion	Some public support for intervention but less for introducing ground troops into conflict. Congress supports Dayton Peace Accords.
Role of United Nations	UN intervention support provided during and after the conflict. Mixed.
Intervention outcome	Phase I: failure to act on "ethnic cleansing." Phase II: mixed. Did U.S. reluctance to get involved extend the conflict?

UN Peacekeeping Forces. United Nations Interim Administration Mission in Kosovo (UNMIK) created on June 10, 1999, after the conflict, with about 9,000 supporting personnel (primarily civilian police), to provide humanitarian and disaster relief, assure safe return of refugees, and promote establishment of substantial autonomy and self-government of Kosovo.

U.S. Intervention. Multilateral, commencing March 24, 1999, when NATO started an air campaign against Yugoslavia. No U.S. ground troops were involved. When the bombing ended, the Kosovo Peacekeeping Force (KFOR) was created. By August 1999, the United States was contributing 4,500 troops to a 28,000 total force (the remainder supplied by other members of NATO).

Mission Objective. To persuade the Serbians to accept the Rambouillet Accords, creating an interim autonomous arrangement for Kosovo and a NATO peacekeeping force in the area consisting of 28,000 troops.

Domestic Situation. Kosovo, an autonomous province inside the Federal Republic of Yugoslavia, hoped to gain independence in the wake of the dissolution of the federation after 1990, and especially after the Dayton Accords over Bosnia were signed in 1995. When that did not happen, some radicalized Kosovars began to support the development of a paramilitary underground force known as the Kosovo Liberation Army (KLA). Serbian-KLA violence escalated between 1996 and 1998. From February 1998 onward, this bitter dispute developed into a full-scale armed conflict between the KLA and the Serbian special police force and regular units of the Yugoslav military.

The 1946 Yugoslav constitution granted Kosovo the status of an autonomous region within Serbia. In 1966 it was classified as an autonomous province, and in 1974 a new constitution granted it extended powers of self-government. Economically, Kosovo was the poorest region in the socialist Yugoslavia in the mid-1980s, with the highest birth rate in Europe and highest rate of unemployment. In 1981, bloody riots took place in Kosovo as Albanians—some 90% of the population—demanded full status as a republic. The minority Serbs in Kosovo felt discrimination, felt they were forced to leave Kosovo and were suffering a kind of political, legal, and cultural genocide. Milosevic, who had assumed headship of the Serbian Communist Party Central Committee in 1986, visited Kosovo, making an impassioned plea to win the battle for Kosovo and face Serbia's enemies.

In 1989, Milosevic became Serb president. He abrogated the right to self-administration of Kosovo. Serbian authorities abolished the province's cultural and political institution. In response, the Albanian majority set up a parallel state structure with a functioning presidency, government, legislature, and education and medical system. Mass demonstrations and violent clashes with the police continued into the spring of 1990, creating anger and fear among the Albanian population. In a 1991 referendum, nearly all of the Albanians in Kosovo supported the idea of an independent state; Serbian officials argued the province should remain within FRY, since, from the Middle Ages, Kosovo has been considered the cradle of Serb nationalism and heartland of its medieval kingdom. After the 1991 referendum, lines of cooperation and contact between the Serb and Albanian communities ceased.

The crisis escalated in 1997 with the influx of small arms into Kosovo following violent social unrest in the country of Albania, and the KLA, a secret guerrilla force that followed a strategy of attacks on police stations and assassinations of Serbian officials, police officers, and those collaborating with the Serbian regime gained strength. Serbian authorities ordered a crackdown and reacted with raids and political trials, and in February 1998, Serbian security forces prepared a military offensive against the KLA aimed at their complete extermination. In March 1998, Serbian police massacred more than 70 Albanians, and afterward started burning Albanian villages, destroying shops and schools. Almost 400,000 persons were displaced, and nearly 2,000 had been killed by October 1998.

U.S. Policy. The UN Security Council imposed an arms embargo and economic and diplomatic sanctions against the Federal Republic of Yugoslavia. In September 1998, NATO issued an activation warning for an air campaign in Yugoslavia. The NATO threat secured an agreement from Serbia to a cease-fire and an end to the repression, and called on Milosevic to cease military and police operations in Kosovo and to withdraw forces that had been moved into the province over the previous seven months. Diplomatic efforts by U.S. envoy Richard Holbrooke led to the creation of the Organization for Security and Cooperation in Europe (OSCE) Kosovo Verification Mission on October 15. A group of about 1,500 unarmed observers were sent to monitor Serbian compliance to withdraw internal security troops and Yugoslav army troops. Neither the Albanians nor the Serbs were willing to abide by the conditions of the agreement and assaults resumed. By January 1999, the cease-fire had fallen apart, and after January 15, with the massacre of 45 ethnic Albanians, the international community decided to act and informed all parties that they were to come to a political settlement for Kosovo by February 20, 1999.

U.S. Secretary of State Madeleine Albright, calling for a peace conference at Rambouillet, France, was intent on solving the problem, taking a stand against state-sponsored violence, sending a message to repressive, criminal country leaders. Both Serbs and Kosovar Albanians were invited. The conference began on February 6. Negotiators presented a "take it or leave it" package calling for broad interim autonomy for Kosovo (but not an independent Kosovo, which NATO did not support, fearing it would destabilize the Balkans further), and 28,000 NATO troops to implement it. The Albanians insisted on a referendum after the interim period, and they opposed the requirement that they demilitarize and surrender their weapons prior to deployment of an international military force; the Serbs were totally against any NATO presence in the province, considering it an assault on their sovereignty. The talks were postponed for a few weeks so the parties could consider these obstacles. After reconvening in March, the Kosovo delegation, under pressure from the United States, agreed to sign the Rambouillet Accords on March 18. The Yugoslav delegation did not. Talks were adjourned on March 19, international monitors were withdrawn from Kosovo on March 20. On that day, Yugoslav forces launched an offensive driving thousands of ethnic Albanians out of their homes and villages, executing some, displacing many others, and setting fire to many houses. U.S. envoy Richard Holbrooke went to Belgrade in a final attempt to persuade President Milosevic to stop attacks on the Kosovar Albanians or face imminent NATO strikes. Milosevic refused to comply.

From the American officials' point of view, the Rambouillet conference demonstrated the U.S. commitment to bring peace to Kosovo; it failed because of Serbian refusal to go along with its provisions, thus making it permissible for NATO to exercise force to bring compliance. The United States believed something had to be done to oppose totalitarianism, ethnic cleansing, and oppression. The U.S. Joint Chiefs of Staff, the White House, and NATO had accepted the idea of bombing the Serbs, and ground troops were being excluded; thus opposition in Congress would be minimized. When the strikes began, Clinton delivered a public speech in which he included the statement, "I do not intend to put our troops in Kosovo to fight a war." The Americans were committed only in a limited way to fighting the cause in Kosovo.

Intervention Action. On March 24, 1999, air strikes against Yugoslavia began. Although it had been expected that Milosevic would back down and sign the Rambouillet Accords after a few days of aerial attacks (as had been the case prior to the cease-fire in Bosnia leading to the Dayton Accords), this did not happen. Rather, Serb forces managed to continue and intensify their war against the KLA and civilian population in Kosovo. The NATO intervention did not avert humanitarian catastrophe. With no ground troops to hinder it, the Milosevic regime used army, police, and paramilitary units to launch campaigns of terror and killings. Refugees fleeing from Kosovo, standing in long chains, made a human barrier against effective NATO air attacks. Refugees also saw the Serb onslaught against them as a direct consequence of the NATO action. Almost one million Albanians were forced from their homes; many were massacred, raped, and tortured. Eight hundred thousand refugees flowed into neighboring countries. Ten thousand Albanians died. The bombing of Serbia continued for almost three months, until June 10. Yugoslavia as a whole, in particular Serbia proper, suffered heavy damage: roads, bridges, industry, and the communication system. The Yugoslav army in Kosovo was not seriously damaged. In the last two weeks before the settlement of early June, NATO began to signal the prospect of a ground operation (in late May, NATO ambassadors improved a plan KFOR-Plus, increasing the projected size of KFOR to 50,000 troops, and the U.S. government had decided to widen the road in Albania along the Kosovo border, conveying that the invasion option was getting serious. These developments influenced ongoing negotiations with Milosevic (Roberts, 1999: 118).

The intervention via a bombing campaign against Yugoslavia over Kosovo was the first sustained use of armed force by the NATO alliance in its 50-year existence. It was undertaken without UN Security Council authorization, and was the first major bombing campaign intended to halt crimes against humanity being committed by a state within its own border. During the NATO campaign, allied pilots flew more than 37,000 sorties, including about 14,000 strike missions.

Intervention Outcome. With Russian mediation assistance, the war was eventually brought to an end; the NATO Secretary-General agreed to suspend the bombing campaign after receiving evidence that Serb forces were withdrawing from northern Kosovo. A UN-led peacekeeping mission established a de facto protectorate in Kosovo, supported by a military presence. NATO deployed the Kosovo Peacekeeping force–KFOR—to reestablish stability and security for the inhabitants of Kosovo during the summer. Refugees returned home, the KLA had been officially disarmed (but not removed from local power and influence) ethnic tensions in Kosovo remained high, and peace was fragile, dependent on extensive outside presence (see Table 5.6).

INTERVENTION IN ISLAMIC REGIONS

Persian Gulf

Triggering Event. Iraqi troops invade and occupy Kuwait on August 2, 1990.

UN Peacekeeping Forces. United Nations Iraq-Kuwait Observer Mission (UNIKOM) created in April 1991 post conflict with about 1,100 troops, following the withdrawal of Iraqi forces from Kuwait, to monitor the demilitarized zone along the border between the two countries, deter border violations and report on hostile action.

Table 5.6
Kosovo Intervention Summary

Cause of the conflict	Civil conflict issue. Social structure, regime leadership in Yugoslavia.
Level of U.S. national interest	Low/medium (after commitment to Bosnian peace, and role in NATO alliance to preserve NATO credibility).
Intervention characteristics	Overwhelming air power, no ground troops, clear objectives.
Public opinion	Congress considered a bill opposing any deployment of ground forces in Kosovo for peacemaking or peacekeeping purposes in February 1999.
Role of United Nations	Intervention was not approved by UN Security Council.
Intervention outcome	Mixed, mission achieved, no exit for KFOR. Did the bombing exacerbate the ethnic cleansing?

U.S. Intervention. Multilateral action (U.S.-led 20+ countries in a coalition), peak strength about U.S. 540,000 within a total force of about 800,000 troops. Operation Desert Shield began on August 7, 1990, when troops were dispatched to Saudi Arabia; Operation Desert Storm, the attack on Iraq, began January 16, 1991.

Mission Objective. To restore and protect worldwide access to Middle East oil resources, to free Kuwait from occupying Iraqi forces, to stabilize security for Saudi Arabia.

Domestic Situation. The Iraqi-Kuwaiti border had been a focus of tension before. In 1961, Britain granted Kuwait independence, and Iraq revived an old claim that Kuwait had been governed as part of an Ottoman province in southern Iraq and was therefore rightfully Iraq's. The claim was not recognized; Iraq recognized Kuwait in 1963. Nonetheless, there were occasional clashes along the border between them. Kuwait assisted Iraq with loans and diplomatic backing during the Iran-Iraq war. The Iran-Iraq conflict ended in a stalemate in 1988 following eight years of fighting, which had a severe impact on the Iraqi economy. The country was deeply in debt and demanded that Kuwait forgive its share of the debt and help with other payments.

In the summer of 1990, the Organization of Petroleum Exporting Countries (OPEC) decided to reduce the price of oil. Saddam argued against this policy, for he needed the money to restore economic conditions of Iraq. Unemployment was high, soldiers would need to be demobilized from the war service against Iran. He began to deploy troops along the Kuwaiti border in July. Several Arab states tried to mediate the dispute, convincing the parties to negotiate their differences. On August 2, 1990, about 150,000 Iraqi troops invaded Kuwait, quickly occupying the entire country and installing a puppet government. Additional Iraqi troops moved towards the Saudi Arabian border.

U.S. Policy. The Middle East is considered a region of undisputed U.S. vital interests. The Carter Doctrine of the late 1970s identifies the continued flow of oil from the Persian Gulf as one of the paramount strategic interests of the United States, to be defended with U.S. military forces if necessary. The doctrine provided the basis for the Reagan administration policy in 1987 of reflagging Kuwaiti oil tankers in the Gulf.

How the United States and the West reacted to Iraq's invasion of Kuwait would have a significant impact upon the character of post–Cold War international relations. Iraq's invasion and occupation of Kuwait was an attack on the core principles of international order. The strategy was to start with diplomatic pressure, and then add economic pressure, then military pressure. Immediately following the invasion, the United States made several decisions. First, the United States decided to involve the United Nations, getting the Security Council to denounce Iraqi actions and impose immediate sanctions. U.S. Ambassador to the United Nations Thomas Pickering was asked to draft a resolution, enacted on August 2 as Resolution 660 by a vote of 14–0 with Yemen abstaining. Resolution 660 condemned the invasion, demanded Iraq's immediate, unconditional withdrawal, called for negotiations between Iraq and Kuwait, and reserved the option of taking further steps to ensure compliance. Second, the United States decided to involve the Soviet Union, to demonstrate a partnership, making it impossible for Saddam to hide behind a possible superpower split. On August 3, U.S. Secretary of State James Baker and Eduard Shevardnadze, U.S.S.R. Foreign Minister, standing before a group of reporters in Moscow, announced an unusual step; "jointly calling upon the rest of the international community to join with us in an international cutoff of all arms supplies to Iraq" (quoted in Beschloss and Talbott, 1993: 248). This was formalized in another Security Council resolution four days later, setting trade and military sanctions on Iraq. At a meeting of the U.S. National Security Council on August 4, 1990, President George H. W. Bush decided the first imperative was to deter an Iraqi movement into Saudi Arabia and to pursue coercive diplomacy against Saddam Hussein. As Lawrence Eagleburger warned, if the aggression were allowed to stand it would send the wrong message: it would tell rogue dictators of the world, the Muammer Quaddafis and the Kim Il Sungs, that with the removal of one of the two superpowers, "pipsqueaks like Saddam Hussein can do more rather than less because they aren't constrained by their Big Brother" (quoted in Beschloss and Talbott, 1993: 249). At the end of the day, Bush had resolved to send 20,000 American troops to Saudi Arabia, providing the Saudis agreed. They granted approval by August 6, and on August 8, 1990, President Bush made a public announcement that U.S. forces would be deployed to the country. In addition, there were more immediate concerns relating to energy interests and the well-being of America's traditional friends in the Middle East.

Intervention Action. Within a week of the Kuwaiti takeover, and continuing for several months, a large international force gathered in Saudi Arabia. In November, forces sent to the region were substantially increased. Secretary of State Baker assembled a multinational coalition of forces—from NATO countries to Arab states—to join in Desert Shield. The United States sent more than 400,000 troops; 200,000 others came from an array of countries; Japan and Germany gave substantial financial support. A UN deadline of Iraqi withdrawal from Kuwait had been set for January 15, 1991. When that date passed, the vast majority of coalition members joined in the decision to attack Iraq, which began early on January 17.

For the first three months of the Gulf crisis, while the United States shipped more than a quarter of a million troops to the Persian Gulf, Secretary of State Baker testified before the Senate Foreign Relations Committee that the administration would consult with Congress if military action were called for but did not feel obliged to get advance approval. Congress held hearings in late November and early December on the advisability of waging war or giving the UN-imposed economic sanctions more time to work. No vote was called. Should Congress authorize the president to take the nation into war pursuant to the United Nations' all-necessary-means resolution? On January 12, the vote was cast: in the Senate, 52 voted in favor, 47 against; in the House of Representatives, 250 yes and 183 no votes were tallied. Some members raised the question whether it was too late to pull the rug out from the expectations of the UN partners and the expectations of the president. Troops were deployed; it would be awkward for them to come home without firing a shot.

The United States showed an eagerness to see the United Nations as a preferred venue through which it would conduct U.S. foreign policy, working to build and sustain Security Council support for an international response to Iraq's invasion and annexation of Kuwait. President Bush, addressing the General Assembly on Oct 1, 1990, said: "The world must know and understand: from this hour, from this day, from this hall, we step forth with a new sense of purpose, a new sense of possibilities. We stand together, prepared to swim upstream, to march uphill, to tackle the tough challenges as they come—not only as the UN but as the nations of the world united....The United Nations is now fulfilling its promise as the world's parliament of peace." For roughly a month prior to adoption of Resolution 678, on November 29, 1990, which would legitimize the use of force by the coalition, Bush, Baker, and UN Ambassador Pickering worked to secure support for the resolution, striving for particular wording to avoid a veto by any of the five permanent members of the Security Council, and to get the support of most, if not all, of the nonpermanent members, to show international unity in their policy-thinking. The final vote for Resolution 678 was twelve in favor, two opposed (Cuba and Yemen), and one abstention (China).

Was the United States merely using the United Nations as an instrument of its own foreign policy, and overwhelming the Security Council with high-pressure tactics? Eleven resolutions specifically concerning the situation in the Gulf had been adopted before Resolution 678 was approved. Only three votes were cast against all of those resolutions, two in Resolution 666 on September 13, 1990, and one of Resolution 670 on September 26 (Cuba and Yemen). No other state either opposed or abstained on any of these resolutions (Gregg, 1993: 111). "The real problem was that leadership turned into headship, where decisions for the group were arrived at unilaterally by a leader whose overwhelming power ensured that subordinates would have few other options than to comply. The leader's preferences quickly became the group's by default, not by consensus. For no member of the coalition was in any position to resist the overwhelming inertial force of Washington's decision-making once it started to roll," states Gregg (p. 113).

When Congress debated the issue, both the administration and congressional supporters of a joint resolution authorizing the use of U.S. military force in the Gulf crises were able to invoke Security council Resolution 678 as a principal rationale for their position. Those who favored authorizing the use of U.S. military force were able to wrap themselves in the UN flag, says Gregg (1993: 117). The Joint Congressional Resolution adopted on January 12, 1991, makes no fewer than five references to the United Nations, and twice links the resolution to Security Council Resolution 678. Operation Desert Storm was launched on January 16, 1991, with an air war. After six weeks of fighting, the coalition initiated a ground campaign in late February, which lasted only a hundred hours.

Intervention Outcome. Successful. By the end of February 1991, Kuwait was liberated, Iraqi armed forces and support establishment decimated. Iraq sustained between 20,000 and 35,000 casualties. Coalition losses were less than 250. The majority were Americans. Saddam Hussein remained in power for more than a decade after the conflict, continuously defied attempts by UN weapons inspectors to carry out their tasks within Iraq, sanctions against the country remained in place, and efforts by the United States and some of its allies to force a successful rebellion against his rule by the Kurdish population in Northern Iraq were not successful. In Kuwait, the prewar regime was restored. Whether the operation can be as counted as complete success is debated by those who judge that the operation should have pursued the war into Baghdad to depose Saddam Hussein to remove his destabilizing presence from the region.

By driving Iraq from Kuwait, the United States achieved its major objectives of countering aggression, securing the independence of Kuwait, restoring a critical level of security to the gulf States, and protecting U.S. citizens. In his address announcing the liberation of Kuwait, President Bush said, "this is a victory for the United Nations, for all mankind, for the rule of law, and for what is right." As Gregg (1993: 135) put it: the president's invocation of a new world order reflected the view that the United Nations would be more important, both in U.S. foreign policy and in global management generally. Less than two years later, the excitement generated by Operation Desert Storm had vanished as had the energy for leadership on behalf of a new world order; Bush was voted out of office (see Table 5.7).

Table 5.7
Persian Gulf Intervention Summary

Cause of the conflict	International issue. Iraq invades and occupies Kuwait, a sovereign state.
Level of U.S. national interest	High (access to oil reserves and flow).
Intervention characteristics	Overwhelming force, clear objectives, quick exit. Multilateral.
Public opinion	Congress supported the President to take the nation to war on a January 12 vote: Senate 52 yes, 47 no; House: 250 yes, 183 no.
Role of United Nations	Intervention approved by UN Security Council beforehand.
Intervention outcome	Successful. Mission achieved.

Afghanistan

Triggering Event. Acts of terrorism against the United States by hijacked airliner crashes in New York at the World Trade Center, in Washington, D.C. at the Pentagon, and in a Pennsylvania field led by members of Osama bin Laden's organization, Al Qaida, headquartered in Afghanistan, on September 11, 2001.

UN Peacekeeping Forces. An International Security Assistance Force authorized in December 2001. United Nations Assistance Mission in Afghanistan (UNAMA) established by UN Security Council March 28, 2002, for nation-building.

U.S. Intervention. U.S. and British forces launched air strikes against targets in Afghanistan beginning on October 7, 2001. Ground troops, roughly 5,000, arrived later. The military action was a coalition effort of mostly NATO countries.

Mission Objective. To locate and destroy the terrorism training groups operated by Osama bin Laden and his organization, Al Qaida, from Afghanistan; to punish the Taliban government for supporting terrorism.

Domestic Situation. Afghanistan has never had national unity. Britain attempted to annex the country during the nineteenth century to protect its Indian empire from Russia, resulting in several wars with the local inhabitants. The last conflict ended with British defeat in 1921. Afghanistan was declared a monarchy in 1926; its king was overthrown in 1973 by a military coup led by pro-Soviet Daoud Khan, his own relative, with the cooperation of some elements of the Afghan Communist party; the republic of Afghanistan was established with strong ties to the Soviet Union. Deposed King Zahir Shah lived in exile in Italy until early spring 2002, when he returned to the country under heavy security to help set up a new government. He was stabbed after arriving, though it was not fatal. In 1978, Daoud Khan was killed in a communist coup. He had begun to move away from the Parcham (one wing of the communist party) and take a more centrist position. The new Marxist regime proclaimed independence from Soviet influence and declared its policies to be based on Islamic principles and Afghan nationalism. A lot of opposition developed. In June, the Mujahadeen guerrilla movement was formed in response to the new government, pledging a holy war. The Soviet Union invaded on December 24, 1979, to bolster the faltering communist regime, in response to a government request. By early 1980, the Mujahadeen rebels had united against Soviet invaders and the USSR-backed Afghan army. Many Afghan citizens fled from the war into Pakistan—nearly three million; another 1.5 million sought refuge in Iran. The guerrillas—supported by arms shipments from the United States, Britain, and China (smuggled through Pakistan)—gained control over rural areas, while Soviet troops held urban centers. Osama bin Laden, a wealthy Saudi Arabian, was part of the Mujahadeen guerrilla movement. By the mid-1980s he had moved to Afghanistan and worked to recruit Islamic soldiers from around the world to join the conflict. This organizational effort later led to the creation of Al Qaida, an international network of fighters..

The conflict in Afghanistan continued until 1988, the Soviet Union's involvement often described as a "quagmire" parallel to the United States' long intervention in Vietnam. The Soviets were unable to defeat local forces. When the war ended, the United States, Pakistan, Afghanistan, and the Soviet Union signed peace accords in Geneva guaranteeing Afghan independence and the withdrawal of 100,000 Soviet troops. Following the withdrawal, the Mujahadeen continued their resistance against the Soviet-backed regime of communist president Najibullah, who was ousted from power in 1992 when an Islamic state was formed. Various rebel groups fought one another for control. Thousands were killed and in Kabul, the capital, one-third of the city had been reduced to rubble by 1995.

In 1996, a newly formed Islamic militia, the fundamentalist Taliban, seized control of Kabul in September and rose to power on promises of peace. Within two years, they took control of nearly all of the country. They cracked down on crime, outlawed cultivation of poppies for the opium trade, stopped the education and employment opportunities for women. Islamic law was enforced rigidly, including public executions and amputations. The Taliban regime imposed harsh rule, engaging in numerous human rights abuses, and isolated itself from the rest of the world; just a handful of states recognized it. Najibullah was publicly executed in 1997 by the Taliban. In the last half of the nineties, continuing drought devastated farming, making many rural areas uninhabitable. Another one million Afghans fled to Pakistan to live in refugee camps. Afghanis live in dire poverty, in a landlocked country with rugged mountains. Afghanistan still leads the world in opium trade, over half of the labor force is in agriculture, and much of the area is covered by several million land mines.

Osama bin Laden, leader of Al Qaida, had returned home after the USSR departure from Afghanistan. He was expelled from Saudi Arabia in 1991 and moved to Sudan, where he was also expelled. Returning to Afghanistan in 1994, he was given sanctuary in 1996, sheltered by the Taliban. From this base, he built a worldwide network of terrorism and terrorist training camps. In 1998, he called for all Americans to be killed.

U.S. Policy. The central link to Afghanistan is due to the relationship between the United States and the violent Islamic movement that has developed there, which started during the Cold War in the 1980s. At the time, the United States backed the Mujahadeen, leaders of the jihad, and was a cosigner to the 1988 peace treaty. That was before the Iraqi invasion into Kuwait and intervention by U.S. forces into Saudi Arabia in great numbers. Bin Laden was incensed that nonbelievers (American soldiers) were stationed in the birthplace of Islam, and he also charged the Saudi regime with deviating from true Islam. (Several thousand troops have stayed on in the country since the Gulf War in 1991, protecting the Saudi regime.)

In August 1998, U.S. cruise missiles struck a terrorist training complex in Afghanistan believed to have been financed by Osama bin Laden. American officials asked for his deportation, for they believed bin Laden was involved in the bombing of the U.S. embassies in Kenya and Tanzania that killed more than 200 people a few weeks earlier. The Taliban refused to extradite him. The United Nations passed two resolutions in 1999 and 2000 demanding that the Taliban cease their support for terrorism and hand over bin Laden for trial. The United States suspected that Osama bin Laden was involved with other attacks against America: the 1996 Khobar military complex in Saudi Arabia that left nineteen U.S. soldiers dead, and the 2000 bombing of the USS *Cole* while it was docked in Yemen.

On September 11, 2001, hijackers commandeered four commercial airplanes in the United States and crashed them into the World Trade Center in New York, the Pentagon in Washington, D.C., and a Pennsylvania field, killing more than 3,000 people. A few days later, American officials declared that Osama bin Laden was the prime suspect in the attack. Policy-makers demanded that the Taliban turn over bin Laden. They refused.

Intervention Action. The Senate passed a resolution authorizing the use of military force on September 14; the vote was 98–0. The next day, the House of Representatives passed a similar measure: 420–1. On October 7, 2001, following unanswered demands that the Taliban surrender Osama bin Laden, U.S. and British forces launched air strikes against targets in Afghanistan. U.S. war planes started to bomb Taliban targets and bases reportedly belonging to the Al Qaida network. On November 13, Afghanistan's Northern Alliance faction, fighting alongside the U.S. forces, entered Kabul, Afghanistan's capital, and the Taliban fled. Some were captured, but most leaders escaped. On December 22, 2001, a provisional government with Hamit Karzai as chairman started running the country for a six-month provisional period. On March 2, 2002, Operation Anaconda started, the largest land campaign of the war, which included 2,000 allied forces, led by 900 U.S. special forces.

Intervention Outcome. The Taliban were defeated, refugees living in Pakistan are returning to Afghanistan, sanctions were lifted, and a new government formed, based on semidemocratic principles. International peacekeeping forces arrived in the capital, at peak around 5,000 troops. The United States pledged more than $300 million worth of humanitarian assistance to rebuild the country. U.S. soldiers continued to occupy the country. Fighting between warlord-controlled groups did not cease. Former King Zahir Shah, returning to Afghanistan to help set up a new government after nearly 30 years in exile, was stabbed, though not fatally. Osama bin Laden remained at large. Counterterrorism measures have been set up to protect Americans via the "homeland security" concept, with substantial public expenditure and a series of complex screening techniques designed to deter the enemy, yet fear of the terrorism network is ever present (see Table 5.8).

Table 5.8
Afghanistan Intervention Summary

Cause of the conflict	International issue. Al Qaida, an independent group, headquartered with sanctuary in Afghanistan, attacks the United States.
Level of U.S. national interest	High, direct attack on American homeland.
Intervention characteristics	Limited force, gradual response.
Public opinion	Congress supported the President to take the nation to war September 14, 2001; November 16, support for efforts in Afghanistan.
Role of United Nations	Intervention approved by UN Security Council beforehand.
Intervention outcome	Partially successful. Afghanistan government ousted, Al Qaida headquarters reduced, bin Laden escapes. Al Qaida attacks continue.

SUMMARY

How might we generalize about these U.S. intervention cases? Which of these interventions looks like an entirely new venture? Which ones illustrate continuation patterns of U.S. behavior of the Cold War period? How were various intervention cases linked together? To begin a comparison, selected intervention characteristics of the eight cases are arrayed in Table 5.9.

Table 5.9
Characteristics of Selected U.S. Interventions: Vietnam and Post–Cold War Cases, 1989–2001

Case Intervention Starts	Vietnam 1960s	Panama 1989	Gulf 1990	Somalia 1992	Rwanda 1994	Haiti 1994	Bosnia 1995	Kosovo 1999	Afghanistan 2001
National interest	disputed	high	high	medium	low	medium	low/medium	low/medium	high
Issues	communism	leadership	oil	anarchy	genocide	leadership	leadership/ genocide	leadership/ genocide	terrorism
Conflict-solving intervention	yes	yes	yes	no	no	yes	yes	yes	yes
Humanitarian intervention	no	no	no	yes	yes	yes	yes	yes/no	yes/no
Multilateral coalition force	no	no	yes	yes	yes	yes	yes	yes	no
UN intervention approval	no	no	yes	yes	yes	yes	yes	no	yes
Overwhelming ground combat troops	yes	yes	yes	no	no	yes	no	no	no
Intervene during conflict	yes	yes	yes	yes	no	no	no	yes	yes
Intervene after conflict	no	no	no	no	yes	yes	yes	yes	yes
Mission under one year	no	yes	no	no	yes	yes	no	no	no

Intervention data on U.S. policy in Vietnam have been included in the table for points of reference in order to evaluate whether lessons learned from participation in that conflict were applied to the post–Cold War situations. Cases are arranged chronologically in order to highlight the introduction of new factors, new strategies, and their longevity. When put together, the record of recent intervention illustrates the following: (1) the United States has intervened in situations where its perceived level of national interest was low; (2) the United States has intervened for a variety of reasons—oil, terrorism, humanitarian assistance—but one factor seems to stand out: bad leadership in the target state; (3) the United States has increasingly used a multilateral force strategy, putting together a coalition of forces, where Americans provide the majority of troops and weaponry and usually direct the operations; (4) the United States has engaged the United Nations in its decision-making on intervention choices—seeing approval via Security Council Resolutions to undertake a mission ("all necessary force") on many occasions, though not all; (5) the United States has followed the Weinberger doctrine of overwhelming force in some intervention instances, though not consistently—it was more true of the first Bush administration; (6) the United States has not always succeeded in its mission, nor have interventions been effectively managed within 12 months. The picture emerging from the U.S. intervention record during this period is notable for its variety and wide range, not for its patterned design. True, the situations were quite different, and three presidents have participated in the intervention decision-making process. There seems to be some relationship between pairs of interventions in certain geographic regions: the Somalia experience played a role in the discussion and decision about reaction to events in Rwanda; Bosnia and Kosovo are linked where slow action in the first case may have influenced speedier action in the second. Panama and Haiti, though both tied to leadership considerations, show very little connection in intervention operations.

Clinton's foreign policy was based on the idea that a world filled with liberal democracies would be one in which everyone could feel secure. Paradoxically, America's own liberalism can make it difficult for the United States to be an effective champion for the promotion of human rights and democracy abroad, argues Peceny (2000: 11). Clinton hesitated before engaging in military interventions that involved the threat of American casualties, sending troops when he was relatively certain those troops would not face combat. The contradictory nature of a liberal intervention principle is this: it encourages intervention in situations where no concrete national security interests exist yet allows strategies that may not be appropriate to the task, emphasizing low risk and low cost but not necessarily matching intervention policies to the actual need requirements. In turn, this pattern damages America's national security interests by tarnishing its reputation as effective leader. Still, if civil wars in peripheral areas are not central to American national interests, public pressure helps remind decision-makers that they should not pay high costs in such conflicts.

Among the interregnum intervention wars, most of them, and most interventions conducted through this period, did not threaten the overall conditions of security of the international system. However, if this trend continues and these types of conflicts become the principal form of contemporary systemic violence, controlling and solving them are likely to be more important, more challenging, and more threatening. This type of conflict is solvable only by long-term, highly committed efforts. The dilemma for intervention is this: such action may be necessary to stop the killing and alleviate the worst situations created by the conflict (starvation, refugee flows), but attacking the underlying causes may take a lot of time which may alienate indigenous peoples who may benefit from a disordered, repressive environment. The longer an intervention continues, the more likely it will become unpopular, the greater the probability for significant dissatisfaction, a chance the affected groups may turn to violent means, including acts of terrorism to oust the intervener. Intervention designed to help may effectively hurt in the end. Long-term intervention, including troop deployment for international peace and security, as is the stated policy for the U.S. presence in the Middle East, may fuel opposition forces among the local constituency. Intervention may breed terrorism, as the link American intervention in Afghanistan shows. By far, the attack on American soil in September 2001 and its ties to an interventionism policy has the most sobering consequences. Whether this situation is an aberration or points to a new norm is hard to say, though it is clearly necessary to rethink traditional notions of security and innovative ways for the international community to respond to violence. Is the U.S. intervention response pattern of the nineties and beyond temporary? The variety of intervention instances coupled with the superpower global obligations and the unipolar world structure means that intervening to achieve foreign policy goals will continue to operate, and most important, that intervention is unlikely to become either less visible or less significant within international politics.

On this point, it is useful to consider a comparison of the four national interest doctrinal proposals from the year 2000 (discussed in Chapter 4) with attendant criteria for U.S. engagement abroad. The eight cases of post–Cold War intervention are evaluated within these parameters, using rough estimations of intervention choices based on the national interests categories of each proposal (see Table 5.10). What becomes clear is that each proposal, if followed, would have led to different intervention choices. Under "Preventive Defense" the United States would have intervened only in the Persian Gulf and in Afghanistan, in both cases managing international security threats of global proportion. This is followed by the National Interest group, where three of the eight cases of intervention would have been advised—namely, the three cases of international threats, and none of the civil conflicts. The White House document on National Security would have led to seven interventions of the eight cases, predicting, naturally, the precise response of the Clinton administration, but also correct response by both Bush administrations. Finally, the bipartisan commission on national security would have been relatively close in line with the White House document. The differences highlight how contested the national interest concept remains, how it leads to a vastly different plan of U.S. military intervention in the post–Cold War age, and whether more or less intervention is advisable for the twenty-first century.

Table 5.10
Recent U.S. Foreign Policy Doctrine Proposals and Post–Cold War Interventions

	Preventive Defense	National Interest	National Strategy	White House	Agreement Level
A. International Conflict Issues. **Would doctrine guidelines encourage intervention?**					
Persian Gulf	yes	yes	yes	yes	unanimous
Afghanistan	yes	yes	yes	yes	unanimous
Panama	no	yes	yes	yes	3–1
B. Civil Conflict Issues. **Would doctrine guidelines encourage intervention?**					
Bosnia	no	no	yes	yes	2–2
Kosovo	no	no	yes	yes	2–2
Somalia	no	no	no	yes	1–3
Haiti	no	no	no	yes	1–3
Rwanda	no	no	yes	no	1–3
Favor Intervention Ratio:					
	2–6	3–5	6–2	7–1	

6

American Intervention:
Evolving Opportunities

INTRODUCTION

The ability of regimes to protect individuals and maintain order within a society is defined by a complex relationship among governmental control, legitimacy, security, and conflict regulation processes. In some countries, the mechanism weakens—when repressive, corrupt leaders meet the increasing power of insurgent groups seeking change, for example—eventually breaking down; conflict escalates into organized violence and spreads throughout the state. With growing fears and rising insecurity, economic conditions deteriorate, institutional services collapse, the diplomatic and foreign business communities evacuate or reduce their presence significantly, and the population flees. A mass exodus creates refugee problems in neighboring areas. At that point, parties to the conflict may request outside assistance: calls originating from the government, or from the rebels (either of whom may be seeking to augment battle strength with military aid, or hoping to get the attention of diplomats in order to negotiate a cease-fire truce) or from the refugees in need of humanitarian help (shelter, food, medicine) mark a threshold defining civil conflict as intervention opportunity.

How do third parties respond to an intervention opportunity? The level of security threat interpreted by policy-makers plays an important role in this respect. Whether outside states decide to become involved unilaterally or as part of a multilateral mission—by participating in combat to help bring a conflict to conclusion or by participating in peace enforcement or peacekeeping to help restore domestic order—will be determined by two lines of security assessment in the international community: (1) what significance is attached to civil unrest within a given context, specifically, the potential for conflict spread and escalation and likely threats to international security, and (2) what are the main sources of the conflict that intervention may bring under control.

Intervention opportunity criteria for identifying events likely to be perceived as sufficiently threatening to the United States to cause the president to consider using military action as a policy option were developed by Ostrom and Job (1986) and Meernik (1994). They include situations involving a perceived current threat to the territorial security of the United States, its current allies, major clients or proxy states; situations posing a danger to the U.S. government, military, or diplomatic personnel, to a significant number of American citizens, or to U.S. assets; events perceived as likely to lead to losses of U.S. influence in regions perceived as within the U.S. sphere of influence (especially in Central and South America); and events involving interstate military conflict of potential consequence, in human and strategic terms, or events, because of civil disorder, threatening destruction of a substantial number of persons.

Analyzing civil unrest from two distinct perspectives, general abstract dimensions and specific manifestations—that is, the prevailing assumptions and dominant beliefs about deeply rooted causes of internal disruption in developing societies, and also the proximate, immediate catalysts of a domestic conflict— becomes important in evaluating an intervention opportunity, affecting policy debate and decision over intervention strategies to stop violence or reduce tensions between combatants, and fundamentally, perspectives on civil conflict causes take on greater significance when long-term consequences of intervention are discussed. The persistence of inherited ways of understanding organized violence within countries limits our view to thinking about current conflict as disorganized, as a form of anarchy, where at best, interveners may try to ameliorate symptoms, argues Mary Kaldor (1999: 14). This approach falls short of constructing a basis for bringing about major social change, taking steps toward greater stability and security.

To understand the nature of contemporary civil conflict and, through intervention, its linkage to global politics is a critical issue of international relations today. Some analysts see post–Cold War instability as a different kind of war than what occurred in the past. Donald M. Snow (1996) labels contemporary internal conflicts "uncivil wars," owing to their more violent, anarchistic nature. Michael Ignatieff (1997) believes the new warriors are paramilitaries, guerrillas, militias, and warlords who are tearing up the failed states of the 1990s. Kaldor (1999) writes about "new wars" as identity politics fought in a context of globalization by a range of organized groups such as criminal gangs, mercenary soldiers, regular armies, and breakaway units from those armies. War experience causes trauma with paralyzing effects, negatively impacting the strength, energy, and will for reconciliation; wars also change local authority mechanisms and the role of significant social groups—shifting power alliances, challenging traditional bases of legitimacy, and repositioning variables of governance.

Intervention is intended to restore peace, promote reconciliation, and if possible, set in place mechanisms to prevent future conflicts. At the start, humanitarian efforts associated with the provision of food and medical assistance or help to noncombatants or the wounded become very important. War is regarded as an emergency requiring disaster relief. During these emergencies illegal economic activities develop, enriching the armed paramilitary units and their connected political elites. Private organized units often conduct violence; the national monopoly of legitimate armed force is eroded.

How does the picture of civil unrest in the post–Cold War period match patterns from the past? How will current patterns of domestic conflict affect the probability of military intervention in the future? In order to build a profile of post–Cold War civil conflict, two steps are necessary. First, to determine whether domestic instability is more widespread and more deadly than in the past, a longer time horizon on civil wars will offer some perspective. Several research studies have explored the problem, charting civil violence growth over time. Second, current theories and research results on civil conflict causes are examined in search of support or refutation of the popular wisdom surrounding the ideas of new wars. The analysis will help answer two central questions, namely, how civil conflict becomes intervention opportunity and, when opportunity is transformed into intervention action, how it shapes the global environment.

GLOBAL TRENDS IN CIVIL WAR

Various waves of state fragmentation occurred over the course of the twentieth century. The first movement accompanied the breakup of the Austro-Hungarian and Ottoman empires at the end of World War I. The second wave was triggered by the dissolution of the great empires after World War II and the ensuing decolonialization process. The third process in this direction, occurring in the early 1990s, came as the Communist empire collapsed in the Soviet Union and Eastern Europe. Much of the civil violence in recent years has been an outgrowth of this transformation. Some scholars have suggested that the end of the Cold War brought an upswing in intrastate conflict (Regan, 1996, 344–345), although others have disputed the existence of a general trend (Gurr, 1994; Wallensteen and Sollenberg, 1995). James Fearon and David Laitin (2001:1) say flatly that the prevalence of civil wars in the post–Cold War world is not due to the effects of the end of the Cold War, nor is it the result of civil wars breaking out in a steadily increasing rate over the period, but a steady, almost linear accumulation of unresolved conflicts since 1945. It would be wrong to imagine that an endless stream of ethnic groups will be vying for statehood in the coming years, says David Callahan (1997: 8).

For an accounting of the frequency and magnitude of civil conflict trends, the Correlates of War data base tracks several classes of war throughout the international system, recording war incidence from 1816 up to the present. An updated typology replaces the original term civil war with intrastate war, where intra-state war is defined as: sustained hostilities (at least 1,000 battle deaths for every year of the conflict) between or among two or more groups within the internationally recognized territory of the state (including civil wars, which involve the state government on one side) who vie for control of the central government or engage in conflict over local issues— issues of governmental change, independence, or regional autonomy (Sarkees and Singer, 2001: 9–10).

The data collected from 1816 through 1997 show 79 interstate wars and 214 intrastate wars. There have been more wars in the twentieth century; intrastate wars have occurred at a rate of 11 or more per decade over the last half-century. And, between 1990 and 1997, 24 new civil conflicts began. The majority were in Africa. The frequency trend indicates a greater number of civil wars have begun in the current age than during most decades of the Cold War era. Significantly greater fatalities have resulted from intrastate wars in the last four decades of the twentieth century, a trend continuing into the post–Cold War period, with between 1.6 million and 4.5 million deaths due to violence during each decade from 1960 forward (Sarkees and Singer, 2001: Appendix).

The trend in these data is pretty clear: a significant increase and continuous high level of intrastate wars over the last 50 years, a proportionately smaller number of international wars (in spite of the expanding number of nation-states since World War II), and hundreds of thousands of deaths due to civil violence. In the brief post Cold–War period, there is no real increase in the intrastate war phenomenon. The ratio of independent states to the number of civil wars reflects a similar situation as that in the past—there are more intrastate wars, but there are also many more independent states raising the possibility of greater numbers of states involved in domestic conflict. The percentage of total war deaths per thousand population in relation to the total international system population is decidedly down; conflict is actually less deadly (see Table 6.1). However, if the creation of smaller and smaller independent units should be an indicator of conflict *reduction* (if we cannot get along let's separate), then the figure is disturbing.

Sarkees and Singer (2001: 17) point out that of the 214 intrastate wars since 1816, only 42, around 20%, were "internationalized" by the intervention of outside states. In the period prior to 1960, 16 or 12% of the 129 intrastate wars were internationalized, which rose to 26 or about 31% of the 85 intrastate wars in the post-1960 time frame.

Post–World War II trends in civil conflict, covering 1945–1996, are examined by William Ayres (2000), who looks at conflicts involving nationalist aspirations—groups of people holding a primary identity who have a history of violence, who think their group can and should have a sovereign state (Ayres, 2000: 107). He includes cases falling below the threshold of 1,000 battle deaths per year; his data consist of 77 conflict episodes. The distribution of starting and ending years for violent intrastate conflicts is presented in Table 6.2.

Conflict episodes start in "waves," says Ayres. Of the 77 conflicts, 36% occurred in states that had either gained their independence in the past five years or were in places about to undergo separation (e.g., the Soviet Union in 1990). But these data also show that nationalist conflict is not solely a product of the end of the Cold War. While the post–Cold War period has seen a number of conflicts, about half of which are attributable to the collapse of Soviet communism, several earlier periods have been equally conflictual.

Has the end of the Cold War changed the intensity of conflict? Dividing the cases into those beginning in 1989 or after (N=18) and those beginning prior to 1989 (N=59), Ayres (2000: 114) discovered that neither fighting intensity, total

Table 6.1
States and Civil Wars: Cold War and Post–Cold War Decades

Decade	States in International System (mid-decade)	International System Population (in thousands mid-decade)	Civil Wars	War Deaths
1950–1959	84	2,525,534	11	158,900*
1960–1969	124	3,268,202	16	2,004,113
1970–1979	150	4,035,169	26	4,581,750
1980–1989	161	4,869,321	19	1,789,232
1990–1997	181	5,426,084	24	1,568,500

*Sarkees and Singer treat the Korean War as an international, not civil, conflict, which affects the fatality figure.

Source: Adapted from Sarkees and Singer (2001), Tables I, III, and IV.

deaths, deaths per month, nor deaths per 1,000 population showed any significant differences between Cold War and post–Cold War conflicts. These findings confirm that the post–Cold War period is not one of unchecked nationalist violence, Ayres concludes.

Do conflict endings have any particular post–Cold War pattern? While 22 conflict episodes *began* from 1985 to 1996, 25 episodes *ended* during the same period, far more endings per year than at any other time in the post–World War II period. Table 6.3 shows a significant relationship between time and type of ending: the absolute largest number of conflicts ended in the first seven years of the post–Cold War decade, including 11 by negotiated agreement, the same number that were negotiated during the 45 years of the Cold War. This suggests that the end of the Cold War, in addition to contributing some new nationalist conflicts, may have brought a wave of peacemaking by negotiation rather than military means.

Greater numbers of conflicts have not occurred in the post–Cold War era; many ongoing conflicts ended during the 1990s. The new age seems not as conflict prone as the earlier period. The picture from Ayres is similar to the sketch of Sarkees and Singer, although precise definitions of civil war varies, the numbers of civil conflict incidents differ, and the time periods, though they overlap, are not identical.

Table 6.2
Distribution of Civil Conflict Starts and Finishes: 1945–1996

Time	Conflict Starts	Total States	New States	Conflict Finish
1945–1949	16	78	13	5
1950–1954	0	83	5	7
1955–1959	5	90	7	1
1960–1964	9	122	32	3
1965–1969	7	133	12	0
1970–1974	1	143	10	6
1975–1979	8	155	12	1
1980–1984	8	161	6	2
1985–1989	8	161	0	5
1990–1996	14	181	20	20

Source: Reprinted by permission of Sage Publications Ltd. from William R. Ayres, "A World Flying Apart? Violent Nationalist Conflict and the End of the Cold War." *Journal of Peace Research* 37(2000): 114. Copyright © International Peace Research Institute (Oslo). PRIO. 2000.

Table 6.3
Type of Conflict Endings: 1945–1996

Time	Inaction	Defeat	Ceasefire	Agreement
Cold War 1945–1989 (45 years)	0	17	2	11
Post–Cold War 1990–1996 (7 years)	2	5	2	11

Source: Reprinted by permission of Sage Publications Ltd. from William R. Ayres, "A World Flying Apart? Violent Nationalist Conflict and the End of the Cold War." *Journal of Peace Research* 37(2000): 114. Copyright © International Peace Research Institute (Oslo). PRIO. 2000.

Peter Wallensteen and Margaret Sollenberg (2001: 629) report more detailed results in their analysis of the Stockholm International Peace Research Institute (SIPRI) data on post–Cold War conflict trends, differentiating major and minor instances on the level of battle-related deaths. They discovered that during the period 1989–2000, there were 111 armed conflicts in 74 locations around the world (see Table 6.4). All those listed had at least 25 battle-related deaths during any year. (For example, in year 2000, there were 9 such conflicts, in 1999 there were 10, and in 1989 there were 15 cases.) For intermediate armed conflicts— more than 1,000 battle-related deaths recorded during the course of the conflict, but fewer than 1,000 in any given year, there is a slight decline in the latter half of the 1990s decade. The trend for war in Table 6.4 shows a curvilinear pattern: civil conflict raged in a greater number of states during the early part of the post–Cold War era, then declined significantly, and rose again in the latter part of the nineties, down slightly in the year 2000. A combination of the intermediate armed conflict and war category shows that this group represents almost three-fourths of the armed conflict recorded in year 2000, and that when compared to the early years of the post–Cold War age, the numbers have decreased. *Major* armed conflicts have not dropped markedly, but episodes of *minor* conflicts have declined significantly. Of 24 major armed conflicts active in 2000 (categorized under "intermediate and "war" in Table 6.4), at least 17 date their origins to the period before 1989. Actors may now be quicker at ending smaller conflicts (often with the use of force) than in coming to grips with the larger and more complex conflicts, Wallensteen and Sollenberg suggest. Thus, the armed conflicts that remain on the list may be those that require more attention and more efforts on the part of the international community.

With respect to a pattern throughout the post–Cold War period, Table 6.5 indicates the number of intrastate wars was considerably higher in the first half-decade than afterward; the instances of foreign intervention have not changed much over the period 1989–2000, except for a high point in 1993, where four civil conflicts experienced intervention from the outside. From Table 6.6, in geographical dispersion, there were more armed conflicts in Europe and Asia in the first half-decade than in the latter part; the same pattern was true for the Middle East and also the Western Hemisphere; in Africa the pattern remained unchanged throughout the entire period. European conflicts were particularly high in 1993: 10 different, specific conflicts within European countries are identified in these data. (Many concerned ongoing conflict in the Balkans.) The basic picture in the dozen years after the Cold War is this: the conflict crescendo period ran from roughly 1989 to 1995: more states in more conflict. Afterward, things changed in a downward direction, though major disputes did continue.

Contrary to conventional wisdom, the number of internal wars did not increase markedly since the end of the Cold War except briefly in the early 1990s. Europe experienced greater growth than any other region in the number of internal conflicts. The emergence of weak states in the former Soviet republics (such as Azerbaijan, Armenia, and Georgia) and the start of civil war in former Yugoslavia largely account for this development. Still, the collapse of

Table 6.4
Armed Conflicts: 1989–2000

Level of Conflict	1989	1990	1991	1992	1993	1994	1995	1996	1997	1998	1999	2000	No. of Different Conflicts
Minor	15	16	18	23	15	16	12	17	13	10	10	9	50
Intermediate	14	14	13	12	17	19	17	13	14	13	13	12	12
War	18	19	20	20	14	7	6	6	7	14	14	12	49
All conflicts	47	49	51	55	46	42	35	36	34	37	37	33	111

Minor conflict: number of battle-related deaths during the course of the conflict is below 1,000.
Intermediate armed conflict: number of battle-related deaths recorded during the course of the conflict is greater than 1,000 but fewer than 1,000 in any given year.
War: number of battle-related deaths during the course of the conflict is greater than 1,000 in any given year.

Source: Wallensteen and Sollenberg (2001), p. 630.

Table 6.5
Civil and International Conflicts: 1989–2000

Type of Conflict	1989	1990	1991	1992	1993	1994	1995	1996	1997	1998	1999	2000	No. of Different Conflicts
Civil conflict	43	44	49	52	42	42	34	33	30	33	33	30	95
Civil with Intervention	1	2	1	2	4	0	0	1	3	2	2	1	9
International conflict	3	3	1	1	0	0	1	2	1	2	2	2	7
All conflicts	47	49	51	55	46	42	35	36	34	37	37	33	111

Source: Wallensteen and Sollenberg (2001), p. 632

155

Table 6.6
Number of Armed Conflicts by Region: 1989–2000

Year	Europe	Middle East	Asia	Africa	Americas
1989	2	4	19	14	8
1990	3	6	18	17	5
1991	6	7	16	17	5
1992	9	7	20	15	4
1993	10	7	15	11	3
1994	5	5	15	13	4
1995	5	4	13	9	4
1996	1	5	14	14	2
1997	0	3	15	15	2
1998	2	3	15	15	2
1999	3	2	14	16	2
2000	1	3	14	14	1

Source: Wallensteen and Sollenberg, p. 632.

the Soviet Union has enhanced only slightly a trend toward more domestic conflicts that has been in evidence since the 1960s. There is no evidence of an increase in the casualties from internal conflicts since the end of the Cold War, yet no one suggests that internal wars are becoming obsolete or will diminish markedly in the post–Cold War era. Instead, there is every expectation that internal conflicts will continue to erupt and fester throughout the world and form ample opportunity for U.S. intervention.

WHAT CAUSES CIVIL WAR?

"Any internal war can be made understandable after the fact by asserting that people were frustrated, or lost confidence in government, or were carried away by emotion," says Steven R. David (1997: 553). These feelings or beliefs are always present and do not indicate why they sometimes produce internal war and sometimes do not. Some internal wars are rational and purposeful; others erupt spontaneously and may be without political goals. Large-scale violence against a government occurs because it is seen as weak or no longer legitimate; weak governments tempt insurgents to challenge a regime's authority. Strong governments, by repression moves designed to reduce opposition power or eliminate insurgent elements, may also lead to civil war.

Why do wars break out in some states and not in others? What is the root of civil conflict? Causes range from structural factors (strength of the state, presence of ethnic minorities) to political factors (fairness in the political system, power divisions) to economic factors (health of the economy, stage of economic development) to cultural/perceptual factors (presence of discrimination against minorities), says David (1997: 573). These factors may explain the underlying sources of internal war, but are not helpful in explaining what triggers domestic conflict.

What brings civil wars to an end? Interestingly, negotiated settlements of civil wars are much less common than negotiated settlements of international war: between 1940 and 1990, only 20% of civil wars were resolved through negotiation, as compared to 55% of interstate wars. Moreover, negotiated settlements are far less likely to endure than are the results of military victory, reports David (1997: 570). Solutions are more difficult to find for an internal war: members of the opposing sides must live together in the same country, often with losers forced to disarm. Negotiated settlements of civil wars may leave disaffected groups in place with the power to challenge the new government's authority while a military victory over another state eliminates a potential rival.

If states cannot resolve problems on their own, there is always the possibility of outside powers intervening to impose order. During the Cold War, the superpowers believed their strategic interests were endangered by several civil conflicts, hence the American involvement in Korea, Vietnam, Lebanon, Nicaragua, and El Salvador, and the Soviet involvement in China, Korea, Vietnam, and Afghanistan, among others. Making sense of internal war will be a critical task of the twenty-first century, states David (1997: 576). The great majority of internal wars do not threaten the security or economic well being of great powers, but the post–Cold War world has created an opportunity for a focus on internal conflicts.

Theoretical Arguments

The question arises why collective violence—destructive acts by groups within a political community against its regime, authorities, or policies—occurs. Harry Eckstein (1980: 137) outlined a number of factors and alternative explanations that make some places more predisposed to violence than others: preconditions or precipitant causes, that is, structural, societal features versus specific, proximate, behavioral events. A first problem in studying conflict cause is whether to regard it as contingent or inherent in political life. Something is contingent if it depends on the presence of unusual, aberrant conditions that occur accidentally; contingencies can be controlled. Something is inherent either if it will always happen or if the potentiality for it always exists. In analyzing civil conflict within contingencies, the puzzle is why the problem developed. The answer is traced back to the aberrant source—a dramatic series of events, a sudden change in political life. In the inherency perspective, the puzzle is why the problem did *not* develop; correlations between low, stagnant, economic conditions and nondemocratic governance may be consistent, but the relationship does not always predict to civil conflict. It occurs in some states, but not others. Why? The two perspectives are almost always intertwined and hard to disentangle; what seems manifestly contingent to one observer may seem just as obviously inherent to another, says Eckstein (1980: 139). Three common theoretical approaches to understand modern causes of civil conflict are discussed here: (1) structural societal explanations (an inherency-based theory), and (2) leadership explanations (a contingency-based theory), and (3) economic base/weak government explanations (a mixture of inherency and contingency perspectives).

Societal Explanations. Relative deprivation theory postulates that violence results from anger produced by frustration caused by an imbalance between what one gets and what one deserves—the discrepancy between value expectations and outcome. Greater scope and intensity of relative deprivation make violent behavior more likely. The balance of coercion between regimes and dissidents produces greatest strife when it is even, where coercion is highly unequal, regimes collapse without being pushed, or dissidents lie low out of fear or are quickly put down, states Eckstein (1980: 145).

Modernization theory is another example of structural, contingency theory pointing toward violence: rapid change leads to system disequilibrium, which produces individual pathologies and results in collective movements. A third example is collective action, where violent conflict is chosen by opposition groups as a tactical calculation to mobilize dissident contenders to challenge the formal access to the political decision-making processes controlled by the elites. Shared interests and a plan of action produce a pattern of networks to carry out a threat against existing authorities, which may include acts of violence. Violence occurs when the costs of action are expected to be especially low, or nonviolent actions in pursuit of highly valued goals are perceived as powerless or unproductive.

A current variant based on inherency theory is the view attributing causes of internal conflicts to "ancient hatreds" many ethnic groups have toward each other. While historical grievances and deep desire for revenge have played important roles in some of the internal conflicts in the post–Cold War world— former Yugoslavia, Rwanda, Chechnya, and Sri Lanka are examples—it is also true that other groups (Ukrainians and Russians, Czechs and Slovaks) have long-term grievances but have abstained from killing each other in large numbers over recent political disputes.

Conditions of inequality, unsatisfied demands, discrimination, and societal cleavages are related to degrees of conflict, yet what remains mysterious is understanding why similar conditions across countries so often have dissimilar results. Although these conditions are common, widely spread across third world states, they do not always lead to domestic instability. Basically, the cause and effect link is not spelled out, posing a theoretical problem: the triggering mechanism in these structural theories is missing. A strict inherency theory orientation is not helpful in either understanding or forecasting civil conflict.

Leadership Explanations. Internal, elite-level actors—bad leaders who are usually the catalysts that turn potentially volatile situations into open warfare, ideological crusades, and criminal agendas, trigger most major internal conflicts, says Michael E. Brown (1996). When it comes to identifying the proximate cause of internal instability and the roles played by elites and leaders in instigating violence, there are three main types of internally driven, elite-triggered conflicts: (1) ideological conflicts driven by the convictions of one or more of the parties; (2) criminal assaults on state sovereignty, driven by the economic motivations of drug barons; and (3) power struggles between and among competing elites, driven mainly by personal, political motivations. Power struggles are most likely to lead to widespread violence when political elites are vulnerable, group histories are antagonistic, and domestic economic problems are mounting. When all three factors are present, permissive conditions and active catalysts come together and the potential for violence is great (Brown, 1996: 573, 576). The emergence of power struggles among elites can be particularly problematic because desperate and opportunistic politicians are particularly prone to employing divisive ethnic and nationalistic appeals.

Elite-level forces are much more important in explaining the proximate causes of domestic conflict than mass-level conditions. Internal wars happen because of the rational and deliberate decisions of bad leaders: heads of state make decisions that lead to war because they are more interested in staying in power than in preserving the peace for their citizens. Brown (1996: 576) says states will be prone to violence if state structures are collapsing due to external developments (sharp reductions in international financial assistance, for example) but if events transpire during a time when regime leadership is weak, leaders are incompetent, politicians opportunistic, or corruption rampant the chance for conflict eruption multiplies.

Leaders both of government and of rebel groups provoke internal wars to stay rich and powerful, says Brown (1996: 564–566): in Russia, Yeltsin's shift from escalating the war with Chechnya to trying to reach a settlement with the insurgents reflected the changing impact of the conflict on his chances of remaining president; in Angola, the civil war provided the rebel leader, Jonas Savimbi, with access to wealth from diamond mines controlled by insurgent forces; in former Yugoslavia, Milosevic, the Serbian leader, helped cause the fighting by inflaming ethnic nationalism, recognizing that he could not hold on to power in a multiethnic state with a Serbian minority. Of the three types of internally driven, elite-triggered conflicts, raw power struggles are clearly the most common, says Brown, who creates a fourfold typology of civil conflict causal elements: whether elite or mass triggered, and whether internally or externally driven, and applies the scheme to current cases of instability (see Figure 6.1).

Into each category Brown places countries currently experiencing internal conflicts. By far, the largest group falls into the elite-triggered/internally driven cell: Algeria, Angola, Bosnia, Burma, Burundi, Cambodia, Colombia, Croatia, Egypt, Guatemala, Indonesia–East Timor, Iran, Iraq, Kenya, Liberia, Peru, Philippines, Russia-Chechnya, Rwanda, Somalia, Sudan, Tajikistan, and Turkey. The overwhelming number of cases, products of decisions and policies of the bad leaders, presumably simplifies the task of isolating cause and formulating a

Figure 6.1
The Proximate Causes of Internal Conflict

	Internally Driven	Externally Driven
Elite-triggered	Bad Leaders	Bad Neighbors
Mass-triggered	Bad Domestic Problems	Bad Neighborhoods

Source: Brown (1996), p. 579.

remedy, including intervention from the outside. A thorny issue, though, remains: intervention to replace leaders violates a most important tenet of state sovereignty. And while leadership may be a culprit in civil conflict, the singular cause presumes motivations of individuals in these positions that may or may not be correct. The leadership story to explain civil conflict cause is intriguing, but still unfinished—it may grant too much autonomy to individuals within a role.

Economic and Government Explanations. A middle ground between structural explanation and leadership causes of civil war is proposed by John Mueller (2000: 1), who focuses on the criminal element as a central reason for instability. He views "new war" as nothing more than opportunistism waged by bands of criminals, bandits, and thugs, whose acts are often scarcely indistinquishable from straight crime. Thuggery, according to Mueller, is an ancient phenomenon: where governments are weak, crime tends to surge, and particularly where there are also exportable resources, primary commodities mainly, crime will require substantial organization and will sometimes look like war. The key to understanding civil unrest is the extent of government effectiveness. Since thugs tend to be opportunistic and cowardly, he continues, policing them would generally not be very difficult or costly. The misguided assumption that such conflicts stem from immutable ethnic hatreds and an extreme aversion to casualties makes international military intervention highly problematic politically.

The violence of "identity politics" arises not from nationalism in the masses, but principally from the actions of recently empowered and unpoliced thugs, Mueller says (2001: 12–14), drawing illustrations from the fighting units in the Balkan conflict. Serbian soldiers were drawn from the pool of prison inmates who were promised shortened sentences, enticed by the prospect that they could take whatever booty they could, and released for the war effort. The collapse of the regular army led to a privatization of the war and loot comprised the chief form of payment. Initial combat forces of Bosnia and of Croatia were also substantially made up of small bands of criminals and violent opportunists recruited or self-recruited from street gangs and organized mobs. Ethnicity was important as an ordering, organizational, sorting, or predictive device or principle, not as a crucial motivating force.

Warfare in the nineties and beyond has been motivated far more by greed than by grievance. By Mueller's interpretation (2001: 16), "There is of course plenty of hate, hostility and animosity between various peoples in the world. However, warfare does not seem to correlate well with these qualities: it is not particularly found in those areas with the most intergroup grievance and cleavage. It tends more reliably to occur in places where governments are weak or incompetent and particularly where there are, in addition, exportable primary commodities, or 'lootable resources,' like drugs, oil, or diamonds."

When governments become weak, it is likely that criminal activity will increase. In places where there is a primary commodity, crime will be organized, often international in scope, and conditions will look like war. The combatants in these conflicts do not want to end the conflict because they are profiting from their illicit business. Contemporary armed conflicts, including Bosnia, have been primarily perpetrated by semi-organized and mostly opportunistic paramilitary predators who are drawn to violence for its own sake and for the personal and material fulfillment it can often supply. "The chief dynamic in what passes for war nowadays is substantially supplied by thugs—combatants who very frequently appear to be more nearly operating as bandits, highwaymen, criminals, bullies, goons, brigands, pirates, mercenaries, robbers, adventurers, and hooligans than as warriors," says Mueller (2001: 17).

If the violence results from criminal opportunism rather than social grievance, control through intervention with policing constabulary forces may be a temporary solution. In the long run, the establishment of competent government is key to engendering and maintaining civil peace. Civil wars are least likely to occur in stable democracies and stable autocracies—that is, in countries with effective governments and policing forces.

Research Findings

Three strands of civil conflict causes—societal structural arguments, bad leadership, and the weak government-criminal activity linkage—represent dimensions along a theoretical continuum, from inherency to contingency. In the end, these perspectives overlap. Structural inequalities may be exploited for political purpose by a bad leader, or result in criminal, violent activity between groups. Bad leaders may foster illegal, economic trade creating strong criminal units in the society. A band of thugs may contribute to the power of bad leaders. What empirical research lends support to these primary ideas? In a perfect world, categorizing leaders as bad or good would permit a look into the future. Taking measure of society's bad leaders would allow us to foresee conflict developments before they occur. But leaders change, policies change, and the strategy of observation may be too elaborate, cumbersome, and unrealistic. The compromised, more common research strategy is to look at cases of civil conflict and determine whether the corresponding leadership was inept, corrupt, and/or repressive. The approach is correlational, rather than causative. Similarly, studies relating structural conditions to civil war onset suffer from focusing on one value of the dependent variable, namely, examining only those cases where significant civil unrest occurred and searching back for prior associated conditions. The true effect of structural conditions on civil conflict onset, as a predictor variable, is rarely evaluated, that is, prospective studies tracking social conditions within states to discover whether or not such countries eventually experience civil unrest. Recent research has focused on societal conditions, including economic development and ethnic groups configuration; the relationship among weak institutions, illicit economic activities, and violent crime; and type of governmental organization—from dictatorship to democracy.

The Cold War Pattern. Errol A. Henderson and J. David Singer (2000) looked at postcolonial states and their civil war experience, noting for each of the 90 cases that fell into their sample, whether a civil war began or continued within all years from 1946 to 1992. They define civil war as sustained, internal military combat, resulting in at least 1,000 battle-deaths per year, pitting central government forces against an insurgent force capable of effective resistance, determined by the latter's ability to inflict upon the government forces at least 5% of the fatalities that the insurgents sustain (Henderson and Singer 2000: 284).

Their essential argument is this: postcolonial civil wars derive largely from tensions related to the challenges of state-building and nation-building; these states have had a much shorter time to build effective state structures and cohesive national identities, and their leaders face a "state-strength dilemma." When they attempt to empower the state, resistance develops because heterogeneous groups within these societies do not have a firm national identity that recognizes central government legitimacy. The elites may turn to repression to ensure regime security and direct resources to the military to ward off insurgency threats, but this results in the very insurgency that such policies were meant to deter. The interaction of economic condition, group composition, and government organization leads Henderson and Singer (2000: 278–284) to formulate the following propositions tested with their data: (1) the greater a state's level of economic development, the lower its likelihood of civil war (confirmed); (2) the presence of ethnopolitical groups increases the likelihood of civil war (yes and no); (3) the greater the cultural polarization in a state, the greater the likelihood of civil war (*not* confirmed); (4) the greater a state's level of military spending, the greater the likelihood of civil war (inconclusive); and (5) the presence of semidemocracy increases the likelihood of civil war (confirmed).

Henderson and Singer found no significant linkage between the presence of an ethnopolitical group and the likelihood of civil conflict, concluding the impact of ethnopolitical variables on civil wars is vitiated by other factors, mainly regime type. Conflict may be reduced in ethnopolitical disputes when the political system is able to provide an accommodating environment to effectively redress the legitimate claims of aggrieved groups, say Henderson and Singer (2000: 291). Their findings indicate that semidemocracy has the greatest impact on the likelihood of civil war (when holding other variables constant), leading them to assert that political factors more than economic or cultural ones appear to have the greatest impact on the probability of civil war. Building viable regimes in the postcolonial world is a demanding, protracted process that requires commitment and close attention.

The Post–Cold War Pattern. Daniel Byman and Stephen Van Evera (1998) analyze seven causes of civil conflict in the Cold War and post–Cold War periods: (1) the collapse of the post-World War II empires, with no rules to define the rights and responsibilities in the former imperial zone, led outsiders to intervene to claim a sphere of influence or disrupt another power's sphere, sparking civil conflict (more important in the post–Cold War era); (2) a lack of regime legitimacy, the growth of restive middle classes in authoritarian states, and a lack of regime accountability lead to corrupt or incompetent state policies, causing violence to erupt (more important in the post–Cold War era); (3) state weakness, spread of modern small arms among third world populations, and end of superpower aid to beleaguered governments weakened authoritarian regimes, making it easier for groups to challenge governments by force (more important in the post–Cold War era); (4) communal hegemonism, aspiration of ethnic, religious, clan, or class groups for power over other groups, leads to violence (common to both the Cold and post–Cold War periods); (5) revolutionary ideology, when groups adopt extreme goals and tactics that preclude peaceful compromise with others, encourages violence (more important in the Cold War period); (6) aristocratic intransigence, the refusal of elites to share power and wealth, may trigger civil war (more important in the Cold War period); and (7) superpower competition for influence in third world states led to proxy wars within countries (more important in the Cold War period) (Byman and Van Evera 1998: 2–8).

Their data, drawn from a variety of sources, include 37 conflicts that broke out between 1989 and 1996 (Byman and Van Evera, 1998: 10). The most significant factors in their analysis are the loss of governmental legitimacy and communal hegemonism: conflict between a hegemonistic ethnic group and other groups helped fuel 25 conflicts; the loss of regime legitimacy was a major cause of 19 wars. In 14 conflicts, governments were too weak, collapse of empire led to 13 conflicts, revolutionary ideologies led to 11 conflicts, superpower competition caused eight conflicts, aristocratic intransigence caused four (Byman and Van Evera 1998: 5.

Much of the post–Cold War violence occurs in states whose governments have lost their legitimacy, whether it is due to poor economic performance, a lack of regime accountability (causing incompetent and corrupt governance) or the rise of a new middle class that seeks a greater political power and presses for demands to democratize. Regimes may become more open to gain broader support or more repressive to manage power. Either route may lead to civil war. Byman and Van Evera (1998: 36–37) offer Algeria as an example of the trap. In 1989, the ruling National Liberation Front (FLN) leaders authorized elections in order to reach out to a hostile society tired of regime corruption, a lack of accountability, and economic stagnation, hoping the process would help regain popular support. The Islamic Salvation Front (FIS) won the election, to the horror of the FLN, who then decided to hunker down, nullifying the vote and banning the FIS. When the FIS resisted, civil war followed.

No new world disorder emerged after 1989, conclude Byman and Van Evera (1998: 45); rather, the net impact of the Cold War's end has been to reduce civil violence. Nearly all of the factors hypothesized as having an impact on domestic instability have been brought under control or vanished completely except for regime legitimacy, which they find worrisome. Effects of reform such as democratization processes may be accompanied by violence. The process is likely to be a part of the political terrain in multiethnic states with an authoritarian tradition—Burma, Iraq, Iran, Indonesia, Pakistan, Angola, Kenya, Liberia, Nigeria, Sudan, Sierra Leone, Congo (Zaire), Guatemala, Kazakhstan, Tajikistan, Uzbekistan. They believe power-sharing would not be a workable arrangement in these societies, hence their grim forecast "democratization is inevitable, but it will often happen in multiethnic states where it will unleash the dogs of war" (Byman and Van Evera, 1998: 48).

Trends: 1960-2000. The World Bank launched a project, "Understanding Civil Wars, Crime and Violence," in February 1999 to study the devastating economic consequences of violence in developing countries. The research sponsored by the group analyzes complex interrelationships among economic, political, and social variables as they affect the probability of conflict outbreak, duration, and intensity. Why are some countries better prepared than others to ward off the pressures that lead to war or that aggravate crime? What distinguishes forces that trigger the incidence of conflict (e.g., external economic shocks) from forces that create the preconditions for imminent violence conflict (e.g., political instability; inequality and oppression)? Can humanitarian aid and economic assistance reduce the risk of civil war recurrence? Is external intervention effective in managing civil wars? Among the findings from this project, studies by Elbadawi and Sambanis (2000); Sambanis (2001); Collier (2000); and Hegre, Ellingsen, Gleditch, and Gates (2001) are discussed here.

The incidence of civil war in 161 Countries using data from 1960–1999 with five-year frequencies on economic, social, and political variables was analyzed by Elbadawi and Sambanis (2000). They use the Correlates of War definition of violent, civil conflict: 1,000 battle-related deaths, in a combat engaging the state with rebels who were able to mount an organized military opposition to the state. Among their variables of interest: per capita real income level, openness of political institutions (average of an index of democracy minus an index of autocracy), ethnic fractionalization, natural resource dependency by primary exports as a percentage of GDP (Elbadawi and Sambanis, 2000: 12). They noticed the percentage of countries experiencing a civil war rose steadily from 7% in 1960–1964 to a staggering 28% in 1990–1994, declining sharply in the following five years (1995–1999) with only 13% of the world affected by civil wars near the end of the twentieth century. However, they caution, the world today is less safe than it was at the midpoint of the Cold War.

Among their results: although indicators of political and economic development have improved considerably over time, mean income per capita has more than doubled, and political rights improved, in terms of average levels, the range of countries along these dimensions spread widely. They found that low levels of political rights are significantly and negatively correlated with the incidence of war; the risk of war is negatively associated with initial levels of economic development and economic growth. Primary exports as a percentage of GPS has a positive, significant association to the risk of civil war. Natural resources present provide an easily "lootable" asset for "loot-seeking" rebels or a convenient source of support of "just-seeking" movements. However, beyond a certain range, natural resources become a formidable instrument in the hands of governments, which can use them to fund armies and buy popular support. Ethnic diversity and the risk of civil war were positively associated, suggesting that ethnic homogeneity actually reduces rather than increases the risk of incidence of war. Population size is positively and robustly associated with the risk of civil war: countries with smaller population size, individually, face lower risk of war (Elbadawi and Sambanis, 2000: 20–23). They suggest that economic diversification, poverty reduction, and political liberalization, separately and together could enhance security in these societies and reduce the likelihood of civil war, but that it may be easier to start in the political arena.

Sambanis (2001), using the same data, searched for differences between the causes of identity (ethnic/religious) and nonidentity civil wars. Seventy-seven cases were classified as ethnic wars, that is, episodes of violent conflict between governments and national, ethnic, religious, or other communal minorities (ethnic challengers) in which the latter sought major changes in their status. Sambanis (2001: 265–268) hypothesized that (1) ethnic war should be positively related to ethnic heterogeity (confirmed); (2) greater levels of economic development should reduce the risk of ethnic civil war by raising the economic opportunity costs of violence (not confirmed); (3) the lack of democracy should raise the probability of ethnic civil war (confirmed); (4) the greater the level of democracy in neighboring countries, the lower the probability of ethnic civil war (confirmed); (5) the presence of war in a neighboring country should increase the risk of more war in the neighborhood (confirmed); and (6) the Cold War should be negatively correlated with the onset of ethnic civil war (no relationship).

Economic variables are negatively associated with civil war onset, Sambanis (2001: 272–273) reports, reinforcing the result of Henderson and Singer. However, for ethnic civil wars, high levels of democracy are robustly significant, and much more important than economic development; moreover, if a country is more heterogeneous, the probability of occurrence of an ethnic war increases, and economic development becomes less critical to mitigating the outbreak of violence. Democracy and economic development have comparable effects on the likelihood of ethnic war onset under some conditions: higher levels of both have roughly equally positive effects and reduce the estimated likelihood of ethnic war onset by approximately the same amount. The observed difference in the risk of war onset between less and more democratic countries or less and more developed countries is significantly greater at higher levels of ethnic heterogeneity. This leads Sambanis (2001: 276) to conclude that democracy and economic development are two good ways to manage ethnic conflict in most societies. Important differences between ethnic war onset and the onset of civil wars more generally indicate that politics—its open or closed nature—is more important than economics in causing ethnic civil war, and ethnic heterogeneity significantly increases the risk of such war. Identity wars are predominantly caused by political grievance and are unlikely to occur in more democratic societies. This research, consistent with Byman and Van Evera (1998) and Henderson and Singer (2000), points to the significance of democratic processes to explain civil war onset.

Disputing the independent role of politics and of democratic processes, Collier (2000) offers an economic perspective on the causes of civil war, based on patterns over the period 1965–1999 of 47 wars. Collier argues that the risk of civil war has been systematically related to a few economic conditions, such as dependence upon primary commodity exports and low national incomes, while objective measures of social grievance, such as inequality, a lack of democracy, and ethnic and religious divisions, have no systematic effect on domestic conflict. This is because civil wars occur where rebel organizations are financially viable. The factors that account for this difference between failure and success are to be found not in the causes that rebel organizations claim to espouse, but in their radically different opportunities to raise revenue.

The conceptualization of causes of civil conflict are reformulated from social-political perceptions of rebellion as a protest motivated by genuine and extreme grievance, where rebels are public-spirited heroes fighting against injustice, into an economic problem which analyzes rebellion more like a form of organized crime. Parties to a civil war offer a discourse of explanations for their actions and work to have good public relations to promote their views, says Collier (2000: 1–2). They will have a litany of grievances against the government for its oppression and unfairness; rebellion will be styled as a protest movement, driven to the extremity of violence by the extremity of the conditions which people face. Alternatively, an economist studying rebellions may think of them as the ultimate manifestation of organized crime: in insurrections the insurgents are indistinguishable from bandits or pirates. The motivation of conflict is unimportant—what matters is whether the organization can sustain itself financially, says Collier (2000: 3), arguing the feasibility of predation, rather than the objective grounds for grievance, determines the risk of conflict. This suggests that greed over grievance dominates the causes leading to a civil war.

Among the risk of civil war factors, Collier (2000: 6–7) includes substantial share of income (GDP) from export of primary commodities, geography (where it is hard for government forces to control by population spread, not concentration), history of civil war in the country, a substantially large American diaspora community, low education levels, fast population growth, economic decline, and a dominant ethnic group (if one group constitutes between 45–90% of the population—enough for control—the risk of conflict doubles). Collier argues the risk of rebellion is connected to three economic conditions: dependence on primary commodity exports, low average income, and slow economic growth (p. 9). His findings: countries earning around 25% of their yearly GDP from the export of unprocessed commodities (gemstones, coffee, oil) face a far higher likelihood of civil war than countries with more diversified economies. Rebel groups in vulnerable countries loot primary commodities to stay financially viable; "lootable" national assets are tied to a single spot like a diamond mine or a coffee plantation. Where rebellions are financially viable, wars will occur. Military needs of the rebel organization create the political conflict rather than objective grievances. Rebel organizations must generate group grievances for military effectiveness, which then politicizes the war, Collier argues (2000: 13–14). Furthermore, diaspora communities help fuel the continuation of the conflict: "they are richer than people in their country of origin and can afford to finance vengeance." Collier challenges the popular perception that civil conflict can be explained through frustration-aggression—an intense political contest fueled by grievances. When the main grievances—inequality, political repression, and ethnic and religious divisions—are measured objectively, his results show they provide no explanatory power in predicting rebellion. By contrast, economic characteristics—dependence on primary commodity exports, low average incomes, slow growth, and large diasporas—are all significant and powerful predictors of civil war. Rebellions either have the objective of natural resource predation, or are critically dependent upon natural resource predation in order to pursue other objectives. Collier concludes that these are the risk of civil war factors that conflict prevention must reduce if it is to be successful.

Following this line of argument, James D. Fearon and David D. Laitin (2001) suggest that better predictors of which countries are at risk for civil war should focus on the conditions that favor insurgency. Insurgency can be harnessed to various political agendas, be it communism (Asia and Latin America), Islamic fundamentalism (Afghanistan, Algeria, Kashmir), right-wing reaction in Nicaragua, or ethnic nationalism (Sri Lanka, Turkey, Sudan, Ethiopia, Indonesia, India). Decolonization from the 1940s through the 1970s gave birth to a large number of financially, bureaucratically, and militarily weak states. These states have been at risk for civil violence for the whole period, almost entirely in the form of insurgency or rural guerrilla warfare.

Fearon and Laitin (2001: 27) state that the prevalence of internal war in the 1990s is for the most part the result of a steady accumulation or protracted conflicts since the 1950s rather than a sudden change associated with a new, post–Cold War international system. The average duration of civil wars in progress has increased steadily from two years in 1947 to about 15 years in 1999 (Fearon and Laitin, 2001: 1), producing a steady upward trend, roughly at a 45-degree angle, in the number of ongoing civil wars from 1945 to 1990, with a significant downturn by the early 1990s that continues into the twenty-first century.

Using "political opportunity structure," a concept highlighting the rules, institutional structure, and elite alliances that make states more or less vulnerable to protest and rebellion, Fearon and Laitin (2001: 2) assert the main factors outlining its cause are not cultural differences and ethnic grievances, but rather the conditions that favor insurgency—military conflict characterized by small, lightly armed bands practicing guerrilla warfare from rural base areas. Insurgency and civil war should be favored in countries with weak central governments—financially, organizationally, and politically, which often means poor local policing or inept and corrupt counterinsurgency practices, sometimes including a propensity for brutal and indiscriminate retaliation that helps drive locals into rebel force. Insurgency is also more likely where rebels, with foreign financial backing or logistical support, have a rural base, preferably in rough, inaccessible terrain, where their knowledge of the local population is superior to the government's. Insurgency need not rely on broad grievances in a population; neither democracy nor the presence of broad civil liberties appears to reduce the incidence of civil war onsets (Fearon and Laitin, 2001: 3).

Insurgents are weak relative to the governments they are fighting. To survive, the rebels must be able to hide from government forces at a distance from the centers of state power; hence, rural locations and the availability of foreign, cross-border sanctuaries are important. To survive, rebels need a supply of arms and materiel, money to buy them, or goods to trade for them. They need a supply of recruits. Insurgents will survive and even prosper if the government and military they oppose are badly financed, organizationally inept, corrupt, and poorly informed about activities in the rural hinterlands (Fearon and Laitin, 2001: 7–11).

They found that terrain matters: a country that is about 10% mountainous has a greater chance of at least one civil war than countries that are relatively flat. The impact of ethnic diversity remains substantively weak, that of per capita income remains strong ($1,000 less in per capita income is associated with 35% greater odds of civil war onset, on average, after controlling for a variety of other factors). All measures for political democracy and ethnic and religious fractionalization are statistically insignificant (p. 17–18). Yet, Fearon and Laitin (p. 26) note that government human rights performance in the prior year is a relatively powerful predictor of the odds of subsequent civil war: thus, a country rated at the top on human rights performance but at peace and at the mean for all other variables has an estimated annual chance of outbreak of 0.37%; the same country with the worst human rights performance has a risk of 5.3%. This may suggest regime brutality could be a factor in civil unrest. The mark of economic effects in ongoing civil wars seems to be well documented. That insurgent groups emerge and sustain themselves not by political grievances but due to the possibilities for private economic support is the central supported thesis of Fearon and Laitin's and also Collier's (2000) research.

What is left of the role of political elements in accounting for the likelihood that conflict will break out? What is the effect of democratization on civil war outbreaks? From a political perspective, violent conflict is causally related to opportunity and grievance. Opportunity relates to a dissatisfied group's ability to organize violently against the state. Grievance reflects a group's dissatisfaction with the state. Extreme autocratic repression can stifle rebellion; democracy allows nonviolent options for protest. Both make civil war less likely. The midpoint between these opposites thus makes civil war more likely. This is the argument of Hegre, Ellingsen, Gleditch, and Gates (2001), who examined civil war trends over three time spans—(1) 1816–1992, (2) 1946–1992, and (3) 1989–1992. They defined civil war as a conflict involving the national government, effective resistance (measured by the ratio of fatalities of the weaker to the stronger forces), military action, and at least 1,000 battle deaths.

Using data from 152 countries, they discovered that harshly authoritarian states and institutionally consistent democracies experience fewer civil wars than intermediate regimes (Hegre et al., 2001: 34–35). They tested four hypotheses: (1) semidemocracies are more likely to experience civil war than either democracies or autocracies (confirmed); (2) institutionally consistent democracies and stark autocracies are equally unlikely to experience civil war (confirmed); (3) countries that have undergone a recent political transition are more likely to experience civil war than countries whose political system has remained stable (confirmed); and (4) the likelihood of civil war in semidemocracies remains higher than in other regime types even a long time after a regime change (confirmed).

Their results show a parabolic relationship between democracy and civil war: regimes ranked near the middle on a democracy-autocracy index have a significantly higher probability of civil war than either democracies or autocracies, which is highest when both opportunity and grievance are present. It holds for the long, short, and shortest period. Semidemocracies are more prone to violent domestic conflict even when they have had time to stabilize from regime change, since when a highly autocratic regime seeks to democratize, the reduction in grievance will not outweigh the increase in opportunity to rebel. In the short run, the countries will also have to live through the unsettling effect of change.

Conclusion. Both economic and political factors fuel civil instability. Democratic, highly industrialized societies rarely evolve into broad scale, conflict-ridden chaos, while poor states, struggling to introduce democratic change in government structure and practice, do. Of the three explanations outlining civil war causes: structural, social factors—an inherency based theory; bad leadership—a contingency based idea; and weak governments and crime—a combination of inherency and contingency perspectives, each one has some validity. No universal, simple theory emerges to cover all instances. In layers of importance, they vary. The empirical research on multiple cases of civil unrest in different contexts suggests that at base, low economic development and slow rate of growth are a significant factor (Collier, 2000; Elbadawi and Sambanis, 2000; Henderson and Singer, 2000; Sambanis, 2001). Cultural and ethnic fragmentation and diversity matter less in feeding a conflict frenzy, a finding in contrast with popular views on civil war causes in the post–Cold War age. While these results lend some support to inherency-based theory, they are least significant in the hierarchy of explanatory perspectives. At the next level, leadership and government regime–type variables emerge. They are more important than the societal-structural level in explaining the outbreak of civil war, although they lack the punch of power of explanation at the upper level. Here, issues of legitimacy, degree of democracy, low political rights, and democratic transition matter. These studies (Byman and Van Evera, 1998; Sambanis, 2001; Hegre et al., 2001) suggest that politics cannot be ignored. In particular, the research by Hegre et. al. strongly indicates the significance of semidemocracy as a predictor for civil war, no matter what time frame is isolated over the nineteenth and twentieth centuries. The most specific, and strongly supported, explanation for civil war onset relates to weak governments and crime—a theoretical perspective joining inherency and contingency causal analysis. The two factors run in tandem: weak government (corruption, lack of organization, poor tax base, little external support) fosters the possibility for outside groups to coalesce into an opposition force; "lootable" resources (gems, diamonds, coffee) make financing possible, and criminal activity enters the picture. Essentially, this is the argument—supported by solid data results—of Collier (2000) and Fearon and Laitin (2001); both studies bracket the cause of major civil war as greed over grievance, emphasizing economic factors and limiting social and political ones.

In all of these studies, it should be noted, methodological limitations exist. In purest form, determining how any group of variables and theoretical explanation has force of explanation is a function of the empirical set of cases forming the analysis. Civil war, while prevalent through history, remains a rare event—it happens relatively infrequently, in a small number of states. Building the relevant conditions for its occurrence becomes an exercise in selectivity where comparisons with other polities with different configurations of variable values are usually not carried out in a thorough fashion. Thus, these explanations remain partial, incomplete, although they do point to two primary elements suggesting where civil wars are likely to break out: situations of government transition into semidemocracy status; and situations of weak government with available, valuable primary commodities to finance rebel activities. Government legitimacy and effectiveness are important, although the relationship among form of rule, application of rule, and economic factors has not been examined. We can safely conclude that contingency theories have greater sway than inherence-based concepts.

CIVIL WAR AND INTERVENTION

The predominance of civil wars has marked the post–World War II period. Civil wars have been terribly bloody, accounting for over 10 million battle-related fatalities during the nineteenth and twentieth centuries. The extensive death and destruction resulting from these civil conflicts has been accompanied by intractability and duration significantly greater than for interstate conflicts. Civil wars are more intense and therefore more difficult to resolve by third-party negotiation than interstate wars, discovered Roy Licklider (1995: 681), who examined 91 civil conflicts between 1946 and 1994. The percentage settled by negotiation is far smaller—somewhere between 15% and 30%. Defining civil war as large-scale violence, killing at least 1,000 or more people per year, in which at least two sides organized for violent conflict before the war started (or the weaker side must have imposed casualties on its opponent equal to at least 5% of its own, to distinguish between civil wars and political massacres), these conflicts end when the violence stops (Licklider, 1995: 682). Most civil wars do not last very long—slightly more than 25% end during the same calendar year in which they begin; over half end within five years, two-thirds end in 10 years. Malaysia, Laos, Vietnam, China—all lasted longer than a decade. Most civil wars end by military victory.

Under what conditions do armed societies disarm, and under what circumstances do outside interventions—military assistance to one or both sides, mediation, humanitarian aid—help or hinder a settlement? Are lasting solutions more likely before or after total military victory by one side? Extremely long civil wars correspond to the equitable distribution of third-party interventions, Dylan Balch-Lindsay and Andrew Enterline (2000: 615) discovered. When third parties raise the stakes of the conflict by engaging in the use of militarized force against the civil war state, the duration of these conflicts is reduced. Nearly one-fourth of the civil wars between 1816 and 1992 involved military intervention by third parties, according to Singer and Small Correlates of War data. Patrick Regan, identifying 138 intrastate conflicts in the post–World War II period (1944–1994), notes more than 60% involved some form of economic or military intervention by a third party. (He includes arms transfers and economic aid both can be difficult to track down.) Interventions may be intended to end a conflict as quickly as possible, but sometimes an intervention actually prolongs it.

Balch-Lindsay and Enterline (2000: 622) consider whether various factors have a strong influence on civil war duration hypothesizing that prior political grievances, larger geographic size of the civil war state (large states are difficult to administer, making it hard for the government to isolate and engage opposition groups in combat, greater sized states may devolve into an urban-rural dynamic in which government forces control cities, oppositions take the hinterlands), and separatist demands increase likely duration of a civil war. Shorter civil wars are positively related to mature domestic political regimes, resources held by the government, and domestic costs of a civil war. Balch-Lindsay and Enterline also predict that the greater the degree of third-party support for the opposition, the shorter the civil war's duration, and they expect third-party support for the government to exert a smaller impact. They see the effect of intervention on civil war duration related to the side the intervening third party supports and the overall balance of interventions in the conflict, expecting a one-sided intervention will shorten the duration of the civil war but when both sides have external support civil war will be significantly prolonged. Balanced third-party interventions create stalemates and lengthen civil war.

Their data sample includes 152 civil wars from 1820–1992. Their results show that prior political grievances have no significant effect on duration, separatist movements tend to increase duration, government strength tends to increase duration, contrary to their predictions, and higher civil war costs reduce duration. Intervention on the side of the opposition lengthens duration of a civil war, opposite to their expectation, and intervention on the side of the government also lengthens duration, again contrary to their hypothesis. A balancing of intervention on two sides increases duration, in line with their predictions (Balch-Lindsay and Enterline, 2000: 632. How third-party interventions are distributed, Balch-Lindsay and Enterline discover, equitably or inequitably across the set of civil war combatants, has a real impact on conflict duration: an equitable distribution of third-party interventions increases the likelihood of a stalemate, which extends the time of violence. They offer the example of the Kosovo conflict in 1999, where NATO members sought to deter

Russia from supporting its Serbian ally fearing that third-party support for both sides would produce a balanced intervention, increasing the duration of the conflict. They conclude that although policy-makers have suggested it is the moral obligation of third-party states to intervene in civil wars to halt the human suffering and physical destruction associated with civil wars, the critical aspect is coordinating interventions among third parties for creating the conditions to balance or unbalance force levels for the combatants in order to reduce conflict duration.

Intervention is complicated by the need to understand the nature of a particular civil conflict that will shape an intervention strategy, whether it is an incremental policy or massive onslaught to assist the government or the opposition. Patrick Regan (2000b) examined 45 conflicts, 274 interventions into 23 of those conflicts, which occurred between 1944 and 1999, discovering, consistent with Balch-Lindsay and Enterline, that outside intervention prolongs the duration of a civil war. His argument, however, was formulated to expect the opposite result: outside intervention in internal conflicts is a form of conflict management, and therefore represent an attempt to control the hostilities rather than exacerbate them. Thus, if the intervention goal is conflict management, it should reduce the conflict duration by convincing both sides that costs of continued fighting are high and the benefits from settlements are preferable. Capability balance between sides will be a major factor determining the willingness of each side to settle now versus continuing to fight until victory. Regan (2000b: 11–16) hypothesizes that (1) unilateral interventions that support government shorten duration; (2) unilateral interventions that support opposition lengthen duration; (3) rapid intervention into ongoing conflict will decrease expected duration; (4) rapid intervention that balances the capabilities between opposing sides lengthens duration, rapid intervention that imbalance will shorten a conflict duration, interventions that attract counter-interventions will increase the expected duration of a conflict; (5) to shorten a civil war a party must intervene in a way that offers benefits to the rebels from settling now versus holding out for victory at some future time, which will increase the expected value of a negotiated settlement, reduce costs, and retard the ability to effectively mobilize forces; and (6) neutral interventions will lead to shorter conflicts than interventions supporting either the government or the opposition.

Regan measures intervention by five categories of military assistance (troops, naval support, equipment or aid, intelligence or advisors, and air support) and by level of contribution in each category (number of troops, dollar value of the aid, number of weapons). The results show that conflicts without interventions are likely to end within the first few months; conflicts with interventions last longer. Neither the total number of casualties nor the average number of casualties per year has any influence on the expected time until the conflict ends. Almost any aspect of an intervention increases civil war duration; only neutral intervention reduces it. Thus, outside interventions prolong rather than shorten a conflict (Regan, 2000b: 22–27).

The likelihood that both the government and the rebels will agree to a settlement rather than continue to fight will vary depending on each party's estimate of its probability of victory, its expected payoff from victory versus those from a settlement, the rate at which it absorbs costs of conflict, and its estimate of how long it will take to achieve victory, state T. David Mason and Patrick J. Fett (1996: 548–549), who in examining 57 civil conflicts (using Correlates of War data) which ended between 1946 and 1992 predicted the longer the duration of the conflict, the greater the probability of the participants seeking a negotiated settlement. Any factors that reduce chances of victory, extend the time required to achieve victory, or increase the utility of settlement will make the participants more willing to agree to a negotiated settlement rather than continue fighting.

Third parties can either enhance the likelihood of a negotiated settlement or prolong the conflict by preventing one side from falling to defeat on the battlefield, due to different reasons underlying intervention in civil wars: when war threatens to expand outside a state's borders, others may intervene to prevent the spread; or when a third party was formerly involved with one of the belligerents, it may feel a moral imperative to intervene. If other nations intervene militarily on one side or the other in a civil war, the likelihood of a negotiated settlement should decrease, they project. Why? The beneficiary of the intervention is likely to experience an increase in its probability of achieving victory, and that party will be willing to fight for a longer time to achieve victory because the intervening party is subsidizing that party's capacity to absorb the costs of additional conflict. Second, the greater the number of participants in a conflict, the longer it will take to reach a settlement through negotiation. Third, interveners may reject the negotiated settlement terms.

Mason and Fett (1996: 558–560) conclude that settlement is very unlikely in civil conflicts lasting 48 months or less, but becomes highly likely if the war drags on beyond four years. Short wars often end in a quick victory by the state, precluding a need for settlement. But if the rebels avoid early defeat but cannot overtake the government, then the longer they hold out, the more likely the government will agree to a settlement. Intervention appears to have no effect on whether a civil war is concluded by a negotiated settlement, state Mason and Fett (1996: 561).

In another approach to the impact of intervention on civil conflicts, Charles King (1997) looks at the conflict structure, drawing data from civil wars in Asia, Africa, and Latin America to understand why some civil wars drag on past a reasonable point. Much of the contemporary debate about intervention in civil wars centers around two issues, says King (1997: 11–12): first, how to define "success" in such operations; and second, how to relate the short-term task of halting the fighting to the longer-term projects of ensuring a stable peace and promoting postwar reconstruction. External involvement is sometimes judged less in terms of its impact on the termination of the conflict and more in terms of its effects on the intervening state. "If an operation can be completed on time, with minimal loss of blood and treasure and with relations between the various members of the intervening coalition in relatively good repair, it is normally seen as successful."

The success of third parties in halting the fighting has been mixed. Interveners have been unable to translate military victory into comprehensive peace settlements. Diverse forms of external involvement have been applied: mediation, election monitoring, traditional peacekeeping, and peace enforcement, although no approach can claim an unqualified success. King (1997: 60–75) outlines what external powers can do to reframe the structure of a civil conflict, among his ideas: (a) promote leadership change, and promote leaders' interests; (b) emphasize the significance of the battlefield—military victory by creating turning points and making war unprofitable; (c) time disarmament programs to reduce the security dilemma, monitor cease-fires, work to generate trust; and (d) build external power legitimacy.

Intervening powers gauge the relative success of their involvement in civil wars less in terms of the effect on warring parties than in the way that intervention experience affects the strategic interests and domestic politics of those powers themselves. The effectiveness of outside powers to stop the disintegration of states and reverse the tide of communal violence is severely constrained by their inability to examine the incentives for violence from the perspective of the belligerents themselves, concludes King (1997: 81-82). Intervening powers can craft more effective strategies for involvement in civil wars by understanding the structure of political, economic, and personal incentives for violence, and recognizing the rationality of violence in many civil wars and the structural obstacles to negotiated settlements. External powers can influence the importance of these structural obstacles, but their ability to do so depends on the political will of the international actors and the nature of the obstacles themselves. On this point, Chaim Kaufmann (1996: 136) notes that the international community has done little and achieved less to halt ethnic wars, where so much violence is directed against armed civilians.

Stable resolutions of ethnic civil wars are possible, but only when the opposing groups are demographically separated into defensible enclaves. Other means—such as peace enforcement by international forces or by a conquering empire—last only as long as the enforcers remain, argues Kaufmann (1996: 137). This means that to save lives threatened by genocide, the international community must facilitate and protect population movements to create true national homelands. "Those considering humanitarian intervention to end ethnic civil wars should set as their goal lasting safety rather than perfect peace. Given the persistence of ethnic rivalries, 'safety' is best defined as freedom from threats of ethnic murder, expropriation, or expulsion for the overwhelming majority of civilians of all groups. 'Lasting' must mean that the situation remains stable indefinitely after the intervention forces leave," states Kaufmann (1996: 151).

Intervention to resolve ethnic civil wars must be guided by two principles, states Kaufmann (p. 161): First, settlement must aim at physically separating the warring communities and establishing a balance of relative strength that makes it unprofitable for either side to attempt to revise the territorial settlement. Second, although economic or military assistance may suffice in some cases, direct military intervention will be necessary when aid to the weaker side would create a window of opportunity for the stronger, or when there is an immediate need to stop ongoing genocide. Unless outsiders are willing to provide permanent security guarantees, stable resolution of an ethnic civil war requires separation of the groups into defensible regions.

One failing of the post–Cold War era has been the West's misunderstanding of the nature of ethnic conflict, suggests Maynes (1999: 20). Analysts assumed that people wanted to live together but were thwarted by bad leaders or foreign intervention. These wars are fought for identity and survival, and are hard to contain. Does this mean that outside powers should avoid involvement? No, says Maynes, for we must try to break the cycle of victimization before the next generation embraces it. But the nature of these struggles means intervening parties must provide reassurance for all sides, taking historical grievances into account rather than simply declaring them irrelevant.

CONCLUSION

The growth of civil conflicts is not exclusively a post–Cold War trend. In fact, the number of intrastate conflicts has increased steadily in both absolute and relative terms since the 1960s. Throughout the Cold War, many of these conflicts were described and analyzed as proxy wars, simple expressions of U.S.-Soviet confrontation. As the Cold War drew to a close, it was widely expected these conflicts would end. This did not happen, so alternative explanations focused attention on the domestic causes. Nationalism, used previously to explain why states wage wars, was reformatted into ethnicity as a primary explanatory factor in civil instability. This time around the identity factor unleashes wars within states rather than between them. Social and economic need constituted a second mainline explanation for civil unrest (continuing the causal theory of development and modernization first presented during tl'he Cold War), and bad leadership coupled with criminal elements— providing incentives for continuation of violence—formed a new, third primary reason for third world instability. These conflicts, along with their causal explanations, have posed the central challenges for crafting an appropriate, widely subscribed U.S. foreign policy on intervention in the modern age.

7

American Intervention: Evolving Trends

INTRODUCTION

Throughout its history, varying contingents of U.S. armed forces have been dispatched to other countries on many occasions with different mission objectives: from small, single-purpose operations composed of a handful of soldiers (the Iranian hostage rescue attempt in 1980) to the deployment of thousands of combat troops to join the fight in an ongoing civil conflict (the Vietnam War). Duration of stay has varied—short, weekend-length visits to arrange peaceful departure for American citizens from volatile environments (Sierre Leone, May 1992; Central African Republic, May 1996) and extended military occupation of several decades (Haiti, 1915–1934; Korea, 1950–present). The types of conflict in which the United States chose to participate include international wars in strategically central regions of the world and isolated domestic disturbances within countries situated in remote, geographic locations.

In what ways have U.S. intervention patterns been linked to the structure of the international system? In one historical study covering the nineteenth and twentieth centuries, Gregory A. Raymond and Charles W. Kegley (1987), examining intervention into civil wars undertaken by the United States and other great powers, found no sharp, consistent relationship, although they noticed a tendency for the international system to be more intervention prone under a unipolar structure, with power concentrated in the hands of one state, and that interventions tended to be undertaken by the preponderant state in support of incumbent governments. Within the Cold War period, Herbert Tillema (1973) discovered norms operated against superpower intervention: only in cases where a direct conflict with the bipolar adversary was unlikely, when there was little internal dissent and no strong, reasonable alternatives to parties to take effective action and request for assistance in response to intervention by another party, would U.S. intervention occur. Tillema's results suggest the U.S.-USSR rivalry balance created major restraints against intervention, suggesting that a bipolar structure is less intervention prone. Hence, structurally different hierarchies in the international system point to divergent patterns in the level of major power interventionary behavior: a unipolar system may lead to greater intervention activity than a bipolar one. The post Cold–War system should have greater levels of intervention.

To understand the U.S intervention record of the post–Cold War period more fully, it is useful to review and compare several lists of historical intervention events to capture the phenomenon over time and to become aware of the variation in the way intervention is construed. For some analysts, intervention is limited to situations of blatant use of military force in another country but where the resistance is not sufficient to constitute war (e.g., U.S. troops landing in Panama in December 1989 to capture General Noriega). Others adopt a different focus and extend the definition to include various forms of involvement and assistance by an external state in an ongoing civil war (e.g., U.S. commitments to Greece in the 1940s and covert aid to Afghan resistance fighters in the 1980s). Military troops may be sent abroad into tense situations for quite different purposes: to engage as partisan units in combat-related activities during an ongoing conflict (U.S. participation in the Persian Gulf War in 1991 and in Afghanistan, 2001–2002), or to serve as impartial peace enforcement or peacekeeping soldiers after a cease-fire has been agreed on (U.S. missions in Bosnia and Kosovo).

Among the studies of intervention trends, two of them cover American military behavior over roughly the nineteenth and twentieth centuries: Small and Singer (1982) present a quantitative analysis of civil wars throughout the world between 1816 and 1980 and accompanying U.S. military troop intervention patterns; Grimmett (1999), using different intervention criteria, provides a brief synopsis of various types of American military actions abroad from 1798 to 1999. Other analysts—Blechman and Kaplan (1978); Tillema (1989); Hermann and Kegley (1998); Pickering (1999); Serafino (1999); Blechman and Wittes (1999); Regan (2000a); and DiPrizio (2001)—concentrate on the Cold War and/or post–Cold War time periods, covering different decades in the last half of the twentieth century. These research efforts apply rigorous, although different, definitions of intervention. Collectively, such studies provide the basis for addressing three questions: (1) to what extent has the United States engaged in intervention? (2) what are the trends in U.S. intervention behavior? and (3) has American intervention in the post–Cold War age set a new course?

LONG-TERM INTERVENTION TRENDS

Although intervention appears continuously in interstate relations, it is infrequent and seems to be a relatively uncommon phenomenon when viewed over a broad sweep of history. There are few cases of large-scale intervention in civil wars; only some of the great powers have achieved significant records in this regard—Britain, France, and the United States. Melvin Small and J. David

Singer (1982: 222) identify 106 civil wars within countries in the international system occurring between 1816 and 1980—occasions when outside states could have decided to become involved in a major way—yet they found just 21 different countries experiencing civil war over the entire period in which interventionary forces were introduced (Small and Singer, 1982: 234). Their data show the United States intervened into six different civil wars: Russia (1917–1920), Lebanon (1958), Vietnam (1960–1965—from 1965 to 1975 it is classified as an "interstate war"), Laos (1960–1962), Dominican Republic (1965), and Cambodia (1970–1975). Five of the six cases occurred during the Cold War, and in four instances the Americans participated on the losing side (Russia, Vietnam, Laos, and Cambodia).

Their operational definitions to qualify and establish thresholds of both civil war and intervention are important in this context: a civil war consists of "any armed conflict that involves (a) military action internal to the metropole, (b) the active participation of the national government, and (c) effective resistance by both sides" (Small and Singer, 1982: 210). Intervention is determined by direct foreign military participation where either 1,000 troops were committed to the combat zone or 100 battle deaths were sustained (p. 234). Parenthetically, Small and Singer note the restrictive parameters of their definition, stating that beyond their purview are "scores of intervention that turned the tide but that did not involve either 100 deaths or 1,000 troops committed to combat. One thinks, for example, of the way the United States could make or break revolutions in Central America with the landing of relatively small marine contingents as in Nicaragua in 1912" (p. 235).

A survey prepared by the Congressional Research Service (CRS) for the U.S. Congress, "Instances of Use of United States Armed Forces Abroad, 1798–1999" (Grimmett, 1999), adopts a more expansive concept of intervention to include instances in which the United States has used its armed forces in situations of conflict or potential conflict or for other than normal peacetime purposes. The list of U.S. military ventures covers overt engagement of forces (without minimum troop or casualty thresholds), excluding disaster relief, routine alliance stationing or training exercises, the use of American troops in covert operation, or exploration and settlement of the western United States. About 230 operations are included; the majority of cases consist of brief Marine or Navy actions undertaken prior to World War II to protect U.S. citizens or promote American interests abroad. The accounting system is far more detailed in the post–Cold War period where the list of intervention "instances" divide into smaller event segments giving an impression that U.S. military behavior has increased significantly over time. What pattern of U.S. military involvement emerges from these data?

Intervention is a common, continuous part of American foreign policy history once smaller operations are incorporated. "Almost every administration since John Adams' has found it necessary to send troops beyond the existing borders of the United States to advance or protect American interests through force, the threatened use of force, or the use of military forces for non-combat missions" is the way Allan Millett (2000: 28) summarized the picture. He extracted six reasons for American intervention over the past two centuries from these data: (1) protection of lives and property of American citizens; (2) protection of national interests that transcend private humanitarian and economic concerns; (3) conduct of retaliatory raids against non-state enemies or against national armed forces that receive tacit or open sponsorship from an antagonistic government; (4) support of continuing diplomatic negotiations with a show of force; (5) support of an incumbent government involved in suppressing a rebellion or to support an insurgent movement that hopes to topple an unfriendly government, or to force both sides to cease military operations through peace-enforcement and peacekeeping efforts; and (6) implementation of governmental, economic, and social reform through the instrument of military occupation, including disarmament of citizen and foreign fighters, creation of new police forces, financial supervision, and economic management (Millett, 2000: 31). The purposes of military interventions have varied over time, although the issue of legitimacy, authorization for the use of force, and the specification of mission and the rules of engagement remained constant. Protracted intervention programs, measured in duration, duties, and achievements, were most likely not anticipated at the time of initial engagement. According to Millett (2000: 31), "When a Marine landing party went ashore at Port-au-Prince, Haiti, in 1915, neither the Wilson administration nor the Marine Corps would have predicted that they had begun an operation to protect foreign lives and property and to stop a civil war that would end *20 years later* (italics in original) with a tacit admission of failure in reforming Haiti's public institutions and political culture."

Throughout the nineteenth century, armed missions focused mostly on piracy issues or ocean-based crimes. Sending troops to resolve a civil dispute or protect American interests within a sovereign territory were less common in that time and through most of the twentieth century, though they did occur on a regular basis in two specific regions: Central America—Panama, Cuba, Haiti, Honduras, and Nicaragua were the main targets—and very frequently China between 1843 and 1949. By Millett's interpretation (2000: 32–34) geostrategic concerns, that is, U.S. sphere of influence policy of the Monroe Doctrine, played a greater role in rationalizing interventions in the Caribbean basin, even if still clothed in the rhetoric of protecting American lives and property. In Asia, "the American military commitment to China in the 1930s in terms of percentages of the American armed forces is analogous to the American commitments to NATO in the 1990s," says Millett (2000: 33). Whatever the expedient rationale, the United States used its armed forces to keep the "Open Door" wide open as long as possible. Overt military intervention stops abruptly in 1949 as the Chinese civil war comes to an end and a communist regime is put into power. However, American intervention into Asia, if not inside China, at least along its borders, continued: in Korea, thousands of U.S. soldiers were deployed during the war in the 1950s, and more than a half-century later, a substantial contingent (around 35,000 troops) was still stationed in South Korea. American troops fought in Vietnam until the mid-seventies. Asian intervention has been a mainstay of U.S. military missions, both in frequency of involvement and by level of intensity through participation in civil wars within the region. Western Hemisphere interventions are also high on the list: U.S. post–Cold War intervention into Panama and Haiti is consistent with this trend. A chronological array and brief description of intervention events in Central America and Asian countries are displayed in Table 7.1.

At the end of World War II, the geographic terrain of U.S. intervention began to expand due undoubtedly to America's transformed position into superpower status and the simultaneous, gradual breakdown of the European colonial system, a process that created a large number of newly independent states as eligible targets of intervention. Cold War geographic locals are more diffuse. What has changed over time, most evident in the post–Cold War period, is American intervention in three geographic theatres; the Middle East, Europe, and Africa.

A noticeable pattern of U.S. direct military involvement in the Middle East begins in the 1980s (although the United States sent Marines to Lebanon in 1958 to curb Arab nationalism, this was a brief, isolated event) starting with the American hostage rescue attempt in Iran (1980), continuing with Marine deployments in Lebanon in 1982 and 1983 and military operations in the Persian Gulf in 1987–1988. The post–Cold War increased U.S. military involvement intensity culminating with the crisis and war in the Gulf in 1990–1991, following the Iraqi invasion of Kuwait and threats against Saudi Arabia—events that would have been unlikely during the Cold War years—and periodic intervention probes in Iraq since then, and the continuous deployment of 5,000 American troops in Saudi Arabia. A strong U.S. military presence in the oil-rich regions of the Middle East is a recent development, a clear change from the Cold War pattern, although historically, great power presence was common to the area.

The pattern of U.S. military intervention in Europe started at the end of World War II when America became an occupying power in several European countries and throughout the Cold War maintained a strong presence, particularly an extensive military force in West Germany, under the NATO alliance. However, the purpose of troop posturing was part of the international bipolar system of threats and stability, not to reduce threats arising from civil disturbance. Only in Greece (where military forces were limited to advising and training tasks; they were not engaged in combat or peacekeeping roles) were Americans troops introduced to deal with a civil conflict. In the 1990s, the locus of activity shifted to ex-Yugoslavia: American forces have participated in conflicts in Bosnia, Macedonia, and Albania, as peacekeeping forces on humanitarian missions to curtail ethnic cleansing, and in Kosovo, Yugoslavia, in both combat and peacekeeping missions. This too represents a departure from previous trends in places and reasons for involvement. In the Cold War, Yugoslavia was an "independent" member of the group of allies affiliated with the Soviet Union. American intervention would have been extremely unlikely.

Table 7.1
U.S. Military Intervention: Selected Countries in Central America and Asia

Intervention in Haiti

Year	Event
1888	A display of force persuaded the Haitian government to give up an American steamer which had been seized on the charge of breach of blockade.
1891	U.S. forces fought to protect American lives and property on Navassa Island.
1914	U.S. naval forces protected American nationals in a time of rioting and revolution.
1915–1934	U.S. forces maintained order during a period of chronic political instability.
1993	U.S. ships began to enforce a UN embargo.
1994	U.S. troops were deployed to restore democracy.

Intervention in Panama

1856	U.S. forces landed to protect American interests during an insurrection.
1865	U.S. forces protected the lives and property of American residents during a revolution.
1885	U.S. forces were used to guard the valuables in transit over the Panama Railroad and the safes and vaults of the company during revolutionary activity. U.S. forces helped reestablish freedom of transit during revolutionary activity.
1901	U.S. forces protected American property, kept transit lines open during serious revolutionary disturbances.
1902	US. placed armed guards on all trains to keep railroad lines open, stationed ships on both sides of Panama to prevent landing of Colombian troops.
1903–1914	U.S. forces fought to protect American interests and lives during and following the revolution for independence from Colombia over construction of the Isthmian Canal.

1904	U.S. forces protected American lives and property at Ancon at the time of a threatened insurrection.
1912	U.S. troops, on request of both political parties, supervised elections outside the Canal Zone.
1918–1920	U.S. forces were used for police duty according to treaty stipulations, during election disturbances and subsequent unrest.
1921	American naval squadrons demonstrated on both sides of the Isthmus to prevent war between Panama and Costa Rica over a boundary dispute.
1925	U.S. troops landed to keep order and protect American interests during strikes and rent riots.
1988	U.S. troops sent to further safeguard the canal, U.S. lives, property, and interests in the area during a period of instability.
1989	U.S. troops sent to augment 11,000 U.S. forces stationed in the area.
1989–1990	U.S. troops sent to protect the lives of American citizens and bring General Noriega to justice.

Intervention in China

1843	Sailors and Marines were landed after a clash between American and Chinese at the trading post in Canton.
1854	American and English ships landed forces to protect American interests in and near Shanghai during Chinese civil strife.
1855	U.S. forces protected American interests in Shanghai and Hong Kong.
1856	U.S. forces landed to protect American interests at Canton.
1859	A naval force landed to protect American interests in Shanghai.
1866	U.S. forces punished an assault on the American consul at Newchwang.
1894–1895	Marines were stationed at Tientsin and penetrated to Peking.
1898–1899	U.S. forces provided a guard for the legation at Peking and the consulate at Tientsin.
1900	American troops participated in operations to protect foreign lives during the Boxer rising, particularly at Peking. For many years after

this experience a permanent legation guard was maintained in Peking, and was strengthened at times as trouble threatened.

1911   Marines were deployed to guard cable stations atShanghai, landing forces sent for protection in Nanking, Chinkiang, Taku and elsewhere.

1912   U.S. forces protected American interests during revolutionary activity.

1912–1941   Landing parties for the protection of U.S. interests continuously and at many points. The guard at Peking and along the route to the sea was maintained until 1941. In 1927, the United States had 5,670 troops ashore in China and 44 naval vessels in its waters. In 1933, the United States had 3,027 armed men ashore. The protective action was generally based on treaties with China concluded from 1858 to 1901.

1916   American forces landed to quell a riot taking place on American property in Nanking.

1917   American troops were landed at Chungking to protect American lives during a political crisis.

1920   A landing force was sent ashore to protect lives during a disturbance at Kiukiang.

1922–1923   Marines were landed five times to protect Americans during periods of unrest.

1924   Marines were landed to protect Americans and other foreigners in Shanghai during Chinese factional hostilities.

1925   American forces were landed to protect lives and property in the International Settlement.

1926   American naval forces were landed to protect American citizens.

1927   American naval forces and marines increased around Shanghai, Nanking, Tientsin.

1932   American forces were landed to protect American interests in Shanghai.

1934   Marines landed at Foochow to protect the American consulate.

1945   U.S. Marines, 50,000 troops, were sent to North China to assist Chinese Nationalist authorities in disarming and repatriating the Japanese in China and in controlling ports, railroads, and airfields. This was in addition to approximately 60,000 U.S. forces remaining in China at the end of World War II.

1948-1949   Marines were dispatched to Nanking to protect the American Embassy when the city fell to Communist troops, and to Shanghai to aid in the protection and evacuation of Americans.

Intervention in Korea

1871   A naval force attacked and captured five forts to punish natives for depredation on Americans, murdering the crew of the *General Sherman* and burning the schooner, later firing on other American small boats taking soundings up the Salee River.

1888   A naval force was sent ashore to protect American residents in Seoul during unsettled political conditions, when an outbreak of the populace was expected.

1894–1896   Marines were stationed at Tientsin and penetrated to Peking for protection purposes during the Sino-Japanese war.

1904–1905   A guard of Marines was sent to protect the American legation in Seoul during the Russo-Japanese war.

1950–1953   U.S. forces were deployed in Korea, responding to North Korean invasion of South Korea. Forces exceed 300,000 during the last year of the conflict. Over 36,600 U.S. military were killed in action.

1976   Additional forces were sent to Korea after two American soldiers were killed by North Korean soldiers in the demilitarized zone between North and South Korea.

Intervention in Vietnam

1964–1973   U.S. military advisors had been in South Vietnam for a decade and their numbers had been increased as the military position of the Saigon government became weaker. Following the Tonkin Gulf Resolution in August 1964, and following a Communist attack on a U.S. installation in central Vietnam, the United States escalated its participation in the war to a peak of 543,000 by April 1969.

1975   U.S. naval vessels, 70 helicopters, and 865 marines had been sent to assist in evacuation of refugees and U.S. nationals.

Source: Adapted from Grimmett (1999), pp. 5–18.

In Africa, the 1990s witnessed numerous instances of civil unrest in various countries—Somalia, Liberia, Sierra Leone, Sudan, Rwanda, Central African Republic, the Congo, Gabon, Guinea Bissau. U.S. forces were sent as rescue missions in some instances, and in Somalia, a substantial contingent of military troops participated in humanitarian relief efforts and undertook some tasks aimed at societal reform. In Rwanda, the genocide failed to bring in U.S. troops until after it was over. Then a short-term disaster response force was sent to help in humanitarian matters.

The recent changes of U.S. intervention in two theatres of operation—the Middle East and former Yugoslavia—are explainable by the international system change; the rules of bipolarism restricted superpower involvement in these arenas and the structural shift cleared the course for intervening. In Africa, one can speculate whether the end of the Cold War, marked in part by states losing support from their former superpower guarantors, was causally related to the increasing levels of instability in the region and helped create military response reactions from the United States. A chronological pattern of U.S. armed force use during the 1980s and 1990s is shown in Table 7.2, documenting the shift in geographic focus in the post–Cold War period.

To account for the general patterns of U.S. intervention frequency over the last 200 years, Brian M. Pollins and Randall L. Schweller (1999: 431), investigating the changes in activism levels in the orientation of U.S. policy, suggested that temporal differences capture periods of "introversion" and "extroversion" moods. The basic argument is that intervention is a function of the state of the U.S. economy. These moods function in relationship to good and bad economic conditions at home: hard times may impel leaders to seek foreign adventure (the "diversionary" hypothesis), abundant finances and military buildups may result in armed entanglements (the "war chest" hypothesis), and economic growth may generate a societal need for foreign expansion (the "lateral pressure" hypothesis).

The shifts in foreign policy orientation are also tied to larger systemic processes that affect the nation's proclivity for foreign engagement and its capability for such activity. This allows the question of national interests and capabilities to be separately examined rather than to take them as given characteristics of autonomous agents, assert Pollins and Schweller (1999: 433). They base their analysis on Frank Klingberg's (1952) mood model identifying alternating introversion-extroversion periods in American foreign policy (with a full cycle lasting roughly 50 years—27 years of extroversion, 20 years of introversion). Klingberg supported his theory with indices including naval spending as a measure of U.S. power projection; events data covering U.S. territorial annexations, armed expeditions, and acts of strong diplomatic pressure; and content analysis of party platforms and presidential inaugural and State of the Union addresses. Klingberg discovered that while America's interest in foreign affairs has steadily risen commensurate with its growth in power, presidents speak measurably less about foreign relations and far less about U.S. foreign activities during introversion phases than they do during extroversion phases. Klingberg (1952: 257–258) reports that during extroversion phases, the

Table 7.2
Instances of Use of U.S. Armed Forces Abroad, 1980–1999*

Year**	Country	Africa	Asia	Europe	Islamic/ Middle East	Western Hemisphere
1980	Iran				●	
1981	El Salvador					●
1981, 1986, 1989	Libya				●	
1982	Lebanon				●	
1982	Egypt (Sinai)				●	
1983–1989	Honduras					●
1983	Chad	●				
1983	Grenada					●
1986	Bolivia					●
1988–1990	Panama					●
1989	Colombia					●
1989	Philippines		●			
1990, 1998	Liberia	●				
1990–	Saudi Arabia				●	
1991–	Iraq				●	
1991	Zaire	●				
1992, 1997	Sierra Leone	●				
1992–1995	Somalia	●				
1993–1999	Bosnia			●		

Table 7.2 Instances of Use of U.S. Armed Forces Abroad, 1980–1999*   **(cont)**

Year**	Country	Africa	Asia	Europe	Islamic/ Middle East	Western Hemisphere
1993–	Macedonia			●		
1993, 1994–	Haiti					●
1994	Rwanda	●				
1996	Central Afr. Rep.	●				
1997, 1998–	Albania			●		
1997	Congo	●				
1997	Gabon	●				
1997	Cambodia		●			
1998	Guinea Bissau	●				
1998–	Kenya	●				
1999–	Yugoslavia (Kosovo)			●		

*Includes rescue mission situations of military conflict or potential conflict to protect U.S. citizens or promote U.S. interests; peacekeeping. Excludes covert actions, occupation forces, training operations.
**Year forces introduced and continued through 1999.

Source: Adapted from Grimmett (1999), pp. 19–29

United States conducted 22 territorial annexations (attempted and successful), 102 armed expeditions, and 75 acts of strong diplomatic pressure; in contrast, in introversion phases, there were no territorial annexations, 12 armed expeditions, and 23 diplomatic pressure acts. Klingberg categorizes America's renewed leadership as the Cold War ends, dating it roughly 1986–1987 as the start of a revived extrovert mood (Klingberg, 1996: 301). Assuming Klingberg is correct, and that the periodicity of the cycle holds, Pollins and Schweller (1999: 435) project the U.S. current extroversion phase should last roughly until 2014. The extroversion times are matched with greater activity, including interventions abroad.

U.S. engagements in foreign conflicts would be more frequent during periods of extroversion and more expansive during the upswing phases of the global economy and introverted during the global downswing, Pollins and Schweller (1999: 435) reasoned. Using Correlates of War Militarized Interstate Dispute Data, which documents all interstate conflicts in which force was used or threatened from 1815 forward, their analysis shows that American involvement in foreign conflict (wars and armed disputes) is associated and patterned with the phases identified in Klingberg's cycles (Table 7.3), although the fit is not as sharp in the most recent periods. At the same time, these periods of extroversion and introversion mirror the four-phase cycle of the global economy identified by Joshua Goldstein (1991)—introversion is matched to a stagnation phase followed by rebirth (cycles of roughly equal duration) and extroversion is matched to an expansion phase followed by stagflation. Goldstein notes growth rates in global economic production and consumption are highest during the rebirth and expansion phases, while levels of such activity peak during expansion and stagflation. Price inflation peaks during stagflation. The probability that the United States is "extroverted" in its foreign policy orientation changes with the phases of the long wave in the global economy. Specifically, state Pollins and Schweller (1999: 441–442), the United States is measurably less likely to be extroverted during the two "down" phases in the global economy (stagnation and rebirth) and more likely to be extroverted during the growth phases, expansion and stagflation.

Pollins and Schweller discover a dramatic rise in the probability of extroversion as the global economy shifts into the expansion phase and a second drop as the system passes through stagflation: a genuine dynamic pattern repeats once every 50 years, roughly speaking, or four times over the course of U.S. history to date. The causal mechanisms linking global economic long-wave cycles to swings in American foreign policy moods and to U.S. conflict behavior suggest military involvement is most likely to occur in prosperous times. This is because armed conflict among nations requires adequate finances, complex organization, and domestic unity. When treasuries are full, countries are willing and able to wage big wars. States expand when they think they can, when they perceive relative increases in national power, and when changes in the relative costs and benefits of expansion make it profitable for them to do so. Realists predict that as states grow wealthier and more powerful, they not only seek greater worldwide political influence (control over territory, the behavior of other states, and the world economy) commensurate with their new capabilities, but they will also be more capable of expanding their interests and, if necessary, of waging large-scale wars for this purpose. Their analysis shows a linkage between U.S. conflict behavior and global economic conditions, supporting theories of domestic policy orientation—the diversionary hypothesis and war chest hypothesis. As further support for the activity cycles of introversion and extroversion periods, intervention levels catalogued in the Congressional Research Service (CRS) report (Grimmett, 1999) closely follow this pattern. Assuming continuation in cyclical projections, a new extroversion phase in American foreign policy started at approximately the same time the post–Cold

Table 7.3
American Foreign Policy Activism Phases since 1776

Introversion Dates	Disputes Entered	Resolved	CRS Interventions	Extroversion Dates	Disputes Entered	Resolved	CRS Interventions
1776–1798 (22 years)	na	na	na	1798–1824 (26 years)	na	na	20
1824–1844 (20 years)	13	10	16	1845–1871 (26 years)	30	27	38
1872–1891 (19 years)	19	17	12	1892–1919 (27 years)	40	33	55
1920–1940 (20 years)	15	10	20	1941–1967 (26 years)	87	58	23
1968–1987 (19 years)	85	67	25	1988–2014 ?	na	na	68*

CRS = Congressional Research Service Study (Grimmett, 1999).
na = not ascertained.
* = through 1999.

Sources: Klingberg (1952); Pollins and Schweller (1999), p. 437; Grimmett (1999).

War era began. The level of U.S. activism is therefore anticipated to be high for some time. Hence, intervention is a more likely policy strategy. The current age of intervention activity around the globe is explainable by cyclical trends, and not unexpected.

COLD WAR INTERVENTION TRENDS

An early study of Cold War intervention patterns by Barry Blechman and Stephen S. Kaplan (1978) was designed to analyze how U.S. armed forces were used as a political instrument of foreign policy. In their survey of interventions covering 1946–1975, Blechman and Kaplan looked for situations where actions by military services were part of a deliberate attempt by the national authorities to influence designated behavior of individuals in another nation without engaging in a continuing contest of violence. Operationally, they searched for incidents where these factors were present: physical movement of soldiers, consciousness of a political purpose, decision-maker intention to reach objectives by gaining influence in the target states rather than by imposing U.S. will, avoidance of violence, and specific behavior desired of the targeted state. Military activities include use of firepower, establishment of a permanent or temporary presence abroad, blockade, military exercises, escort or transport services of another actor's armed forces or supplies, evaluations, patrol missions, and changes in readiness status, but they exclude situations of armed forces as a martial instrument, when a military unit acts to seize territory or defeat an army (they ruled out both the Korean and Vietnam wars), uses of U.S. military power deployed to defend directly U.S. property, citizens, or military positions, routine activity to maintain or improve combat readiness, provisions of military assistance, and relief efforts following national disasters (Blechman and Kaplan 1978: 12–15). Their data include 215 incidents in which the United States employed its armed forces for political purposes between 1946 and 1975.

Most interventions during the 30-year window occurred within the Western Hemisphere and in Asia, consistent with the 200-year patterns identified by the CRS study. A few types of situations in each world region accounted for a large proportion of the incidents in which the United States used its armed forces for political objectives: most incidents in sub-Saharan Africa involved internal strife in Zaire or Tanzania; in Central America, nearly half involved Cuba (the rise to power of Fidel Castro, attempts to oust him from power) and domestic conflicts in either Haiti or the Dominican Republic; in the Middle East, a third of the incidents related to internal strife in Jordan and Lebanon (Blechman and Kaplan 1978: 24).

Blechman and Kaplan divide the data into four time periods to evaluate how attention in U.S. foreign policy has moved across the geographic terrain over time (see Table 7.4). At the start of the Cold War period, the intervention focus on Europe is highest, but shifts downward over time; the Middle East not a focal point in early years, commands greater attention in the 1970s; intervention activity in the Western Hemisphere appears cyclical across the 30-year period; the focus on East Asia remains relatively consistent. From their analysis, Blechman and Kaplan project the end of the war in Vietnam and changing perceptions of U.S. interests in Southeast Asia would render new actions in that area unlikely. By contrast, they predict the Middle East will not be a neglected arena: "The Arab-Israeli conflict continues, regimes in the area remain fragile, intra-Arab conflicts abound, and the oil issue looms large in calculations of U.S. decision-makers," say Blechman and Kaplan (1978: 33).

They find a correlation between the frequency of U.S. armed force use and the number of opportunities presented by the international system, and also a positive correlation between the intervention activity and the popularity of the President, and with the nation's sense of confidence. An optimistic national spirit creates more intervention. Increasing opportunities presented by the international environment and high levels of national confidence suggest higher levels of intervention, a conclusion fully supportive of Pollin and Schweller's motivational perspective to buttress trends in activism levels in the history of U.S. foreign policy. In a related point, when they divided the list of incidents of armed force use into categories that were essentially international and those that were civil based (Blechman and Kaplan 1978: 34), they discover a sharp increase in the share of incidents attributable to civil-based events during the period of greatest U.S. activism (1956–1965), offering further evidence for the extroversion hypothesis (see Table 7.5). The United States tended to become involved in domestic conflicts mainly when violence was threatened or actually occurred, that is, civil conflict constitutes intervention opportunity, a finding entirely consistent with the post–Cold War period. In the periods around the Korean and Vietnam Wars, they discovered policy-makers employed U.S. armed forces in discrete political operations far less often than they did at other times, not a surprising result, for fewer unengaged forces were available and officials would be reluctant to become involved in situations which might have resulted in new demands on their resources (Blechman and Kaplan 1978: 26–31).

Tillema (1989), extending the Cold War time frame by 10 years to cover 1945–1985, looked at intervention trends by all states in the international system but applied a more restrictive meaning of the term than Blechman and Kaplan. Tillema was interested in the frequency of "foreign overt military intervention," which consists of direct combatant or combat-preparatory military operations conducted on foreign territory by units of a state's regular military forces— conventional deployments of ground combat units, commando or small unit raids, aerial bombing, ground-based artillery, or rocketry. Less blatant forms of international interference—covert operations, military alerts, shows of force, military assistance, activities of police units, irregular forces, multinational peace forces, observer groups, encounters in the air or at sea—were excluded (Tillema 1989: 187). Any set of sporadic events occurring within six months of one another were packaged into one intervention (Tillema 1989: 183).

These data include 97 states initiating 591 intervention events within 269 armed conflicts. U.S. interventions are identified in just seven armed conflicts among the total set of the world's violent crises across the 40-year time span. All of the cases deal with problems of domestic governance: South Korean Occupation (1945–1948), North China Occupation (1945–1946), the Korean

Table 7.4
U.S. Political Use of Armed Forces: Distribution over Time and Region

Time	Western Hemisphere	Europe	Middle East and North Africa	South Asian sub-Saharan Africa	Southeast and East Asia
1946–1948	21%	63%	13%	0%	4%
1949–1955	13%	29%	8%	4%	46%
1956–1965	37%	12%	15%	9%	27%
1966–1975	13%	15%	32%	4%	36%

Source: Blechman and Kaplan (1978), p. 33.

Table 7.5
U.S. Political Use of Armed Forces: Distribution over Time and Political Situation

Time	Intranational	International Initially involving U.S.	International Not initially involving U.S.
1946–1948	33%	38%	29%
1949–1955	38%	20%	42%
1956–1965	52%	25%	23%
1966–1975	34%	26%	40%

Source: Blechman and Kaplan (1978), p. 35.

War (1949–1953), the Lebanese Civil War (1958), the Second Indochina War (Vietnam, 1962–1975) the Lebanese Conflict (1968 on), and the Occupation of Grenada (1983). The level of intensity, specifically troops stationed abroad, bombing campaigns, and so on, are not part of this analysis; rather, the real interest is geographic spread and resort to defense forces to deal with problems facing states in the international community.

Superpower intervention restraint operated throughout the Cold War, Tillema (1989: 185) concludes: The United States and Soviet Union conducted 13 interventions (4%) between September 1945 through October 1965, of 298 total instances; they carried out 11 (4%) interventions from November 1965 through December 1985 of 293 total interventions. Britain, France, Israel, China, and

India all intervened far more frequently. More interventions conducted by states acquiring their independence in 1945 or later increased over time. These data show that the two superpowers contributed relatively little to the overall frequency of foreign overt military intervention during the Cold War, if not in the magnitude of their military operations, at least in the number of times and places where they resorted to arms. "There appears to be an 'intervention gap' between the disproportionate military capabilities of the superpowers, which have consistently commanded a majority of world military expenditures, and the frequency with which they have directly exposed their armed forces to the immediate prospect of combat abroad," writes Tillema (1989: 185). One might add a second feature of the "intervention gap," which is the contradictory viewpoints between general impressions of high-level superpower interventionary involvement through the Cold War years and the low-level involvement revealed in the Foreign Overt Military Intervention data set. Surely discrepancy lies in the way the term *intervention* was applied. Tillema is interested in one primary aspect situated at the far end of the intervention scale—military, overt behavior, without other, more subtle forms of military use—he focuses on frequency rather than intensity. When applied to the post–Cold War period, Tillema's conceptualization shows the United States is decidedly more active in recent times: within roughly 10 years, there are five cases where American troops were sent abroad to engage in foreign, overt military intervention activity—Panama, the Gulf War, Somalia, Kosovo, and Afghanistan (the U.S. military role in Haiti, Rwanda, and Bosnia fall into peacekeeping operations, categories excluded by Tillema). By sharp contrast, during the previous 40 years, armed forces intervened into just seven cases. It must be concluded, from this perspective, that the United States engages more frequently in interventionary behavior in the new age, that is, the United States appears to be more willing to brandish its military might into wider environments.

Regan (2000a) designed an alternative basis for judging the extent of U.S. intervention in the last half of the twentieth century, asking whether intervention was a direct function of changes in levels of violence and instability around the world. As violence spreads, the possibilities for intervention policies also increase. More states need help, more assistance will be provided. Regan created a file of "intervention opportunities" consisting of intrastate, civil conflicts between 1944 and 1994, specifically, "armed combat between groups within state boundaries in which there are at least 200 fatalities" (Regan, 2000a: 21). Intervention refers to third-party involvement of a form that is "convention-breaking military and/or economic activities in the internal affairs of a foreign country targeted at the authority structures of the government with the aim of affecting the balance of power between the government and opposition forces" (Regan, 2000a: 10). Military interventions encompass the supply or transfer of troops, hardware, intelligence, air or naval support, and logistical support to the parties in conflict, or the cutoff of any such aid currently in place. Economic interventions involve various forms of economic aid and economic sanctions or embargoes. The Regan definition of intervention is more encompassing than

Tillema's, not quite as detailed as Blechman and Kaplan's description. The chief difference in Regan's approach is establishing a baseline, by setting parameters for intervention choices: he identified 138 civil conflicts—111 started during the Cold War, and 29 developed from 1989 forward (22 began in the 1991–1994 period). Altogether, 89 conflicts included at least one outside intervention; 49 did not. Unilateral decisions to intervene are much more common than collective efforts, notes Regan (2000a: 25, 17).

These data indicate nearly 40% of all interventions were carried out by major powers. The United States, leading the list, had 35 interventions. The Soviet Union followed with 16 (next on the list were France, 10 instances; Britain, 9; China, 6) (Regan 2000a: 28). From the analysis, it appears that during the Cold War there were fewer intervention opportunities but there was greater U.S. intervention; in the post–Cold War the relationship is reversed: considerably more civil conflicts and hence greater opportunities to intervene, yet a lower level of intervention response rate by the U.S. forces—a result that contradicts a popular view of expanded U.S. interventionary action in the new age and shows a different conclusion than trends identified by Tillema. Again, the source of difference in result is probably the circumscribed definition of civil conflict (setting the fatality toll at 200 minimum deaths) and expanding the designation of intervention, which includes military and economic acts.

Regan's central interests focused in two areas: whether the intervener was successful in achieving its goals (measured by cessation of military hostilities for a period lasting at least six months) and identifying whether an intervener entered to support the government or opposition forces. Regan found roughly half of the interventions were in support of government forces, and successful strategies tended either to support the government through military intervention or to provide economic intervention to the opposition. For conflicts that have been settled and had intervention, the average time period is seven years, while conflicts in which there was no intervention had a mean duration of just 18 months. Regan cannot say whether this difference is because multiple interventions make resolution more intractable or because third parties generally intervene in conflicts of long duration rather than contributing to the length of the conflict. Conflicts with intervention tend to be bloodier. Regan also discovered some inconsistencies: "The list of intrastate conflicts with and without intervention is relatively long and there does not seem to be any intuitive criteria to determine when an intervention is most likely to take place: The United States intervened in Colombia in the 1950s but not in the failed revolution of 1948; neither did it intervene in Paraguay in 1947 but did in Guatemala seven years later. Rwanda has experienced a number of internal conflicts since the 1960s but only the most recent one led to a unilateral intervention. The US essentially intervened twice in the Somalia conflict prior to 1991, once in support of the opposition forces, and then switching sides to support the government. Chad attracts outside interventions to its civil wars, yet nobody intervened in the Nigerian conflicts throughout the 60s, 70s and 80s" (Regan 2000a: 39).

A well-designed intervention strategy affects the climate that will increase the effectiveness of the effort; operational criteria will contribute to the building of trust between combatants and the interveners, yet a changing environment may lead interveners to rely on ad hoc measures, which can challenge the authority of the mission itself, concludes Regan (2000a: 116). Among other predictors of success: neutral posture intervention and mutual consent by warring parties to the intervention and its terms. In addition, interventions are considerably more likely to be successful when the conflict is quite intense, although the more intense the conflict, the less likely are outside actors to become involved in it: "Given a set of base conditions an intervention into a highly intense conflict has about a 70% chance of successfully stopping the fighting" (Regan, 2000a: 141). The most important outcome from the study is that the strategy for intervening has the largest influence on the outcome of the intervention, and support for the government is more effective than similar support for an opposition.

Regan challenges the common perception that intervention into civil conflicts has increased significantly since the end of the Cold War, granting that the public seems to be considerably more aware of the phenomenon, which may contribute to this impression. His evidence demonstrates that unilateral interventions were more likely during the Cold War than after it and the data show that it is not clear that a new trend is evolving since the end of the Cold War. He also doubts whether civil conflicts, "intervention opportunities," are actually following an upward trend in the new era, noting that the immediate aftermath of the Soviet collapse did result in an upswing in conflicts but that trend quickly tapered off (Regan, 2000a: 142). Multilateral peacekeeping efforts administered through the United Nations showed a similar upward trend in the brief period following the Cold War's demise, though this too was a short-lived, temporal spike.

Is intervention a wise policy choice in the post–Cold War age? Regan is not so sure. Constraints on decisions and actions limit intervener options: supporting a government in its struggle against an opposition's challenge may be the most effective method of stopping the fighting, yet depending on the political alignments of the groups, supporting the government may not be an acceptable option. Regan cites the NATO response to the conflict in Kosovo in 1999 between the Albanian independence movement and Serbian government reactions, in which the Western alliance supported the opposition forces, diminishing likelihood of success. From this experience, Regan forms an inductive argument: "The approach then—if a state decides to intervene—might be to design a strategy that is most effective given the political constraints. Equally plausible is that given the conditions of the conflict and the orientation of the groups involved, the prospects for a successful outcome is (sic) so low that in spite of political imperatives, the best strategy is not to intervene. Intervening, it may turn out, simply increases the level of conflict without any reasonable prospect of achieving a desirable outcome" (Regan, 2000a: 148). This argument directly counters the elemental, implicit assumption of policy-makers, namely that intervention helps security enhancement.

Why did the United States intervene during the Cold War? The research reviewed to this point has focused primarily on identifying changes in patterns of geographical interest, the up-and-down periods of activity, and very general reasons for American foreign policy behavior. Margaret Hermann and Charles Kegley (1998: 94) examine the political consequences of 89 U.S. interventions—the direct use of overt American military force in other countries—that occurred between the end of World War II and 1992. Hermann and Kegley define intervention as "forcible interference by a state in the affairs of another state, calculated to impose certain conduct or consequences on the other state." It is a form of coercive diplomacy, focused on changing or preserving the structure of political authority in the target society. Hermann and Kegley were specifically interested in actions where at least one major purpose was to protect or promote democracy in the target state (the action involved military force used either to support a government that was leaning toward or in the liberal democratic community or to oppose an autocratic government). Sixty-four interventions involved varying degrees of U.S. troop commitments ranging from sending military advisors and equipment to assist one combatant in a civil war to shows of force with naval warships to moving large numbers of U.S. ground forces into the target country. There were 25 other times when the United States employed military force that did not meet their definition of intervention, which focuses on government reform as a primary goal. Hermann and Kegley (1998) assessed changes in the institutions of governments in countries experiencing outside intervention using scales of democracy and autocracy, measuring the degree of democraticness of the target regime at the start and at the end of an intervention. The data show that U.S. interventions intended to protect or promote democracy in the target have generally led to an increase in the democraticness of those targets' political regimes (Hermann and Kegley, 1998: 97–98) and interventions with other purposes resulted in the target states' becoming more autocratic. Hermann and Kegley conclude that the U.S. government targets pro-liberalization interventions toward countries where it stands a chance of promoting democratic reform in situations where the risks are acceptable. When the motivation for an intervention is to *promote* democracy (38 cases), not only to *protect* democracy (26 cases), within a target country, the change toward democraticness is significantly stronger. Reform intervention can be effective as a foreign policy strategy, conclude Hermann and Kegley (1998: 101–102) and change toward more democratic political institutions was greater during the shorter intervention periods—under one year. They also discover different amounts of reform were associated with various levels of commitment: minimal *and* large commitments resulted in greater change in the democraticness of the target than those used in modest forces. Moreover, the United States stayed with minimal commitments when the target was already somewhat democratic and went with largest commitment when the target was autocratic.

Dividing the data into two eras, 1955–1974 and 1975–1992, Hermann and Kegley found a significant increase in the degree of democraticness of American targets following interventions intended to protect or promote democracy during the recent period of democratization in the international system, suggesting that intervention may be a more effective instrument for democratization when democracy is preferred more generally in the international arena (Hermann and Kegley 1998: 107). This helps explain why American presidents have combined military intervention and democracy promotion despite the apparent contradictions involved in promoting self-determination through coercion: pro-liberalization policies help to legitimate a rationale for employing American troops abroad, they suggest. In the first 12 years of the post–Cold War age, the United States has been involved in democracy promotion interventions in Panama (replacing the national dictator and restoring democratic principles of free elections), Haiti (restoring the freely elected president to power), and Bosnia, Kosovo, and Afghanistan (putting institutional arrangements in place after conflict)—in sum, five of the cases of heaviest interventionary actions fit the projections of Hermann and Kegley.

Will intervention patterns evolving over the course of the Cold War decades persist in the post–Cold War era? To what extent will the United States continue to be motivated to intervene abroad? Jeffrey Pickering (1999: 363–364) takes up these questions, noting that two wholly distinctive worlds have emerged in the contemporary international system with regard to conflict, reminiscent of Fukuyami's vision that the entire world is gradually turning toward democracy and peace and the opposite perspective of Kaplan, who sees more anarchy and disorder in developing countries: democratic societies, those in the center who exist in a "zone of peace," and non-democracies confined to the periphery, living in a "zone of turmoil," the locale of much of the world's violence and conflict over the past half-century. Pickering (1999: 369) examines intervention activities into the turmoil zone—the developing world—by 24 members of the Organization of Economic Cooperation and Development (OECD)—the developed world—which he labels center states and conceives the use of force as employing the military to protect states' interests abroad to secure various foreign policy objectives. Foreign military intervention refers to the purposeful dispatch of national military personnel into other sovereign countries designed in pursuit of political or economic goals. Pickering's data cover 50 years, 1946–1996, which are divided into three periods—1946–1966, 1967–1986, and 1987–1996, temporal markers highlighting most generally transformations that have had the greatest effect on center-periphery relations over the past half-century, the slow winding down of the colonial period, the end of the Cold War (post-colonial period), and the post–Cold war era.

Pickering traces the structural shape that interstate force has taken roughly over the past half-century, 1946–1996—the level, intensity, and overall patterns of military force both within and between the central and peripheral systems. Are interventions likely to increase or diminish in the future? Pickering looks at two main arguments. One argument holds that levels of intervention will increase; center actors will continue to use military force in the periphery at fairly significant levels in the post–Cold War era. Levels of center military intervention in the developing world may gradually rise as the post–Cold War period continues, largely because center actors (OECD members) will increasingly be compelled to use force to try to mitigate instability inherent in the "zone of turmoil." International policing and humanitarian suffering may warrant limited military action in peripheral lands, suggesting intervention will continue to increase.

An alternative view suggests that levels of intervention will remain steady or decrease. With the end of colonialism, former colonial powers have found themselves with fewer commitments and therefore less involvement in the hinterlands. With the dissolution of superpower rivalry, center states have fewer vital strategic interests in the periphery. Also, there are new perils that make center actors more reluctant to intervene militarily in the hinterlands—the growing intensity of ethnic tension and the increasing spread of sophisticated weaponry throughout the developing world. Accordingly, center states have become less involved in low-scale conflicts in the periphery.

Is center use of force in the periphery increasing or declining? While levels of force have fluctuated, they increased considerably between 1987 and 1996. The evidence indicates that intervention is rising *and* that it is declining. Pickering (1999: 372) notes that force has not been used more often in post–Cold War era. While absolute frequency of forceful intervention did rise somewhat, controlling for the proliferation of new actors in the international system over the post-1945 era, the aggregate proclivity to intervene actually decreases after 1987. Moreover, both the scale of troop levels and the duration of interventionary force declined consistently over time. Military interventions lasting over one year and involving more than 1,000 troops were less frequent in the latter half of the Cold War era (1967–1986) than in the first half (1946–1966), and both were even less typical the post–Cold War era (1987–1996).

Military intervention in the developing world has occurred at high levels over the past half century. The United States was the most active intervener, with 81 uses of force in the periphery over the entire period (see Tables 7.6 and 7.7). accounting for nearly 40% of OECD interventions from 1946–1996. Initiation of center-periphery interventions peaked in the mid-1960s hit a low point in the 1970s, rose briefly in the early 1980s, and surged in the 1990s (Pickering, 1999: 376). From his analysis, Pickering (1999: 384–385) concludes that the center's use of interventionary force in the periphery continuing in the post–Cold War era suggests that interests and activities in the periphery will persist regardless of changes in the structure of the international system, yet it may not be permanent. The center's increased activity in the periphery may be due to expanded notions of security and to the periphery domination of the center. And, although there are consistent opportunities to intervene, the willingness to do so must be considered a function of many factors, including attitudes about the utility of force in the international community, and especially in the United States.

POST–COLD WAR INTERVENTION TRENDS

What vision of armed force use appears to dominate U.S. policy in the post–Cold War world? Nina M. Serafino (1999) examined nine cases where the U.S. military has intervened, either unilaterally or together with other nations, and

Table 7.6
Center State Intervention in Developing Countries

Interventions	1946–1966	1967–1986	1987-1996	Total 1946–1996
All interventions (by OECD states)	279 (34%)	370 (44%)	183 (22%)	832
Large interventions (more than 1,000 troops)	91 (44%)	103 (36%)	61 (34%)	255
Long duration (more than 1 year)	111 (40%)	125 (35%)	56 (31%)	292
Goal: Support host government	79 (39%)	104 (41%)	31 (40%)	214

Source: Adapted from copyright © 1999 from "The Structural Shape of Force: Interstate Intervention in the Zones of Peace and Turmoil, 1946–1996." *International Interactions* 25 (1999): 374 by Jeffrey Pickering. Reproduced by permission of Taylor & Francis, Inc., http://www.routledge-ny.com.

Table 7.7
United States Intervention in Developing Countries

Interventions	1946–1966	1967–1986	1987-1996	Total 1946–1996
All interventions	36	29	16	81
Large interventions (more than 1,000 troops)	6	4	9	19
Long duration (more than 1 year)	11	4	0	15
Goal: Support host government	16	11	5	32

Source: Adapted from copyright © 1999 from "The Structural Shape of Force: Interstate Intervention in the Zones of Peace and Turmoil, 1946–1996." *International Interactions* 25 (1999): 380 by Jeffrey Pickering. Reproduced by permission of Taylor & Francis, Inc., http://www.routledge-ny.com.

assessments of the operation relevant to the use of force. Six of them occurred in the post–Cold War period: Panama, Iraq, Somalia, Rwanda, Haiti, and Bosnia. Data about each operation include number of U.S. forces, period of deployment, battle-related deaths, mission objective, and outcome (see Table 7.8). Most missions had several objectives—the need to reverse aggression, to maintain regional stability, protect U.S. citizens, economic interests, human rights; restor-

Table 7.8
Comparative Data on U.S. Military Interventions

Case	No. U.S. forces (peak approx.)	Deployment Period	Deaths from Hostilities	Intervention Outcome
Vietnam	546,000	1961–1973	59,000	U.S. withdrawal in unstable peace Eventual collapse of supported government
Lebanon	1,900	1982–1984	260	U.S. withdrawal in unstable situation Six more years of civil war
Grenada	8,800	1983	19	U.S. withdrawal after restoring stability, democracy
Panama	27,000	1989–1990	23	U.S. withdrawal after restoring stability, democracy
Iraq	541,000	1990–1991	147	U.S. partial withdrawal after Iraqi aggression reversed; continued efforts to contain hostile regime
Somalia	25,800	1992–1994	29	U.S. withdrawal in unstable situation. Continued instability
Rwanda	3,600	1994	0	U.S. withdrawal in unstable situation. Continued instability
Haiti	21,000	1994–1996	1	U.S. withdrawal after restoring constitutional order Later, continued instability
Bosnia	16,500	1995–on	0	U.S. peacekeeping troops present Humanitarian relief provided, peace agreement Implementation proceeding slowly

Source: Adapted from Serafino (1999), pp. 9–10.

ation of constitutional order or rule of law, enforcing political or peace settlements. Rwanda was undertaken only to provide relief to refugees in the midst of a civil war. Only Panama was a unilateral action; for others, the United States sought allies. Serafino marks two successful cases: Iraq and Panama; Somalia is regarded as a failure. Outcomes in Haiti, Rwanda, and Bosnia produced mixed results.

Among lessons learned regarding these interventions is the use of overwhelming force as a major factor in successful operations and the lack of adequate force as a major factor contributing to mixed results, says Serafino (1999: 1). For mixed results or failed interventions, the amount of force deployed and exercised fell considerably short of the force needed. "Sometimes this force was applied gradually or incrementally, giving an appearance of hesitation or reluctance to its use. This applies to both conventional operations where the goal was to win by inflicting a military defeat, as well as to operations where the objective was to force parties to negotiate their differences, as well as peace operations where it was to ensure or enforce an agreed upon peace settlement" (Serafino 1999: 3). Judgments concerning the amount of force needed were easier to reach in cases where the objective was to defeat an opposing armed force and more difficult in cases where the objective was to present a credible threat to back diplomatic efforts to achieve a negotiated solution. Force levels and mission objectives are related to "mission creep," that is, the perception that the intervening forces, once committed, get assigned ever greater military tasks. Serafino (1999: 3–5) says this results from a failure to anticipate the amount of military effort that would be required, or a willingness to commit sufficient forces and resources at the outset. Successful interventions either were undertaken to restore the status quo ante which had been disrupted by an event or were conducted on behalf of an existing and long-standing constitutional order with broad public support, while failed interventions attempted to establish a new order or support a relatively recently adopted new order which did not have a cultural or institutional basis or perceived legitimacy to sustain it and where the intervening force left before such conditions were attained. Serafino notes that some situations may not be winnable with "limited" force because the opponent has a much greater interest in the outcome than the intervening parties, and thus is willing to sustain greater costs and to cede only in the face of a crushing defeat. Serafino hence recommends the United States develop better doctrine about the use of force and diplomatic efforts to back it. Force commitment is important, even though forces may not actually be deployed.

Why is it difficult for American military intervention missions to achieve their objectives in the post–Cold War age despite the political and military dominance it has enjoyed since 1989? One hinderance, state Barry Blechman and Tamara Cofman Wittes (1994: 4) is the U.S. experience in Vietnam, which they say left a heavy burden on future decision-makers: "There is a generation of political leaders throughout the world whose basic perception of US military power and political will is one of weakness, who enter any situation with a fundamental belief that the US can be defeated or driven away. This point of view was expressed explicitly and concisely by Mohamed Farah Aideed, leader of a key Somali faction, to Ambadssador Robert Oaklely, U.S. Special Envoy to Somalia during the disastrous U.S. involvement there in 1993–1995: 'We have studied Vietnam and Lebanon and know how to get rid of Americans, by killing them so that public opinion will put an end to things.' Aideed, of course was proven to be correct. The withdrawal from Mogadishu was a humiliating defeat for the US and it reinforced perceptions of America's lack of resolve and further complicated US efforts to achieve its goals through threats of force alone".

Blechman and Wittes examined all cases during the first Bush and first Clinton administrations in which the United States utilized its armed forces demonstratively in support of political objectives in specific situations. They identified eight cases, several of which included multiple uses of force: Panama, Iraq, Somalia, Macedonia, Bosnia, Haiti, North Korea, and Taiwan. While they admit the U.S. armed forces have been used demonstratively in support of diplomatic objectives in literally more than a thousand incidents during this period, ranging from major humanitarian operations to joint exercises with the armed forces of friendly nations to minor logistical operations in support of the United Nations or other multinational or national organizations, Blechman and Wittes studied the handful of specific incidents in which U.S. armed forces were used deliberately and actively to threaten or to conduct limited military operations in support of American policy objectives in specific situations. They suggest two primary factors facilitate effective use of military threats: the credibility that America will use force, and the degree of difficulty of meeting U.S. demands   (Bleckman and Wittes, 1999: 5–9). They propose eight conditions where coercive uses of military power are most likely to be successful: (1) a precedent: when the United States acts in a historical context, with precedent for its demands and actions; (2) public support: the presence and wide public support among members of Congress; (3) third-nation support: the presence of third-nation support for the United States; (4) urgency of the threat: a sense or urgency and deadlines for noncompliance for target tangible military action—deployment of forces on the ground in the potential theatre of operations; (5) articulated threat: clearly articulated in terms the target understands, specific demand content; (6) content of the demand: what is being demanded? (7) visibility of retreat required: a retreat that is visible and humiliating may be perceived as something to resist at any cost; (8) positive incentives: features to improve the target's perception of a U.S. demand, providing political excuse to back down and accept the U.S. demand. The target must perceive that the threat if carried out would result in a situation in which the target would be worse off than if it had complied with the U.S. demand. The context and character of the threat and degree of difficulty of the demand contribute to the target leader's understanding of the cost of complying or not.

They conclude that U.S. threats failed in Somalia, and succeeded with great difficulty in Panama, Iraq, Bosnia, and Haiti. In Bosnia and Haiti the underlying political conflict remains unresolved. Nothing alone appears to be a sufficient condition for success. A relationship between the difficulty of the demand and positive outcomes shows that the U.S. posture in most successful uses of military power included positive incentives, further reducing the difficulty of the demand as perceived by the target. Public support for a threat cannot guarantee its success, but a lack of public support apparently can make it difficult to make threats credibly, say Blechman and Wittes (1999: 21). Potent threats are important; in Iraq, Panama, and Bosnia the unwillingness of the United States to make threats that would clearly offer the target the prospect of an unacceptable cost seems to have been an important reason for the failure of U.S. policy, they argue (p. 21), noting a dilemma. "The problem that the United States faces, therefore, is very clear. It is rare that it can both make potent threats and retain public support. Potent threats imply greater risks. And the American public's aversion to risk, particularly the risk of suffering casualties, is well known; the legacy of Vietnam is real" (Blechman and Wittes, 1999: 24).

U.S. presidents have been reluctant to take appropriate actions in order to achieve objectives in the post–Cold War conflicts because of the problems associated with building and maintaining public support. They understand the need to act but are unwilling to get the sacrifices to meet the goal. Instead, they pursue a satisfying strategy: take some action, but not the most effective possible action to challenge the foreign leader threatening American interests, according to Blechman and Wittes. Presidential discretion operates in a way that is intended to curtail the extent and potential cost of the confrontation by avoiding the most serious type of threat and therefore the most costly type of war if the threat were challenged. This reduces the possibility for a successful operation. "Bosnian Serb leaders, Haitian paramilitary leaders, Saddam Hussein and Somalia's late warlord all banked on their ability to force a U.S. retreat by inflicting relatively small numbers of casualties on U.S. forces. That places American presidents attempting to accomplish goals through threats in a dilemma" (Blechman and Wittes, 1999: 24). Tentative policies reinforce the prejudices of foreign leaders leading them to stand firm, and domestic opinion rarely supports forceful policies at the outset. Vietnam's legacy abroad tends to push greater demonstrations of U.S. will, more tangible U.S. force actions, and stronger, more potent threats in order to succeed. Vietnam's legacy at home increases the difficulties for American presidents to take such forceful actions without risking significant political costs. Presidential choice to assert American strength will continue to be a primary determinant in successful intervention situations. Selecting cases carefully, proposing relatively easy demands and positive incentives will be very important. Acting decisively with clear, urgent demands and demonstrations of military power should also enhance success.

What key factors account for intervention in the post–Cold War period? Public support and presidential leadership are especially important in this post–Cold War era where there are fewer widely accepted clear threats to vital national interests, says Robert C. DiPrizio (2001: 2). What about public opinion? The mass media and public emotion might force the United States into imprudent interventions, but the parochial concerns of Congress and the military serve as major impediments to intervention: they prefer not to risk battle casualties. Conventional wisdom holds that mass media coverage of humanitarian crises forces policy-makers to act in ways they otherwise would not. The purported power of this so-called CNN effect emanates from the media's supposed ability to mobilize public emotions and the politician's sensitivity to public opinion. What is the interrelationship between presidential choice and intervention decisions and the influence of the media as public opinion support for an intervention?

Presidential evaluation of three particular factors determines an intervention policy, says DiPrizio (2001: 2–6). They are: (1) soft security (refugee flows, regional stability, alliance credibility, interalliance tension), (2) humanitarian concerns, and (3) domestic political issues (the public, media, and Congressional opinion factors in electoral politics). The president is the only person authorized to send military troops into action. DiPrizio evaluates six cases of post–Cold War intervention, concluding different combinations of forces explain each case. In Northern Iraq, soft security was primary; in Somalia, it was humanitarian concern; for Rwanda, domestic political concerns dominated the decision not to intervene; in Haiti, domestic political concerns—including the refugee issue—dominated; Bosnia was dominated solely by soft security issues; and Kosovo was seen similarly with humanitarian impulses and soft security operating as prime motivators. Whatever the concern to intervene, humanitarian plight was usually not a sufficient motivation force, yet the responses were humanitarian, promoting goals of delivering aid and quelling the crisis causing conflict. The actual effects of media influence are limited, and public opinion support (or lack of it) is not a key motivating factor. The role of Congress in these cases suggests neither strong encouragement nor strong opposition: for Northern Iraq or Somalia, there was no real encouragement nor effective opposition; in Rwanda, Congress was perceived to be influential (Clinton didn't want to go there for support fearing it wouldn't exist); in Bosnia and in Kosovo, Congress was deeply divided about the intervention; for the case of Haiti, Congress did play an important role. There is military opposition to humanitarian operations abroad—in every occasion they opposed the intervention but the president decided to go ahead in spite of the Pentagon's preferences. In none of the cases was military opposition the deciding factor in delaying or abdicating action.

"Despite the growing importance of human rights in global and national politics, it is unlikely that the humanitarian impulse will become a motivation for action on par with hardcore security concerns any time soon," predicts DiPrizio (2001: 15). Yet, there is no simple formula for predicting how a president will respond when faced with a humanitarian crisis. Everything depends on context—location and timing of the crisis, values and priorities of the president, vagaries of domestic politics.

How do presidential decisions to intervene in the post–Cold War environment compare with choices made by U.S. leaders in the past? James Meernik (1994) conducted a comprehensive study of presidential impact on interventions covering the Cold War, discovering that American presidents have used military force in support of U.S. foreign policy quite often. Meernik, examining 458 international crises from 1948 through 1988, categorized 213 events where

American presidents would be expected to consider using force but where no military action was taken and 245 situations where there was an opportunity and a subsequent decision made to use the military for political purposes. Only specific and extraordinary circumstances during ongoing crises were considered likely to lead the president to consider using military force, and were included in the data set. Five groups of different groups of events were constructed: (1) cases of major threats to the United States itself, its NATO allies, Japan, South Korea, and other states with whom the United States has particular close relations; (2) cases of actions by governmental or nongovernmental actors regarding U.S. military forces, governmental personnel, civilians, property, or economic assets (e.g., takeover of the U.S. embassy in Iran in 1979); (3) cases where the Soviet Union or other communist guerrilla groups attempted to advance their interests (e.g., in Vietnam and Afghanistan; (4) cases in the Western Hemisphere (insurgency movements in El Salvador, military coups in Brazil, Chile); and (5) major wars of concern to the United States for their potentially disruptive effects, for example, disputes between India and Pakistan, the Arabs and Israel (Meernik 1994: 125). Regional distribution of opportunities is shown in Table 7.9. Table 7.10 shows presidential distribution of opportunities to use force over the 40-year period.

Meernik composed a set of predictions for intervention, suggesting that the most visible demonstration of U.S. commitment, namely, the level of American military involvement in the area in which an opportunity takes place is perhaps the best predictor. U.S. military involvement includes: an established U.S. military base in the area, military aid, and prior use of force in the country. In situations where there is an established U.S. military presence, the most important indicator of involvement is an increase in the level of military response. Second, opportunities to use force in states that have been recent recipients of American military aid also increase the level of the military response. Third, previous use of U.S. military force in the area is important in the president's decision for earlier deployments are evidence of U.S. interest in the region. Finally, threats or violence to American citizens increases the level of the military response. All of these factors were confirmed in the analysis.

Meernik (1994: 131) also proposes a "presidential discretion" element, projecting that presidents "suffering in the polls will not wish to risk further deterioration of their public standing by failing to take decisive action during international crises." Presidents lacking significant public support in general ratings, seeking to improve their reputation among voters as a protector of American interests, might look upon the opportunity to use force as an opportunity to improve their own domestic standing. Meernik postulates that presidents are more likely to use force the lower the percentage of the public approving of their job performance, and that presidents are more likely to use greater levels of military force in the immediate period before national elections. Domestic political conditions appear to exercise little influence on presidential decisions to use force, Meernik (1994: 135) discovered. Presidents' decisions are more often motivated by national interest than personal political gain.

Table 7.9
Regional Opportunities for U.S. Military Force Use: 1948–1988

Region	Frequency	Percent
Central America	93	20.3
South America	41	9.0
Western Europe	27	5.9
Eastern Europe	21	4.6
Middle East	126	27.5
Sub-Saharan Africa	44	9.6
South Asia	20	4.4
Southeast Asia	54	11.8
East Asia	32	7.0
TOTAL	458	100.0

Source: Meernik (1994), p. 125.

Table 7.10
Presidential Opportunities for U.S. Military Force Use: 1948–1988

Administration	Frequency	Percent
Truman	40	8.7
Eisenhower	82	17.9
Kennedy	52	11.4
Johnson	65	14.2
Nixon	51	11.1
Ford	23	5.0
Carter	41	9.0
Reagan	104	22.7

Source: Meernik (1994), p. 126.

Yet, in an updated analysis through the period 1948–1990, Meernik (2000: 554–555), discovered that U.S. involvement in crises is determined by leaders' beliefs about the possibility of winning in a dispute, and that opportunities to use force are more likely to occur the higher the president's approval rating, that presidents are more likely to use it the greater their level of popularity, that as approval ratings slip, the likelihood of a use of force increases, and as inflation and unemployment increase, so does the probability of a crisis. This seems to suggest that the role of public opinion, in its relation to U.S. intervention decisions, may be more significant in the post–Cold War period.

The relationship between public opinion and intervention is not completely clear. For example, if the role of media coverage is added, we need to ask two questions: How is public opinion formed from media stories? How do the media influence intervention policy? Generally, research into the CNN effect oninterventionn has tended to reach contradictory conclusions regarding media influence. One model outlined by Piers Robinson (2000: 616) argues that media coverage causes intervention during humanitarian crisis, if we find policy uncertainty and critical empathizing media coverage preceding intervention. Media influence on intervention policy occurs when two factors exist: there is official policy uncertainty within the government, and strong media coverage that empathizes with suffering people, suggesting the need for intervention. Media coverage of violence may be framed to urge readers and viewers to empathize with suffering people, identifying them as "victims." This type of framing, empathy framing, contains implicit or explicit criticism of a government opposed to intervention. Alternatively, coverage may be framed to influence the public to maintain emotional distance by classifying suffering people as members of warring "tribes." This type of framing, distance framing, is implicitly supportive of a government opposed to intervention (Robinson, 2000: 616).

Policy-makers, uncertain of what to do and without a clearly defined doctrine basis or position, can be pushed to intervene during a humanitarian crisis due to media-driven public pressure or the fear of potential negative public reaction to government inaction. Observable implications of policy uncertainty are: no policy line (no official policy in place regarding an issue); wavering policy line (when a policy line changes frequently); and an inconsistent policy line (when the subsystems of the executive may be divided over policy and pursue or advocate different policies), states Robinson (2000: 617).

Robinson analyzed the press briefings of three key U.S. executive subsystems, the White House, the State Department, and the Defense Department, to see the extent to which government was feeding a certain policy line to the media, checking for consistency as a measure of policy certainty. To examine the CNN effect, that is, that media coverage causes intervention during humanitarian crisis, two cases, U.S. intervention in Bosnia in 1995 to protect the Gorazde "safe area" and U.S. intervention in Kosovo in 1999 (Operation Allied Force), were chosen. In the first case, the theory was applied to try to explain why U.S. policy-makers decided to defend the area; in the second case, the model was used to help explain why, despite criticisms of the NATO air war and emotive coverage of suffering refugees, the Clinton Administration did not deploy either ground troops or close air support to protect Albanian Kosovars.

In the Bosnian situation, Robinson found that critical media coverage and policy uncertainty following the fall of the Srebrenica safe area helped cause the U.S. intervention policy decision to defend Gorazde. After the fall of the safe area, the Americans took over military leadership of the Western response to the war, followed by a renewed U.S. diplomatic effort in August and a sustained bombing campaign later that month. By the end of September, the war in Bosnia had ended. What effect did media coverage have on this policy change? From critical media coverage and policy uncertainty preceding the decision to defend Gorazde, Robinson predicted the media should have been a factor in causing the policy outcome. Alternatively, if policy certainty and media coverage were observed following the decision to defend Gorazde, the media coverage is unlikely to have been a factor in causing the policy outcome. In fact, the media treated the fall of Srebrenica as an event of preeminent importance devoting extensive coverage to the story. An empathy frame prevailed in media reports, which encouraged concern with the victims as opposed to emotional distance, and a failure frame predominated in reports that highlighted failure of Western policy in Bosnia. In the government, there were indications of no policy line regarding the use of force, indicating the presence of policy uncertainty. Robinson (2000: 624) concludes that these findings shows that policy uncertainty, critical media coverage, and the decision to defend Gorazde were correlated; that media coverage influenced the policy process and helped cause the intervention.

In the case of Operation Allied Force (March–June 1999), an air campaign against Serbia to force Milosevic to withdraw troops from Kosovo led to a debate in the United States throughout April over whether air strikes were sufficient for this purpose or whether a ground war would be required; it was reflected in critical coverage in the media. The Clinton administration maintained policy certainty against escalation to a ground war through most of the campaign. As the air campaign progressed, a massive refugee crisis developed when Milosevic accelerated the expulsion of Albanian Kosovars from the region. At that point, Western governments justified the bombing as an attempt to prevent ethnic cleansing and ensure the safe return of the expelled citizens. The air campaign ended in early June with the deployment of over 40,000 NATO troops in Kosovo and the complete withdrawal of Serbian forces from the province. Robinson (2000: 627) argues that when policy-makers have decided on a particular course of action, critical media coverage is unlikely to influence policy. Government policy certainty meant that critical media coverage could not influence policy and as a result neither ground troops nor close air support was used to provide immediate protection to Albanian Kosovars. But did media coverage of the refugees force a policy change by the Clinton Administration? Media reports encouraged empathy with the victims as opposed to emotional distance, and highlighted failure of Western policy was prominent during the month of April, but coverage in May became mixed. The policy line regarding the use of force—specifically there was no intention to use ground troops—was consistently and clearly articulated across all bodies of the U.S. executive, indicating the presence of policy certainty. As Robinson states, if we observe policy uncertainty and critical media coverage and find evidence of a change in policy, then we would expect media coverage to have been a factor in the policy outcome. If we observe policy certainty and find no evidence of a policy change, then we would not expect the media to have been a factor in the policy outcome. The findings here support the prediction that when policy certainty exists, media coverage is unlikely to influence policy outcomes.

Peter Viggo Jakobsen (2000) decided to investigate the media influence on intervention decisions in another way. He looked at the previolence phase when the goal is to prevent organized, armed violence from breaking out; the violence phase with efforts to limit or end armed violence; and the postviolence phase when conflict managers seek to promote peace building. Jakobsen discovered that during the previolence period, the impact of media is negligible: there is usually no interest before violence or mass starvation kills lots of people. Governments tend to ignore calls for preventive action when media coverage does occur; preventive diplomacy such as UN troops in Macedonia receive little coverage. In the violence phase direct impact of the media is greatest, says Jakobsen (2000: 133–134), although it remains limited. Many violent conflicts are not covered: Abkhazia, Afghanistan, Angola, Azerbaijan, Burundi, Kashmir, Liberia, Moldova, Nagorno Karabakh, Sierra Leone, Sudan, and Tajikistan are among cases in the 1990s that were not exposed to broad media coverage. A trigger event such as an exodus of refugees or a massacre is usually required, and the crisis must be photogenic and dramatic—a short bloody war is better than a drawn out stalemate, states Jakobsen. Finally, media influence is irrelevant when governments have decided to intervene. The CNN effect comes into play only when Western governments oppose military intervention in conflicts where massive human rights violations occur. The CNN effect did not cause the interventions in northern Iraq, Somalia, or Rwanda. It did matter in helping officials in favor of an intervention to win the argument with the administration, Jakobsen argues (pp. 134–135). Without the media, some officials believe that the intervention would not have taken place in Somalia; yet the media did not cause the intervention. Actually, the intervention in Somalia was perceived as low-risk operation, with few casualties expected, promising a humanitarian and political payoff by outgoing President Bush.

Media pressures on governments to intervene in humanitarian emergencies are limited when the risk of casualties are perceived as high and/or exit points seem uncertain. Jakobsen (2000: 135–136) believes these factors played a major role for Western states to resist involvement in Bosnia between 1992 and May 1995; in Chechnya in November and December 1994 (where it would have triggered a confrontation with Russia) in Burundi in July 1996; in the Great Lakes region in November 1996; and in Kosovo in June 1998. Moreover, Jakobsen believes the importance of casualties and exit points can also be inferred from the Western intervention practice: reliance on air power in Bosnia in 1995 and Kosovo in 1999 was designed to reduce the risk of casualties; interventions in Somalia, Rwanda, and Albania were all minimalist and limited in time. "In conflicts where Western governments are reluctant to intervene and perceive the risk of casualties associated with military intervention on the ground as unacceptable, media generated pressures are likely to result in minimalist policies, which are primarily aimed at demonstrating to their action-demanding publics that 'something is being done' so that ground deployments can be avoided." Thus, the CNN effect has only a limited impact on Western intervention decisions (Jakobsen, p. 136).

During the postviolence phase, media coverage of a conflict is nearly impossible to sustain unless Western troops are killed or massacres of civilians occur, writes Jakobsen (p. 137). If an intervention succeeds in stopping the fighting, the media quickly lose interest in it. After the successful deployment of troops in Somalia in December 1992, media coverage quickly dropped. Of the 1,300 journalists who had gone to Haiti in September 1994 to cover the U.S. intervention, only a handful remained a month later. Postviolence-phase conflicts receive very little media attention. This leads to the conclusion that the CNN effect will influence government policy only at the peak of the violence. A systematic assessment of media influence on policy choices on intervention indicate that direct impact of the media on conflict management is quite limited; coverage is confined to a small number of conflicts in the violence phase, and government policy may already be set and immune to major revisions.

CONCLUSION

Combining the predictors of intervention, reasons for intervening, and factors of intervention success throughout these studies, it is easier to understand which cases fall within the ongoing pattern of U.S. policy, reflecting continuity in the transition from Cold War into the post–Cold War period, and which instances suggest a new direction. In the first 12-years of the new era, substantial numbers of U.S. forces were sent abroad on at least eight occasions for varying purposes, from combat operations to peacekeeping tasks. In Figures 7.1 and 7.2, factors of involvement and success are predicted in crude dichotomized variables. In Table 7.11 these elements are rated relatively for each intervention. Five situations focused on civil disturbances in foreign lands and how the United States might assist in conflict resolution; forces sent to these areas were designed as peacekeeping and peace-enforcement missions: Haiti, Somalia, Rwanda, Bosnia, and Kosovo; three concerned international problems, that is, conflicts between the United States (alone or in concert with the global community) and the party abroad: Panama (General Noriega was involved in massive illegal drug trafficking into the United States); Iraq (Saddam Hussein's forces had occupied Kuwait and deployed troops near the Saudi Arabian border, threatening the flow and supply of oil around the world); and Afghanistan (Osama bin Laden ran terrorist training operations, responsible for the attack on America in New York City and Washington, D.C., that were permitted by the ruling Taliban regime). Are the American intervention destinations unusual? Are the types of conflicts drawing U.S. intervention unpredictable? Is the frequency of intervention activity atypical? Would the crisis have evolved if there had been no change in the global structure, the bipolar pattern?

Figure 7.1
Predicting Intervention Involvement

Prior Involvement in Region

Level of National Interest	Extensive	Minimal
Vital interests	highest probability	high probability
Non Vital Interests	lower probability	lowest probability

Figure 7.2
Predicting Intervention Success

Mission Objective

Level of Ground Combat Forces Committed	Simple	Complex
Overwhelming force strength	highest probability	high probability
Minimal force strength	lower probability	lowest probability

On the international cases: it is beyond any identified historical trend of overseas crises or U.S. intervention patterns to have predicted two major international problems that drew heavy American involvement would unfold shortly into the post-Cold war era, namely the Gulf War in 1990–1991, when Iraq invaded Kuwait, and the War in Afghanistan starting in October 2001, caused by a direct terrorist hit on American soil. Both instances raise the immediate question whether these events could have happened during the previous global structure of U.S.-USSR bipolar tension and nuclear threat. Were parties simply willing to take greater risks to achieve their goals in an environment that seemingly posed few restraints on their behavior? Did the United States choose to respond by forming a coalition force against Iraqi troops and effecting withdrawal from Kuwait because of the fresh new age developing, whereas under Cold War rules they might not have taken action? (The United States and Soviet Union were officially neutral toward the Iran-Iraq conflict fought between 1980 and 1988, although the Iran Contra affair revealed partisanship on the U.S. side.) Was the international terrorist network made easier by the removal of travel and information barriers, and facilitated by a redirected intelligence motivation—changing the basic functioning rules of the U.S.-USSR governed global system after the breakdown in late 1989? Or, were

Table 7.11
Predicting U.S. Military Intervention in Post–Cold War Cases

Case	National Interest Level	Prior Involvement In Region*	Mission Objective	Ground Combat Force Strength	Intervention Involvement Probability	Intervention Success Probability
Persian Gulf	vital	extensive	simple	overwhelming	highest	highest
Afghanistan	vital	minimal	simple	minimal	high	lower
Panama	nonvital	extensive	simple	overwhelming	lower	highest
Haiti	nonvital	extensive	simple	overwhelming	lower	highest
Somalia	nonvital	extensive	complex	minimal	lower	lowest
Rwanda	nonvital	minimal	simple	none	lowest	not rated
Bosnia	nonvital	minimal	complex	none	lowest	not rated
Kosovo	nonvital	minimal	complex	none	lowest	not rated

*Includes military ties from prior intervention to financial assistance to arms sales.

these conflicts just a product of the times: Saddam Hussein needed a diversion focus to avoid the economic hardships of his country following the long war with Iraq in the 1980s and increasing unemployment; terrorism developing out of a radical version of Islam reflects long-standing extreme economic and political frustration with ruling regimes in the Arab world to manage social problems. Changes in technology brought speed and globalization, meaning the new world would operate at a faster pace, crises with global implications developing more quickly than before. We cannot know with certainty how to sort out these contributing elements. With respect to Panama, the third international case, the intervention action is hardly atypical; The United States has a long history of sending troops to the country. Thus, in two of three cases, the level of intervention to deal with major international problems shows a real change in the 1990s and beyond. Whether this represents a new, more or less permanent direction, though, is hard to tell. Terrorism seems an ongoing problem, which suggests the war in Afghanistan is the beginning of a new trail of intervention decisions. Major war about oil politics may be less likely in the near future. The focus on Middle East politics and U.S. involvement seems here to stay for a while, continuing a trend starting in the final decade of Cold War life.

On the civil conflict cases: in the post–Cold War period, we have seen U.S. armed forces deployed to five countries to assist in solving domestic social and governmental problems. As a general policy, this represents no departure from previous mission goals—intervention in Lebanon, in the 1950s and 1980s, in the Korean conflict, from 1950 to 1953, and in Vietnam during the 1960s and 1970s were all tied to issues of governance and local opposition. The geographic locales for U.S. intervention show some continuity, and some surprises. The intervention into Haiti would not be regarded as unusual, given the heavy and frequent pattern of American involvement in Caribbean countries over the past century. The interventions in ex-Yugoslavia are different. The U.S. involvement in southern Europe over the entire Cold War period was confined to Greece— where U.S. military and economic aid was extensive—a country serving as the defining moment for the Truman Doctrine which launched a new international system. But, through diplomatic involvement to negotiate the end of the Bosnian conflict and participation in a multinational peacekeeping force, and engaging in military acts in concert with NATO forces in Kosovo—a province within a sovereign state–American intervention patterns departed significantly from previous policy and behavior. Intervention into sovereign territory without invitation had not been the U.S. posture; workable peacekeeping forces were largely nonexistent throughout the Cold War, to say nothing of U.S. willingness to contribute actively to them. In Europe, then, both locale and purpose of the interventions represent real change. Finally, the mission to Somalia was an attempt to try a new idea: that America engage in humanitarian interventions and work closely with the United Nations to carry out such missions. Somalia represented the test case, where the U.S. troops, positioned within the UN operation, would help to stabilize a country, which, at the time, was in civil turmoil and suffering extreme food shortages. The United States had not been engaged in Africa much, had selected to remain on the sidelines in situations of anarchy. Although the earlier Somalia mission was successful, the second one (UNISOM II) was not. In policy, in operation, and in organization, everything about intervention in Somalia showed a new picture, but in the end, its lack of success showed it was a short-lived policy. When genocide in Rwanda broke into sudden violence in April 1994, soon after the intervention mission in Somalia failed to achieve its objectives (coupled with American humiliation in the October 1993 televised version of Mogadishu battle aftermath), the United States consciously chose not to follow a humanitarian intervention strategy. In fact, the Americans blocked the United Nations from sending a peace enforcement mission to Rwanda. Only later, in July 1994, did the United States deploy a unit of peacekeepers to facilitate transportation and logistical operations of relief agencies, who stayed for a brief, two-month period. Deciding for nonintervention in the Rwandan crisis was not surprising; deciding in favor of Somalian humanitarian intervention was the new twist.

In conclusion, intervention into Panama and Haiti represent policy continuation. Intervention into Somalia, Rwanda, Bosnia, and Kosovo represent policy change—in purpose (humanitarian intervention), in form (peacekeeping), and in norms of sovereignty respect (attacking an independent state). Intervention in the Gulf (Saudi Arabia and Iraq) and Afghanistan are responses to global issues—protecting access to oil reserves and subduing terrorist attack strength—that may have developed whether the Cold War ended or not, depending on the perceived nature of superpower tension and areas of agreement. Real change in the pattern of intervention has occurred in the post–Cold War time. In priority of threat assessment, though, the role of national interest still outweighs humanitarian concerns with respect to U.S. intervention choices.

Conclusion:
Intervention Impact—An Assessment

THE LEGACY

In the search for lessons of guidance in U.S. post–Cold War intervention choices, American experience in Vietnam lingers as the benchmark for evaluating and debating action. The operative slogan, "no more Vietnams," popularized in the late 1960s (Pfeffer, 1968), captured precisely and simply divergent opinion reflecting the meaning and mistakes of the engagement. It humbled policy–makers by dispelling the illusion of American omnipotence and the illusion of American innocence. The message continues to resonate in the post–Cold War period, influencing U.S. strategic intervention decisions. In their nationwide survey of U.S. leaders' attitudes toward the Vietnam War, conducted in 1976 and 1980, which included nearly 5,000 responses to a detailed questionnaire, Ole R. Holsti and James M. Rosenau (1984: 20) discovered two dominant, different interpretations of the conflict related to appropriate goals of American policy, sources and consequences U.S. policy failure, and the lessons to be learned from the war. Holsti and Rosenau predicted these views would evolve into belief systems—configured ideas and attitudes bound together by forms of constraint and functional interdependence—and continue to influence U.S. foreign policy decisions.

One perspective holds the view that American intervention in the Vietnam War was justifiable in the context of U.S. security commitments and that America's international credibility and reputation suffered as the troops were withdrawn. The warning for the future is that the United States might fail to protect its legitimate interests rather than risk the trauma of another Vietnam-like experience. The country could be paralyzed by the "Vietnam syndrome" to the detriment of its vital national interests, and ultimately pull back from its duties and responsibilities to help maintain a stable world order (Holsti and Rosenau, 1984: 16–17).

A second perspective sees American intervention in Southeast Asia as unjustified, based on a distorted appraisal of the national interest, unrealistic premises, and faulty logic. The end of American involvement in Vietnam permits the United States to turn its attention and resources to real threats to national security, including a full agenda of social, economic, and environmental problems (Holsti and Rosenau, 1984: 17–18). The United States must assess the scope and substance of its role in the world more realistically, avoiding interventions in most third world conflicts because they do not threaten basic national interests.

In the aftermath of Vietnam, elite opinion formed into three distinct modes of thinking with respect to the third world role and U.S. obligations, Holsti and Rosenau (1984: 130–133) assert: (1) "Cold War Internationalism"—the United States should protect the global universe from aggression and terrorism, but on a selective basis to strategically important countries (e.g., oil producers), and rebuild and maintain military strength. An active U.S. role in the world is a necessary but not sufficient condition to create a stable and just world order; (2) "Post–Cold War Internationalism"—the United States should provide economic and other forms of nonmilitary assistance and play a leading role in structural systemic change and free resources for dealing with North-South issues. An active U.S. role in the world is a necessary but not sufficient condition to create a stable and just world order; and (3) "Semi Isolationism"—the United States has few, if any, obligations for either security or economic development in the international system and should reduce commitments and dependencies abroad, in order to free resources for dealing with domestic issues. American retrenchment is a necessary but not sufficient condition to ensure that U.S. democracy will survive; the power of example is the best American contribution to the welfare of other nations.

The Vietnam syndrome, a national reluctance to commit U.S. forces to combat, has been a defining feature of U.S. foreign policy since the early 1970s and had an impact on American intervention policy in the first post–Cold War test in 1990. When Iraq invaded Kuwait, President George H.W. Bush—whose experience predated those who came of age in the Vietnam generation—decided real leadership required a willingness to use military force. Yet, he preferred that it not be used unilaterally. Throughout the crisis in the Persian Gulf, Bush repeatedly stressed that he did not want the conflict to become another Vietnam, suggesting that pursuing objectives such as removing Saddam Hussein were likely to have minimal international support and little support from Congress and the American public and would alienate the Iraqi people (Hurst, 1999: 101–111). As General Norman Schwarzkopf said, summing up the U.S. military's lack of enthusiasm for the idea, had the United States gone into Iraq, it would probably still be there, like a dinosaur in a tar pit (Hurst, 1999: 121). Bush declared after the war that "by God, we've kicked the Vietnam syndrome once and for all." According to Hurst (1999: 125), though, "Despite the fact that the Iraqi threat to Middle East oil in many ways posed a far clearer challenge to U.S. interests than the rather indeterminate danger posed after the fall of Vietnam to communism, the U.S. public was far more reluctant to support the use of force in 1990 than it had been three decades earlier. Bush was constantly aware of the fragility of public support and the need to maintain it, hence the popular but dubious rationales advanced to justify USA sanctions in the Gulf. His decision to end the war when he did was driven in large part precisely by the fear of getting entangled in 'another Vietnam' inside Iraq."

The specter of Vietnam had not been dispelled by the Gulf conflict, and memories of Vietnam clearly influenced the U.S. response to the Yugoslav crisis. At the Pentagon, talk of military intervention in Bosnia looked exactly like the kind of "limited" mission with vague and unachievable objectives that had brought so much grief in the past. The Gulf crisis had applied lessons of Vietnam: the intervention should have clearly defined military objectives, the opportunity to apply overwhelming force, and terrain ideally sited to conventional warfare, but Yugoslavia offered none of those advantages. And Bush, in reference to the Bosnian situation, said, "I do not want to see the United States bogged down in any way into some guerrilla war. We lived through that once" (quoted in Hurst, 1999: 218).

The Vietnam experience has much to recommend it, says Michael Lind (1999: 284), but to the extent that it influences U.S. foreign policy it is dangerous. Twice in 35 years, American armed forces engaged in massive military intervention in a civil war in a peripheral region in order to demonstrate the credibility of the United States as a military power and as an alliance leader: in Korea and in Vietnam. The domestic result of the Vietnam War was a neoisolationist consensus in the 1970s, causing an increase in the relative power, influence, and ambition of the Soviet empire, according to Lind (1999: 258), a trend reversed by increased U.S. activism in the 1980s, the last decade of the Cold War.

What lessons can be derived from the U.S. experience in Indochina? Lind (1999: 262–265) suggests two. First is a military lesson: low–intensity conflicts demand tailored operations designed with high efficiency and low casualty costs to fit both the country's overall grand strategy and its domestic political tolerance and culture. Second is a public support lesson: "Americans want 'real' wars, like World War II and the Gulf War, not limited wars like Korea and Vietnam. They want American soldiers to be sent into battle, if at all, to take territory, not to prop up weak and tyrannical regimes threatened by civil war, in order to signal American resolve in great–power showdowns....They want world wars to end with the enemy capital in smoking ruins under U.S. military administration, not in a seismic shift of allegiance on the part of governments that leaves the world superficially looking much the same as it did before. Above all, Americans do not like quagmires like the half–century conflict in Indochina." Lind extends the argument into the post–Cold War age:

If the characteristics of a quagmire are low–intensity conflict, political chaos, and moral ambiguity, then avoiding quagmires means avoiding intervention in most wars in which the world–order interests of the United States and its allies are likely to be at stake in the twenty–first century. And avoiding those wars means sooner or later ceding world leadership to a nation, liberal or (more likely) illiberal, whose political culture does not paralyze its military policy. If the United States is to continue to be the dominant world power, or even one of several great military powers, then American soldiers must learn to swim in quagmires. (Lind, 1999: 265)

If the Vietnam War holds a lesson for domestic politics, it is the importance of preserving American public support for both grand strategy and military tactics, argues Lind (1999: 271). The Clinton administration policy in Kosovo reflected a failure to learn the tactical and political lessons of Vietnam: ground troops should have been deployed on Serbia's borders to deter Serbs from emptying Kosovo by ethnic cleansing, or, if deterrence failed, to invade Kosovo to protect the ethnic Albanians. Instead, President Clinton publicly ruled out the use of ground troops. A reluctance to commit U.S. ground troops who might be killed and wounded in large numbers led American officials to hope that an air war would be a sufficient intervention strategy for achieving their goals. Perhaps the American public would not have supported a ground war in Yugoslavia in which significant numbers of U.S. soldiers were killed. However, says Lind (1999: 279), the lesson about public attitudes from the Vietnam War is that there is a limit to the number of American casualties the U.S. public will tolerate, not that preserving public support for a war means ensuring no American soldiers at all are killed in combat.

How have lessons of Vietnam shaped the policy choices of contemporary foreign policy-makers? Andrew J. Taylor and John T. Rourke (1995) examined the impact of the Munich and Vietnam analogies on decisions made by members of Congress about U.S. policy toward Iraq in 1991. They discovered analogies are mostly utilized as post-hoc justifications for policy choices determined by ideology and partisanship and are not causal agents in the policy process. In their analysis of the Persian Gulf crisis debates that took place between January 10 and January 12, 1991, including words spoken on the House floor and remarks revised and extended for *The Congressional Record* on specific resolutions (to continue sanctions against Iraq, to authorize the president to use force to rid Kuwait of Iraq, to maintain Congressional authority to declare war), of 552 members who had the opportunity to participate, 119 used the Munich or Vietnam analogies to help explain why they supported continuing the sanctions or using force. The analysis shows, however, that analogies legitimize, not drive the policy choices of members of Congress (Taylor and Rourke, 1995: 466).

The long, visible shadow the Vietnam experience continued to cast over the American intervention debate in the post–Cold War age affected civilian–military relations and had a significant impact on the strategic choices advocated by key policy-makers throughout the 1990s. David Halberstam in *War in a Time of Peace: Bush, Clinton, and the Generals*, emphasizes this point when he writes, "I did not go looking for the ghosts of Vietnam, but they were often there, most notably in the damage done to two institutions critical to general public health and disproportionately affected by that war, the U.S. Army and the Democratic Party" (Halberstam, 2001: 497). An example: by mid-1992, Bosnia was under siege: 7,200 inhabitants were dead, small villages were subject to ethnic cleansing by Serb irregular forces, Muslims were driven from their homes, their property confiscated, and the men transported to camps, often never seen again. The United States stood on the sidelines. It was slow to act, says Halberstam (2001: 32–36), for the ghosts of Vietnam, the resistance of the Pentagon toward direct military involvement with ground troops intervention, and the great fear of being sucked into a Balkan quagmire. The intervention troop estimate needed for a successful mission was always high, in the 200,000 range or more. Those most enthusiastic about intervention wanted to use American airpower against the Serbs. Participating in a conflict in Yugoslavia— a distant, peripheral war from the perspective of American people and American politicians—might lead to a Vietnam-like entanglement. It was not a high priority for American national security; it was not worth the price of implementation if the consequences, turned out to be more severe than imagined.

In the old days, says Halberstam (2001: 37–38), the Pentagon had tended to be gung ho about military involvement, the Department of State, cautious. Vietnam changed that and now the roles were reversed. The memory of Vietnam lingered in the Pentagon: almost all of the top army people had served directly in the war and the experience had been bitter. At State, the activists were younger officials who had come along after the Vietnam experience. The American military, therefore, remained dubious about military intervention in the Balkans. The Pentagon was also nervous about assuming any simple humanitarian role that might be poorly thought out and too open-ended and might somehow draw the country into an unwanted combat commitment. The counter argument was that America was a great power, standing well above all others in the world, which meant on occasion it had to use its power. The situation in Bosnia demanded action. If America did not act with its unique military dominance in a conflict like that, then what other country would? Confining the use of military force to only those situations where America's strategic interests were directly threatened was far too limiting for a global leader. The world's only superpower had to be prepared to act in more ambiguous circumstances. The world had changed, which meant the military would have to figure out how to use their forces in smaller wars. But the complicated civil war in Yugoslavia with no easy mission or exit strategy meant responding with ground troops.

U.S. interventions at the start of the post–Cold War system, were not handled fresh; the Vietnam legacy from the old global order bore a heavy mark. The test of U.S. leadership was to grasp how the world had changed, and whether the emphasis of American foreign policy should be on maintaining stability or adopting a new vision in a dynamic world. To inaugurate the post–Cold War era and designate a role for the United States within it, President Bush in September 1990 presented his concept of the "new world order," where peace, democracy, free trade, and rule of law prevail. A world in which nations recognize the shared responsibility for freedom and justice; where the strong respect the rights of the weak. A world where aggression would meet a collective international response, articulated through the United Nations which would be fundamental in the shaping of the new world order. It was based on balance of power, global management, and principles of idealism. Victory in the Gulf War meant the world had passed the first test of a post–Cold War order, where the United

Nations, freed from Cold War stalemate, could fulfill the vision of its founders. Yet, it was never clear whether Bush was promising a new structure of international relations based on respect for international law—ushering in a new set of rules—or using the phrase "new world order" as a bid for public support for American intervention policy—playing the card of traditional power politics. One of the principal criticisms of the Bush administration was that it failed to articulate a viable strategy for U.S. foreign policy in the post–Cold War era, implying that the new world order concept failed. The concept, more an optimistic slogan than grand design, faded from view once Bush left office.

The defining policy statement introduced by the Clinton administration shortly after coming to power was based on the idea that "enlargement of democracies" would replace the doctrine of the containment of communism; abstract moral and ethical concepts would be elevated to the same level as national security interests. Morality was the broad rationale for peacemaking (as opposed to peacekeeping), for "humanitarian" intervention, and for conducting foreign policy that rested not on American power but on the international legitimacy of multilateral institutions such as the United Nations (Hyland, 1999: 24). By the start of Clinton's second term, much of the early enthusiasm for this program began to wane. Little was heard of the doctrine of "assertive multilateralism," or as Senator Trent Lott, majority leader, put it, "big code words for international nanny" (quoted in Schneider, 1996: 2). When he left office, Clinton also was criticized for failing to articulate an operational theory of foreign policy for the post–Cold War period. The policies were seen as lacking strategic center, conviction, and steadiness, writes William Hyland (1999: 139). It was often charged that Clinton was responsible for making the defining feature of American engagement in the world in the years since the Cold War one of confusion. Jacob Heilbrunn (1996: 1) argues that U. S. policy has always been confused and ad hoc. No grand strategy is required or recommended since muddling through has long been the norm.

MODERN DEBATE

More than a decade into the post–Cold War era, following foreign policy theme efforts and the intervention record of Presidents George H. W. Bush and Clinton, three rival schools of foreign policy tradition, consistent with the categories developed by Holsti and Rosenau, form the debate parameters on America's intervention future. In updated visions outlined by Patrick Buchanan (1999: 355–368), they are: (1) "The Hegemonist Temptation" school (America should exploit its hour of power to impose a Pax Americana, whether it be through air strikes on belligerent states—as in Iraq—or U.S. intervention abroad, including Bosnia and Kosovo, a parallel to Maynes' "controllers"); (2) "The Global Democracy Panacea" school (America can be truly secure only within a world system where democracy has spread over the planet and a global government has emerged capable of securing justice for all nations and keeping the peace, which shares some commonalities with Maynes' "shapers"); and (3) "The Enlightened Nationalism" school (American foreign policy should be first a shield, only then a sword; maintain the power to defend U.S. territory from all enemies, stay out of wars that are not ours but be prepared to confront enemies that threaten us; the perspective of Maynes' "abstainers"). The first two views of global activists see the world as a dangerous place, full of enemies anxious to exploit American weakness, believing U. S. security rests on its own power and the will to use it. In this vision, the United States should impose a benevolent global hegemony across the world. The third position, the semi-isolationists, encourages retrenchment into the new century.

Global Activists

Anthony Lake, national security advisor to President Clinton from 1993 to 1996, discusses the most pressing threats to U.S. national security in *6 Nightmares* (2000). How should America prepare "when the next Rwanda, Bosnia, Haiti, or Kosovo teeters on the brink—will we step in early enough to pull it back before it falls into the abyss? In the age of CNN, can we say no? Are our purposes in our peacekeeping efforts clear enough, or are these operations Band–Aids that we will never dare remove?" asks Lake, (2000: xiii–xiv). The worst of the nightmare is for the millions of people suffering directly from violence and disorder. But, says Lake (2000: 112), unless we learn to act with greater efficiency in conducting peacekeeping operations—and with much greater clarity about the long–term purposes of such efforts—these conflicts will become something of a nightmare for us, as well. In addition, there is a moral imperative with our superpower status. Can America sit on the sidelines when innocent civilians are being slaughtered, or starved, or made to suffer? We should do all we can to prevent conflicts, but when they occur, we all should take a hard look not only at *whether* to get involved but *how*, states Lake (2000: 16). This means focusing on three issues: how to pursue diplomatic solutions to internal conflicts, how to conduct peacekeeping operations to reinforce diplomatic agreements, and deciding the proper *purposes* of our diplomatic and peacekeeping efforts. It is imperative that a national debate on peacekeeping and "humanitarian interventions" not be a partisan clash of competing doctrines (never intervene versus near automatic intervention); properly conceived, well-executed peacekeeping missions can be an important and useful tool of American foreign policy, according to Lake, who urges a build up of the capacity of the United Nations to supply police constabulary forces who can accompany military peacekeepers. The key issue for Lake is the difficulty in distinguishing between helping, through narrowly defining U.S. interests and involvement, and getting caught in more general involvement levels (p. 167). Establishing military security, instituting economic development programs, and supporting elections and viable democratic institutions is a start, but these activities must be limited. Further, the United States must make the effort to firmly establish a clear strategic goal that defines "success" before rushing in with troops to solve the problems of conflicted societies. America must size its ambitions to reflect appropriate relationships among national interests, resources, and real responsibilities in foreign policy. But if we act only on the narrowest calculations of national interest dismissing efforts to redress such wrongs as mere "social work," we will diminish ourselves, Lake advises (2000,

p. 174). No other nation can provide the experience and capabilities of the United States. America's willingness to do its part can make or break a mission (Lake, 2000: 285). In sum, an active United States engaged on intervention issues, working within the UN framework on peacekeeping, is key to the security of a post–Cold War order.

A second internationalist perspective is outlined in *Global Focus: U.S. Foreign Policy at the Turn of the Millennium* (Honey and Barry, 2000), a publication of the Foreign Policy In Focus project, which pushes new principles (an earlier version, edited by Barry and Honey, appeared in 1996) further in this direction, arguing that the United States should use its status to encourage more participation in global decision-making. Honey and Barry urge the United States to become a more responsible, generous, and collaborative global partner and leader by promoting social and economic equality, human rights, democratic institutions and participation, demilitarization, environmental protection, and sustainable and socially responsible development. They see the U.S. role to facilitate more multilateral consideration and action on global peace and security issues. "The United States as global peacekeeper is untenable: morally, financially and politically. Washington is not an impartial arbiter and enforcer of global peace and security. It is a globocop but a selective one. No longer does it maintain the pretension of being willing to 'bear any burden' or 'pay any price' but instead it has become highly selective about where and when it intervenes. Evaluations of U.S. national interests and the potential for U.S. casualties are primary considerations. Don't count on the globocop to stop genocide in a backwater state like Rwanda, where U.S. interests are few" (Honey and Barry, 2000: xx). The United States should adopt a new strategy aimed at preventing, containing, and abating ethnic and sectarian violence that entails economic aid to distressed societies, stepped–up mediation and diplomacy and participation, and where warranted, in multinational peacekeeping operations. Honey and Barry believe strongly that U.S. foreign policy should work harder to build peaceful societies and be ready to act in that capacity.

If a new system of multilateral engagement is to take hold, the United States should support a broad range of measures to make peacekeeping an effective tool that advances both American and global interests. They recommend a two–tiered UN force for that purpose. The first tier, responsible for traditional peacekeeping tasks, would consist of a permanent, directly recruited, and specially trained force with at least 10,000 military, police, and civilian personnel. The second tier, responsible for preventive deployments and the establishment of safe areas to protect civilian populations, would be composed of more militarily capable units, remaining under the jurisdiction of national governments but available to the United Nations on short notice. Honey and Barry suggest the United States should conclude a standby agreement with the United Nations, where a government designates specific personnel and equipment that will be on call for peacekeeping services.

A third perspective of the internationalists is represented by Condoleezza Rice, National Security Advisor to George W. Bush, in "Campaign 2000: Promoting the National Interest," published in *Foreign Affairs* (2000). Rice adopts a counterpoint to the views of Lake and Honey and Barry. It takes courage to set priorities, to separate the important from the trivial issues, says Rice. "The absence of an articulated national interest either produces a fertile ground for those wishing to withdraw from the world or creates a vacuum to be filled by parochial groups and transitory pressure" (Rice, 2000: 2). The key tasks in U.S. foreign policy are to ensure that America's military can deter war, project power, and fight in defense of its interests if deterrence fails; to focus U.S. energies on comprehensive relationships with the big powers, particularly Russia and China, that can and will mold the character of the international political system; and to deal decisively with the threat of rogue regimes and hostile powers, which is increasingly taking the forms of the potential for terrorism and the development of weapons of mass destruction (Rice, 2000: 2).

U.S. interests can be promoted within the United Nations, but multilateral solutions are not always in America's interest (Rice, 2000: 3). Some worry that this view of the world ignores the role of values, particularly human rights and the promotion of democracy, but Rice (2000: 4) argues otherwise: "There are those who would draw a sharp line between power politics and a principled foreign policy based on values. This polarized view—you are either a realist or devoted to norms and values—may be just fine in academic debate, but it is a disaster for American foreign policy. American values are universal."

The military mission of the United States must be refocused. What does it mean to deter, fight and win wars, and defend the national interest? Some small-scale conflicts clearly have an impact on American strategic interests, argues Rice, such as Kosovo, "which was in the backyard of America's most important strategic alliances: NATO." The United States had an overriding strategic interest in stopping Milosevic. In the absence of concerns based on the interests of the alliance, the case for intervention would have been more tenuous. Humanitarian intervention cannot be ruled out a priori, but "Humanitarian problems are rarely only humanitarian problems, the taking of life or withholding of food is almost always a political act. If the U.S. is not prepared to address the underlying political conflict and to know whose side it is on, the military may end up separating warring parties for an indefinite period. Because the military cannot, by definition, do anything decisive in these 'humanitarian' crises, the chances of misreading the situation and ending up in very different circumstances are very high" (Rice, 2000: 5). A president entering these situations must ask whether decisive force is possible and is likely to be effective and must know how and when to get out. These are difficult criteria to meet, so U.S. intervention in these "humanitarian" crises should be, at best, exceedingly rare. This does not mean that the United States must ignore humanitarian and civil conflicts around the world, but the military cannot be involved everywhere. Using the American armed forces as the world's "911" will degrade capabilities, bog soldiers down in peacekeeping roles, and fuel concern among other great powers that the United States has decided to enforce notions of "limited sovereignty" worldwide in the name of humanitarianism. American military power is a special instrument—it is neither a civilian police force nor a political referee, nor designed to build civil society. The problem today is that in the absence of a compelling vision of the national interest, parochial interests are filling the void. A firm ground of the national interest, not from the interests of an illusory international community, is necessary (Rice, 2000: 6).

The Internationalist school of U.S. foreign policy advocates a strong activist role for America in international politics to build world security. In three versions presented here, differences exist with respect to the definitions of national interest, the role of military intervention, and how security can best be achieved. Lake and Honey and Barry advocate a multilateral approach, including an emphasis on humanitarianism. Rice believes traditional state–based power politics is a better basis for principled policy.

Semi-Isolationists

Patrick Buchanan, in *A Republic, Not an Empire: Reclaiming America's Destiny* (1999) argues that American security could best be attained by a pull back and adjustment to the Western Hemisphere rather than spreading its wings worldwide, asserting that the United States by compiling commitments to nations around the world is essentially reenacting the ancient folly of imperial overstretch. Buchanan argues for limited involvement, where the United States pursues its own vital interests, advocating a narrow criterion for American intervention abroad. The role for the United States is not to right the wrongs of a sinful world, but to threaten none so long as we are neither threatened nor intruded upon. Hence, the United States should avoid wars in places where it has no interests that its citizens will accept as reason to fight. Buchanan's outline for American foreign policy is this: reinstall the Monroe Doctrine—legitimating intervention in Central and South America under a sphere of influence concept of a great power; disengage militarily from the Far East, including full withdrawal of troops from Korea. The only way for Americans to shake their "imperial habit" is to quit, yet, having acquired a position of global dominance, it is not a direct, easy step to walk away, says Buchanan (1999:4).

The United States desperately needs a review of all its commitments to determine which remain vital to our security and which we must let go in order to stay out of future wars. "If we continue on this course of reflexive interventions, enemies will one day answer our power with the last weapon of the weak—terror and eventually cataclysmic terrorism on U.S. soil with weapons of mass destruction," predicted Buchanan (1999:46).

True foreign policy must be rooted in the nation's vital interests—"which the people of the nation are agreed they must defend at the risk of their lives," states Buchanan (1999: 368), who recommends that since Americans have always been prepared to fight to prevent any hostile power from establishing a strategic beachhead in the Western Hemisphere, the United States should restate the position that the Monroe Doctrine is the cornerstone of American foreign policy, while disavowing any right or intention to intervene in a Latin American country that does not threaten us or its neighbors. "So long as authoritarian regimes, military and civilian, of the Left and Right do not align themselves with hostile powers and do not threaten us or their neighbors, they should be left to deal with their own internal problems. Buchanan advocates America ground troops should be withdrawn from Europe and the NATO treaty should be amended so that involvement in future European wars is an option, not an obligation.

The perspective of Chalmers Johnson in *Blowback: The Costs and Consequences of American Empire* (2000) is similar. Ten years after the end of the Cold War, hundreds of thousands of American troops, supplied with the world's most advanced weaponry, sometimes including nuclear arms, are stationed on over 61 base complexes in 19 countries worldwide, according to Johnson (2000: 4). With the disappearance of any military threat faintly comparable to that posed by the former Soviet Union, these costs have become easily avoidable. Perpetuating Cold War structures gives overseas deployment a new twist. Johnson (p. 5) believes the waste of our resources on irrelevant weapons systems, the continuous trail of "military accidents" and of terrorist attacks on American installations and embassies, are all portents of a twenty-first-century crisis in America's informal empire, an empire based on the projection of military power to every corner of the world and on the use of American capital and markets to force global economic integration on our terms, at whatever costs to others.

The term "blowback," which the CIA invented for its internal use, refers to the unintended consequences of policies that were kept secret from the American people. Johnson sees a strong correlation between U.S. involvement in international situations and an increase in terrorist attacks against the United States. The United States now faces an agenda of problems that simply would not exist except for the imperial commitments and activities, open and covert, that accompanied the Cold War. Johnson (2000: 29) discredits the common government argument for such continued imperialist activism as a version of the old "domino theory" often articulated to justify intervention during the Vietnam War: America's armed forces have no choices but to hold off instability wherever it may threaten to protect peace in the world.

Military interventions in Somalia, Haiti, Bosnia, and Kosovo, where the United States may have no vital interests in the outcome of ethnic, religious, or internecine struggles are unwise. Given its wealth and power, the United States will be a prime recipient in the foreseeable future of all of the more expectable forms of blowback, particularly terrorist attacks against Americans in and out of the armed forces anywhere on earth, including within the United States, Johnson (2000: 224) predicted. Eventually, the international system will break down because declining powers, rather than adjusting and accommodating, try to cement their slipping preeminence into an exploitative hegemony.

Johnson advises the United States should withdraw its military bases overseas and adapt to conditions in a changing world. That means leading through diplomacy rather than through military force and economic bullying. The United States should put welfare of its citizens ahead of the pretensions of its imperialists (Johnson, 2000: 229). Johnson expects world politics in the twenty-first century to be driven primarily by blowback from the second half of the twentieth century, that is, from the unintended consequences of the Cold War and the crucial American decisions to maintain a Cold War posture in a post–

Cold War world. Even though the United States has a strong sense of invulnerability and substantial military and economic tools to make such a feeling credible, the fact of its imperial pretensions means that a crisis is inevitable.

The semi-isolationist school of U.S. foreign policy, promoted by Buchanan and Johnson, encourages American retrenchment and reduction of international commitments with a strong refocus on U.S national interests. Unless it affects vital interests, military intervention is ill–advised.

Assessment

U.S. foreign policy perspectives are examined somewhat differently by Walter Russell Mead (2001: xvii), who sees four schools that have shaped the American foreign policy debate from the eighteenth to the twenty-first centuries. Hamiltonians emphasize the importance of U.S. participation in the global economy on favorable terms. Wilsonians believe the United States has a moral obligation and important national interest in spreading American democratic and social values throughout the world, creating a peaceful international community that accepts the rule of law. Jeffersonians hold that American foreign policy should be concerned about safeguarding democracy at home. Jacksonians believe the most important goal of the U.S. government should be the physical security and economic well being of the American people and avoiding foreign quarrels.

According to Mead (2001: 268–269), Hamiltonians and Wilsonians, the globalists, believe construction of a global order is the fundamental task of American foreign policy. Both schools thought in 1989, as in 1919 and 1945, that the end of a major international conflict created a valuable opportunity to build a new world order. For Wilsonians, this meant promoting the rule of law, spreading democracy, and protecting human rights by international police actions, and even the creation of a permanent armed body at the disposal of the UN Security Council. For Hamiltonians, it meant a unique opportunity to develop a worldwide trading and finance system based on the unchallenged might of America's military forces and the dynamism of its economy. Jeffersonians and Jacksonians believe globalism goes too far. The end of the Cold War allows the United States a chance to reduce its international commitments; national interest could be better served by pursuing less ambitious, far reaching projects than the globalist visions of a new world order. Would a global order mean U.S. policy-makers were willing to sacrifice the interests of the American people for the sake of that order?

The story of the rise and fall of the globalist coalition, the waning of American commitment to a Hamiltonian and Wilsonian "new world order," is the story of the 1990s, says Mead. The Gulf War reinforced the notion that the two programs could be simultaneously achieved at low cost: the intervention halted actions of a rogue state in a region of vital national interest. Wilsonians could call it a war for international law, conducted, as it was, with a multinational force and the approval of the UN Security Council. For a while after 1989, the foreign policy establishment saw few obstacles to using

American power to build a world order that satisfied the internationalist agenda of both Hamiltonian and Wilsonian goals.

U.S. foreign policy has a peculiar relationship to world order, says Mead, who views this situation as a weakness. The chief international concern of the American people through the centuries has been the relationship of the United States to the growing and changing global economic and political order. When that relationship is clear and reasonably satisfactory, the American foreign policy system works well (e.g., the Cold War). In other eras, the United States has lacked a clear consensus about its relationship to the global system, and different schools have stood for fundamentally different strategic approaches to the core issues of American foreign policy. "These periods have historically been much more difficult for the United States, and our foreign policy has been much less effective" (Mead, 2001: 313). The challenge for the United States is to develop a coherent, sustainable, realistic strategy for American world leadership in peacetime. The United States will be expected to provide vigorous farsighted leadership, and our continued power and security will depend on the wisdom, courage, and resolution that the country shows in choosing and pursuing its goals. As Mead (2001: 325) states, "The reality today is that our national security and prosperity depend on the health of the world system—and the health of that system depends on the wisdom, strength and foresight of American foreign policy."

Strategic elegance, says Mead (2001: 333–334), may be the single most needed quality in American foreign policy. What is essential is a set of directions and goals that serve "the concrete interests of the American people, that respects and serves their moral values, and that at the lowest possible costs in blood, treasure and political concentration of power secures their lives, their fortunes, and their sacred honor." In the end, strategic elegance emerges from strategic clarity. How might this be achieved? Several political analysts suggest starting positions that fit into Mead's schema. Fukuyama and Kaplan, representing the Hamiltonian and Wilsonian perspectives, respectively, continue to peddle their ideas; a Jacksonian, Charles Krauthammer, and a Jeffersonian, Gore Vidal, round out the counter point of view. William Buckley works outside of this framework, preferring a more inductive approach.

Francis Fukuyama: "The old world of power politics does rear its head occasionally, in peripheral areas like the Balkans or Transcaucasus; and it may come roaring back in a big way among the great powers at some point in the future. ... Today, internationalism and engagement are more properly matters of how the U.S. and the international financial institutions can help Russia or China or Ukraine build free markets and democracy rather than the conditions under which the U.S. will or will not use military force." (Fukuyama, 2000: 9)

Robert Kaplan: Humanitarian crises in Africa will worsen in the near future, even as the United States pays less attention to the continent, because of other foreign-policy concerns and because America's diminished affluence will temper national idealism. If NATO does not begin to work through the United Nations to organize a global constabulary force for select humanitarian interventions, the applications of American power against terrorists will run the risk of seeming narrowly self-serving—undermining

America's reputation and thus its ability to be a benevolent global power. (Kaplan, 2002: 56)

Charles Krauthammer: "The only sound theory of global engagement for the post–cold–war world is a dry–powder theory of intervention. In a country with strong isolationist tendencies, you do not squander blood and treasure on teacup wars. This is an anti–isolationist theory of (relative) noninterventionist, or as I would prefer, of prudent and selective intervention. Why? Because one needs to preserve one's strength for major exertions. In an era or relative quiet, you do not run around putting out small fires just because they are the only ones burning. You save your resources for the real strategic threats." (Krauthammer, 2000: 22)

Gore Vidal: "Fifty year ago, Harry Truman replaced the old republic with a national–security state whose sole purpose is to wage perpetual wars, hot, cold, and tepid. Exact date of replacement? February 27, 1947. ... Republican senator Arthur Vandenberg told Truman that he could have his militarized economy only *if* he first 'scared the hell out of the American people' that the Russians were coming. Truman obliged. The perpetual war began. ... Although we regularly stigmatize other societies as rogue states, we ourselves have become a large rogue state of all. We honor no treaties. We spurn international courts. We strike unilaterally wherever we choose. ... We have allowed our institutions to be taken over in the name of a globalized American empire that is totally alien in concept to anything our founders had in mind." (Vidal, 2002. 158–159)

William Buckley: "...The comprehensive problems of foreign policy—what to do when, to whom, under what circumstances—a priori. That is the intellectually challenging way of doing things, to seek out policy templates. As in, 'When a nation threatens other nations, we will intervene.' Or even, 'When a nation threatens its own people, we will intervene.' Or maybe even, 'When a nondemocratic nation can reasonably be assumed to be developing an ABC (atomic/biological/chemical) weapons capability, we will intervene.' How to intervene, at risk of how much sacrifice, is a subordinate question, and of course subordinate questions generate sub–subordinate questions.... I am going to proceed not a priori, but a fortiori: not by laying down constitutional formulations, but by asking one question. What are we going to do about Taiwan? In exploring that, perhaps light will be shed on structural questions as well." (Buckley 2000: 3–4)

INTERVENTION LESSONS

If the foreign policy doctrine search cannot be settled, due to lack of consensus or because the exercise is futile, it is still appropriate and helpful (perhaps more so) to pull together strands of lessons from the U.S. post–Cold War intervention experience in its first dozen years. What has been learned? What has been modified in response to problems encountered? Evidence of lessons and guidelines have emerged in at least three areas: Doctrine, Decision-Making, and Humanitarian Commitment.

Military Doctrine Lessons

Unlike general foreign policy doctrine, both the strategy and tactics of U.S. military doctrine have been updated over time, usually as a result of evaluating suitability and/or success of a particular plan in the context of current situations. From the Truman doctrine in 1947, which provided substantial military aid to anticommunist forces in Greece, though its message was stated more generally: helping free people everywhere, U.S. policy-makers sought to make an amendment allowing for the *direct use* of U.S. forces in resisting Soviet/communist gains abroad. The policy was explicitly proposed in NSC–68, and put to the test in Korea in 1950. But when communist China entered the conflict, introducing a significant risk of nuclear confrontation, U.S. leaders pulled back from further escalation and chose to fight a conventional military campaign restricted to the Korean peninsula. This decision produced a stalemate on the ground and domestic discontent in the United States.

Following the Korean stalemate, Eisenhower decided to adopt a new defense posture, "massive retaliation," to deter Soviet probes into the third world, ordering a substantial cut in U.S. conventional capabilities, particularly the army's ground forces. Some, including General Maxwell Taylor, began to question the logic of the posture, saying it was inappropriate to insurgencies and low–level military challenges; it did not maintain the little peace—that is, peace from disturbances which are small only in comparison with the disaster of general war. Taylor argued for a buildup of nonnuclear forces and a strategy of "flexible response" to any given challenge—views embraced by John Kennedy, who decided to test the new program by authorizing a substantial increase in U.S. military presence in South Vietnam. Vietnam was a laboratory for its application. Because it was a proving ground, it was important that the United States not fail, for it would send messages to other countries. But it did fail, and the United States withdrew by the mid–1970s. The Carter administration undertook a major review of U.S. strategy in the third world, at a time when the Americans were recovering from the deep crisis induced by the Vietnam War.

The new military doctrine was a commitment to use U.S. military power to protect key economic resources in the third world, especially oil, the activation of the Rapid Deployment Forces earmarked for intervention in the third world, the acquisition of new basing rights in the Indian Ocean (Oman, Kenya, and Somalia), and permanent deployment of a carrier battle group in the Indian Ocean. The Carter doctrine, which specified that "an attempt by any outside force to gain control of the Persian Gulf will be regarded as an assault on the vital interests of the United States of America and such an assault will be repelled by any means necessary, including military force," continued to govern U.S. military action in the region.

President Reagan denounced the Vietnam syndrome as an aberration and implemented a policy of resurgent intervention, reviving U.S. commitment to intervention in the third world during the 1980s in the doctrine of "low–intensity conflict." Its two assumptions were that vital U.S. interests are threatened by radical and revolutionary violence and the United States must be prepared to use military force to protect against such threats. Police actions, peacekeeping missions, and counterinsurgency were treated as an extension of the same continuous conflict perspective.

The end of the Cold War came at virtually the same time that American military forces had defeated the Iraqi army. The success of the American units in the Persian Gulf was savored as an ending for the period of frustration and self–doubt caused by the embarrassment of military defeat in Vietnam. American forces could not be pushed around again. The Gulf War, however, had little staying power; it was a war without legacy. Land combat lasted just four days; it had been conducted by an elite professional army.

The next doctrine came with the election of Bill Clinton, ushering in the era of "Precision Strikes" (Noonan and Hillen, 2002: 3), built on these assumptions: that most conflicts in which the United States decided to intervene involved very low geopolitical stakes—Americans would not want to suffer casualties, and technological advances allowed the United States to hit targets with great precision from long ranges, with minimal risk to military personnel. For ethnic conflicts and humanitarian disasters, the United States came to favor multilateral action, and when unilateral force was necessary, high–tech means (air strikes, cruise missiles) were used—as in Kosovo, Afghanistan, and Sudan.

The twenty-first-century Bush administration "Decisive Action" doctrine (as labeled by Noonan and Hillen, 2002: 3) combines precision force with overwhelming force and decisive combat engagements. Under this plan, single-action engagements are out; long conflicts, fought with smaller units, are in. Unmanned armed drones and combat air vehicles are becoming more popular; major deployments of ground troops are unlikely.

Although U.S. grand strategy may be elusive in the post–Cold War environment, there is real evidence of experiential learning documented in military doctrine updates in response to changing conditions in the global environment. This is not to suggest the newer doctrines are effective, rather that efforts in modification are made. From the Truman Doctrine based on communist insurgency, through massive retaliation, flexible response, the Carter doctrine, low-intensity conflict, precision strikes, to decisive action, there is continuing evidence for changing plans to fit the current environment.

Decision–Making Lessons

In the first decade of the post–Cold War world, there was a "paradox of policy principles," according to Arnold Kantor (1996), who worked in the Bush administration in the early 1990s. During the transition period from Cold War to post Cold War, there were situations where the United States had to decide whether, when, and how to intervene with military force. Principles were needed to provide both internal guidance to the bureaucracy and public rationales to explain the intervention decisions taken and not taken. The absence of a relatively consistent set of decision guidelines added to the confusion and controversy that surrounded an intervention issue, and the absence of principles contributed to accusations of inconsistency. This complicated the decision process to reach, implement, and defend an intervention in a particular situation because intervention issues have become more complicated and less orderly. Uncertainty about whether or not to intervene has increased. Furthermore, the United States is unable to predict or control ways to deter the newer types of conflict. Among the characteristics of the decision-making process and guidelines for making choices, Kantor (1996: 2–5) points to the following:

1. The manner in which intervention cases get on the U.S. decision agenda is relatively idiosyncratic and unpredictable. Media coverage helps advertise—the human tragedy in Somalia was broadcast widely, a similar situation in Sudan was not—but it does not necessarily lead to a decision to intervene. Ad hoc assessments by officials is another way candidates for intervention rise to the top of the agenda.

2. The U.S. decision-making process on intervention is ad hoc. Crisis issues arise in a nonroutine manner leading to nonroutine discussions about intervention in an atmosphere where there is no clear intervention policy; little precedence guides action.

3. The decision-making process on intervention issues frequently begins at relatively senior levels and works up via informal discussion. Problems initially addressed were not supported by substantial written analyses, due to time constraints and a fear of leaks.

4. There are distinguishable agency perspectives on issues related to intervention. The State Department tends to be more willing than others to threaten, deploy military forces, and take risks. The Defense department is much more conservative, viewing the use of force as a last resort, when diplomacy and other policy instruments have been tried and failed. The Joint Chiefs of Staff argue that if the United States is going to commit military forces, we should be prepared to bring overwhelming force to bear to ensure victory.

5. Personal beliefs, experiences, and perceptions of the participants play an unusually large role in the intervention decisions. U.S. policy toward Bosnia was shaped by President George H. W. Bush's determination not to put U.S. ground forces into Bosnia under virtually any circumstances, and General Powell's regularly insisting on an answer to the question, "What is the *military* objective we are trying to accomplish?"

6. "Slippery slopes" are always a source of concern, the fear that the U.S. role, however modest initially, would expand into growing political responsibility for the outcomes which emerge and increasing military intervention to ensure that the outcomes are satisfactory. There is concern over loss of control, difficulty in terminating military involvement short of having achieved success, or setting an arbitrary deadline for withdrawal. (The U.S. airlift of relief supplies to Somali airfields seemed a modest operation with clear limits, but it paved the way for UNITAF. Given the overwhelming U.S. responsibility for UNITAF it proved to be impossible politically to do a clean hand–off to UNISOM.)

7. Planning is often shortsighted: if a decision is made to intervene, the worries, concerns, and risks expressed by those who have been overruled tend to be forgotten or ignored.

8. Decision-making is context dependent. The decision to take military action to drive the Iraqis out of Kuwait was neither certain nor obvious in advance. The decision to

intervene in Somalia caught most people inside and outside the government by surprise.

There were no formal policy guidelines for intervention decisions during the Bush administration, Kantor (1996: 6–7) says. Several informal rules were used to structure the issues and inform choices, including: (a) do not intervene unless highly confident the intervention will be brief, inexpensive, cause minimal casualties and minimal collateral damage, and there is high probability of success; (b) decide intervention choices without involving Congress in order to enhance presidential flexibility and changes of involvement; (c) minimize the need for political support and the risk of negative political consequences: the greater the chances of controversy, the greater the probability that the United States will intervene, and the higher the premium on keeping the intervention quick, clean, and cheap; (d) avoid committing U.S. ground forces; (e) retain operational control over U.S. combat forces, particularly ground combat forces; (f) secure authorization by the United Nations or other international organizations; and (g) obtain multilateral participation.

The picture of decision-making emerging from the early post–Cold war period is one which is very insular and also highly constrained by external factors, says Kantor (1996: 8). Yet, the informal decision process reveals relatively stable characteristics, and some form of "learning" through convergence on tactical guidelines and rules of thumb is occurring.

Humanitarian Commitment Lessons

A government report, "Interagency Review of U.S. Government Civilian Humanitarian and Transition Programs" (2000: 3–9), evaluated the success and failure of four humanitarian interventions in Kosovo, Sudan, Afghanistan, and in Central America following Hurricane Mitch. In its conclusions, the report states:

- Since the end of the Cold War, the humanitarian factor has become central to senior policy makers' deliberations over U.S. foreign policy priorities and possible diplomatic, economic or military interventions to ease crises and facilitate humanitarian relief.

- As global humanitarian interests become more complex and vital to U.S. foreign policy, the need has grown for the government to have a unified, coherent humanitarian leadership. In Rwanda, Bosnia, Kosovo, Timor, Sudan and elsewhere, major foreign policy challenges typically feature, at their very center, complex humanitarian emergencies that demand coherence in our policy response.

- The global demand for humanitarian relief will not subside, we should anticipate more crises, and an ever greater demand for humanitarian assistance in the future. U.S. leadership, with respect both to internally norms and commitment of resources and personnel, is essential.

- The line separating the U.S. government humanitarian stakes from our other key foreign policy goals has been erased: these issues have become deeply embedded in one another. In Bosnia, Kosovo, Haiti, Somalia, North Korea, northern Iraq and Mitch (Hurricane Mitch in Central America) our actions to ameliorate humanitarian crisis have become conspicuously interlinked with other US foreign policy goals: democratization, respect for human rights, regional stability and control over weapons of mass destruction, protection of sustainable development investments and consolidation of fragile transitions from war to peace. ... Increasingly, multilateral humanitarian interventions must be integrated with peacekeeping strategies. The increasing role of the U.S. military in assisting with humanitarian operations significantly elevates the need to ensure timely, effective coordination mechanisms among State, USAID and DOD (Department of Defense).

- Humanitarian crises have changed profoundly in the past decade and have become, for better or worse, a central facet to our foreign policy. We struggle today—institutionally and conceptually—to catch up with harsh new external realities. ... There are no easy answers, but it is clear that we must give humanitarian issues full consideration when key political and military decisions are taken—through unified humanitarian leadership.

Rather than serving as guidelines for action, the official message is presented that the U.S. role of providing humanitarian assistance in an international context is both new and firmly ensconced in the post–Cold War world. For example, in data gathered by the United Air Forces in Europe (USAFE), a list of humanitarian military operations between 1945 and 1997 shows a significant increase in missions conducted in the 1990s from earlier periods, illustrating the expanded role of humanitarian operations in treating civil instability (and also natural disasters) in the post–Cold War era (see Table C.1). While it may not be the vision of U.S. foreign policy, humanitarian–based policy is likely to figure into any future issue.

INTERVENTION DECISION TEMPLATE

From the lessons and guidance discussed, we still do not get a firm grasp of when and where to intervene and whether any pattern marks the post–Cold War experience. James F. Goodby (1998) has sanguine advice about lessons of intervention in the modern era. Although the goal is conflict prevention and deterrence and early intervention, circumstances almost always make early intervention difficult, especially in cases of civil war. The basic dilemma is familiar: as events move from a minor dispute to a major crisis, greater efforts are required to deal with the situation. Yet, at the earliest stage of a dispute, the case for external intervention cannot be convincingly made. Nor is there a clearly definable point at which outside forces—great powers, international organizations—should begin to concert their policies to deal with a potential conflict. Nations are mostly unwilling to use coercive measures before violence has occurred and then only if the level of violence shocks the international community into action. There is no method for the international community to gauge the ultimate impact on international peace and security of a slowly developing crisis. There are few criteria to determine whether a better course would be to contain and isolate a dispute or to attempt to settle it. And, if a

Table C.1
U.S. Humanitarian Military Operations: 1945–1997
Relief Efforts by United States Air Forces in Europe (USAFE)*

Cause	Civil War, Instability**	Location	Natural Disaster, etc.	Total
Year				
1997	1	Albania	0	1
1996	6	Liberia, Iraq (3) Central African Republic Rwanda	2	8
1995	0			
1994	3	Bosnia, Rwanda (2)	7	10
1993	1	Bosnia	1	2
1992	7	Somalia (2), Sierra Leone (2), Croatia, Bosnia, Angola	4	11
1991	2	Iraq, Zaire ('Congo)	0	2
1990				0
1989				0
1988			1	1
1987				0
1986				0
1985				0
1984				0
1983	1	Lebanon		1
1982			1	1
1981				0
1980			1	1
1979	2	Iran (2)	3	5
1978	1	Zaire (Congo)		1
1977				0
1976	1	Lebanon	2	3
1975				0
1974	1	Cyprus	1	2
1973			1	1
1972			1	1
1971	1	Bangladesh	2	3
1970	1	Jordan	1	2
1969			5	5
1968			7	7
1967			4	4
1966			1	1
1965	1	Cyprus	3	4
1964	2	Cyprus, Congo (Zaire)		2
1963			10	10

Table C. 1 (cont.)
U.S. Humanitarian Military Operations: 1945–1997
Relief Efforts by United States Air Forces in Europe (USAFE)*

Cause	Civil War, Instability**	Location	Natural Disaster, etc.	Total
Year				
1962			9	9
1961	1	Congo (Zaire)	9	10
1960	2	Congo	3	4
1959			2	2
1958				0
1957			1	1
1956	1	Hungary	5	6
1955			3	3
1954			6	6
1953			6	6
1952			1	1
1951			2	2
1950			1	1
1949				0
1948				0
1947			1	1
1946				0
1945	1	Greece		1

*This list includes only civil instability-related humanitarian operations, and natural disaster, medical problems—floods, earthquakes, disease. It excludes international conflict relief efforts. (There are few, though the most outstanding effort was the Berlin Airlift in 1948.)

**Operations include relief supplies for refugees—food; clothing; shelter; rescue operations; transportation support for peacekeepers; medical evacuation; American expatriate evacuation.

Source: "USAFE Humanitarian Operations 1945–1997," Federation of American Scientists (*www.fas.org*).

nation's interests are not clearly and directly damaged by a crisis, substantial grounds substantial grounds always exist for governments to prefer the nonintervention approach.

The role of America in the post–Cold War world is not yet clearly defined, but the sum total of experiences throughout the nineties is shaping the future choices and policies of decision-makers. Memories linger. The Vietnam War shaped military intervention decisions on Bosnia; the engagement in Bosnia shaped the intervention decision in Kosovo; humanitarian intervention in Somalia affected American nonintervention in the case of Rwanda. The public opinion emotions that carry a policy tend to be unreliable: first, an enthusiastic urging to "do something," to intervene to alleviate citizen suffering in areas where there is not an immediate threat to American vital interests; later, an enthusiastic cry, when they see dead and wounded American soldiers returning stateside, to ask loudly why we are involved.

Debate continues about the merits of describing conflict and peace as a linear or cyclical model and about the merits of involvement in distant lands beset with internal violence and unrest. The potential for violence can be defused through early, integrated application of intervention through political, diplomatic, economic, and military measures. There remains, however, a gap between long-term intervention as a solution to handle structural problems in domestic societies and quick, short–term responses in conflict situations, including complex emergency humanitarian assistance. Intervention may be the solution; the trick is knowing what tools to apply in what stage in what setting. We need a template of appropriate interventionary strategies.

When is it in the interests of third parties to intervene? Under what conditions will low–intensity missions succeed? How can an unsuccessful intervention become a successful one? David Carment and Dane Rowlands (1998: 573) address these questions using a game-theory model in which an intervener's utility of escalation is derived from an assessment of the relationship between four variables: (1) the *salience* level of the dispute to the third party, (2) the *capabilities* of the combatant, (3) the *expected gains* to the combatant from continued fighting, and (4) the *level of intensity* of the third-party intervention. The intensity of the intervention is the only factor that varies, it is not determined in the game, while salience, combat strength, and expected gains are assumed to be given features rather than choices. The model prescribes how core concerns for the intervener affect the costs and benefits associated with each strategy and point to the conditions of a mission that should facilitate a better understanding of the conditions under which intervention will and will not succeed. They focus on UN intervention efforts through peacekeeping, but their formal model can be applied easily to American foreign policy choices.

A third party responds to a conflict in one of three ways: by resisting any military involvement, concentrating instead on mediation, fact finding, preventive diplomacy, and sanctions; by committing troops to a low-intensity conventional peacekeeping mission; or by engaging in forceful intervention that requires substantial and favorable military capabilities. The challenge a third party faces is identifying how much force is needed to deploy in an intervention to ensure that basic objectives are achieved at minimal cost. The trade-offs between these basic strategies are clear: high-intensity interventions may be more effective in forcing a settlement, but are costly; less forceful interventions are cheaper, but less effective. Choosing a level of intervention somewhere in between may be the worst solution, raising costs without improving outcomes (Carment and Rowlands, 1998: 577–579).

The third party must evaluate the outcomes of the civil conflict in terms of its own interests. The payoff of an outcome depends on both the benefits associated with a particular settlement and the costs endured to achieve it. In this evaluation, the salience of the conflict is critical to the ranking of different outcomes in terms of their benefits because it determines the willingness to absorb costs to achieve a particular settlement. The salience of a conflict to an intervener and the cost that intervener is willing to pay to secure a favorable outcome are directly related, state Carment and Rowlands (1998: 579), who differentiate the concept from threat. "Threats to an intervener arising out of a combatant's willingness to use violence to challenge core values such as life, territory, or resources do indeed change over the lifetime of a conflict. However, the importance or weight of these threats can be understood only in terms of their implications and relevance to the third party. Thus, we define salience in a geostrategic context by referring to its implications for structural change and its proximity to major power centers and intense conflict zones and the risks it poses both regionally and globally." Salience, in their model, is only marginally sensitive to policy choices or manipulation and cannot quickly be changed by policy-makers. Nor can it be artificially proclaimed, for it would fail to generate the sustained credibility and commitment essential to bring an end to an internal conflict. Third-party intervention works only when the belligerents believe that the third party is there to fulfill its mission. Salience is the only means of establishing this political credibility. When applied to American intervention choices, salience is a factor perhaps best conceptualized within the broad framework of national interest.

Using the model's four variables, Carment and Rowlands display the eight combinations of dichotomous variation: whether the salience level of the issue for the third party is high or low, whether the combatant fighting capabilities are high or low, whether any of the combatants expect to gain from a continuation of the conflict (rather than settlement brought about by a third party), and the best strategy for an intervener under these conditions. They applied their model to several cases of conflict, including post–Cold War events in Bosnia, Rwanda, and Somalia, and compared the UN intervention mission's intensity with the best solution recommended from their analysis. The results are displayed in Table C.2

High-intensity intervention is recommended regardless of the conflict's salience to the intervener, when the combatant strength overall is weak and the gains from continuing the conflict expected by any of the combatants are low, suggesting that a fatigue factor may bring the conflict to a ripe moment for resolution through decisive action coming from the outside. High-intensity

Table C.2
Template for Intervention Decisions

Recommended Decision	Intervener Issue Salience Evaluation	Combatant Fighting Capability Assessment	Combatant Expected Gains from Conflict
High Intensity Intervention to resolve the conflict	high	low	low
	low	low	low
	high	high	high
Low Intensity Intervention to resolve the conflict	high	low	high
	low	low	high
No Intervention to resolve the conflict	low	high	low
	low	high	high
	high	high	low

Source: Adapted from Carment and Rowlands (1998), p. 586.

intervention is also optimal when there is high-issue salience for the intervener and a strong combatant who anticipates further advantage through continued fighting. Here, only strong intervention will be sufficient to deter the combatant from seeking to prolong the conflict. Issue salience for the intervener is generally important in high-level military interventions, but, as the analysis shows, it is not always the decisive factor.

Low-intensity intervention is recommended in two situations. First, where the issue has high salience for a third party and combatant expectations of gain for continued fighting remain high despite their low capabilities to do so. The strategic calculus, according to Carments and Rowlands (1998: 589), is that the "intervener has sufficient credibility regarding its willingness to escalate that the combatant would cooperate regardless of the intervener's strength, and thus the intervener chooses the lowest cost option." In the second situation where the issue has low salience, the intervener's credibility in making threats of escalation are challenged, and a different decision logic enters. Because the intervener is unwilling to allow the combatant to dominate in the conflict, possibly acquiring high gains, the selected strategy is to "send a small force to modify the results but not overpower the combatant." Low-intensity interventions are recommended when combatant power is weak, regardless of issue importance to the third party.

A decision not to intervene is best when the cost of opposing a strong opponent is simply too high given the rather low importance of the outcome (low salience and strong combatant combinations), and in cases in which, despite the high salience of the conflict to a third party, the strength of the combatant makes the intervener unwilling to absorb the costs of certain resistance to ensure an outcome that is not strongly valued, but only marginally preferred. Combatant strength deters outsiders from intervening.

Their model addresses the question of resource allocation by examining the conditions in which cheaper low-intensity interventions will be sufficient to bring about peace. In general, low-intensity interventions will be more likely to succeed when deployed against weak combatants who have an expectation of high gains to continued conflict. They advise against the expense of a larger and more intense intervention. Sometimes low-intensity interventions will be unsuccessful. They caution that interveners have no guarantee that their actions can generate the desired outcome. In their model, if issue salience, combatant capability, and the fighters' expected gains from continued conflict are weighed equally in a decision to intervene, it appears that combatant fighting power (consistently low for low-intensity recommended interventions and consistently high for decisions not to intervene) is more important for third-party choices than issue salience, which varies under all three levels of recommendations. If these factors are not given equal weight, highlighting the significance of any one over the others would influence policy choice. Here, the evaluation of issue salience becomes more critical and complex. Which crises demand a decisive military response from the United States and which do not will depend on the framework of salience within the defining parameters of American national interest in the post-Cold War environment. Although somewhat helpful, the ultimate limitation in this template formula is that salience is derived from American national interest evaluation, an assessment that is subjectively determined within the context of the changing world system. The emerging global structure is affecting how the United States evaluates its national interests and how American intervention is shaping the global structure. If U.S. policy-makers and the public come to agreement on issue salience for various world problems, and the concept were to be defined operationally and usefully and weighed more precisely with qualified distinctions established a priori, then the possibilities for applying this decision template expand.

SHAPING THE GLOBAL ORDER

Paul Kennedy wrote at the eve of the Cold War (1987: 534–535), "The task facing American statesmen over the next decades, therefore, is to recognize that broad trends are underway, and that there is a need to 'manage' affairs so that the *relative* erosion of the United States' position takes place slowly and smoothly, and is not accelerated by policies which bring merely short–term advantage but longer–term disadvantage....The American position is a very special one. It remains the decisive actor in every type of balance and issue.

Because it has so much power, because it is the linchpin of the western alliance system, and the center of the existing global economy, what it does, or *does not do* is so much more important than what any of the other Powers decides to do." Kennedy was writing about the possibility of America's decline. Instead, the United States turned out to be the most powerful defining agent shaping the global order. The international system has consequences, and agent and structure are interlinked. What are those linkages?

In the decade following the 1979 Soviet invasion of Afghanistan (a Cold War intervention), which was designed to assist the communist government in power, Saudi Arabia funds, along with covert U.S. training and military support, backed the Mujahadeen, the opposition forces. The Pakistani army provided the logistical support, and religious schools at the foot of the Khyber Pass guaranteed a steady flow of Islamic missionaries and fierce, devout fighters for the battle against the USSR intervention in Afghanistan. As the Soviets were withdrawing near the end of the 1980s, Osama bin Laden, who had been part of the Mujahadeen, founded Al Qaida, "the base," a cluster of military–ideological camps. The major turning point in his work came when Iraq invaded Kuwait leading to the 1991 Gulf War: bin Laden proposed to launch a jihad against Saddam Hussein and his Iraqi soldiers, but he was turned down by the Saudi authorities who sought U.S. military assistance instead. Large numbers of American troops were sent to Saudi Arabia. Bin Laden's disapproval of the American intervention turned into open hostility with the stationing of American armed forces on Saudi soil. A U.S. military presence continued throughout the 1990s, withdrawing in the summer of 2003. Was the purpose of mustering a grand coalition against Iraq to push American national interests, in particular, to secure safe and continued flow of oil? Was the objective of U.S. policy to guarantee the continuation of the Saudi regime, which seemed out of step with the proper values of social life of Islam? The Saudi authorities revoked Osama bin Laden's passport and froze his assets. Later, Washington succeeded in pressuring Sudan to deny him safe haven. He sought refuge with the Taliban in Afghanistan, who had taken control of Kabul in 1996, in exchange for his financial and logistical support. The Taliban movement took root among the dislocated and deprived children of the Afghan refugees trained in the religious schools of Pakistan financed by private Saudi funding. Bin Laden and associates declared war against the United States, deciding that to attack giant structures representing superpower economic and military might would subdue the interventionist tendencies of the most powerful country in the world. Their intervention—a large, simple but sophisticated, terrorist attack against America —was carried out on September 11, 2001.

Is terrorism a new kind of challenge, the result of arrogance of a national interest-based, interventionist foreign policy? Can America do anything effective against such a threat, since the enemy thrives in shadowy corners of the world, contriving schemes beyond the reach of our intelligence capabilities and military might? The challenge is not new. The United States has been confronting terrorism since the 1970s (American ambassadors assassinated abroad, airplanes hijacked, hostages taken in Iran). But defeating terrorism will mean patience, fortitude, and willingness and ability to undertake diverse and difficult tasks. Among the strategic objectives: draining the swamp, frightening perpetrators into the open, and enlisting the help of others. In the twenty–first century, the George W. Bush administration announced in March 2002 a plan: that the United States was willing to train and provide military aid to governments everywhere for the fight against terrorism, beyond the borders of Afghanistan. Accordingly, Americans sent 600 troops to the Philippines to train forces to stamp out a Muslim extremist group; 150 military trainers were sent to Georgia to eradicate terrorists; Yemen received about 100 U.S. troops to fight terrorism. In short, the United States expanded its intervention network.

What is the future of civil unrest? In the wake of the attacks on America in 2001, Thomas Friedman in a *New York Times* editorial (November 7, 2001) portrayed the elements of Arab states' domestic instability problem in this way: first, the regimes fail to build a real future for their people, triggering a seething anger; second, young people who can get visas escape oversees but those who cannot turn to protest, often in the mosque, using Islam as an ideology; third, the regimes must control the violent Muslim protesters, but to avoid being accused of being anti-Muslim, they give money and free rein to their most hard-line, but nonviolent, Muslim clerics; fourth, the regimes redirect their public's anger onto America through the (government controlled) press. As a result, America is hated and Islam gets handed over to the most antimodern forces. Civil instability of this nature is not likely to be remedied soon. Whether rich or poor, countries saddled by low economic growth, corruption, and nonaccountability are candidates for internal crises. Such crises may drag the United States into the impending conflict with far-reaching consequences. For example, a collapse of a country like Pakistan into anarchy or revolution would cripple the on-going global campaign against terrorism. These situations pose serious issues for U.S. intervention policy. The examples of unrest and U.S. intervention tie back to nation-building and whether it is an appropriate task for the United States to ensure a state does not succumb to a civil war. Does it make sense to force U.S. western-style democracy? That takes a lot of education, time and training, and financial support. Moreover, violence often accompanies democratization. Elections may strengthen people who are armed, like warlords, who can use their weapons for power. Democracies may be peaceful; getting there is not. There is a further issue of U.S. strategy of involvement (or noninvolvement) to bring regional security. Together, the set of problems associated with civil unrest and its relation to international security will continue to influence many aspects of American intervention choices both in immediate application and over the long term.

What was the effect of the Cold War's end on civil conflict? What was its effect on U.S. intervention policy? What new patterns of intervention are emerging? What is the role of UN peacekeeping under the new system? How does one explain the transition into the post–Cold War system in terms of structural arrangement impact on global order units? Complexity theory sees life forms existing on a spectrum ranging from ultrastability (ordered hierarchy) to instability (chaos). Fitness is found in the middle range of the spectrum.

When organisms associate in a symbiosis, the resultant structure is called an "emergent property." It is "order for free," since the cooperation seems self-organized and self-imposed. The collective behavior that emerges from a group of social arranging units is called "swarm intelligence," offering an alternative way of designing systems that traditionally required centralized control and extensive preprogramming (Clemens, 2000: 10). Complexity theory application is strictly inductive. The weakness lies in its ad hoc assumptions and flexibility that may encourage intellectual sloppiness, says Lars-Erik Cederman (1997: 62). It has no unique predictions and its outcomes are fragile, an artifact of specific parameter configurations.

Applying a complexity systems perspective would seem to suggest the following: If the Cold War had continued, Iraq would not have invaded Kuwait, a massive troop deployment in Saudi Arabia would have been unnecessary, and there would have been no Persian Gulf War. If the Cold War had continued, U.S. aid to Somalia would probably not have ended when it did, and conditions of anarchy would not have developed as they did, leading to eventual intervention. If the Cold War had continued, the Yugoslav state would not have disintegrated the way that it did. There would have been no extensive war in Bosnia, and no war in Kosovo. Without the conflicts, no intervention would have occurred. If the Cold War had continued, and the Gulf War had not occurred, the Al Qaida forces would not be as powerful, bin Laden would not have been running extensive military camps in Afghanistan, the attack on America would have been unlikely, and the United States would not have been involved in the war in Afghanistan at the start of the twenty–first century. With respect to civil conflict and U.S. intervention in Haiti, Panama, and Rwanda: whether the global order was defined in Cold War or post–Cold War terms, these conflicts would have proceeded. Intervention might have been more cautious, scaled down, or perhaps directed differently. Overall, if the Cold War had continued, less *overt* U.S. military intervention would have been expected, but *covert* action, long a staple in American policy, might have expanded, or at the very least, might have remained at its given plane. What changed in the post–Cold War world was the expanded level and range of civil disturbances. International action, unrestrained by earlier bipolar superpower competition, expanded openly—that is, by using overt military intervention tools—in response. The interventions were largely reaction to opportunity, and the opportunities changed. Essentially, as intervention opportunity rose, so did intervention action; military intervention expanded to fit the occasion, not to exploit it.

Table C.3 shows post–Cold War system adaptability along three dimensions related to the global order: running totals of new civil conflicts; new UN peacekeeping missions to deal with them; and U.S. military intervention behavior from 1980 to 2000, divided into three-year time frames. Magnitude of the violence, extent of peacekeeping, and combat intervention commitments are not indicated. A pattern seems to be forming between civil conflict occurrence and UN peacekeeping response in the post–Cold War period. Greater levels of

Table C.3
Adaptability in the Post–Cold War International System

Years	New Civil Conflicts[1] (1,000+ deaths)	New UN Peacekeeping[2] Missions for Civil Conflicts	U.S. Overt Military Intervention[3] Civil	International
1980–1982	10	0	Lebanon	
1983–1985	10	0	Grenada	
1986–1988	8	0	Panama[4]	
1989–1991	14	7	Panama	
				Persian Gulf
	15	11	Somalia Rwanda Haiti	
1995–1997	6	11	Bosnia	
1998–2000	2	7	Kosovo	Afghanistan

[1]Includes conflicts begun during the specified time period with at least 1,000 annual conflict-related deaths.
[2]Includes peacekeeping operations for civil conflicts begun during the specified time period.
[3]Includes military intervention with 1,000 or more troops committed for combat and/or peacekeeping purposes. Lebanon, Somalia, Rwanda, Bosnia, and Kosovo were cases of more than 1,000 annual civil conflict deaths.
[4]The United States sent troops to Panama in 1988 (as reinforcement) and 1989 (for the attack). Panama crisis contained both domestic and international issues.

Sources: Regan (2000a) Appendix; Wallensteen and Sollenberg (2001) Appendix 1; United Nations Peacekeeping Operations, Completed Peacekeeping Operations, Current Peacekeeping Operations (*www.un.org.Depts/DPKO*).

multilateral peacekeeping activities are in view; there is no sign this will disappear. The path of violent civil conflict outbreak is steady throughout the 1980s as the Cold War is winding down, peaks upward from 1989 to 1994, and moves to much lower points thereafter. In UN peacekeeping operations, it is notable that absolutely no missions were approved throughout the 1980s (until late 1989) in line with the bipolar stalemate at the Security Council. From 1989 forward, each period includes a number of UN peacekeeping operations, and consistent with the peak in civil conflicts, a larger number were approved during the 1992–1994 period. The picture of U.S. intervention over time likewise shows a high point of involvement in the early 1990s—operations in Somalia, Rwanda, and Haiti all commenced between 1992 and 1994. However, when compared to the parallel trends in civil conflicts and UN peacekeeping operations, the U.S. picture seems a little out of step. In relative terms, America has not engaged more frequently in intervention operations in the post–Cold War period; nor is there an upward pattern. Notably, in just four instances (Somalia, Rwanda, Bosnia, and Kosovo) did the United States intervene in response to serious cases of civil war, although many instances of violent domestic conflict—nearly 40—marked the 1990s.

The current age is neither a time of chaos, a totally unpredictable, violent, uncertain world, nor of ultrastability, a rigidly controlled operation in the international system reminiscent of Cold War bipolarity. Rather, the pattern of activity between the emerging global order structure and its primary agent, the United States, falls somewhere between the extremes. It shows an element of fit. In terms of a U.S. role, "unipolar guardian" rather than "hegemonic leader" seems a better characterization.

What evidence of "swarm intelligence" exists in other features of the post–Cold War system? Very little. There is no convergence of opinion on world views. Both Fukuyama's optimism, that the universe is becoming a democracy haven, and Kaplan's pessimism, that the world is hopelessly pushing toward anarchy, have sway. No movement toward consensus of the U.S. role in the world is on the horizon. Significant camps advocate that America should (a) seek primacy, (b) participate but not seek control, or (c) pull back from a strong internationalist stance. Settlement on a foreign policy doctrine is not in sight; the country has not moved closer to adopting a particular plan designed around a twenty-first-century national interest set of concept most appropriate in the contemporary setting. By default, the lack of consensus in these areas brings "selective engagement" into focus as an active slogan. It's a flexible position, suitable for any occasion, from broadcasting a general message to the world about U.S. involvement preference to providing a rationale for decisions made and actions taken. It is not a vision.

Is the shape of world order one of deliberate design or adaptation? Shape comes from two levels of international interaction: dramatic superpower involvement (the Persian Gulf War and the terrorist attacks on America leading to the war in Afghanistan), and accumulated extension—the spread of military forces into small interventions around the globe. The collected evidence leans toward adaptation. On its record, the United States has success (Persian Gulf War), failure (Somalia), mixed results (Bosnia, Kosovo), and unfinished work (Afghanistan, and more generally, the war on Terrorism). Principles of involvement are hard to find, but the idea of selective engagement—if it is a real policy, not just post hoc justification for action or inaction—comes closest.

If we must be selective, what are the guidelines? From the American post–Cold War experience in the first twelve years of the new age, at least three points surface: (1) intervention practice appeared to be driven by reaction to crises and not informed by grand vision or advanced planning; (2) intervention practice appeared to be driven by reluctance to enter civil conflicts early or with an overwhelming force (Somalia, Rwanda, Haiti, Bosnia); and (3) intervention practice appeared to be *less* driven by resoluteness: the use of an overwhelming force and a quick, clear exit strategy, for example, have varied.

In the near future, it seems that U.S. intervention choice will not be solved by principles, although the template formula, pragmatic ideas, and evolving lessons presented here will contribute to the discussion and guidelines. Inconsistencies are likely to continue and will be explained under the rubric of a selective engagement rationale. The problem of making U.S. intervention choices will not be solved by a foreign policy doctrine, for opinion will not unite around an idea expressing American interests. Presidents will try out slogans and themes, and these will generally be expected to last as long as the administration is in power. U.S. intervention choice will not be resolved by UN collectivist thinking or debates on multilateral engagement. As chief UN donor, America will continue to exercise significant control in the international institution, guiding peacekeeping plans and discouraging vastly expanded missions. The post–Cold War era, with respect to intervention and how it is shaping the global order, will be understood gradually, by experience of engagement plus the conventional wisdom of lessons learned. There will be more intervention opportunities, and U.S. debates on the subject will not cease. Intervention choices will be handled case by case. Peacekeeping will not diminish in importance, but may not expand in the near future as the world struggles to deal with the terrorism phenomenon and its relation to intervention as a first order priority.

What is the future of U.S. military intervention? If terrorism against America is a result of "blowback" as Johnson argues, then we should expect reduced levels of intervention in the near future, under the premise that extended global reach breeds resentment in affected populations. If terrorism is an open, worldwide danger that must be eliminated, then enhanced levels of intervention could result under the premise that aggressive action is required to stoke it out. Together, these contradictory policies may cancel one another, producing no change at all with respect to levels of intervention.

If the Cold War story is largely a tale of intervention, what about the post–Cold War sequel? To be sure, there are changing visual images and conceptualizations for understanding transition in the international system. The old structure broke down. The ideology clash broke down. The balance of power broke down. The enemy images broke down. In the 1990s, there were critical cases of intervention, of challenges, of defining the new scene, and efforts to work out new norms of behavior in response to the breakdown. Intervention in the Cold War was important in creating and perpetuating the system, but intervention in the post–Cold War seems less of a definer in forming exact system shape. It operates under new rules and a more ambiguous picture, with potentially greater opportunity for experimentation.

The start of World War II, the middle of the Vietnam War, the end of the Cold War, and a decade into the post–Cold War era—these were times of major debate about intervention in U.S. foreign policy circles. It was not that the conflicts that arose were necessarily different, but the logic of the structure-agent relationship—of the American role in shaping or reshaping the global order—that was at issue. Civil disorder is a constant; what varies is how this form of instability is allowed to develop and emerge in the political climate of authority and grievance and ultimately how it is treated as a security problem on the agenda of the international community and its global leader. Under such constraints, the complexity theory of adaptation offers a reasonable conceptualization for understanding these processes.

Bibliography

Abolfathi, Farid, John J. Hayes, and Richard E. Hayes. "Trends in United States Response to International Crisis: Policy Implications for the 1980s." In Charles W. Kegley, Jr. and Patrick McGowan, eds. *Challenges to America: United States Foreign Policy in the 1980s*. Beverly Hills, Calif.: Sage Publications, 1979.

Abrams, Elliott. *Security and Sacrifice: Isolation, Intervention, and American Foreign Policy*. Indianapolis, Ind.: The Hudson Institute, 1995.

Acheson, Dean. *Present at the Creation: My Years at the State Department*. New York: W.W. Norton, 1969.

Allison, Graham, and Gregory F. Treverton, eds. *Rethinking America's Security: Beyond Cold War to New World Order*. New York: W.W. Norton, 1992.

Ambrose, Stephen E. *Rise to Globalism: United States Foreign Policy Since 1938*. 4th Ed. New York: Viking Penguin, 1985.

Annan, Kofi A. "The Peace-Keeping Prescription." In Kevin M. Cahill, ed. *Preventive Diplomacy: Stopping Wars Before They Start*. New York: Basic Books, 1996.

—. *Towards a Culture of Prevention: Statements by the Secretary-General of the United Nations*. A Report to the Carnegie Commission on Preventing Deadly Conflict. New York: Carnegie Corporation of New York. December 1999.

Art, Robert J. "Geopolitics Updated: The Strategy of Selective Engagement." *International Security* 23 (Winter 1998–99): 79–113.

—. "Geopolitics Updated: The Strategy of Selective Engagement." In Michael E. Brown, Owen R. Coté, Sean M. Lynn-Jones, and Steven E. Miller, eds. *America's Strategic Choices: An International Security Reader*. Rev. Ed. Cambridge, Mass. The MIT Press, 2000.

Aspen Strategy Group. *The United States and the Use of Forces in the Post-Cold War*. Queenstown, Md.: The Aspen Institute, 1995.

Avant, Deborah D. "The Institutional Sources of Military Doctrine: Hegemons in Peripheral Wars." *International Studies Quarterly* 37 (1993): 409–430.

Axelrod, Robert. *The Complexity of Cooperation: Agent-Based Models of Competition and Cooperation.* Princeton, N.J.: Princeton University Press, 1997.

Ayres, R. William. "A World Flying Apart? Violent Nationalist Conflict and the End of the Cold War." *Journal of Peace Research* 37 (2000): 107–117.

Bacevich, Andrew J. "Policing Utopia: The Military Imperatives of Globalization." *The National Interest* 56 (1999): 5–13.

—. "A Less than Splendid Little War." *The Wilson Quarterly* 25 (2001): 83–94.

Baker, James A., III. *The Politics of Diplomacy: Revolution, War and Peace.* New York: Putnam, 1995.

—. "Selective Engagement: Principles for American Foreign Policy in a New Era." In Keith Philip Lepor, ed. *After the Cold War: Essays on the Emerging World Order.* Austin: University of Texas Press, 1997.

Balch-Lindsay, Dylan, and Andrew J. Enterline. "Killing Time: The World Politics of Civil War Duration, 1820–1992." *International Studies Quarterly* 44 (2000): 615–642.

Barber, Benjamin. *Jihad vs. McWorld: How Globalism and Tribalism Are Reshaping the World.* New York: Ballantine Books, 1996.

Barnett, Michael N. "Peacekeeping, Indifference, and Genocide in Rwanda." In Jutta Weldes, Mark Laffey, Hugh Gusterson, and Raymond Duvall, eds. *Cultures of Insecurity: States, Communities, and the Production of Danger.* Minneapolis: University of Minnesota Press, 1999.

Barry, Tom, and Martha Honey, eds. *Global Focus: A New Foreign Policy Agenda 1997–1998.* Albuquerque, N.M.: Interhemispheric Resource Center, 1997.

Bert, Wayne. *The Reluctant Superpower: United States' Policy in Bosnia, 1991–1995.* New York: St. Martin's Press, 1997.

Beschloss, Michael, and Strobe Talbott. *At the Highest Levels: The Inside Story of the End of the Cold War.* Boston: Little, Brown, 1993.

Betts, Richard. "The Delusion of Impartial Intervention." *Foreign Affairs* 73 (1994): 20–33.

Blacker, Coit D. "A Typology of Post-Cold War Conflicts." In Arnold Kantor and Linton F. Brooks, eds. *U.S. Intervention Policy for the Post–Cold War World: New Challenges and New Responses.* New York: W.W. Norton, 1994.

Blechman, Barry M. "The Intervention Dilemma." *The Washington Quarterly* 18 (1995): 147–157.

Blechman, Barry M., and Stephen S. Kaplan. *Force Without War: U.S. Armed Forces as a Political Instrument.* Washington, D.C.: Brookings Institution, 1978.

Blechman, Barry M., and Tamara Cofman Wittes. "Defining Moment: The Threat and Use of Force in American Foreign Policy Since 1989." Occasional Paper No. 6. Washington, D.C.: The Henry L. Stimson Center, May 1998.

—. "Defining Moment: The Threat and Use of Force in American Foreign Policy." *Political Science Quarterly* 114 (1999): 1–30.

Bonneuil, Noël, and Nadia Auriat. "Fifty Years of Ethnic Conflict and Cohesion: 1945–94." *Journal of Peace Research* 37 (2000): 563–581.

Boutros-Ghali, Boutros. *An Agenda for Peace: Preventive Diplomacy, Peacemaking and Peacekeeping.* New York: United Nations, 1992.

—. *An Agenda for Peace: Preventive Diplomacy, Peacemaking and Peacekeeping.* 2n Ed. New York: United Nations, 1995.

Boyd, Charles G. "The U.S. Commission on National Security/21st Century: The Progress of a Nation." Address at Rice University, April 10, 2000.

Bowker, David. "The New Management of Peace Operations Under PDD-56." *The Fletcher Forum of World Affairs* 22 (1998): 57–72.

Brands, H. W. *What America Owes the World: The Struggle for the Soul of Foreign Policy.* New York: Cambridge University Press, 1998.

Brown, Chris. "History Ends, Worlds Collide." In Michael Cox, Ken Booth, and Tim Dunn, eds. *The Interregnum: Controversies in World Politics 1989–1999.* Cambridge, United Kingdom: Cambridge University Press, 1999.

Brown, Michael E. "The Causes and Regional Dimensions of Internal Conflict." In Michael E. Brown, ed. *The International Dimensions of Internal Conflict.* Cambridge, Mass.: The MIT Press, 1996.

Brown, Michael E., and Richard N. Rosecrance, eds. *The Costs of Conflict: Prevention and Cure in the Global Arena.* Lanham, Md.: Rowman and Littlefield, 1999.

Brown, Michael E., Owen R. Coté, Jr., Sean M. Lynn-Jones, and Steven E. Miller, eds. *America's Strategic Choices: An International Security Reader.* Cambridge, Mass.: The MIT Press, 2000.

Brzezinski, Zbigniew. *Game Plan: A Geostrategic Framework for the Conduct of the U.S.-Soviet Contest.* Boston: Atlantic Monthly Press, 1986.

Buchanan, Patrick J. *A Republic, Not an Empire: Reclaiming America's Destiny.* Washington D.C.: Regnery Publications, 1999.

Buckley, William. "American Power—For What? A Symposium." *Commentary Magazine.* January 2000: 23–24.

Bull, Hedley. "Intervention in the Third World." In Hedley Bull, ed. *Intervention in World Politics.* New York: Oxford University Press, 1984.

Burg, Steven L., and Paul S. Shoup. *The War in Bosnia-Herzegovina: Ethnic Conflict and International Intervention.* Armonk, N.Y.: M.E. Sharpe, 1999.

Bush, George H.W., and Brent Scowcroft. *A World Transformed.* New York: Knopf, 1998.

Buzan, Barry. "The Timeless Wisdom of Realism?" In Steve Smith, Ken Booth, and Marysia Zalewski, eds. *International Theory: Positivism and Beyond.* New York: Cambridge University Press, 1996.

Byman, Daniel. "After the Storm: U.S. Policy Toward Iraq." *Political Science Quarterly* 115 (2000–01): 493-516.

Byman, Daniel, and Stephen Van Evera. "Why They Fight: Hypotheses on the Causes of Contemporary Deadly Conflict." *Security Studies* 7 (1998): 1–50.

Byman, Daniel, and Matthew Waxman. "Defeating US Coercion." *Survival* 41 (1999): 107–120.

Cahill, Kevin M., ed. *Preventive Diplomacy: Stopping Wars Before They Start.* New York: Basic Books, 1996.

Callahan, David. *Unwinnable Wars: American Power and Ethnic Conflict.* New York: Hill and Wang, 1997.

Campbell, David. "Why Fight: Humanitarianism, Principles, and Post-structuralism." *Millennium: Journal of International Studies* 27 (1998): 497–521.

Carment, David, and Patrick James. *Peace in the Midst of Wars: Preventing and Managing International Ethnic Conflicts.* Columbia: University of South Carolina Press, 1998.

Carment, David, and Dane Rowlands. "Three's Company: Evaluating Third-Party Intervention in Intrastate Conflict." *Journal of Conflict Resolution* 42 (1998): 572–599.

Carpenter, Ted Galen. "Direct Military Intervention." In Peter Schrader, ed. *Intervention in the 1980s: United States Foreign Policy in the Third World.* Boulder, Colo.: Lynne Rienner Publishers, 1989.

—. "Uncle Sam as the World's Policeman: Time for a Change?" *USA Today Magazine* (January 1991).

—. "Setting a Dangerous Precedent in Somalia." *Cato Foreign Policy Briefing* 20 (December 18, 1992). www.cato.org/pubs/fpbriefs/fpb-020.html. (Accessed June 25, 2003.)

Carpenter, Ted Galen, and Doug Bandow. "Foreign Assistance and U.S. Foreign Policy." U.S. Congressional Testimony. Washington, D.C., March 13, 1997.

Carter, Ashton B. "Adapting US Defense to Future Needs." *Survival* 41 (1999–2000): 101–123.

Carter, Ashton B., and William J. Perry. *Preventive Defense: A New Security Strategy for America.* Washington, D.C.: The Brookings Institution, 1999.

Cederman, Lars-Erik. *Emergent Actors in World Politics: How States and Nations Develop and Dissolve.* Princeton, N.J.: Princeton University Press, 1997.

Chomsky, Noam. *World Orders Old and New.* New York: Columbia University Press, 1994.

Christopher, Warren. "America's Leadership, America's Opportunity." *Foreign Policy* 98 (1995): 6–27.

Clarke, Jonathan. "The Conceptual Poverty of U.S. Foreign Policy." *The Atlantic Monthly Digital Edition* (September 1993): 1–20.

Clarke, Jonathan, and James Clad. *After the Crusade: American Foreign Policy for the Post Superpower Age.* Lanham, Md.: Madison Books, 1995.

Clemens, Walter C., Jr. *America and the World 1898–2025: Achievements, Failures, Alternative Futures.* New York: St. Martin's Press, 2000.

Coats, Daniel R. "Should the Senate Support the Use of U.S. Ground Forces in Bosnia-Herzegovina? CON." *Congressional Digest* 75 (February 1996): 43–47.

Cohen, Warren I. "Compromised in Korea: Redeemed by the Clinton Administration?" *Foreign Affairs* 76 (1997): 106–112.

Cole, Wayne S. *America First:The Battle Against Intervention 1940–41.* Madison: University of Wisconsin Press, 1953.

Collier, Paul. "Economic Causes of Civil Conflict and Their Implications for Policy." Working paper. Washington, D.C.: World Bank, June 2000.

Collier, Paul, and Anke Hoeffler. "On Economic Causes of Civil War." *Oxford Economic Papers* 50 (1998): 563–573.

—. "Justice-Seeking and Loot-Seeking in Civil War." Working paper. Washington, D.C.: World Bank, February 1999.

—. "Greed and Grievance in Civil War." Working paper. Washington, D.C.: World Bank, March 2000.

Commentary Magazine. "American Power—For What? A Symposium." Vol. 109, January 2000: 21–47.

Commission on America's National Interests. *America's National Interests.* Cambridge, Mass.: Harvard University Belfer Center for Science and International Affairs, 2000.

Conry, Barbara. "U.S. 'Global Leadership': A Euphemism for World Policeman." *Cato Policy Analysis* No. 267. February 5, 1997.

Couloumbis, Theodore A. *The United States, Greece, and Turkey: The Troubled Triangle.* New York: Praeger, 1983.

Cox, Michael, Ken Booth, and Tim Dunn, eds. *The Interregnum: Controversies in World Politics 1989–1999.* Cambridge, United Kingdom: Cambridge University Press, 1999.

Cumings, Bruce. *Child of Conflict: The Korean-American Relationship, 1943–1953.* Seattle: University of Washington Press, 1983.

—. *Korea's Place in the Sun: A Modern History.* New York: W.W. Norton, 1997.

—. "Still the American Century." In Michael Cox, Ken Booth, and Tim Dunn, eds. *The Interregnum: Controversies in World Politics 1989–1999.* Cambridge, United Kingdom: Cambridge University Press, 1999.

Damrosch, Lori Fisler, ed. *Enforcing Restraint: Collective Intervention in Internal Conflicts.* New York: Council on Foreign Relations, 1993.

Danchev, Alex, and Thomas Halverson, eds. *International Perspectives on the Yugoslav Conflict.* New York: St. Martin's Press, 1996.

David, Steven R. "The Necessity for American Military Intervention in the Post–Cold War World." In *The United States and the Use of Force in the Post Cold War World: A Report by the Aspen Strategy Group.* Queenstown, Md.: The Aspen Institute, 1995.

—. "Review Article: Internal War: Causes and Cures." *World Politics* 49 (1997): 552–576.

—. "Saving America from the Coming Civil Wars." *Foreign Affairs* 78 (1999): 103–116.

Debrix, François. *Re-Envisioning Peacekeeping: The United Nations and the Mobilization of Ideology.* Minneapolis: University of Minnesota Press, 1999.

Denemark, Robert A. "World System History: From Traditional International Politics to the Study of Global Relations." *International Studies Review* 1 (1999): 43–76.

Diehl, Paul F. *International Peacekeeping.* Baltimore, Md.: Johns Hopkins University Press, 1993.

Diehl, Paul F., Jennifer Reifschneider, and Paul R. Hensel. "United Nations Intervention and Recurrent Conflict." *International Organization* 50 (1996): 683–700.

DiPrizio, Robert C. "US Humanitarian Interventions in the Post-Cold War Era." Paper presented at the Annual Meeting of the American Political Science Association, San Francisco, August 29–September 2, 2001.

Doob, Leonard. *Intervention: Guides and Perils.* New Haven, Conn.: Yale University Press, 1993.

Dore, Isaak I. *International Law and the Superpowers: Normative Order in a Divided World.* New Brunswick, N.J.: Rutgers University Press, 1984.

Doyle, Michael W., and G. John Ikenberry. *New Thinking in International Relations Theory*. Boulder, Colo.: Westview Press, 1997.

Dulles, John Foster. "Policy for Security and Peace." *Foreign Affairs* 32 (1954): 353–364.

Dunér, Bertil. *Military Intervention in Civil Wars: The 1970s*. New York: St. Martin's Press, 1985.

Dunnigan, James F., and Austin Ray. *A Quick and Dirty Guide to War: Briefings on Present and Potential Wars*. New York: William Morrow and Co., 1985.

Durch, William J. *The Evolution of UN Peacekeeping: Case Studies and Comparative Analysis*. New York: St. Martin's Press, 1993.

——. *UN Peacekeeping, American Politics, and the Uncivil Wars of the 1990s*. New York: St. Martin's Press, 1996.

Eckstein, Harry. "Theoretical Approaches to Explaining Collective Violence." In Ted Robert Gurr, ed. *Handbook of Political Conflict*. New York: The Free Press, 1980.

Elbadawi, Ibrahim A., and Nicholas Sambanis. "External Interventions and the Duration of Civil Wars." Princeton, N.J.: Paper presented at the World Bank Conference, March 18–19, 1999.

——. "How Much War Will We See? Estimating the Incidence of Civil War in 161 Countries." Washington, D.C.: Paper presented at the World Bank Conference, July 2000.

Fakiolas, Efstathios T. "Kennan's Long Telegram and NSC-68: A Comparative Analysis." *East European Quarterly* 31 internet version (1998): 1–14. *www.mtholyoke.edu/acad/intrel/fakiolas.html*. (Accessed August 14, 2001.)

Falk, Richard. "Recycling Interventionism." *Journal of Peace Research* 29 (1992): 129–134.

Farer, Tom J. "Harnessing Rogue Elephants: A Short Discourse on Foreign Intervention in Civil Strife." *Harvard Law Review* 82 (1969): 511–541.

——. "Intervention in Unnatural Humanitarian Emergencies: Lessons of the First Phase. *"Human Rights Quarterly* 18 (1996): 1–22.

Fautua, David T. "The 'Long Pull' Army: NSC-68, the Korean War, and the Creation of the Cold War U.S. Army." *Journal of Military History* 61 internet version (1997): 1–22. *www.mtholyoke.edu/acad/intrel/Longpull/html*. (Accessed March 12, 2001.)

Fawcett, Louise, and Yezid Sayigh, eds. *The Third World Beyond the Cold War: Continuity and Change*. New York: Oxford University Press, 1999.

Fearon, James D., and David D. Laitin. "Ethnicity, Insurgency and Civil War." Paper presented at the Annual Meeting of the American Political Science Association, San Francisco, August 30–September 2, 2001.

Feste, Karen A. *Expanding the Frontiers: Superpower Intervention in the Cold War*. New York: Praeger, 1992.

Fetherston, A.B. *Towards a Theory of United Nations Peacekeeping*. New York: St. Martin's Press, 1994.

Fisher, David. "The Ethics of Intervention." *Survival* 36 (1994): 51–59.

Forbes, Ian. "Beyond the State." In Ian Forbes and Mark Hoffman, eds. *Political Theory, International Relations, and the Ethics of Intervention*. New York: St. Martin's Press, 1993.

Forbes, Ian, and Mark Hoffman, eds. *Political Theory, International Relations, and the Ethics of Intervention*. New York: St. Martin's Press, 1993.

Freedman, Lawrence, ed. *Military Intervention in European Conflicts*. Cambridge, Mass.: Blackwell Publishers, 1994.

Friedman, Thomas. "Arabs Must Quell bin Ladenism." *The New York Times*, November 11, 2001.

Fromkin, David. *Kosovo Crossing: American Ideals Meet Reality on the Balkan Battlefields*. New York: The Free Press, 1999.

Fukuyama, Francis. "The End of History?" *The National Interest* No. 16 (1989): 3–18.

—. *The End of History and the Last Man*. New York: Free Press, 1992.

—. "Second Thoughts: The Last Man in a Bottle." *The National Interest* No. 56 (1999): 16–33.

—. "American Power—For What? A Symposium." *Commentary Magazine*, January 2000: 25–26.

Gaddis, John Lewis. *Strategies of Containment: A Critical Appraisal of Postwar American National Security Policy*. New York: Oxford University Press, 1982.

—. "Toward the Post–Cold War World." *Foreign Affairs* 70 (1991): 102–122.

Gardner, Lloyd. "Old Wine in New Bottles." In Charles Kegley, ed. *The Long Post War Peace: Contending Explanations and Projections*. New York: HarperCollins, 1991.

Gaubatz, Kurt Taylor. "Intervention and Intransitivity: Public Opinion, Social Choice, and the Use of Military Force Abroad." *World Politics* 47 (1995): 534–554.

George, Alexander L. "American Policy-Making and the North Korean Aggression." *World Politics* 7 (1955): 209–232.

George, Alexander L., David K. Hall, and William E. Simons. *The Limits of Coercive Diplomacy*. Boston: Little, Brown, 1971.

Gergen, David. *Eyewitness to Power: The Essence of Leadership Nixon to Clinton*. New York: Simon and Schuster, 2000.

Gerson, Joseph, and Bruce Birchard, eds. *The Sun Never Set...Confronting the Network of Foreign U.S. Military Bases*. Boston: South End Press, 1991.

Gibbs, David N. "Realpolitik and Humanitarian Intervention: The Case of Somalia." *International Politics* 37 (2000): 41–55.

Gilboa, Eytan. "The Panama Invasion Revisited: Lessons for the Use of Force in the Post Cold War Era." *Political Science Quarterly* 110 (1995): 539–562.

Glennon, Michael J. "The New Interventionism: The Search for a Just International Law." *Foreign Affairs* 78 (1999): 2–7.

Goldstein, Joshua S. *Long Cycles: Prosperity and War in the Modern Age*. New Haven, Conn.: Yale University Press, 1988.

Good, Robert C. "National Interest and Moral Theory: The 'Debate' among Contemporary Political Realists." In Roger Hilsman and Robert C. Good, eds. *Foreign Policy in the Sixties: The Issues and the Instruments*. Baltimore, Md: The Johns Hopkins Press, 1965.

Goodby, James E. *Europe Undivided: The New Logic of Peace in US-Russian Relations*. Washington, D.C.: United States Institute of Peace, 1998.

Goodpaster, Andrew. *When Diplomacy Is Not Enough: Managing Multinational Military Interventions*. A Report to the Carnegie Commission on Preventing Deadly Conflict. New York: Carnegie Corporation of New York, July 1996.

Gottlieb, Gidon. *Nation Against State: A New Approach to Ethnic Conflicts and the Decline of Sovereignty*. New York: Council on Foreign Relations Press, 1993.

Graber, Doris A. "The Truman and Eisenhower Doctrines in the Light of the Doctrine of Non-Intervention. *Political Science Quarterly* 73 (1958): 321–334.

Graybill, Lyn. " 'Responsible. ... By Omission': The US and Genocide in Rwanda." Paper presented at the Forty-first Annual Convention of the International Studies Association, Chicago, February 20–24, 2001.

Gregg, Robert W. *About Face? The United States and the United Nations*. Boulder, CO: Lynne Rienner Publishers, 1993.

Grimmett, Richard F. "Instances of Use of United States Armed Forces Abroad, 1798–1999." CRS Report for Congress. Washington, D.C.: Congressional Research Service, Library of Congress, May 17, 1999.

Grossman, Mark. *Encyclopedia of the Persian Gulf War*. Santa Barbara, Calif: ABC-CLIO Press, 1995.

Gurr, Ted Robert. "The Internationalization of Protracted Communal Conflicts since 1945: Which Groups, Where and How." In Manus Midlarsky, ed. *The Internationalization of Communal Strife*. London: Routledge, 1993a.

—. *Minorities at Risk: A Global View of Ethnopolitical Conflicts*. Washington, D.C.: United States Institute of Peace Press, 1993b.

—. "Peoples Against States: Ethnopolitical Conflict and the Changing World System." *International Studies Quarterly* 38 (1994): 347–377.

—. "Communal Conflicts and Global Security." *Current History* (May 1995): 212–217.

—. *Peoples versus States: Minorities at Risk in the New Century*. Washington, D.C.: United States Institute of Peace Press, 2000.

Gurr, Ted Robert, Monty G. Marshall, and Deepa Khosla. *Peace and Conflict 2001: A Global Survey of Armed Conflicts, Self-Determination Movements and Democracy*. College Park, Md.: Center for International Development and Conflict Management, University of Maryland, 2000.

Haass, Richard N. *Intervention: The Use of American Military Force in the Post–Cold War World*. Washington, D.C.: The Carnegie Endowment for International Peace, 1994.

Halberstam, David. *War in a Time of Peace: Bush, Clinton, and the Generals*. New York: Scribner, 2001.

Halliday, Fred. *The World at 2000: Perils and Promises*. New York: Palgrave, 2001.

Hawthorn, Geoffrey. "Liberalism Since the Cold War: An Enemy to Itself?" In Michael Cox, Ken Booth, and Tim Dunn, eds. *The Interregnum: Controversies in World Politics 1989–1999*. Cambridge, United Kingdom: Cambridge University Press, 1999.

Hegre, Håvard, Tanja Ellingsen, Nils Petter Gleditch, and Scott Gates. "Towards a Democratic Civil Peace? Opportunity, Grievance, and Civil War 1816–1992." Paper presented at the World Bank, Washington, D.C., February 22–23, 1999.

—. "Towards a Democratic Civil Peace?" *American Political Science Review* 95 (2001): 33–48.

Heilbrunn, Jacob. "TRB from Washington: Univisionary." *The New Republic,* November 11, 1996: 6.

Heisbourg, François. "American Hegemony: Perceptions of the US Abroad." *Survival* 41 (1999–2000): 5–19.

Helman, Gerald B., and Steven R. Ratner. "Saving Failed States." *Foreign Policy* 89 (Winter 1992/93): 3–20.

Henderson, Errol A., and J. David Singer. "Civil War in the Post-Colonial World, 1946–92." *Journal of Peace Research* 37 (2000): 275–299.

Henrikson, Alan K. "Mental Maps." In Michael J. Hogan and Thomas G. Paterson, eds. *Explaining the History of American Foreign Relations.* New York: Cambridge University Press, 1991.

Hermann, Margaret, and Charles W. Kegley, Jr. "The U.S. Use of Military Intervention to Promote Democracy: Evaluating the Record." *International Interactions* 24 (1998): 91–114.

Hilsman, Roger, and Robert C. Good, ed. *Foreign Policy in the Sixties: The Issues and the Instruments.* Baltimore, Md.: The Johns Hopkins Press, 1965.

Himmelfarb, Gertrude. "Responses to Fukuyama." *The National Interest* No 56 (Summer 1999): 37–38.

Hinckley, Ronald. "Public Attitudes toward Key Foreign Policy Events." *Journal of Conflict Resolution* 32 (1988): 295–318.

Hirsh, Michael. "At War with Ourselves: In Kosovo, America Confronts Its Own Ideals." *Harper's Magazine* 150 (July 1999): 60–69.

Hitt, Jack. "Is there a Doctrine in the House?" *Harpers Magazine* (January 1994): 57–64.

—. "Calling All Regio-Cops." *Foreign Affairs* 79 (November/December 2000): 2–8.

Hoffman, Stanley. "Comments." In Richard Pfeffer, ed. *No More Vietnams? The War and the Future of American Foreign Policy.* New York: Harper and Row, 1968.

—. *World Disorders: Troubled Peace in the Post–Cold War Era.* Lanham, Md.: Rowman and Littlefield, 1998.

Hogan, Michael J. *A Cross of Iron: Harry S. Truman and the Origins of the National Security State, 1945–1954.* Cambridge, United Kingdom: Cambridge University Press, 1998.

Holbrooke, Richard. *To End a War.* New York: Random House, 1998.

Holsti, Ole R., and James N. Rosenau. *American Leadership in World Affairs: Vietnam and the Breakdown of Consensus.* Boston: Allen and Unwin, 1984.

Honey, Martha, and Tom Barry, eds. *Global Focus: U.S. Foreign Policy at the Turn of the Millennium.* New York: St. Martin's Press, 2000.

Howe, Irving, ed. *A Dissenter's Guide to Foreign Policy.* Garden City, N.Y.: Doubleday, 1968.

Humanitarian Intervention: Effectiveness of U.N. Operations in Bosnia. Briefing Report to The Honorable Robert S. Dole, U.S. Senate. Washington, D.C.: General Accounting Office, April 1994.

Humanitarian Intervention: Crafting a Workable Doctrine. New York: Council on Foreign Relations October 2, 2000.

Hunter, Allen, ed. *Rethinking the Cold War.* Philadelphia: Temple University Press, 1998.

Huntington, Samuel. "The Erosion of American National Interests." *Foreign Affairs* 76 internet version (September–October 1997): 1–12. *www.htholyoke.edu/ acad/intrel/ hunting3.html.* (Accessed March 7, 2001.)

—. "The Lonely Superpower." *Foreign Affairs* 78 (March/April 1999): 35–49.

Hurst, Steven. *The Foreign Policy of the Bush Administration: In Search of a New World Order.* New York: Cassell, 1999.

Hyland, William. *Clinton's World: Remaking American Foreign Policy.* Westport, Conn.: Praeger, 1999.

Ignatieff, Michael. "Introduction: Intervention by Proxy." Alex Danchev and Thomas Halverson, eds. *International Perspectives on the Yugoslav Conflict.* New York: St. Martin's Press, 1996.

—. *The Warrior's Honor: Ethnic War and the Modern Conscience.* New York: Henry Holt, 1997.

—. *Virtual War: Kosovo and Beyond.* New York: Henry Holt, 2000.

"Interagency Review of U.S. Government Civilian Humanitarian and Transition Programs." Washington, D.C.: George Washington University Gelman Library National Security Archive, April 2000.

Jacquin-Berrdal, Dominique. "Ethnic Wars and International Intervention." *Millennium: Journal of International Studies* 27 (1998): 127–139.

Jaggers, Keith, and Ted Gurr. *Polity III Data.* Internet Document. *http://wizard.ucr.edu/~wm/Polity/polity.html,* 1996. (Accessed February 10, 2002.)

Jakobsen, Peter Viggo. "National Interest, Humanitarianism or CNN: What Triggers UN Peace Enforcement After the Cold War?" *Journal of Peace Research* 33 (May 1996): 205–215.

—. "Focus on the CNN Effect Misses the Point: The Real Media Impact on Conflict Management Is Invisible and Indirect." *Journal of Peace Research* 37 (2000): 131–143.

Jentleson, Bruce W. "Who, Why, What, and How: Debates over Post–Cold War Military Intervention." In Robert J. Lieber, ed. *Eagle Adrift: American Foreign Policy at the End of the Century.* Reading, Mass.: Longman, 1997.

—. ed. *Opportunities Missed, Opportunities Seized: Preventive Diplomacy in the Post–Cold War World.* Lanham, Md.: Rowman and Littlefield, 2000.

Jervis, Robert. *System Effects: Complexity in Political and Social Life.* Princeton, N.J.: Princeton University Press, 1997.

Jett, Dennis C. *Why Peacekeeping Fails.* New York: St. Martin's Press, 1999.

Job, Brian, and Charles Ostrom, Jr. "Opportunity and Choice: The U.S. and the Political Use of Force: 1948–1976." Paper presented at the Annual Meeting of the American Political Science Association, Washington, D.C., 1986.

Johnson, Chalmers. *Blowback: The Cost and Consequences of American Empire.* New York: Henry Holt, 2000.

Jones, Joseph M. *The Fifteen Weeks (February 11–June 5, 1947)*. New York: The Viking Press, 1955.

Juddah, Tim. "Kosovo's Road to War." *Survival* 41 (Summer 1999): 5–18.

Kaldor, Mary. *New and Old Wars: Organized Violence in the Global Era*. Stanford, Calif: Stanford University Press, 1999.

Kantor, Arnold. "Intervention Decision Making in the Bush Administration." In Jeremy R. Azrael and Emil A. Payin, eds. *Conference Report: U.S. and Russian Policymaking with Respect to the Use of Force*. RAND. 1996. *www.rand.org/publications/CF/CF129.chapter10.html*. (Accessed August 15, 2001.)

—. "U.S. Policy on 'Armed Humanitarian Intervention': Guidelines for Managing Painful Dilemmas." *Miller Center Report* 17 (Winter 2001): 12–17.

Kantor, Arnold, and Linton F. Brooks, eds. *U.S. Intervention Policy for the Post–Cold War World: New Challenges and New Responses*. New York: Council on Foreign Relations, 1994.

Kaplan, Morton. *System and Process in International Politics*. New York: John Wiley, 1964.

Kaplan, Robert D. "The Coming Anarchy." *The Atlantic Monthly* (February 1994): 44–76.

—. *The Coming Anarchy: Shattering the Dreams of the Post Cold War*. New York: Random House, 2000.

—. "The World in 2005." *The Atlantic Monthly* (March 2002): 54–56.

Kapstein, Ethan B., and Michael Mastanduno, eds. *Unipolar Politics: Realism and State Strategies after the Cold War*. New York: Columbia University Press, 1999.

Kaufmann, Chaim. "Possible and Impossible Solutions to Ethnic Civil Wars." *International Security* 20 (Spring 1996): 136–175.

Kennedy, Paul. *The Rise and Fall of the Great Powers*. New York: Random House, 1987.

Keohane, Robert O. *After Hegemony: Cooperation and Discord in the World Political Economy*. Princeton, N.J.: Princeton University Press, 1984.

Kessler, Bart R. "Bush's New World Order: The Meaning Behind the Words." Paper presented at U.S. Air Command and Staff College, Montgomery, Ala., March 1997.

Khadhafi, Muammar. "A Revolutionary Perspective on the New World Order." In Keith Philip Lepor, ed. *After the Cold War: Essays on the Emerging World Order*. Austin: University of Texas Press, 1997.

Khalizad, Zalmay. "Losing the Moment? The United States and the World After the Cold War." *The Washington Quarterly* 18 (1995): 57–77.

King, Charles. *Ending Civil Wars*. Adelphi Paper 308. Oxford, United Kingdom: Oxford University Press, The International Institute for Strategic Studies, 1997.

—. "The Myth of Ethnic Warfare: Understanding Conflict in the Post-Cold War World." *Foreign Affairs* 80 (November/December 2001): 165–170.

Kissinger, Henry. *American Foreign Policy*. 3rd Ed., New York: W.W. Norton, 1977.

Klare, Michael. *Beyond the "Vietnam Syndrome": U.S. Interventionism in the 1980s*. Washington, D.C.: Institute for Policy Studies, 1982.

—. "The Development of Low-Intensity Conflict Doctrine." In Peter Schrader, ed. *Intervention in the 1980s: United States Foreign Policy in the Third World.* Boulder, Colo.: Lynne Rienner Publishers, 1989.

Klingberg, Frank. "The Historical Alternation of Moods in American Foreign Policy." *World Politics* 4 (1952): 239–273.

—. *Positive Expectations of America's World Role: Historical Cycles of Realistic Idealism.* Lanham, Md.: University Press of America, 1996.

Krauthammer, Charles. "The Short, Unhappy Life of Humanitarian War." *National Interest* No. 57 (Fall 1999): 5–8.

—. "American Power—For What? A Symposium." *Commentary Magazine* (January 2000): 34–35.

Kull, Steven. "What the Public Knows that Washington Doesn't." *Foreign Policy* No. 101 (Winter 1995–96): 102-115.

Kull, Steven, and I.M. Desler. *Misreading the Public: The Myth of a New Isolationism.* Washington, D.C.: Brookings Institution Press, 1999.

Kull, Steven, and Clay Ramsay. "The Myth of the Reactive Public: American Public Attitudes on Military Fatalities in the Post–Cold War Period." In Philip Everts and Pierangelo Isernia, eds. *Public Opinion and the International Use of Force.* New York: Routledge, 2001.

Kuperman, Alan J. "Rwanda in Retrospect." *Foreign Affairs* 79 (January/February 2000): 94–118.

Kurth, James. "Models of Humanitarian Intervention: Assessing the Past and Discerning the Future." Foreign Policy Research Institute Wire 9. (*fpri@fpri.org*). (August 2001): 1–8. (Accessed August 3, 2001.)

LaFeber, Walter. "Rethinking the Cold War and After: From Containment to Enlargement." In Allen Hunter, ed. *Rethinking the Cold War.* Philadelphia: Temple University Press, 1998.

Lairson, Thomas D. "Revising Postrevisionism: Credibility and Hegemony in the Early Cold War." In Allen Hunter, ed. *Rethinking the Cold War.* Philadelphia: Temple University Press, 1998.

Lake, Anthony. *6 Nightmares: Real Threats in a Dangerous World and How America Can Meet Them.* Boston: Little, Brown, 2000.

Lamborn, Alan. "Theory and the Politics of World Politics." *International Studies Quarterly* 41 (1997): 187–214.

Lapidoth, Ruth. "Sovereignty in Transition." *Journal of International Affairs* 45 (1992): 325–346.

Lepgold, Joseph, and Thomas G. Weiss, eds. *Collective Conflict Management and Changing World Politics.* Albany: State University of New York Press, 1998.

Lepor, Keith Phillips, ed. *After the Cold War: Essays on the Emerging World Order.* Austin: University of Texas Press, 1997.

Levite, Ariel E., Bruce Jentleson, and Larry Berman. *Foreign Military Intervention: The Dynamics of Protracted Conflict.* New York: Columbia University Press, 1992.

Licklider, Roy. *Stopping the Killing: How Civil Wars End.* New York: New York University Press, 1993.

—. "The Consequences of Negotiated Settlements in Civil Wars, 1945–1993." *American Political Science Review* 89 (1995): 681–690.

Lieven, Anatol. "The Pressures on Pakistan." *Foreign Affairs* 81 (January/February 2002): 106–118.

Lind, Michael. *Vietnam the Necessary War: A Reinterpretation of America's Most Disastrous Military Conflict.* New York: The Free Press, 1999.

Lischer, Sarah Kenyon. "Refugee Crises and the Spread of Civil War." Paper presented at the Annual Meeting of the American Political Science Association, San Francisco, August 30–September 2, 2001.

Little, Richard. *Intervention: External Involvement in Civil Wars.* Totowa, N.J.: Rowman and Littlefield, 1975.

Livingston, Steven. "Beyond the CNN Effect: An Examination of Media Effects According to Types of Intervention." Cambridge, Mass.: Kennedy School of Government, Harvard University, 1997.

Lund, Michael S. *Preventing Violent Conflicts: A Strategy for Preventive Diplomacy.* Washington, D.C.: United States Institute of Peace Press, 1996.

MacFarlane, S. Neil. "Taking Stock: The Third World and the End of the Cold War." In Louise Fawcett and Yezid Sayigh, eds. *The Third World Beyond the Cold War: Continuity and Change.* New York: Oxford University Press, 1999.

Mahnken, Thomas G. "America's Next War." *The Washington Quarterly* 16 (Summer 1993): 171–183.

Makin, John H., and Donald C. Hellman, eds. *Sharing World Leadership? A New Era for America and Japan.* Washington, D.C.: AEI Press, 1989.

Malcolm, Noel. *Kosovo: A Short History.* New York: New York University Press, 1998.

Mandela, Nelson. "Toward the Twenty-first Century." In Keith Philip Lepor, ed. *After the Cold War: Essays on the Emerging World Order.* Austin: University of Texas Press, 1997.

Mandelbaum, Michael. "Foreign Policy as Social Work." *Foreign Affairs* 75 (1996): 16–32.

Mason, T. David, and Patrick J. Fett. "How Civil Wars End: A Rational Choice Approach." *Journal of Conflict Resolution* 40 (1996): 546–568.

Mastanduno, Michael. "Preserving the Unipolar Moment: Realist Theories and U.S. Grand Strategy After the Cold War." In Ethan B. Kapstein and Michael Mastanduno, eds. *Unipolar Politics: Realism and State Strategies after the Cold War.* New York: Columbia University Press, 1999.

Matthews, Jessica T. "Power Shift." *Foreign Affairs* 76 (January/February 1997): 50–66.

Mayall, James. *The New Interventionism: 1991–1994.* New York: Cambridge University Press, 1996.

Maynes, Charles William. "Squandering Triumph: The West Botched the Cold War World." *Foreign Affairs* 78 (1999): 15–22.

—. "Contending Schools." *The National Interest* No. 63 (Spring 2001): 49–58.

McCalla, Robert B. "Constraints on Adaptation in the American Military to Collective Conflict Management Missions." In Joseph Lepgold and Thomas G. Weiss, eds. *Collective Conflict Management and Changing World Politics.* Albany: State University of New York Press, 1998.

McCormick, James M. *American Foreign Policy and Process.* 2nd Ed. Itasca, Ill.: F.E. Peacock Publishers, 1992.

McCuen, Gary E. *Foreign Intervention and Global Security: Ideas in Conflict.* Hudson, Wis.: Gary E. McCuen Publications, 1995.

McSweeney, Bill. *Security, Identity and Interests: A Sociology of International Relations.* New York: Cambridge University Press, 1999.

Mead, Walter Russell. *Special; Providence: American Foreign Policy and How It Changed the World.* New York: Alfred A. Knopf, 2001.

Meernik, James. "Presidential Decision Making and the Political Use of Military Force." *International Studies Quarterly* 38 (1994): 121–138.

—. "Modeling International Crises and the Political Use of Military Force by the USA." *Journal of Peace Research* 37 (2000): 547–562.

Mermin, Jonathan. *Debating War and Peace: Media Coverage of U.S. Intervention in the Post-Vietnam Era.* Princeton, N.J.: Princeton University Press, 1999.

Midlarsky, Manus I. *The Internationalization of Communal Strife.* New York: Routledge, 1993.

Millett, Allan R. "The Parameters of Peacekeeping: U.S. Interventions Abroad 1798–1999." *Strategic Review* 28 (2000): 28–38.

Milliken, Jennifer. "Intervention and Identity: Reconstructing the West in Korea. In Jutta Wettes, Mark Laffey, Hugh Gusterson, and Raymond Duvall, eds. *Cultures of Insecurity: States, Communities, and the Production of Danger.* Minneapolis: University of Minnesota Press, 1999.

Minear, Larry, Colin Scott, and Thomas G. Weiss. *The News Media, Civil War, and Humanitarian Action.* Boulder, Colo.: Lynne Rienner Publishers, 1996.

Mitchell, C.R. "Civil Strife and the Involvement of External Parties." *International Studies Quarterly* 14 (1970): 166–194.

Moore, Mike. "How George Bush Won His Spurs." *Bulletin of the Atomic Scientists* 47 (October 1991): 26–33.

Morganthau, Hans J. "To Intervene or Not to Intervene." *Foreign Affairs* 45 (April 1967): 425–436.

Mueller, John. "The Catastrophe Quota: Trouble after the Cold War." *Journal of Conflict Resolution* 38 (September 1994): 355–375.

—. "The Remnants of War: Thugs as Residual Combatants." Paper presented at the Euroconference, Uppsala, Sweden, June 8–9, 2001.

Muravchik, John. *The Imperative of American Leadership.* Washington, D.C.: American Enterprise Institute Press, 1996.

A National Security Strategy of Engagement and Enlargement. Washington, D.C.: The White House, February 1996.

A National Security Strategy for a New Century. Washington, D.C.: The White House, January 2000.

Nelson-Pallmeyer, Jack. *Brave New World Order.* Maryknoll, N.Y.: Orbis Books, 1992.

Neumann, Robert. "This Next Disorderly Half Century: Some Proposed Remedies." *The Washington Quarterly* 16, No. 1 (Winter 1993): 33–49.

Niebuhr, Reinhold. *"Christian Realism and Political Problems.* New York: Scribner, 1953.

Nincic, Miroslav, and Donna Nincic. "Virtuous Intent, Unintended Outcomes: Humanitarian Intervention and U.S. Moral Authority." Paper presented at the 42nd Annual Meeting of the International Studies Association, Chicago, February 2001.

Noonan, Michael P., and John Hillen. "The Coming Transformation of the U.S. Military?" Foreign Policy Research Institute: A Catalyst for Ideas. E-notes distributed via fax and email exclusively. (*fpri@fpri.org*). (Accessed February 2, 2002.)

Novak, Robert D. *Completing the Revolution: A Vision for Victory in 2000.* New York: The Free Press, 2000.

NSC-68: United States Objectives and Programs for National Security. A Report to the President January 31, 1950. *Naval War College Review* 27 (May–June 1975): 51–108.

Nuscheler, Franz. "Multilateralism vs. Unilateralism: Cooperation vs. Hegemony in Translantic Relations." Policy Paper 16. Development and Peace Foundation. Bonn, Germany: Stifung Entwicklung und Frieden, January 2001.

Nye, Joseph, Jr. *Understanding International Conflicts: An Introduction to Theory and History.* New York: HarperCollins, 1993.

Nye, Joseph S., Jr. "Redefining the National Interest." *Foreign Affairs* 78 (July–August, 1999): 22–35.

Odell, J. "Correlates of U.S. Military Assistance and Military Intervention." In S. Rose and J. Kurth, eds. *Testing Theories of Economic Imperialism.* Lexington, Mass.: D.C. Heath, 1974.

Odom, William E. "Intervention for the Long Run: Rethinking the Definition of War." *Harvard International Review* (Winter 2001): 48–52.

Oliver, April. "The Somalia Syndrome." In Roderick K. von Lipsey, ed. *Breaking the Cycle: A Framework for Conflict Intervention.* New York: St. Martin's Press, 1997.

Ostrom, Charles W.J., and Brian L. Job. "The President and the Political Use of Force." *American Political Science Review* 80 (1986): 541–566.

Peceny, Mark. "Two Paths to the Promotion of Democracy During U.S. Military Interventions." *International Studies Quarterly* 39 (1995): 371–401.

—"The Democratic Peace and Contemporary U.S. Military Interventions." Paper presented at the Forty-first Annual Convention of the International Studies Association, Los Angeles, March 14–18, 2000.

The Pentagon Papers. New York: Bantam Books, 1971.

Pfaff, William. "The Case Against Interventionism." In Irving Howe, ed. *A Dissenter's Guide to Foreign Policy.* New York: Doubleday and Company, 1968.

—. "The Question of Hegemony." *Foreign Affairs* 80 (January/February 2001): 221–233.

Pfeffer, Richard M., ed. *No More Vietnams? The War and the Future of American Foreign Policy.* New York: Harper and Row, 1968.

Phillips, Robert L., and Duane L. Cady. *Humanitarian Intervention: Just War vs. Pacifism.* London: Rowman and Littlefield, 1996.

Pickering, Jeffrey. "The Structural Shape of Force: Interstate Intervention in the Zones of Peace and Turmoil, 1946–1996." *International Interactions* 25 (1999): 363–391.

—. "War Weariness and Cumulative Effects: Victors, Vanquished, and Subsequent Interstate Intervention." Paper presented at the Annual Meeting of the International Studies Association, Chicago, February 20–24, 2001.

Policy on Reforming Multilateral Peace Operations (PDD 25). *Bureau of International Organizational Affairs.* Washington, D.C.: U.S. Department of State, February 22, 1996.

Pollins, Brian M., and Randall L. Schweller. "Linking the Levels: The Long Wave and Shifts in U.S. Foreign Policy, 1790–1993." *American Journal of Political Science* 43 (April 1999): 431–464.

Posen, Barry R., and Andrew L. Ross. "Competing Visions for U.S. Grand Strategy." *International Security* 21 (Winter 1996/97): 5–53.

Powell, Colin L. "U.S. Forces: Challenges Ahead." *Foreign Affairs* 71 (1992–93.): 32–45.

—. *My American Journey.* New York: Random House, 1995.

Power, Samantha. "Bystanders to Genocide: Why the United States Let the Rwandan Tragedy Happen." *The Atlantic Monthly* (September 2001): 84–108.

PDD 25 White Paper. Executive Summary of Presidential Decision Directive 25 (PDD-25), "The Clinton Administration's Policy on Reforming Multilateral Peace Operations," May 1994. *http://www.whitehouse.gov/wh/EOP/html/documents/NSCDoc1.html.* (Accessed December 18, 2000.)

PDD 56 White Paper. Presidential Decision Directive 56 (PDD/NSC 56), "Managing Complex Contingency Operations." May 1997. *http://www.au.af.mil/au/awc/awcgate pdd/pdd56.html.* (Accessed April 17, 2003.)

Ramsbotham, Oliver and Tom Woodhouse. *Humanitarian Intervention in Contemporary Conflict: A Reconceptualization.* Cambridge, Mass.: Blackwell Publishers, 1996.

Raymond, Gregory A., and Charles W. Kegley, Jr. "Long Cycles and Internationalized Civil War." *The Journal of Politics* 49 (May 1987): 481–499.

Reed, Laura W., and Carl Kaysen, eds. *Emerging Norms of Justified Intervention: A Collection of Essays from a Project of the American Academy of Arts and Sciences.* Cambridge, Mass.: American Academy of Arts and Sciences, 1993.

Regan, Patrick M. "Conditions of Successful Third-Party Intervention in Intrastate Conflicts." *Journal of Conflict Resolution* 40 (June 1996): 336–359.

—. *Civil Wars and Foreign Powers: Outside Intervention in Intrastate Conflict.* Ann Arbor: University of Michigan Press, 2000a.

—. "Third Party Interventions and the Duration of Intrastate Conflicts." Paper presented at the World Bank Conference, Princeton, N.J., March 18–19, 2000b.

Reitzel, William, Morton A. Kaplan, and Constance G. Coblenz. *United Sates Foreign Policy 1945–1955.* Washington, D.C.: The Brookings Institution, 1956.

Rengger, N. J. "Contextuality, Interdependence and the Ethics of Intervention. In Ian Forbes and Mark Hoffman, eds. *Political Theory, International Relations, and the Ethics of Intervention.* New York: St. Martin's Press, 1993.

Rice, Condoleezza. "Campaign 2000: Promoting the National Interest." *Foreign Affairs* 79 internet version (January/February 2000): 1–16.

Roberts, Adam. "The Road to Hell....A Critique of Humanitarian Intervention." *Harvard International Review* (Fall, 1993). Reprinted in Paul Winter, ed., *Interventionism.* San Diego, Calif.: Greenhaven Press, 1995.

—. *Humanitarian Action in War: Aid, Protection and Impartiality in a Policy Vacuum.* Oxford University Press: The International Institute for Strategic Studies, 1996.

—. "NATO's 'Humanitarian War' over Kosovo." *Survival* 41 (Autumn 1999): 102–123.

Roberts, Brad, ed. *Order and Disorder after the Cold War*. Cambridge, Mass.: The MIT Press, 1995.

Robinson, Piers. "The Policy-Media Interaction Model: Measuring Media Power During Humanitarian Crisis." *Journal of Peace Research* 37 (2000): 613–633.

Robinson, William I. *Promoting Polyarchy: Globalization, U.S. Intervention and Hegemony*. New York: Cambridge University Press, 1996.

Rockefeller, Nelson A. "Widening Boundaries of National Interest." *Foreign Affairs* 29 (July, 1951): 523–538.

Rondos, Alex. "The Collapsing State and International Security." In Janne E. Nolan, ed. *Global Engagement: Cooperation and Security in the 21st Century*. Washington, D.C.: The Brookings Institution, 1994.

Rosati, Jerel A., Michael W. Link, and John Creed. "A New Perspective on the Foreign Policy Views of American Opinion Leaders in the Cold War and Post-Cold War Eras." *Political Research Quarterly* 51 (June 1998): 461–479.

Rosenau, James N. "The Concept of Intervention." *Journal of International Affairs* 22 (1966): 165–175.

Rubinstein, Alvin Z., Albina Shayevich, and Boris Zlotnikov. *The Clinton Foreign Policy Reader: Presidential Speeches with Commentary*. Armonk, N.Y.: M.E. Sharpe, 2000.

Ruggie, John Gerard. "Third Try at World Order? America and Multilateralism after the Cold War." *Political Science Quarterly* 109 (Autumn 1994): 553–570.

Sambanis, Nicholas. "Do Ethnic and Nonethnic Civil Wars Have the Same Causes?" In *Journal of Conflict Resolution* 45 (June 2001): 259–282.

Samuelson, Robert J. "Responses to Fukuyama." *The National Interest* (Summer 1999): 40–42.

Sarkees, Meredith Reid, and J. David Singer. "The Correlates of War Warsets: The Totality of War." Paper presented at the International Studies Association Annual Meetings, Chicago, February 21–24, 2001.

Schnabel, Albrecht, and Ramesh Thakur, eds. *Kosovo and the Challenge of Humanitarian Intervention*. New York: United Nations University Press, 2000.

Schneider, Bill. "Analysis: Albright Made the Right Political Moves." *CNN: All Politics: Play of the Week*, December 6, 1996.

Schrader, Peter, ed. *Intervention in the 1980s: United States Foreign Policy in the Third World*. Boulder, Colo.: Lynne Rienner Publishers, 1989.

Schweller, Randall L., and David Priess. "A Tale of Two Realisms: Expanding the Institutions Debate." *Mershon International Studies Review* 41 (1997): 1–32.

Seabury, Paul. *The Rise and Decline of the Cold War*. New York: Basic Books, 1967.

Serafino, Nina M. "Military Interventions by U.S. Forces from Vietnam to Bosnia: Background, Outcomes, and 'Lessons Learned' for Kosovo." CRS Report for Congress. Washington, D.C.: Congressional Research Service, Library of Congress. May 20, 1999.

Shacochis, Bob. *The Immaculate Invasion*. New York: Viking Press, 1999.

Shalom, Stephen R. "Gravy Train: Feeding the Pentagon by Feeding Somalia." *Z Magazine*, February 1993.

—. *Imperial Alibis: Rationalizing U.S. Intervention after the Cold War.* Boston: South End Press, 1995.

Shawcross, William. *Deliver Us from Evil: Peacekeepers, Warlords and a World of Endless Conflict.* New York: Simon and Schuster, 2000.

Sheehan, Neil, Hedrick Smith, E. W. Kenworthy, and Fox Butterfield. *The Pentagon Papers.* New York: Bantam Books, 1971.

Shultz, George. "The Ethics of Power: Address at Yeshiva University." *Bureau of Public Affairs.* Washington, D.C.: U.S. Department of State, December 9, 1984.

Sibley, Katherine A.S. *The Cold War.* Westport, Conn.: Greenwood Press, 1998.

Singer, J. David, and Melvin Small. *The Wages of War 1816–1965: A Statistical Handbook.* New York: John Wiley and Sons, 1972.

SIPRI YEARBOOK: Armaments, Disarmament and International Security. New York: Oxford University Press, 1995, 1996, 1997, 1998, 1999, 2000.

Sisk, Timothy D., and Donald Rothchild. "Beyond United Nations Peace Operations: Changing International Responses to Intrastate Conflicts." Paper presented at The Annual Meeting of the American Political Science Association, Washington, D.C., August 29–September 2, 1997.

Small, Melvin, and J. David Singer. *Resort to Arms: International and Civil Wars 1816–1980.* Beverly Hills, Calif.: Sage Publications, 1982.

Smith, Anthony. *America's Mission: The United States and the Worldwide Struggle for Democracy in the Twentieth Century.* Princeton, N.J.: Princeton University Press. 1994a.

—. "In Defense of Intervention." *Foreign Affairs* 73 (November/December 1994b): 34–47.

Smith, Gaddis. *The Last Years of the Monroe Doctrine 1945–1993.* New York: Hill and Wang, 1994.

Smoke, Richard. "Analytic Dimensions of Intervention Decisions." In Ellen P. Stern, ed. *The Limits of Military Intervention.* Beverly Hills, Calif.: Sage Publications, 1977.

Snow, Donald M. *Uncivil Wars: International Security and the New Internal Conflicts.* Boulder, Colo.: Lynne Rienner Publishers, 1996.

—. *When America Fights: The Uses of U.S. Military Force.* Washington, D.C.: CQ Press, 2000.

Starr, Harvey, and Benjamin Most. "Patterns of Conflict: Quantitative Analysis and the Comparative Lessons of Third World Wars." In Robert Harkavy and Stephanie Newman, eds. *The Lessons of Recent Wars in the Third World.* Lexington, Mass.: Lexington Books, 1985.

Stedman, Stephen John. "The New Interventionists." *Foreign Affairs* 72 (1992–1993): 1–16.

Stern, Ellen P., ed. *The Limits of Military Intervention.* Beverly Hills, Calif.: Sage Publications, 1977.

Stimson, Henry L. "The Challenge to Americans." *Foreign Affairs* 26 (1947): 5–14.

Stremlau, John. *Human Rights, Humanitarian Action, and Preventing Deadly Conflict.* A Report to the Carnegie Commission on Preventing Deadly Conflict. New York: Carnegie Corporation of New York, July 1996.

Strobel, Warren P. *Late-Breaking Foreign Policy: The News Media's Influence on Peace Operations*. Washington, D.C.: United States Institute of Peace Press, 1997.

Talbott, Strobe, and Nayan Chanda, eds. *The Age of Terror: America and the World After September 11*. New York: Basic Books, 2001.

Taylor, Andrew J., and John T. Rourke. "Historical Analogies in the Congressional Foreign Policy Process: A Research Note." *Journal of Politics* 57 (1995): 460–468.

Tesón, Fernando R. *Humanitarian Intervention: An Inquiry into Law and Morality*. 2nd Ed. Irvington-on-Hudson, N.Y.: Transnational Publishers, 1997.

Tillema, Herbert K. *Appeal to Force: American Military Intervention in the Era of Containment*. New York: Crowell, 1973.

—. "Foreign Overt Military Intervention in the Nuclear Age." *Journal of Peace Research* 26 (1989): 179–195.

Trubowitz, Peter. *Defining the National Interest: Conflict and Change in American Foreign Policy*. Chicago: University of Chicago Press, 1998.

Trubowitz, Peter, Emily O. Goldman, and Edward Rhodes, eds. *The Politics of Strategic Adjustment: Ideas, Institutions, and Interests*. New York: Columbia University Press, 1999.

United Nations General Assembly. *www.un.org/documents/ga*. (Accessed June 25, 2003.)

United Nations Peacekeeping. *www.un.og/DPKO*. (Accessed June 25, 2003.)

United Nations Security Council. *www.un.org/documents/ga*. (Accessed June 25, 2003.)

United States Commission on National Security/21st Century. *Seeking a National Strategy: A Concert for Preserving Security and Promoting Freedom*. Washington, D.C.: The United States Commission on National Security/21st Century, 2000.

—. *New World Coming: American Security in the 21st Century*. Washington, D.C.: The United States Commission on National Security/21st Century, 2000.

U.S. Congress, Senate Foreign Relations Committee. Historical Series, *Legislative Origins of the Truman Doctrine: Hearings Held in Executive Session*, 80th Congress, 1st Session (Washington, D.C.,1973).

U.S. Congress. "Bill Summary and Status." http:/thomas.loc.gov/cgi-bin. (Accessed June 25, 2003.)

Urquhart, Brian. "The Rusty Tools of Peace." *World Policy Journal* 17 (Winter 2000/01): 2–5.

Vaccaro, J. Matthew. "The Politics of Genocide: Peacekeeping and Disaster Relief in Rwanda." In William Durch, ed. *The Evolution of UN Peacekeeping: Case Studies and Comparative Analysis*. New York: St. Martin's Press, 1993.

Van Creveld, Martin. *The Transformation of War*. New York: Free Press, 1991.

Van Evera, Stephen. "The United States and the Third World: When to Intervene?" In Kenneth Oye, Robert Lieber, and Donald Rothchild, eds. *Eagle in a New World: American Grand Strategy in the Post-Cold War*. New York: HarperCollins, 1992.

Vertzberger, Yaacov Y. "National Capabilities and Foreign Military Intervention: A Policy-Relevant Theoretical Analysis." *International Interactions* 17 (1992): 349–373.

—. *Risk Taking and Decisionmaking: Foreign Military Intervention Decisions*. Palto Alto, Calif.: Stanford University Press, 1998.

Vidal, Gore. *Perpetual War for Perpetual Peace: How We Got to Be So Hated."* New York: Thunder's Mouth Press/Nations Books, 2002.

Vincent, R.J., and Peter Wilson. "Beyond Non-Intervention." In Ian Forbes and Mark Hoffman, eds. *Political Theory, International Relations, and The Ethics of Intervention.* New York: St. Martin's Press, 1993.

von Hippel, Karin. *Democracy by Force: U.S. Military Intervention in the Post-Cold War World.* New York: Cambridge University Press, 2000.

von Lipsey, Roderick K., ed. *Breaking the Cycle: A Framework for Conflict Intervention.* New York: St Martin's Press, 1997.

Wallensteen, Peter, and Margareta Sollenberg. "After the Cold War: Emerging patterns of Armed Conflict 1989–94." *Journal of Peace Research* 32 (August 1995): 345–360.

—. "Armed Conflict, 1989–2000." *Journal of Peace Research* 38 (September 2001): 629–644.

Walt, Stephen M. *The Origins of Alliances.* Ithaca, N.Y.: Cornell University Press, 1987.

—. "Musclebound: The Limits of US Power." *The Bulletin of the Atomic Scientists* (March/April 1999): 44–48.

Walter, Barbara F. "Designing Transitions from Civil War: Demobilization, Democratization, and Commitments to Peace." *International Security* 24 (1999): 127–155.

Walter, Barbara F., and Jack Snyder, eds. *Civil Wars, Insecurity, and Intervention.* New York: Columbia University Press, 1999.

Waltz, Kenneth N. *Theory of International Politics.* Reading, Mass.: Addison-Wesley, 1979.

Weber, Cynthia. *Simulating Sovereignty: Intervention, the State, and Symbolic Exchange.* Cambridge, United Kingdom: Cambridge University Press, 1995.

Weinberger, Caspar. "U.S. Defense Strategy." *Foreign Affairs* 65 (1986): 676–697.

Weiss, Thomas G. *Military-Civilian Interactions: Intervening in Humanitarian Crises.* Lanham, Md.: Rowman and Littlefield, 1999.

Weiss, Thomas G., and Cindy Collins. *Humanitarian Challenges and Intervention: World Politics and the Dilemmas of Help.* Boulder, Colo.: Westview Press, 1996.

Weldes, Jutta, Mark Laffey, Hugh Gusterson, and Raymond Duvall, eds. *Cultures of Insecurity: States, Communities, and the Production of Danger.* Minneapolis: University of Minnesota Press, 1999.

Wendt, Alexander. *Social Theory of International Politics.* New York: Cambridge University Press, 1999.

Wilkinson, David. "Unipolarity Without Hegemony." *International Studies Review* 1 (1999): 141–172.

Winters, Paul, ed. *Interventionism: Current Controversies.* San Diego, Calif.: Greenhaven Press, 1995.

Wittner, Lawrence S. *American Intervention in Greece, 1943–1949.* New York: Columbia University Press, 1982.

Wohlforth, William C. "The Stability of a Unipolar Moment." *International Security* 24 (Summer 1999): 5–41.

Wolfers, Arnold. " 'National Security' as an Ambiguous Symbol." *Political Science Quarterly* 67 (1952): 481–502.

Wright, Robin. "Ethnic Strife Owes More to Present than to History." *Los Angeles Times*, June 8, 1993.

Young, Oran R. "Intervention and International Systems." *Journal of International Affairs* 22 (1968): 177–187.

Zakaria, Fareed. "A Framework for interventionism in the Post–Cold War Era." In Arnold Kantor and Linton F. Brooks, eds. *U.S. Intervention Policy for the Post–Cold War World: New Challenges and New Responses.* New York: W.W. Norton, 1994.

Zelikow, Phillip D. "Force Without War." *Journal of Strategic Studies* 7/1 (1984): 29–54.

Index

About the Author

KAREN A. FESTE is Associate Professor and Associate Dean of the Graduate School of International Studies at the University of Denver.